IN SEARCH OF NEW YORK

Edited by Jim Sleeper

Transaction Publishers
New Brunswick (U.S.A.) and Oxford (U.K.)

Library of Congress Catalog Number: 88-23562
ISBN: 0-88738-767-5
Printed in the United States of America

Library of Congress Cataloging in Publication Data

In search of New York / edited by Jim Sleeper.
    p. cm.
    Originally published as a special issue of Dissent, Fall 1987.
    ISBN 0-88738-767-5
    1. New York (N.Y.)—Civilization.   2. New York (N.Y.)—Economic conditions.   3. New York (N.Y.)—Social conditions.   I. Sleeper, Jim.
F128.55.15 1988
974.7—dc19   88-23562
                                                                   CIP

Contents

Among our Contributors

JEWEL BELLUSH is professor emeritus of political science at Hunter College, City University of New York and co-author of the book *Union Power and New York*.

THOMAS BENDER, who teaches American history at New York University, is the author of the recently published *New York Intellect: A History of Intellectual Life in New York City, from 1750 to the Beginnings of Our Own Time* (Knopf).

MARSHALL BERMAN teaches political science at the City University Graduate Center and is the author of *All That Is Solid Melts Into Air*, a study of postmodernism in America. He is working on a book about urban decay and rebirth.

PAUL BERMAN is a writer for the *Village Voice*.

ANTHONY BORDEN is a writer whose work has appeared in the *Nation, In These Times*, and *Dissent*.

WESLEY BROWN is a native New Yorker and is the author of a novel, *Tragic Magic*, and a play, *Boogie Woogie and Booker T.* He teaches literature and creative writing at Rutgers University.

JIM CHAPIN is a longtime political activist in the Democratic party. He taught history at Yale and Rutgers and is chairman of the board of World Hunger Year.

JEROME CHARYN's most recent books are *Metropolis: New York as Myth, Marketplace, and Magical Land* and *Periodic Man*. He is working on a new novel and a book about Hollywood.

MORRIS DICKSTEIN is a writer and critic, author of *Gates of Eden: American Culture in the Sixties*. He teaches English at Queens College.

ROSALYN DREXLER is a novelist, playwright, and painter. Her latest book, *Bad Guy*, was issued in softcover in spring 1988 (PAJ Publications). She is currently at work on a new novel.

JUAN FLORES teaches in the department of sociology at Queens College and the *Centro de estudios puertorriqueños* at Hunter College.

PAULA FOX is a novelist who lives in Brooklyn. Among her novels are *Desperate Characters, The Widow's Children*, and *A Servant's Tale*.

THERESA FUNICIELLO is co-director of Social Agenda, which brings the point of view of people who experience poverty into debate on public policies. She is a Revson Fellow with the Center for Women in Government.

MICHAEL HARRINGTON, co-chair of Democratic Socialists of America, is best known for his path-breaking study of poverty, *The Other America*, but has written many books, among them *The Accidental Century* and *Socialism*.

IRVING HOWE, founder and co-editor of *Dissent*, is the author of many books, among them *Socialism in America, World of Our Fathers, Politics and the Novel*, and *A Margin of Hope*.

ADA LOUISE HUXTABLE was architecture critic for the *New York Times* before her retirement.

PHILIP KASINITZ teaches sociology at Williams College and has recently completed a book on New York's West Indian community. He has served as a consultant to the New York City Board of Education.

MARTIN KILSON, Frank G. Thomson Professor of Government at Harvard University, is the author of *Neither Insiders Nor Outsiders: Blacks in American Society*.

LEONARD KRIEGEL is working on a new novel and on a collection of essays. He is director of the City College of New York Center for Worker Education.

ROBERT LEKACHMAN is Distinguished Professor of Economics at Lehman College of the City University of New York in the Bronx, and the author, most recently, of *Greed is Not Enough: Reaganomics*, and *Visions and Nightmares: America After Reagan*.

ELLEN LEVY is a poet and journalist living in New York City.

DEBORAH MEIER is director of Central Park East School, a public elementary and secondary school in East Harlem, and a 1987 MacArthur Prize recipient.

CARLIN MEYER is a past president of the New York City chapter of the National Lawyers Guild, and former chief of the Labor Bureau of the New York State Attorney General's office.

NICOLAUS MILLS is professor of American Literature at Sarah Lawrence College. His most recent book is *The Crowd in American Literature* (Louisiana State University Press).

JOHN MOLLENKOPF teaches political science at the City University Graduate Center. He is editor of the forthcoming *Power, Culture, and Place: Essays on New York City*, sponsored by the Social Science Research Council Committee on New York City.

JO-ANN MORT, a poet and writer who lives in New York, is active in Democratic Socialists of America.

BRIAN MORTON, an editor of *Dissent*, is at work on a novel.

MICHAEL ORESKES, former labor editor of the New York *Daily News*, is now a Washington correspondent for the *New York Times*.

MAXINE PHILLIPS, managing editor of *Dissent*, was conference and public relations director for the Child Welfare League of America.

JAN ROSENBERG teaches sociology at Long Island University and has written about Jamaican women in New York. She is the author of *Feminism into Film*.

JIM SLEEPER is deputy opinion editor of *New York Newsday*, one of the city's four major newspapers, and a writer,

teacher, and consultant on urban affairs. He has written about New York City politics for *Dissent* magazine since 1980.

XAVIER F. TOTTI is an anthropologist at the Department of Puerto Rican Studies, Lehman College, City University of New York.

GUS TYLER, is assistant president of the International Ladies' Garment Workers' Union and director of the union's Departments of Politics, Education, and Staff Training. A veteran organizer, agitator, and talk-show host on WEVD-FM in New York, he is the author of twelve books.

ROGER WALDINGER is assistant professor of sociology at City College, CUNY. He is the author of *Through the Eye of the Needle: Immigrants and Enterprise in New York's Garment Trades* (NYU Press).

Acknowledgments

This book owes its central inspiration to IRVING HOWE, *Dissent* magazine's founder and editor, who first proposed it as a special Fall 1987 issue of the magazine—twenty-six years after *Dissent's* first special issue on New York City. Without his constant guidance and the generous support of the J.M. Kaplan Fund and the New York State Council on the Arts, *In Search of New York* would not have come to fruition.

Dissent managing editor MAXINE PHILLIPS, business manager SIMONE PLASTRIK and BRIAN MORTON worked with sophistication and dispatch to produce the original magazine publication, from copyediting through distribution. EMIL ANTONUCCI designed the page format.

JOANNE BARKAN, MARSHALL BERMAN, WILLIAM KORNBLUM, CAROL O'CLEIREACAIN, and FRED SIEGEL were particularly helpful in recruiting writers and artists. JAN ROSENBERG initiated the competition in photographs of immigration to New York that produced more than a dozen of the photographs in this book. DAVID WILLIAMS of Long Island University was unfailingly gracious as we worked with the competition entries.

Of the many photographers who have contributed their work, several deserve special mention for their engagement with the larger project. DAN WEAKS, who has photographed every street in midtown Manhattan using a camera he designed and built, modeled after a U.S.A.F. aerial strip-mapping camera, was extremely generous in making available some of his four million negatives. His photos appear on pp. 26, 27, 29, 164, 165, 174, 175, 186, 191, 199, 202, 204, 205, and 211.

MIKE STEIN worked creatively against tight deadlines to photograph subjects to accompany several of the essays in this volume. His photographs are on pp. 14, 17, 20, 22, 99, 206, and 207. MICHAEL KAUFFMAN of Impact Visuals and PAUL BAER were very helpful in finding appropriate photographs from their files. DAN OCHIVA photographed the round-table participants pictured on pp. 220–224.

Finally, we are grateful to IRVING LOUIS HOROWITZ, SCOTT BRAMSON, ESTHER M. LUCKETT, and the staff of Transaction Publishers for the vision and professional support that have smoothed the often difficult, in this case delightful, transition from magazine to anthology.

OTHER PHOTO CREDITS: Impact Visuals: Donna Binder, p. xii; James Cuebas, p. 6; Jim West, p. 81; Agnes Zellin, "Children Playing in a New York City-run Shelter for the Homeless," p. 144; Martha Tabor, p. 150; Cindy Reiman, p. 158; Mel Rosenthal, pp. 56, 162; Tony Savino, p. 217. The image on p. 30 is of an art work by Jenny Holzer, photographed by John Marchael. This project is an ongoing Public Art Fund, Inc. program entitled "Messages to the Public." It is made possible through the cooperation of Spectacolor, Inc. with support from the National Endowment for the Arts and the New York City Department of Cultural Affairs; Model of Trump Television City/Courtesy the Trump Corporation, p. 48; From the Regional Plan of the City of New York, 1929, p. 49; TIM, Louis Mitelberg, p. 51; Campaign poster, p. 87; Picture of David Jones/Courtesy CSS, p. 125; Alfredo Gonzales/From the New Immigrants Photography Exhibition, p. 130; Mel Rosenthal, New Immigrants Photography Exhibition, p. 95. Richard Landry, Mabou Mines, p. 181; Babette Mangolte, Mabou Mines p. 183.

IN SEARCH OF NEW YORK

Irving Howe

SOCIAL RETREAT AND THE *TUMLER*

> *". . . the inner darkness in high places*
> *that comes with a commercial age."*
>
> —E. M. Forster

Human nature didn't change once Ed Koch became mayor of New York, but it soon began to display its shabbier sides. The mood of the city seemed to grow sullen, as if in contempt of earlier feelings and visions. . . .

Quick to sense the change, Koch attached himself to it. The mood of the city now revealed a weariness with the language of idealism, a coarsening of social sentiments, a resignation before inequities that had once troubled consciences. The city, we were told, was in bad financial shape and so belts had to be tightened (*whose* belts?) while major concessions were to be made to the real estate developers in Manhattan. A budget crisis, no doubt constraining expenditure, became the occasion, though hardly the sole cause, for a rightward shift in social policy. Some called it realism.

Low rationales for Koch, often provided by Koch himself, carried a sharp message: enough chatter about reforms, enough weeping over the blacks, listen instead to the wisdom of Queens streets and make deals with Stanley Friedman and Donald Manes. There were also sophisticated versions of this message: life is unfair and what can you do about it, meanwhile it's better to have a rough sort of social peace, graced by Koch's vaudeville, than to continue with the tensions and irruptions of earlier years.

But there is another reading of what has been happening in New York. We have been witnessing

• the gradual disintegration of the New Deal tradition, once vibrant in the city, but over the years suffering the failures of its success and then an inability to cope with such barely definable problems as stagflation, the black lumpen proletariat, and the drawing apart of the city's ethnic communities into suspicion, fear, and contempt;

• the turning inward of the Jewish community, not to the neoconservatism of a few intellectuals but to a gradual "conservatizing" of its liberalism;

• the growing reaction against the protests and excesses in the cultural styles of the late 1960s;

• the collapse of the New York left, never strong enough to make policy but once a significant prod for liberal coalitions;

• the withdrawal of many blacks to their own areas, partly as a nursing of wounds incurred during the black-nationalist phase of the late 1960s, but mainly as a sign of disappointment with the failure of the liberal promise (Kennedy, Johnson, Lindsay) to deliver;

• and as both cause and reflex of the above, the near-collapse of liberalism, as both political force and voice of protest.

These were local manifestations of a national political trend, climaxed by the victory of Reaganism, the most explicit effort we have yet seen to hobble the welfare state.

Reaganism's triumph was registered most vividly in ideological atmosphere and social tone. In New York, through the chatter of the mayor, it was "translated" into an abandonment, first embarrassed and then defiant, of social feeling. You no longer had to feel "bad" or "guilty" about the blacks and the poor, you no longer had to agonize about Vietnam.

As a contribution of far-right ideologues, there began also to appear a peculiar kind of social nastiness, a pseudoaristocratic Ivy League disdain for the plebes. You no longer had to be weighed down by conscience. In fact it was good, it was American, to revel in your indifference to the plight of the weak and the losers. What mattered now was personal assertiveness, the aggression of winners, the coolness of top dogs—a style blending bluff social Darwinism with button-down superiority.

None of this was initiated by Koch, and much of it he could not have imitated even if he had wanted to. He had been a mainstream liberal who had gone south to join the protests against Jim Crow. When I encountered him during the early 1960s as a neighbor in an apartment building, he seemed a quiet, somewhat withdrawn chap. But now he was the mayor. He sensed that activism was out of fashion and he realized that to remain a liberal would mean to pit himself, maybe hopelessly, against the powers of Washington and without much support from the people of his city.

From playing along with this new social mood, Koch after a time began to play it. Once begun, such adaptation has a rhythm of its own. Koch's "comic" style embodied the street wisdom that you can't fight City Hall, a notion especially convenient when you happen to be running City Hall. He was not a villain and he was not a reactionary. Nor was he stupid. Gradually showing that streak of skepticism which, like a gray underside, had run parallel to the idealism of the immigrant Jews, he came to enjoy the violation he was staging of his earlier self. He was to Reaganism as LaGuardia had been to Roosevelt's New Deal—the municipal broker for the dominant social force in the country. And he had his rewards: popularity in the city, large sales for a rather mean-spirited book, an increasingly cozy relationship with old-line Democratic pols like Donald Manes and Stanley Friedman, and the warm blessing of the *New York Post,* Rupert Murdoch's vile sheet. Nor was Koch lacking in gratitude: he nominated the *Post* for a Pulitzer Prize in 1981.

If the mood was indigo; if there really wasn't much you could do about municipal problems in a moment of social retreat (and who can doubt that if there had been a liberal president Koch would have been glad to adapt to *him*?); if you had to deal with Reagan's gang and even with a picklehead like Senator D'Amato—then Koch would not only play the role, he would play it to the hilt. He had a gift for touching the half-hidden sentiments of lower-middle-class whites in Queens and Brooklyn who had come to fear and despise blacks. He became rather cunning in his ability to insinuate unsavory messages without using unsavory words. The Koch who announced that "blacks [are] basically anti-Semitic," who described Congressman Ron Dellums as a "Watusi," and who (his finger to the wind) changed his condemnation of Bernhard Goetz's subway shootout to a statement that a grand jury's decision not to indict Goetz for murder was "right"—this Koch knew something about the uses of popular prejudice. It was as if a message were coming out of City Hall: "All right, let the blacks have their welfare, but let's not hear any more talk about discrimination or injustice. Enough already!"

For several years a gray, uneasy social peace settled over the city—a peace resting not on integration or genuine sentiments of community but on strict separation of ethnic, racial, and class turfs.

Koch became what the Borscht Belt calls a *tumler,* the sort of entertainer whose gift for comedy isn't always to be distinguished from his ability to make noise. Once he spoke, people could unbutton their petty contempts.

Until, that is, Howard Beach. Then it was as if Ed Koch looked into the mirror of New York and turned pale. He now spoke out forcefully, describing the incident as a "lynching." He hated the hooliganism and the killing. The *tumler* had wanted to lull and divert, not arouse anyone—certainly not see anyone hurt.

But did he find himself wondering what

connection there might be between the snarling hatreds of the Howard Beach hoodlums and the social tone, the vibrations of attitude, marking his years in office? Did he ask himself: What has happened to me? What have I become?

About the Rich and the Poor

There is statistical evidence that the contrast between wealth and poverty in New York has recently grown sharper. Statistics apart, the signs of social and economic polarization seem more visible, more gross than in earlier years. Those sleek, dark-curtained limos driving through streets in which thousands of people are homeless on winter nights; Madison Avenue below 96th Street and Madison Avenue above; the glitz of midtown contrasted with the devastation of large sweeps of Brooklyn and the Bronx—a few of the signs. This of course is an impression, and impressions can be overstated.

What is not overstated, I'm convinced, is that the shared perception regarding extreme inequities of wealth and poverty—the perception shared among both "ordinary people" and cultivated elites—has changed. You can find reports in the papers about the poor or the difficulties of working-class families trying to scrape by. But what seems to have all but vanished from the discourse of the city, perhaps even its consciousness, is the stress liberals and radicals used to place on the outrage, the violation of moral norms and democratic values that the extremes of wealth and poverty represent. One rarely hears any longer expressions of social dismay or anger or even guilt. If the developers tighten their grip on Manhattan, driving out small storekeepers and booksellers and offbeat movie houses, and the city, dispensing tax breaks and helpful indifference, acquiesces with at best a weary version of the "drip-down" argument—why that's the way things are, the way they've always been. We live, as Dickens once wrote, with "a loose belief that if the world go wrong, it was, in some offhand manner, never meant to go right."

Social guilt is not the most helpful of sentiments, but if there is reason for guilt, then better that it should be visible than not. The old cry of American rectitude—*it's wrong, it's unfair*—hardly provides a sufficient analysis of society in the age of the multinationals, but now, when that voice sounds dimly and infrequently, one realizes how much it can be missed.

There are important ways in which life in New York has improved over the last several decades, but in one crucial respect, especially to be noted at a time when the Constitution is being celebrated, I see regression. A democratic society must rest on the persuasion that politics is essential to the life of its citizens, that through politics they express their interests and values, and that it is finally through an unencumbered participation that citizenship becomes a reality. Such a persuasion seems more in question today, as one looks at the life of the city, than a few decades ago. It's hard to know to what degree the breakdown of political life is the consequence of technological changes largely beyond immediate social controls and to what degree it reflects an "inner" political development that may, in time, change. But clearly the state of the city's political life ought to dismay even conservatives, at least those who genuinely care about democratic politics as a process of activity rather than a mere ritualistic vote every few years.

It is television, of course, that seems mainly responsible for the changes in political life. Gone, or almost gone, is the public meeting that required only the cost of hiring a hall and printing leaflets. Entirely gone is the street meeting, the soapbox oratory favored by left-wing groups but also practiced by Democrats and even Republicans. A mere memory is the full-length (say 30-to-40-minute) speech that major candidates felt obliged to make. What have replaced all these are the slick 30-second TV ad, the vacuous one-sentence "statement" for the evening news, and "debates" in which candidates are given two minutes to respond to questions that (assuming they knew the answers) ought to take twenty minutes to answer. And with these changes, politics becomes increasingly the province of the rich, for only they can afford to buy, or finance, "time" on the tube.

Again, I don't want to romanticize. Much of the soapbox oratory was wind, but at least it gave audiences a chance (which they often seized) to fire questions and heckle. If people sometimes talked nonsense, at least they talked directly, face to face. (Try heckling a TV set: it's small satisfaction.) Many of the formal meetings held by political parties were occasions for bull and hoopla, but people like Franklin Roosevelt and Adlai Stevenson—to say nothing of Norman Thomas—did now and then say something significant. Attending a public meeting at least meant that you had to leave the house and go to a hall. Back in the 1930s, when there was still a Socialist party, we would hold, before election day, meetings of a few thousand people in Hunts Point Palace in the Bronx, where people waited patiently for Norman Thomas to arrive while lesser comrades talked or mumbled; and whatever their flaws, such meetings signified a degree of participation and interest that TV simply cannot elicit.

New York today is no longer even a one-party town; it has become a no-party town, with the barest participation in primaries and little more in elections. Perhaps it's the feeling of the Reagan and Koch years that "nothing can be done" that led to such passivity. Perhaps things will improve. But the profound changes brought about by television in our political life remain, and it would be foolish to suggest that anyone, left or elsewhere, quite knows how to cope with them.

New York becomes harder and harder to live in. Maybe, I tell myself, you feel that way because you're getting older and old people are notoriously cranky. But it can't be bad character alone that's responsible for my alienation from a city where I've spent most of my life and about which I used to say that a day away was a day lost.

What is it then? I hate the fast-money greediness that's taken over Manhattan. I share the anxieties of other New Yorkers about violence. I rage against the snarls of traffic in a Manhattan where the Koch administration encouraged a wildly excessive concentration of luxury towers but did nothing to save the subway system. I grow sad when the Thalia movie house—where I first saw *Grand Illusion*—is closed down because the developers are closing in.

What made New York a place one loved—its diversities, its unconventionalities—is being swept away by the forces of money, the developers and foreign investors, the corporations with their sleek facades.

The Culture of the City

There are good things, also. In the cultural life of New York during the decades since the Second World War, there were two major outbursts of creative talent—the first in art, with the abstract expressionists of the 1950s, and the second in dance, particularly through the genius of Balanchine. The abstract expressionists owed a great deal to earlier artistic groups, first the school of Paris and then,

City of Despair

" While New York remains a city of gold for those at the top of the economic ladder, it has become a city of despair for many elderly, for the homeless, for women and children barely subsisting on public welfare."

This was the conclusion of a 1984 study commissioned by the Community Service Society, a New York City social welfare organization. A new study commissioned by the society has found that the situation has become even worse.

In 1984, 1.7 million New Yorkers—almost a quarter of the city's population—were trapped below the poverty line, as defined by the federal government. For Hispanic New Yorkers, the poverty rate was 43 percent; for blacks, 32 percent. Thirty-eight percent of the city's children were poor. Only 70 percent of poor families were insured by

Medicaid; and 50,000 families were below the poverty line even though their main wage earner was working full time.

David Jones, the society's general director, now believes that the number of poor New Yorkers may approach two million by the end of the decade—despite an economic boom that has brought the city's unemployment rate to its lowest point since the 1970s. "We all expected some trickle-down effect," Jones told the *New York Times*, "and it's not working."

The city's elected officials, according to Jones, "seem to have given up on the notion that they can do very much" to help the poor. "I don't see anybody charging down to Washington, and that starts to make it questionable how serious they are. I think they've given up even before they've made the fight."

during the war, the many European artists who came to New York as exiles. Within the world of dance there was a similar internal flowering—something that takes on a dynamic of its own, quite apart from the larger society—but to a considerable extent this was due to the gifts of one man, George Balanchine. As long as he was alive and working, that seemed an important reason to stay in the city.

These two developments showed that the city could still be a place of cultural vitality. Can one say as much for our literary life? I doubt it. The old *Partisan Review* group broke down into a number of bitterly antagonistic cliques, often assailing one another. The beat writers brought something new to the culture of the city—you had to engage with them whether you liked them or not—but only one of them,

Allen Ginsberg, has remained as a significant figure.

Serious, devoted, and good-spirited writers continue to live and work in New York. They struggle with impossible rents; they dream about escaping the noise, the dirt and the dangers of the city, though not many move away. But what has been lacking now for some years is a fresh surge of energy, a new direction or a new idea, a shared and irresistible impulse that could give writers the feeling that they are part of a "movement" or "trend" that might, if only slightly, reinvigorate American culture. It's not exactly a bad time, it's only a flat time.

Still, who can say? Not yet visible, impulses of renewal may be gathering. The days of Reagan and Koch are coming to an end, and a new "American newness" may be waiting to be born. □

BOODLING, BIGOTRY, AND COSMOPOLITANISM

The Transformation of a Civic Culture

Like the mountains that labored and brought forth a mouse, the ongoing eruptions of charges against New York City officials for bribery, extortion, and racketeering over the past two years have brought forth two quips.

The first belongs to Murray Kempton, long-suffering watchman of the city's civic virtue. Remarking the frequency with which Mayor Ed Koch stood before the City Hall press corps last year saying, "I am shocked" by some revelation of corruption, Kempton discovered that the great seal of the City of New York bears no motto and proposed that whatever is Latin for "I am shocked" be promptly affixed, in backhanded tribute to the deep public apathy that has itself become an aspect of the corruption.

The second came from journalist Sidney Zion. Watching U.S. Attorney Rudolph Giuliani in titanic struggle with defense counsel Thomas Puccio at the trial of Bronx boss Stanley Friedman, Zion noted that, for the first time in anyone's memory, "all the defendants are Jewish and all the lawyers are Italian." This inversion of "natural" order was soon righted with the indictments of former Transportation Commissioner Anthony Ameruso, former Brooklyn Democratic boss Meade Esposito, and Representative Mario Biaggi; but that left undisturbed an irony in a mayoral administration that had come to power pledged to purge minority "poverty pimps" allegedly coddled by its predecessors: with the exception of indicted Representative Robert Garcia, all the major malefactors in the recent probes are white.

The racial and ethnic role reversals anticipated in Zion's quip may help explain the seemingly invincible public indifference implicit in Kempton's. New Yorkers of all races seem to sense that, on the other side of the current upheavals, the city's once-vibrant, predominantly white ethnic and proletarian political culture—progenitor of the New Deal, the 1939 World's Fair, Hollywood, the interracial Brooklyn Dodgers, municipal unions, myriad bohemias, and even the early Levittowns prototypical of the suburban American Dream—will lie dead or dying. The city is in the grip of demographic and economic sea changes, deeper than the fiscal and political cycles noted by some observers, that could make the New York of 1995 unrecognizable to keepers of the civic flame ignited by Al Smith and Fiorello H. LaGuardia. If the scandals arouse little outrage, it is not only because they partake of the spirit of the times on Wall Street and in the White House, but because they are part of an old local order's melancholy, long withdrawing roar.

In its place must come a new political culture responsive to the burgeoning, unfocused vitality of aliens—the bearers of a black, Latin, and Asian cosmopolis emerging from a hundred immigrant streams deluging the city at levels unprecedented since the 1920s. That tide has been slow gathering strength partly because of its own mind-boggling diversity. After all the talk about a "majority-minority" city that became less than half white at some point during the mid-1980s, New York is only slowly coming to realize that, unlike predominantly black Atlanta or Detroit, it will never, ever have an ethnic or racial majority. A third of its 1.9 million blacks are Caribbeans whose experiences and agendas mesh imperfectly with those of native American blacks; a varied Asian population of 350,000 is expected to grow 150 percent by 1995 with revolution in Korea and the defenestration of Hong Kong; nearly a million Puerto Ricans have been joined by almost as many other Hispanics, including Dominicans, Cubans, and South Americans. This Asian and Hispanic growth seems to be holding blacks' own slower expansion to under 30 percent of the whole, while even the city's white population has been augmented in recent years by 200,000 Russian Jews, Israelis, Poles, Italians, Irish, and Greeks, to say nothing of the young professionals, managers, artists, and activists from the American heartland.

As important as the diversity of these 2.5 million newcomers is the brevity of their time in New York. Most are not English-speaking citizens, let alone registered voters. Scrambling for shelter, taxi medallions, and career training of every sort, they haven't yet constituted themselves politically. Asians make up 25 percent of the city's elite public Stuyvesant High School, but as a substitute teacher there for a few days in 1983 I couldn't make them stop studying chemistry in a class on American labor history. Recently off the boat from Hong Kong or Seoul, they seemed to have had their fill of history and to be intent on rocketing themselves out of its tragedies as scientists or computer magnates. Who could blame them? Not every young Jew who warmed a seat here before them and whose parents labored in sweatshops as do theirs was inclined to build the International Ladies' Garment Workers Union. But then, enough young Jews were indeed so inclined that one can't help wondering how the differences in culture and historical expectation now visible in the schools will shape the city's future. It is too soon to know.

There may be one or two more Jewish mayors, and after that this American world city will be read only by those unafraid to look into dark young faces.

There is, for some, a certain romance to the prospect. Think of New York as a great human heart which draws into itself those immigrant bloodstreams and, after working its strange alchemy, pumps them back out again across America and the world bearing athletes, impresarios, engineers. The city has done this uncomplainingly for so much of the country for so long that one in eight Americans can trace family ties to Brooklyn alone. A question posed by the old order's decay is whether New York's great heart can keep beating. Uncertainty about the answer may be all the newcomers have in common.

Here the romance of immigration sometimes fades for liberals as much as xenophobes: it is noted that blacks resent Korean merchants, or that Russians are as racist as American "rednecks," or that many Chinese won't join unions. Racial succession in labor organizations, boardrooms, nonprofit organizations, and political offices has been erratic, at best; the ominous language of separatism is more prevalent than that of liberal pluralism, let alone proletarian solidarity. Where is the new LaGuardia, himself not only Italian and Jewish but Spanish-speaking, whose passionate leadership helped fuse new New Yorkers into a polis? Where are the touchstones and training grounds for such leadership and a citizenry responsive to it?

These questions are complicated by an erosion in the status of cities themselves as foci of national cultural and political concern and as centers of locally committed wealth. What is the political meaning of a city when increasingly fluid market forces move capital and leadership cadres worldwide at whim? Since its earliest days as a Dutch-run, polyglot trading port, New York has always been a conduit for such forces and populations; but even the maintenance of a conduit would seem to require some political consensus, some ability to influence or make claims upon new configurations of technology, investment, employment, consumption, demographics, and immigration. To say nothing of a federal urban policy whose ignorance and bad faith regarding New York's mission have been appalling, the more so when compared to the resources other nations lavish on their premier cities. Who can reconstitute the New York conduit on terms America can support?

White Rage

As these questions lie unanswered in the interregnum between the old order and the new, confusion about the meaning of civic responsibility and belonging is evident in other racial role reversals, not only in the corruption dramas but also in the streets, where an impressive number of last year's rioters were white. In Howard Beach just before Christmas 1986, bat-wielding whites attacked three blacks, one of them killed as he fled into the path of an oncoming car. That horror recalled one four years earlier when whites pummeled to death a black transit worker coming off his shift. "I love you, Mom!" cried one assailant as the jury convicted him of "manslaughter-two" in that incident. None of his sobbing neighbors, who'd backed Koch in part because of his support for the death penalty, could be heard calling for a murder conviction.

Bernhard Goetz came to trial this year for gunning down four black youths who he said had menaced him on an IRT train, paralyzing one of them from the waist down for life by shooting the youth a second time after saying, "You don't look so bad, here's another." Goetz's victims were found to have police rap sheets as long as their arms, except for the one who will never walk again and whose own father was murdered years earlier while trying to wrest his taxi from a thief. The brutal strangling of young Jennifer Levin in the summer of 1986 prompted her uncle to pronounce New York "a social experiment that has failed," an observation that assumed an interesting aspect when the killer turned out to be Levin's white preppie escort, Robert Chambers.

New York's Year of White Crime continued in The Bronx, a borough half-leveled in the 1970s by tax write-off and arson-for-insurance scams perpetrated upon hapless welfare tenants by a cabal of sociopathic white real estate agents and slumlords. Hispanic entrepreneur John Mariotta became so successful a minority defense contractor, lionized by Ronald Reagan, that he sought help with his booming business from former presidential counsel James E. Jenkins, former White House communications director Lyn Nofziger, and other well-connected white professionals, some of whom fired him, took over his stock rights, and ran his company, Wedtech, into the ground along with the jobs of more than 1,000 workers.

That was child's play beside the rompings downtown of Ivan Boesky and kindred spirits, who sent tremors through the edifice of finance capital, which only recently had been extended out into the Hudson on landfill dumped there as if in arrant mockery of all the square footage and infrastructure abandoned in the Bronx and on Main Streets all over the country whose assets had been liquidated by the arbitrageurs. Meanwhile, a professor of ethics at New York University's Business School told the MacNeil-Lehrer News Hour that 80 percent of his students chose, in a simulation of corporate decision making, to fight the FDA rather than stop marketing a drug known to have killed twenty-two people. As more of the city's "elite" work force engages in the manipulation of words and symbols that consolidate corporate power, abstracted from the rewards and constraints of union and neighborhood roots, the social and political basis for LaGuardia's vision of a just, integrated city dissolves.

In a purely tactical sense, public silence about corruption suggests that whites, who still dominate established politics and media, are themselves immobilized by the charges. It is

The Joys and the Blessings

Joyous are the large corporations, for they shall benefit from the deduction value of the 46 percent corporate tax rate in their mergers and acquisitions.

"Joyous are the stock speculators, for they shall inherit tremendous dividends.

"Joyous are the corporate raiders, for they shall reap the profits of liquidation.

"Joyous are the corporate lawyers, for wealthy salaries shall be theirs.

"And blessed are the working people of thy country for it is they who subsidize these takeovers.

REPRESENTATIVE SILVIO CONTE, Massachusetts

hard to champion capital punishment for murderers and long sentences for boodlers when the boy next door is a candidate for death row and the avuncular clubhouse captain down the block is sweating a subpoena from the grand jury.

But that silence also reflects an embitterment, beyond words, of white ethnics suddenly marginal to civic cultures they struggled hard to make their own. Expressions of moral outrage assume a consensus that has been violated but to which one can still appeal. For whites who think such a consensus has unraveled, and who felt their claims upon it tenuous in the first place, outrage gives way to simple rage—to street violence and lawless plunder of the commonweal. The decay of white ethnic political culture reflects not just demographic change, but also the conviction of many white New Yorkers that the rules have been changed against them.

Overall, it isn't minorities they're losing ground to—Boesky and the yuppie managerial class come to mind. But try to tell that to people driven out of "the old neighborhood" by muggings and decay. The connections they make between racial change, rising crime, and their plummeting property values are empirically valid and seared into personal experience. The fact that racism itself, including the machinations of unscrupulous white brokers, helps make self-fulfilling prophecies of such fears seems beside the point to people trapped by the consequences.

To them, the real municipal scandal isn't the fixing of government contracts but the unchecked rise of street crime and social and physical disintegration among encroaching poor minorities, as well as the rigid, often naïve illogic of redistribution imposed on them by liberal jurisprudence and politicians like John Lindsay, who, they feel, preferred to spend their taxes on siting public housing in their areas rather than on police. Such impositions seem extortions of gains they've won by following the disciplines of an upward mobility that many of them were willing to share with minorities, until they began to believe that minorities preferred a "free ride" from liberals.

That these "extortions" reached their peak in the mid-1970s, just as inflation and urban disinvestment were undermining their own upward mobility, only compounded their desperation. What Jonathan Rieder, the sympathetic ethnographer of Brooklyn's white-working-class Canarsie, calls "indignation, an emotion born of the perception of injustice," lay at the heart of their transformation. Even now—and the Italian and Jewish lower-middle-class residents of places like Canarsie are furious at us for not understanding this—what distinguishes their rage from the reactionary ideologies or blood racism of the Nazis or the Klan is its focus against specific, wrenching interventions in their neighborhood turf. The perceptions of injustice fueling their indignation may not always be accurate, but neither are the values they believe to be under assault always invalid.

Since the mid-1970s, then, there has been a decay in the city's white-working-class idiom, from one that could express its grievances in tart humor, irony, and flashing insight into one of sullen, evasive rationalization for attacks on blacks. Compared to that, the transmutation of Jackie Gleason's Ralph Kramden, the garrulous, decent "Big Mouth," into Carroll O'Connor's Archie Bunker, quiver of barbed retorts, was a triumph of human spirit.

By contrast, the new silence is so eerie, so ominous that I was almost relieved to hear it broken on a Brooklyn street one recent warm summer dusk by a bloodied, hard-muscled Italian teenager who came tearing down the block and spun around to face his black pursuers from the safety of the sidewalk counter of a pizzeria where some of his buddies worked. The black youths faded back into a deepening pool of shadows down the block as the boy's white-clad pizza parlor friends stepped wordlessly into the street, brandishing bats. The veins in his neck throbbed as, finding his breath, he cried out to the blacks in a register so deep from the gut it seemed to tap a bottomless hurt more startling than his anger.

"You *muh*-tha . . . *fuck*-in' . . . *nig*-guhs. You're *all shit*! *Eh*-very *one*-a' yous! They otta *ship* yous *all back*!" He doubled over, gasping for air, hands on his knees, then straightened up, not satisfied. "I don' care, I tell ya da trut'.

I wish *eh*-very *one*-a'yous was *dead*. You ruin *eh*-very *fuck*-in' *thing*," he moaned in a despair so deep it riveted everyone on the street. "I *spit* on ya *muh*-thas," he shrieked, "I wish you was *nev*-veh *ee*-ven *born*!"

Black Rage

What startles about the white youth's rage is its utter conviction that blacks "ruin" the social compact, as if white ethnic organized crime and "machine" corruption hadn't also diminished every benign form of citizenship by making force and fraud the never-distant arbiters of social order. However exalted LaGuardia's notions of justice and community, millions of New Yorkers have always passed their lives in complex webs of complicity with enemies of liberal virtue. It wasn't only the orthodox Marxist left that considered bourgeois citizenship a sham and organized violence the reality; the harsh logic of protected group "turf," both geographically in neighborhoods and economically in industry and bureaucracies, always shaped the contours of liberal citizenship in New York.

Even so, if one measure of civility is the degree to which force and fraud are kept at bay in the calculations of daily life, then New York is a place less civilized today than it was in the 1950s and early 1960s, though not, perhaps, in earlier times. Some would argue that even LaGuardia managed to construe liberal institutions not as bourgeois heavens of meaningless, "rights" but, in today's parlance, as a "level playing field" where ordinary people might mobilize against greed and reactionary nationalisms. It's that sense of engagement and dialogue across racial and ethnic lines that seems to have diminished.

What the recent racial role reversals in courts and streets suggest is that, if we except the crimes committed by young males, most blacks have kept LaGuardia's faith better than whites, whether it be in the courageous, sometimes heartbreaking simplicity of elderly churchgoers and civil rights marchers or the sophisticated electoral decisions of black voters who have supported worthy white incumbents against facile black challengers when it seemed to them appropriate to do so. Blacks came to New York

in large numbers after the war seeking jobs, not welfare, so much so that Irving Kristol, inventor of the insidious little *mot* that a neoconservative is a liberal who's been mugged by reality, wrote in a 1958 Sunday *New York Times Magazine* essay that blacks would in the course of another generation assimilate, like all other groups, to the blessings of economic security and citizenship. One may even say that, in the immediate postwar years, white migration to suburbia wasn't so much a "flight" from minority crime and decay as a response to the lure of privately marketed, publicly subsidized greener pastures.

As the middle-class tax base slipped and jobs left New York for the Sunbelt, however, minorities—last hired, first fired—bore the brunt of a downward spiral of unemployment, shrinking tax revenues, curtailed services based on those revenues, along with increased dependency on the curtailed services. It's important to make distinctions: black women benefited more than black men from the new service economy; more whites lost jobs than blacks. Still, indicators of social distress—infant mortality, welfare dependency, truancy, alcoholism, drug addiction, crime, housing abandonment—began edging upward among blacks, both absolutely and in comparison to whites.

Nor, when all is said and done, can the role of unemployment and discrimination in deepening that suffering be overemphasized. When the full history of the agony of the South Bronx and central Brooklyn in the 1970s is written, the pathologies of "multi-problem" speculators and other, mostly white, schemers will assume greater prominence alongside the pathologies of the large welfare families who were the ultimate victims of bank redlining, blockbusting, and mortgage insurance scams. And not only the minority poor: the true Job of neighborhood racial change in New York is the black lower-middle-class family that scrimps to buy a home in a predominantly white area only to find its own arrival used by brokers as a signal to disinvest, prompting general white flight.

All of this leads to a black embitterment and to black defection from civic consensus, a defection evident since the 1968 "community control" battles in the schools not only among poor but also among middle-class blacks. Some of the latter could be found in 1984 applauding Louis Farrakhan at Madison Square Garden and in 1987 cheering Alton Maddox, Jr. at a "blacks only" rally at a public high school in the wake of the Howard Beach incident. According to Nat Hentoff, the New York Civil Liberties Union was at first confused about how to respond to the use of a public school building for a racially exclusive meeting; the progressive civic culture of the past has been routed as whites embrace varieties of privatization and so feel disarmed when blacks indulge in separatist gestures.

What models of empowered, integrated citizenship might bridge the gaps in communication and trust, avoiding both doomed black separatism and terminal white cynicism? As always, in a nation virtually tone-deaf to either side in the tragedy of urban polarization, we find ourselves grasping at straws.

A New Cosmopolitanism?

On a freshly fenced ballfield in Brooklyn's devastated Brownsville section in October 1982, gaily colored banners mark off a milling throng of 8,000 American and West Indian blacks, Hispanics, and a small minority of whites by congregations: Lutheran Church of the Risen Christ, Community Baptist, Our Lady of Consolation, R.C., and so on. Their umbrella group, East Brooklyn Churches (EBC), is breaking ground for 1,000 single family homes it's building with an ingenious package of subsidies on fifteen abandoned blocks delivered free by the city. Half the buyers—nurses, paralegals, teachers' aides, transit workers—have come from the neighboring high-rise public housing projects, bearing small nest eggs they'd dreamed of investing in their community.

The new "Nehemiah" housing, now almost completed, was named for the biblical prophet who convinced his despondent neighbors to rebuild Jerusalem's battered walls. It represents a triumph of urban republican virtue across years of patient community organizing by East Brooklyn Churches. EBC representatives stunned the local political establishment by handing the Brooklyn borough president their resig-

nations from do-nothing community boards and demanding a meeting with his shadow boss, the county Democratic party leader, to talk about city services. EBC registered 10,000 new voters, 70 percent of them black, without once using slogans about black power or anyone's time having come. It also doubled local turnout in the November 1984 presidential elections.

"Contrary to common opinion," cries the Rev. Johnny Ray Youngblood at the rally, "we are not a 'grassroots' organization. Grass roots grow in *smooth* soil. Grass roots are *shallow* roots!" His incantatory power catches his listeners, summoning their strength and spontaneous "Amens." "*Our* roots are *deep* roots!" ("Aw-right!" "Praise God!") "Our roots have fought for existence in the shattered glass of East New York and the blasted brick of Brownsville! And so we say to you, Mayor Koch, We Love New York! And we say to you, Council President Bellamy"—the crowd joining him now, on its feet, thundering, "WE LOVE NEW YORK!," shifting the emphasis gradually to "WE," as in "Listen to us: *WE* Love New York!"

The mostly white dais is stunned. The bishop of Brooklyn is blinking back tears. Here, in 1968, watching people pick their way to the elevated IRT past rows of abandoned buildings and over rubble-strewn lots prowled by wild dogs, visiting Boston Mayor Kevin White made the *Times*'s Quote of the Day by sputtering that he'd just seen "the beginning of the end of our civilization." In 1975, with virtually nothing left standing but public housing, the then city-housing commissioner Roger Starr proposed "planned shrinkage" of the area—the calculated withdrawal of services and resettlement of population. Then in 1979, EBC began building a "power organization" and turned the city fathers' assumptions upside down. In hundreds of house meetings and lay leadership training sessions run by the late Saul Alinsky's Industrial Areas Foundation (IAF), EBC studied the structure of local power. It began simply, with winnable goals: new street signs, cleanups of local food stores under polite but daunting threats of boycott; crackdowns by the district attorney on local "smoke shops."

The group's growing clout caught the attention of its national parent church bodies, which together contributed almost $9 million for the Nehemiah project. The city donated the land and a $10,000 federal Community Development subsidy to write down the purchase price of each house. The state provided low-interest mortgages. But the initiative and ownership is EBC's—and its individual buyers', whose probity and discipline have made local bankers, contractors, politicians, and bureaucrats seem predatory by comparison; often it was only the bishop of Brooklyn who helped EBC embarrass or intimidate local elites into doing their civic duty.

Now, at the rally, the mayor leads the crowd in a dramatic countdown and a bulldozer roars, opening the earth for the homes. Huddled at the edge of the crowd are a couple hundred dazed-looking middle-aged whites who might have stepped out of Archie Bunker's neighborhood—and who, in fact, have come by bus from "his" area of Queens. They are members of the Queens Citizens Organization (QCO), another IAF affiliate. QCO's president Pat Ottinger takes the mike and cries, "Our trip to Brooklyn today has reinforced our belief that there is no boundary between us. We are all one neighborhood, one great city. Your struggles are our struggles! Your heartaches are our heartaches! Your victories are our victories!"

The crowd roars back its welcome. The Queens visitors loosen up, smile, wave. The elected officials, accustomed to shuttling two-faced back and forth across the color line, are visibly impressed. "Two years ago," Ottinger later confides, "you couldn't have gotten my neighbors here in a tank."

The EBC effort—doggedly interracial yet almost Jeffersonian in its community-based well-springs of virtue and power—is but a straw in the wind. There are others: replicable models of public/private sector collaboration, "learning curves" shared now by varied actors involved in neighborhood change—the lenders, developers, brokers, residents, planners, and media image makers and interpreters who for so long have worked at cross-purposes to make a wasteland of urban promise. The contradictions in their interests cannot be glossed over, yet the lesson of community organizing is that they can be negotiated. There are the beginnings of con-

structive racial succession in the leadership of unions like AFSCME and the ILGWU. Even the oftnoted mismatch between new white collar jobs and an unprepared populace may not be as stark as it seems, because of unanticipated economic developments and new cultural resources among immigrants.

But none of these encouraging developments, and not even all of them together, yet herald a new civic culture. What the Queens visitors to Brownsville experienced would have to happen to tens of thousands more like them to change a city the size of New York; and any viable new politics would have to acknowledge and somehow address some white ethnic grievances, if only because their anguish resonates so deeply throughout the powerful suburbs and the larger national culture upon whose solicitous regard the health of the city depends. Even those New Yorkers who've all too easily dispersed to suburbia carry within them pockets of civic loss and longing, and are slow to understand how something like the EBC rally in Brownsville can contribute to restoring their souls.

What's worth remarking about that event is that 8,000 mostly black and Hispanic poor people instructed white officials and onlookers in the rebuilding of civic consensus and a decent America. *That* kind of racial role reversal is part of the new tide that must gather strength. The city is blessed with two and a half million newcomers innocent of its recent mistakes and ancient feuds, and another two million "outsiders" uninitiated into its subtler corruptions and cynicisms. Even thousands of young white Americans from the Heartland keep bypassing Manhattan for outermost Brooklyn and kindred locations to cast their fates with the urban struggle. "New York is the most fatally fascinating thing in America," wrote James Weldon Johnson at the turn of the century; "She sits like a witch at the gate of the country." She still does. An embodiment of our worst fears about ourselves, but also of our deepest strengths, New York offers abundant instruction to a nation becoming as diverse and interdependent as the city herself. Merely coming to know her better would constitute a reasonable return on the investment the nation ought to make in her future.   □

Marshall Berman

RUINS AND REFORMS

New York Yesterday and Today

We beg delinquents for our life.
Behind each bush, perhaps, a knife;
each landscaped crag, each flowering shrub,
hides a policeman with his club.
　　　　　　　—Robert Lowell, "Central Park"

. . . the block is burning down on one side of the
street, and the kids are trying to build something on
the other.
　　　　　　—Grace Paley, "Somewhere Else"

There are all sorts of ironies in a *Dissent* issue devoted to New York City. In one sense, nothing could be more obvious. Most of *Dissent*'s editors have spent most of their lives in or near this city. Indeed, the strong vertical form of our masthead resembles nothing so much as a New York apartment house. [*Editors' note*: With this issue, the masthead changes to a low-rise model.] Examined at closer range, this mostly but not wholly Jewish masthead—"Howe, Walzer, Geltman, Phillips, Carpenter, Plastrik, Avishai, . . . Schapiro, Sexton, Steinberg, Steinfels, Wrong"—evokes the rows of doorbells on the thresholds of the Bronx and Brooklyn apartment houses where many of us grew up, or in the lobbies of the more formidable piles of the Upper West Side where many of us live now. In scrutinizing New York, we are buzzing our own bells to get us to come out in the open.

It may sound obvious, but it hasn't come easy. Our founders, growing up in immigrant families and neighborhoods, and coming of age in the various radical movements of the 1930s, prided themselves on taking the whole world as their province. They saw quite early that they would never storm the Winter Palaces of the world; instead, they asserted the intellectual power to penetrate into that world's remotest corners and to grasp it as a whole. But, somehow, that whole did not include themselves, or the world they came from and moved in; they couldn't imagine that their homes, or their streets, or their city, could have meaning for anybody but themselves. They showed amazing aptitude for seeing the big picture, and yet failed to put themselves and their own history into the picture.

In 1961, however, that first generation made what we might call a great leap inward, and produced a splendid issue on New York. That Summer 1961 issue of *Dissent* is still exciting a quarter century later. It features a memoir by Irving Howe, "New York in the Thirties"; an overview of the city's political economy by Daniel Bell; a portrait of contrasting modes of urban poverty by Dorothy Day; an exposé of Robert Moses's politico-bureaucratic empire by Fred Cook; an eminently sensible "Utopian proposal" by Percival and Paul Goodman to ban private cars from Manhattan; "Harlem, My Harlem," Claude Brown's first published piece; Norman Mailer, living life on the edge with a Brooklyn gang; and twenty other pieces, almost every one of which still stands up today. What makes *Dissent*'s first New York issue so special is the passion that drives it, and the willingness of the writers to affirm the ties that bind them to a particular place; they are happy to identify themselves as New Yorkers, rather than trying to sound like universal beings. They seem to understand instinctively how the personal is political.

One of the most striking things about our

first New York issue is how much of its political analysis still rings true today. Daniel Bell complains that the city lacks a procedure, or even a vocabulary, for assessing public priorities. "Where politics is played as a brokerage game, all groups defend private interests" against social needs. Dorothy Day distinguishes between stable poverty in which "the poor have some hope," and destitution, "habitation of the ill, the lonely and the hopeless ones" who "suffer the torments of hell." Daniel Friedenberg begins his "Real Estate Confidential" with the assertion that "The most stunning fact about New York is the realty boom," and concludes, "As long as the laws deliberately subsidize the rich and rapacious, a frenzy of building and speculation will be a permanent aspect of American life." Edward Chase paints a picture of neighborhoods increasingly segregated by class and race, and the city as a whole polarized increasingly between rich and poor. Mary Perot Nichols sees the success of municipal reform movements as shallow and transient, and portrays a political machine increasingly adept at coopting its enemies. Percival Goodman

Koch & the Developers

Once, there was a time when the city of New York saw its responsibility for physical planning as a simple mandate: to limit growth. The idea was not to restrict us unreasonably, or to meddle excessively with the forces of capitalism, but to guarantee that those qualities of urban living that are of public benefit, such as light, air, sunshine and a sense of comfortable scale, did not disappear. It was implicitly understood that the private sector, acting on its own, had little incentive to preserve these things, and that it was the responsibility of the city to do so instead. . . .

The city is no longer our protector, but a full-fledged participant in the orgy of Manhattan real-estate development. This is the sad truth—that the municipal government, which at its best should be a moral force for good development, has shown so little interest in anything except accommodation. It is not the job of private developers to set limits; it is their job to make money. It is the function of the city to represent the public interest and forge into the building process the values that matter, which often means drawing the line. And that is just what the city has chosen *not* to do.

PAUL GOLDBERGER
New York Times, May 31, 1987

shows how city and state governments pour lavish subsidies into culture as a luxury industry and imperial spectacle (in the 1960s it was Lincoln Center), even as Nat Hentoff and Mary Otis show how the jazz musicians and theater groups that are New York's real culture heroes face endless harassment from landlords, government bureaucracies, the mob, and the police.

In important structural ways, then, New York hasn't changed much in the last quarter century. And yet, rereading our Summer 1961 issue, we can't help but notice the great gulf in experience and sensibility between those days and our own. Those writers were often bitter or sad, but not traumatized or shocked. They saw New York deteriorating in all sorts of ways; but the trouble they feared was entropy, not catastrophe. They saw themselves as part of a large, growing, increasingly self-confident reforming public, a public that cared passionately about the city and had the energy to make real changes, if it could just understand what was going on. The élan of that public comes through in the issue's cover, a brilliant expressionist montage by Elaine de Kooning, deploying torn newspaper headlines ("Larger Capacity!", "Tigers," "Man," "Murderers," "Rage," and other familiars of daily life), shredded Christmas wrappings, and fragments of industrial debris, leaping off the page in bold black and white and fuchsia and purple. Below the exploding chaos, "New York, N.Y."; above it, boldest of all, like a billboard flashing in Times Square, DISSENT. De Kooning's cover expresses—we might even say, it helps to invent—the spirit of the 1960s. It proclaims that we can let all the city's eruptive forces live and thrive.

We have come a long way since then. The experience of looking back to New York in the summer of 1961 is a little like Philip Larkin's poem about pictures of England in August 1914. The poet's refrain: "Never such innocence again." Those of us who lived through the 1960s and 1970s in New York often felt like soldiers in that Great War: under fire for years, assaulted from more directions than we could keep track of, pinned down in positions from which we couldn't seem to move. These were years when violence, and violent death, became everyday facts of city life. The number of homicides in New York, which had remained remarkably constant at around 300 per year since 1930 (when reliable statistics begin), quintupled in the course of the 1960s; it has fluctuated between 1,500 and 1,800 per year ever since. The frequency of assault, robbery and rape, and of drug-related death seems to have increased even more. So many ordinary, decent people like ourselves, who had worked all their lives to stay clean, suddenly found themselves entangled—as victims, witnesses, or survivors—in ferocious crimes. There was nowhere you could get away from it. We all learned (often without noticing that we were learning) to be very alert in public places, to respond to subliminal signs. Yet our defense systems, adept in protecting us against strangers, might totally fail to alert us to what our loved ones were doing just behind the door; we would only learn when the knock or call came from the police.

We were used to shabby, impoverished, neglected neighborhoods all around the town— some of us worked in them, others drove through on the way out of town; nothing prepared us for the burning down and virtual destruction of many of these neighborhoods, the flames shooting up around us night after night, the metamorphosis of teeming streets and overflowing buildings—sometimes the streets and buildings we'd grown up in—into deserts of burnt-out hulks and vast emptiness. We were used to photographic images of ragged, distressed people down on the Bowery or uptown in Harlem; we weren't prepared to see them face to face, flooding our own streets and doorways and subway stations, and sleeping out in the cold and rain because they had no place to go. We were used to walking through streets full of quiet desperation; we had to learn to negotiate streets full of people shrieking in rage and despair at the top of their voices, and often directing their shrieks at us.

Now we should not forget that, since the early 1960s, the sky has been falling all over America. It would be a sign of our often-remarked provinciality for New Yorkers to think that it has fallen on us alone. Neverthe-

less, there are certain features of New York that have made these general troubles particularly traumatic. Ironically, these are precisely the qualities that have also made New York such a thrilling and beloved place.

First of all, there is our city's intense and vibrant street life. Our nineteenth-century street system, built for pedestrians to walk around in, and our early-twentieth-century mass transit system, built to move streets full of people *en bloc*, have been overtaxed and undermaintained for a long time now. Still, they have held up over the long haul, and most New Yorkers use them every day. They constitute public space of a breadth and intensity probably unsurpassed in the world, and not even dreamt of in the rest of the U.S.A. A random walk in the street or ride on the train can give us a remarkably full view of the richness, diversity, and color of New York life. All our people's energy and beauty can be instantly seen, heard, felt in the street. But that also means that all our strains and tensions are instantly visible, audible, palpable—and, moreover, because the streets are our lifeline, there is nowhere we can go to get away from it all. This openness is one of the things that makes New York so endlessly exciting. But all the tensions that have been seething throughout American society—tensions between races, classes, sexes, generations—have boiled over instantly on the sidewalks of New York. At such times, our

wonderfully open city has felt like a great, festering open wound.

Even as New York's street life has intensified our collective troubles, the city's preeminence as a world communications center has blown them up into something mythical. Things that happen in New York are beamed instantly all over America, indeed, the world, thanks to all the mass media that are located here. Facts become symbols instantly—often long before they are understood. In the late 1960s, New York came to symbolize "urban violence." This wouldn't have been so bad if it had enabled Americans to confront the rapidly rising tide of violence throughout American society. But the symbolism took on an insidiously twisted form: poverty, racism, easy access to drugs and guns, desperate rage exploding into mayhem, were considered uniquely *our* problems; out-of-towners seeing our town come apart concluded complacently that it could never happen to theirs. And when it did happen, instead of learning to scrutinize their own towns more closely, they attacked

New York even more violently, as if we had afflicted all America with its spreading blight. Our own media mythicized us into America's Other, which could be blamed for everything that the country didn't want to see in itself. The demonization of New York reached orgiastic heights in the mid-1970s, during our fiscal crisis, when many politicians and media pundits spoke as if social peace would return to all America if only New York could somehow be wiped off the map.

Another severe blow to New Yorkers came from a direction where we had felt most secure: our city's public sector. New York's public services included enormous housing and hospital complexes, the most generous welfare allowances in the country, and a city university that not only dwarfed all existing state systems (except perhaps California's) but was free. The upkeep of these services helped to make New York the most highly taxed city in the U.S.A. But New Yorkers were willing to pay for them, in part because they appreciated the benefits they brought, in part because these services

Carlin Meyer

Whose Windfall?

Every couple of years friends of friends from Denmark come to visit. When they leave I always ask them, "What impressed you the most about New York City?" Always, I hear the same reply. Not the Statue of Liberty, the World Trade Center, or Wall Street. Not the architecture or the food or the jazz or the theater. What has impressed them about New York City is the appalling disparity of wealth. "How can you stand to live in such a place?" they always ask me.

Sometimes I wonder how I can. Last week I had lunch with a friend who told me about his best law school buddy, now a senior partner in a major Wall Street law firm. His buddy's "draw" (annual salary) is $800,000. His expense account is $100,000, or about $2,000 a week.

My Danish friends are teachers, or carpenters, or government employees. They earn small salaries ($15,000 to $25,000—they can never afford hotels when they come to the United States); they pay 50 percent of those small salaries in income tax so that

all Danes can have medical care, food, and basic necessities. They don't have expense accounts.

I think of the Wall Street partner and of my Danish friends whenever I pass a homeless person, a streetwalker, a beggar, a junkie. I wish for, I dream of, a 50 percent income tax that might pay for the housing for the homeless that no one can seem to build, or the food for the hungry that we pay midwestern farmers not to grow. Of a 50 percent inheritance tax that might pay for free college tuition, or adequate staffing, equipment, and buildings for our elementary and high schools. I look around me at the decaying city structures and at the thousands of unemployed, young and old, and imagine having the funds to hire those unemployed to accomplish all of the public works so desperately needed just to hold our crumbling infrastructure together, let alone to make the city a glorious place to live in (planting flowers and trees, painting murals, supporting free theater and concerts all year round).

And then I listen sadly as the politicians of our

were a source of civic pride. First, because they contained world-renowned people and institutions; second, because they provided formidable social support for people in need and generated a sense of civic solidarity.

By the end of the 1960s, however, all the city's public services found themselves overwhelmed by floods of people who were in far more trouble than the city's resources could even begin to cope with. Anybody who lived in a housing project, took the subway to work, sent a child to public school, tried to use a city hospital or summon the police for help, came face to face with institutions that were, or seemed to be, on the point of breakdown. This was dreadful, not just for the immediate suffering it caused (which was plenty), but for the revelation that, after all the expense and care we had lavished on our public services, we were as endangered and helpless as if we had spent the last twenty years asleep. Our whole public sector, which was supposed to form a structure of solid walls binding New Yorkers together into a community, seemed to be crashing down on our heads.

Nothing in our collective civic consciousness prepared us for this sudden vulnerability. There was nothing in that first *Dissent*—or in any other American source—to warn us. We assumed that although we as individuals were bound to die, our city would live forever. Like citizens of so many cities through the ages, we discovered, to our shock, the precariousness of urban life. The shock was greatest, probably, for the more than half a million New Yorkers who, between 1968 and 1980, saw their own homes and neighborhoods—large parts of Brownsville, East New York, Bedford-Stuyvesant, the Lower East Side, Harlem, a dozen neighborhoods in the Bronx—go up in flames. But our city life was shattering and exploding in so many ways, that all New Yorkers were burned by the heat. In 1984 I coined a word for this dreadful process: URBICIDE, the murder of a city.

Why did everything in the city seem to be collapsing at once? For years nobody seemed to

great city and state race each other to the microphones to announce with great fanfare that they will be the first to return to the individual taxpayer the "windfall" gain to government tax coffers that has resulted from slight adjustments in the federal tax laws (adjustments that *lower* the basic income tax rate for the $800,000-a-year partner!). I try to imagine what I and hundreds of thousands of other average New Yorkers will buy with the $50, or $500 or even $1,000 that we will gain. And I wish I could stop each one of us as we spend those "windfall" dollars on the new Easter hat, or the night on the town, or the video cassette we'll watch twice, or the trip to the Bahamas—stop each one of us and ask if we'd be willing to give it back if it meant fewer homeless in the subways and bus stations, fewer dropouts and drug addicts, fewer hungry and desperate.

I know what every one of us would say and do, if someone stood next to us as we received that "windfall" refund (or set out to spend it) and asked for the return of that small gift to our city and its people. I know that virtually every one of us would gladly give it up. I'd like to put a referendum on the ballot.

But whenever I tell this dream, this vision, to the ones in the know—the politicians and the academics and the planners and the pundits—they tell me that it's

not that simple. They tell me that the issues require an understanding of microeconomics and macroeconomics and inflation and deflation and conflagration. They've tried to convince me that even though there is much work to be done to enable our city to survive, and even though there are thousands of unemployed ready, willing, and eager to do it, it somehow isn't possible to put work and worker together.

They've tried to convince me that though we're capable at this moment of producing vastly more food to feed our thousands of hungry (and, indeed, hunger activists tell me that we already produce enough), it is nonetheless necessary to pay farmers not to plant and to let cheese and butter and grain rot in storage bins. Some of them have even tried to show me why it would be economically counterproductive for the wealthiest nation in the world to redistribute its wealth so that children are not born malnourished and do not grow up to turn to suicide and drugs. They've drawn graphs and pictures and charts. But no matter how they try to explain it, I just can't seem to get it.

I have a sneaking suspicion that it really isn't about numbers or graphs or statistics. I have the feeling somehow that it's about choices. About political and personal and yes, even moral choices. Maybe it's even about choosing which side you are on. □

have a clue. It was only in the late 1970s, after our fiscal crisis, that we developed a comprehensive analysis that did justice to the longterm complexity of our troubles, and brought to light the deep structural forces at their root. One of the crucial historical forces working against New York—and, indeed, against all industrial cities more than a generation old—is the vastly accelerated mobility of capital, propelled by breakthroughs in information technology. This mobility, which no government in the world has as yet figured out how to regulate, is fast bringing about the deindustrialization of America. The first wave broke over the cities of the Northeast. One irony of our history is that this coincided precisely with a human wave of mass migration, in which millions of poor and uneducated blacks and Hispanics came to northern cities in search of industrial jobs that were going the other way. In 1958 the U.S. Navy relocated the Brooklyn Navy Yard to the Gulf Coast, taking with it not only thousands of jobs but a whole complex of satellite industries that supported thousands more.

Meanwhile, the federal highway system, probably the biggest public works project in history, was creating massive incentives for businesses and industries to leave city locations. (Robert Moses's Cross-Bronx Expressway, which displaced about 50,000 people, made the Bronx seductively easy to get out of, and increasingly difficult to stay in.) Federal Housing Administration lending policies, which effectively blacklisted cities (and all locations with large minority populations), created similar incentives for families to relocate. Banks

followed by redlining (i.e., refusing mortgage or construction loans in) large areas of the city. Meanwhile, the American economy as a whole was becoming increasingly militarized, further inflating the power of the Sunbelt. A multibillion dollar, cost-plus, militarized economy virtually guaranteed spectacular profits to investors in the West and South. The Sunbelt became skillful at transforming its economic power into political power; the federal budget was focused more and more on guns, and the social expenditures which, starting in the Great Society years, had helped so many poor people and their neighborhoods survive, were slashed. All these converging forces put us—along with dozens of other cities—up against the wall.

It was, and still is, a desperate predicament. There was probably nothing New York could have done to avert the crash of 1975, because it depended so heavily on decisions made at a national and international level by elites utterly indifferent to the fate of the city. Yet it might have made some difference—even now it still could make a difference—if we were blessed with political leaders honest enough to explain to the people the shape and weight of the forces we are up against. Then we might at least begin to develop a new civic consciousness, appropriate to an age of deindustrialization and dematerialized capital. Then, too, we could take a first step toward a new social contract, in which New Yorkers could share in both the sacrifices that are necessary and the benefits that are still possible.

So how come we're still waiting for a preface to a new social contract? Why, in a city full of smart people who love the city, haven't we moved beyond the urbanism of the summer of 1961? I think that New York intellectuals are stuck because the inner wounds we suffered through the 1960s and 1970s, when we saw our city shake and break, still have not healed. To help things happen, we need to examine some of these old wounds once again.

In 1971, at one of New York's darkest moments, Bernard Malamud published a brilliant parable, *The Tenants*, that came close to the heart of our darkness. Malamud's protagonists are a Jewish writer and a black writer, the sole inhabitants of a collapsing East Side tenement that the landlord is trying to tear down. Each man is imaginative and talented, but profoundly blocked and unable to work through what he is trying to say. (The Jew, Lesser, can hardly bear to go out.) At first, they are delighted to meet. They talk of James Joyce and Bessie Smith, share space, smoke dope, feel like brothers, help each other survive. By and by, however, accumulated pain, rage, and despair poison the friendship. Each comes to believe that it is the other's very existence that blocks him. As the book plunges toward its end, the two men stalk each other with lethal weapons through the building's ruins. In deepest night,

> Neither could see the other but sensed where he stood. Each heard himself scarcely breathing.
> "Bloodsuckin Jew niggerhater."
> "Anti-Semitic ape."
> Their metal glinted in hidden light. . . .

They attack each other, and as they lie dying— this is the book's last line—"Each, thought the writer, feels the anguish of the other." At the end, Levenspiel, the old landlord, finds the bodies, and cries and cries for *rachmones*, mercy for us all.

In *The Tenants*, as in all his best fiction, Malamud was a master of imprisonment. Here he captured the tragic pathos of Jews and blacks clinging to our crumbling city when so many others had given up on it. They are briefly aware of each other's anguish, and alive to the possibility of empathy and mutual aid; in the end, however, they lose themselves in the sure joys of martyrdom, even at the price of self-destruction, rather than staying alive and running the risks of solidarity. It would be silly to restrict the scope of this novel's meaning to Jews and blacks, or for that matter to New York. Still, if we want to think about the costs of isolation, New York's Jews and blacks in the past fifteen or twenty years are not a bad place to start. People who have been chronically victimized often glory in their wounds and fear a future without them. Sometimes victims turn into vicious chauvinists who try to monopolize suffering, and erupt with rage at anybody who might hope to heal or even to share their pain.

Now, as a matter of fact, very few New Yorkers have turned themselves into brutal chauvinists, monopolizers of suffering, empty of empathy or *rachmones*—that's the good news. The bad news is that one of those few is our mayor.

Much of this issue of *Dissent* examines Edward Koch's policies and strategies: the spectacular giveaways to real estate developers; the attacks on the poor, depriving them of industrial work, low-income housing, public hospitals; the trained incapacity to see the city as a human environment, or as anything more than a machine for generating money; the casual brutality that has come to permeate our public life, as in the recent wave of mass arrests to drive homeless people out of the railway terminals that the city's own development policies have driven them into; the triumphal march of the city's rejuvenated political machines, whose movers and members have made the 1980s one long carnival of white-collar crime; the rescue of the city from the clutches of a hostile federal government, by selling it (or giving it away) to rapacious real estate empires that will tear down anything or throw up anything, if it pays; the long-term transformation of New York into a place where capital from anywhere in the world is instantly at home, while everybody without capital is increasingly out of place.

Koch could never have done so much for New York's plutocrats without his demagogic flair for dividing and demoralizing its people. He has been remarkably adept at polarizing blacks and Jews, exploiting their pain and vulnerability, opening and deepening their inner wounds, nourishing their resentments and dreams of revenge, entrenching them in the death frieze of *The Tenants*, ensuring that they will not learn to unite. In life as in art, the landlord steps over the bodies; only in life the landlord is not Malamud's kindly old Levenspiel, an outsider like his tenants, but Donald Trump, who treats all New Yorkers as so much slag, to be discarded fast when we get in the way of his gold mines.

If we look hard at New York's civic culture as it is today, the view is bleak. Hustlers and haters fight for hegemony; the city lurches between sophisticated nihilism and crude eruptions of tribal fear and rage. The worst part is the dearth of alternatives. The generosity of spirit, the reforming vision and energy of the 1960s seem to be gone with the wind. The dominant modes of civic consciousness today help to keep New Yorkers unconscious of the gigantic development deals that will blow them all away tomorrow. No doubt Mayor Koch and his henchmen, and the media that adored him uncritically until last year, deserve plenty of blame for this. But we ourselves, New York's intellectuals, have to take a major share of responsibility for what New Yorkers know and when they know it. If they don't know that the city is controlled by a development machine that is eating up their neighborhoods, their livelihoods and their culture, and if they don't know that they have the power to fight the machine and change the city's course, then we haven't been doing our job. Civic culture was born, in ancient Athens and Jerusalem, when intellectuals took their stand in public spaces, and took it on themselves to act as the consciousness and conscience of their cities. New York's intellectuals haven't done much

lately to live up to this legacy. We've stayed indoors, upstairs, while more and more of our city has been sold and bulldozed out from under us.

I've argued that this long absence springs not from ignorance or indifference, but from impacted pain and grief. But there's no reason for our paralysis to be terminal. After all these years, aren't we sick of it? We still have plenty of brains and energy, and we still love New York. If we expose some of our inner wounds to the air, we can not only discover their sources, but see how widely they are shared. Knowledge is power; understanding pain can help us work our way toward a stronger civic identity. If New Yorkers can come to feel how much we all have lost, it can help us work together fast before we lose it all. We need first to mourn, then to reform: to go through our grief together, and then to move beyond the work of mourning, to create a framework that can bring our city's future development under its citizens' control. Then we will be able to let go of our pain, and to build over the ruins a city we can share. □

Thomas Bender

NEW YORK AS A CENTER OF "DIFFERENCE"

How America's Metropolis Counters American Myth

When people speak of New York as being different, something other than America, they seem to have in mind a special quality of the city's culture and politics, perhaps associated with its ethnic makeup. Such perceptions, however imprecise, have a ring of truth. Culture and politics in New York are based on premises not quite shared by the dominant American culture.

The most influential myths of America, those that have been incorporated into the culture, are easily identified in their origins with specific regions: Puritan New England and Jeffersonian Virginia. Neither place is really as representative of America as are the more difficult-to-characterize middle colonies. Yet in spite of the narrowness and purity of the Puritan dream of "a city upon a hill" and of agrarian Jeffersonianism, these myths have come to be associated with America, evoking the virtues of the small town and the agricultural frontier.

It is puzzling but true that the outlook associated with New York's cosmopolitan experience has been unable to establish itself as an American standard. The other two myths or, to use a more contemporary terminology, these other two representations of the American ideal, have managed to deflect, if not completely obliterate, the alternative standard that since the eighteenth century has been an abiding theme of cultural and political discourse in New York City.

Scholars a generation ago devoted themselves, perhaps too much, to the study of the communitarian myth of the American town and the agrarian myth of the American landscape. It is worth returning to the theme and point of that scholarship. Our acceptance of these myths—whether passively or, as in the case of recent national political leaders, aggressively and exploitatively—has been consequential, limiting our ability to grasp the value or distinctiveness of the culture and politics of New York City.

When we examine these myths we can better see what makes New York City uncomfortable with America and America uncomfortable with, even fearful of, New York City. Although the New York experience and the outlook associated with that experience posit a political and cultural life based upon *difference,* the myth of rural and small town America excludes difference from politics and culture. Such exclusion impoverishes civic life, thinning and trivializing the notion of a public culture.

Can one really bracket Puritanism and Jeffersonianism? Everything about them, it seems, is different: one religious, the other secular; one hierarchical, the other egalitarian; one town-oriented, the other rural; one reminiscent of the medieval worldview, the other drawing upon the Enlightenment. More differences could be enumerated, but I want to point out a crucial similarity: *both reject the idea of*

© 1987 Thomas Bender. A slightly different version of this essay will appear in *America in Theory*, edited by Denis Donoghue, Luke Menand, and Leslie Berlowitz, to be published by Oxford University Press.

difference. Neither can give positive cultural or political value to heterogeneity or conflict. Each in its own way is xenophobic, and that distances both of them from the conditions of modern life, especially as represented by the historic cosmopolitanism of New York and, increasingly, other cities in the United States.

Few phrases reverberate more deeply through American history than John Winthrop's celebration of the Massachusetts Bay Colony as "a Citty upon a Hill." "We must," Winthrop urged his party as they sighted Massachusetts Bay, "be knitt together in this worke as one man." Never has the ideal of community been more forcefully stated in America. The Puritans envisioned a single moral community, one that acknowledged no distinction between private and public values. "Liberty," Winthrop explained in his famous "Little Speech" in 1645, permits "that only which is good, just, honest"—something to be determined by the consensus of the community.

Contrary to much American mythmaking, neither individualism nor democracy was nourished in the New England town. Its significance, Michael Zuckerman has argued, is rather that it nourished "a broadly diffused desire for consensual communalism as the operative premise of group life in America." You had a place in a Puritan village or town only if your values coincided with those of your neighbors. Rather than incorporating difference, Puritan town leaders were quick to offer strangers the "liberty to keep away from us."

The myth of consensus and sameness was sustained in the towns by a peculiar pattern of "democratic" practice. Votes were, of course, taken at town meetings, but the minutes of those meetings offer no evidence of split votes, thus making a single opinion the only recorded history. The ideal of concord and sameness underlay religion as well. When Jonathan Edwards described heaven for his congregation, it was the New England town ideal made eternal. Heaven, he explained, is a place "where you shall be united in the same interest, and shall be of one mind and one heart and one soul forever."

Although the social basis for such an experience of consensus had been undermined by the beginning of the nineteenth century, enough remained to sustain belief in it for many Americans. The ideal of a covenanted community persisted, as Page Smith has demonstrated, especially in the midwest.[1]

Even in the seventeenth century, this theory of America could accommodate inevitable difference, but only in a quite limited way. You cannot stay in our town, but you are free to establish your own town, with your own people and beliefs. This sort of pluralism, argued before the Supreme Court as recently as 1982 (in defense of school library censorship in the suburban Long Island district of Island Trees), is a pluralism of many supposedly consensual communities. So the dream of living surrounded by sameness, with all differences kept at a distance, persists. It is at the heart of much suburban development, but it is also to be found, as Frances FitzGerald has shown, in a diverse group of self-segregating communities, ranging from the "Castro" in San Francisco to Jerry Falwell's Virginia Church.[2]

The dark side of the New England communal ideal is intolerance, as many a seventeenth-century New England Quaker accused of witchcraft learned. Otherness is a problem for such communities; difference becomes indistinguishable from subversion.[3]

Thomas Jefferson, of course, was less worried about subversion. He even recommended frequent revolutions, always trusting the democratic practice of the living. It is this spirit that prompted Alexis de Tocqueville to refer to Jefferson as "the most powerful advocate democracy ever had." But however much we are moved, and properly so, by Jefferson's magnificent democratic professions, we must also attend to the theory of society that underlay them. Jefferson could trust democracy because he assumed a societal consensus on values, and he opposed places like New York, calling them "cancers" on the body politic, in part because they would produce citizens whose values and interests would be marked not only by difference but even serious conflict.

It is only lately, since Garry Wills publicized the Scottish influences on Jefferson, that the communitarian basis of his social thought has become evident. Jefferson believed men were naturally endowed with a "sense of right and wrong" because they were "destined for society." Yet this "moral sense" was honed by actual social relations, making common sense, as Wills put it in *Inventing America*, actually "communal sense." The approbation of the community provided the basis for assessing virtue. For example, Jefferson granted blacks a moral sense, going on to explain that it was "their situation" that accounted for their evident "disposition to theft."

Jefferson's admiration for Native American tribal cultures has been much remarked. But we must grasp more fully the centrality of such communalism to his general theory of society. It was the basis for his confidence that in the agrarian society he envisioned Leviathan was not needed. Sociability and affection, not the artifice of government, would make the good society. All of this depended, however, upon shared values. That is why he encouraged territorial expansion, which would replicate America. He sought a common experience in a nation of relatively equal yeoman farmers. On the negative side, his commitment to uniformity made Jefferson very hesitant about immigration. Arguing against a policy of encouraging immigration, he explained that "it is for the happiness of those united in society to harmonize as much as possible in matters which they must of necessity transact together." For Jefferson, homogeneity and the duration of the republic seemed closely linked.

Jefferson's fear of the heterogeneity he associated with immigration provides a clue to his inability to contemplate a republic made up of former masters and former slaves. Historians have long tried to determine the sources of Jefferson's peculiar position on slavery and freedom: he strongly criticized slavery but declined to become publicly identified with any antislavery movement. Even in his private dreams he always assumed that freed blacks would have to be deported. Some Jefferson scholars have focused on his racist language and assumptions, others upon economic interest, still others on his inability to transcend the worldview of his time, place, and class. Some have even suggested that slavery was fundamental to his republicanism: freedom was defined by slavery. All such explanations contain part of the answer, but no one, to my knowledge, has noted the way in which his theory of society as necessarily conflict-free made an interracial republic of former masters and former slaves impossible.

Jefferson himself gave this kind of explanation. In his *Notes on the State of Virginia* (1784), he explained why freed slaves, if ever there was such a population, must be removed from society:

> Deep-rooted prejudices entertained by the whites; ten thousand recollections by the blacks, of the injustices they have sustained; new provocations; the real distinctions which nature has made; and many other circumstances, will divide us into parties and produce convulsions, which will probably never end but in the extermination of the one or the other race.

Writing in 1820, Jefferson observed that "we have a wolf by the ears, and we can neither hold him, nor safely let him go. Justice is in one scale, and self-preservation in the other." When faced with real conflicts of interest and values, the happy revolutionary retreated to the conservative standard of self-preservation. He even feared the divisiveness of public antislavery agitation, hoping, quite unrealistically, for a natural and conflictless moral progress that would somehow remove the blot of slavery. There was nowhere else for Jefferson to go.

Certain elements of the Jeffersonian tradition may thus appear in a new light. We can now see why Jefferson wanted a happy and undifferentiated yeomanry and why he opposed the development of cities, with their complex social structures, diverse values, and conflicting interests. The great defender of democracy based upon sameness, Jefferson could find no way to accommodate difference. He found himself compelled to discourage immigration, to maintain slavery, and to oppose urbanization. Hardly a democratic theory for our time.

Both the Puritan and the Jeffersonian myths nourish a distrust of democracy, at least any democracy that proceeds from difference, whether of culture or interest. Both undermine a theory of democracy that proposes to use politics to determine the allocation of societal resources, since they cannot accommodate the conflicts implied by such politics. New York, operating on different cultural premises, historically has proposed an alternative redistributional politics. One cannot claim as much success for this approach as one might hope for, but New York has at least trusted in democracy amidst difference. And there are some successes, including nearly a half-century of progress until the fiscal crisis of 1975.

When New York has been stopped or even turned back in such ambitions, it has been in the name of dominant American values, not in the name of its own values. As early as the 1830s, Tocqueville suggested that the blacks and immigrants in cities (what he called the "rabble" of New York) be governed by an "armed force" under the "control of the majority of the nation" but "independent of the town population and able to repress its excesses." In 1840, the conservative Philip Hone, a former mayor, recorded in his diary that universal suffrage might work in the American countryside, but not in New York, with its "heterogeneous mass of vile humanity." After the Civil War, E.L. Godkin, the founding editor of the *Nation*, insisted that economic and social relations were beyond the legitimate reach of politics. If the mass of urban workers could not be dissuaded from pursuing interest politics, he was prepared to disenfranchise them, thus removing them from municipal politics.

Most recently, it has been Felix Rohatyn who has taken aim at New York's best traditions. In place of the tumult of a politics of difference, he proposes to rescue the city and even the nation from New York's excessive democracy with an elite council of conciliation, much like the leaders of a Puritan church, charged with winning the wayward to the one true way. For Rohatyn the only way to make New York City acceptable to America is to depoliticize the city, substituting—in the Municipal Assistance Corporation and the Emergency Financial Control Board—a suprapolitical authority, "publicly accountable but . . . run outside of politics."

Myths of sameness inevitably misrepresent the condition of life in a modern and urban society. Not only do they favor provincialism over cosmopolitanism, but they undermine our ability to bring economic life within the purview of a democratic politics.

If there are fully shared values—either as a fact of nature, as Jefferson would have it, or as a result of very strong communal institutions, as Winthrop proposed—the market need not be an arena of conflict. It would be no more than a mere mechanism of exchange, essentially without implications for power relations. If, however, the assumption of consensus is false, then the market, unless politically controlled, becomes autonomous and self-legitimating—an all-too-faithful representation of modern power relations. Just this happened in the course of the nineteenth century, but for many Americans the myth of equality and of natural harmony masked the implications of this development, allowing the bulk of economic

decisions to be insulated from political control. Americans, more than any other people, came to accept the market as a law of nature, as a public philosophy.

Although there have certainly been New York intellectuals of both radical and conservative persuasion who have put their faith in the market on the basis of these mythical assumptions, the broader political culture of the city—grounded upon an experience marked by the idea of difference—has energized attempts to bring economic decisions within the sphere of democratic politics. To the extent that modern America is more like New York than it is like Jefferson's America, New York's history may become prophetic. An America victimized by the illusion of the market as a public philosophy—which in fact facilitates corporate manipulation—may well find in its beleaguered metropolis an alternative myth.

But can we identify a tradition of cultural and social thought in New York City that suggests an alternative to the dominant American myths? A more vital politics? A richer notion of public culture? Does New York offer even a rudimentary alternative myth that deserves recovery? I think it does.

The special character of New York was evident from the beginning. If religion inspired the Puritans and the dream of wealth drove the Virginians, the practicality of trade engaged the first settlers of New Amsterdam. If churches and regular church service came quickly to both Massachusetts and Virginia, it was the counting house, not the church, that represented early New Amsterdam. There was little impulse to exclusion; trading partners were sought no matter what their background. Already in the 1640s eighteen languages were spoken in the area that is now New York City.

This very different history became the material for an alternative vision of society, one that embraced difference, diversity, and conflict. By the middle of the eighteenth century William Livingston, who would later be a signer of the Constitution, was beginning to articulate in New York City a theory—remarkable for its time—of society and culture.

Born in 1723, Livingston graduated from Yale College before beginning the study of law in New York City in 1742, the year before Jefferson's birth. A decade later the trustees of the proposed King's College (today's Columbia) requested a charter of incorporation that privileged one religion at the expense of others (it prescribed an Anglican president in perpetuity). Livingston responded with an innovative vision of city culture that was cosmopolitan and pluralistic.

At a time when all colonial intellectual life was organized within denominational institutions, Livingston proposed a radically different premise for culture. Writing in his own magazine, *The Independent Reflector*, Livingston described a "free" college, one not tied to any private group. It would be governed by the people in their public character, that is, through public authorities.

> While the Government of the College is in the Hands of the People . . . its Design cannot be perverted. . . . Our College, therefore, if it be incorporated by Act of Assembly, instead of opening a Door to universal Bigotry and Establishment in Church, and Tyranny and Oppression in

the State, will secure us in the Enjoyment of our respective Privileges, both Civil and religious. For as we are split into a great Variety of Opinions and Professions; had each Individual his Share in the Government of the Academy, the Jealousy of all Parties combating each other, would inevitably produce a perfect Freedom for each particular Party.

This sense of city culture not only tolerated difference but depended upon it.

Almost exactly one hundred years later Walt Whitman transformed these same social materials into a work of art that at once reveled in and reconciled difference. But Whitman's achievement was aesthetic, and its glue was emotion, not ideas. An ideological expression of New York found its best voice another half century later, in the person of Randolph Bourne.

The symbolic leader of the first generation of American writers to call themselves intellectuals, Bourne was in fact the prototype of the later New York intellectual, working at the intersection between politics and culture. Bourne gave ideological expression to the cosmopolitan ideal that would distinguish New York from the provincial values of America. He supplied the context for the emergence, as David A. Hollinger has pointed out, of a left intelligentsia in New York between the wars.[4]

Seeking to liberate himself and his generation from the Anglo-Saxon parochialism of the dominant culture, Bourne embraced the immigrants who were transforming New York City. His essay, "Trans-National America," published in the *Atlantic* in 1916 amid the intolerance of war, combined an acceptance of enduring particularism with a commitment to a common or public culture. He envisioned America in the image of New York City—a federation of cultures. Rejecting the Anglo-Saxon tradition, he declared that American culture "lies in the future," it shall be "what the immigrant will have a hand in making it."

This was an audacious claim when made, and it could have been made only in New York. The editor who published the piece, Boston's Ellery Sedgwick, stood for more traditional and homogeneous American ideals.

He had agreed to publish the essay only because of his long-standing relationship with Bourne, a regular contributor, and because it was so well written. But he informed Bourne in his letter accepting the article: "I profoundly disagree with your paper." In the incredulous voice of genteel Boston confronted by cosmopolitan New York, he admonished: "You speak as if the last immigrant should have as great effect upon the determination of our history as the first band of Englishmen." Insisting that the United States had neither political nor literary lessons to learn from Eastern Europe, he bridled at Bourne's equation of an old New Englander and a recent Czech as "equally characteristic of America."[5]

If we may now leap to the present—and toward a conclusion—it is precisely Bourne's vision of New York and America that is endangered by both national and local cultural and political developments. No local cultural and political issue better illustrates these stakes than does the controversy over the future of Times Square. Is it to remain and be renewed as a New Yorkish public space, or is it to be transformed, with vastly over-scaled corporate towers designed by Phillip Johnson, into a mere episode in crass government-sponsored but private real estate development that could occur anywhere in America?

A government that seemingly recognizes only one constituency is trying to give to that constituency a space that has historically represented all classes. What Johnson proposes, and what the political and financial elite sponsoring the scheme desire, is the transformation of a public space historically marked by a multivoiced public culture into a monotonal space without public significance.

To thus destroy Times Square is to destroy our most potent symbol of New York's peculiarly cosmopolitan politics and culture. Times Square, like Union Square before it, has historically represented the complexity of the city's culture. Here for all to see, for all to experience, the city has represented itself in all its fullness to itself and to the world. No other American city has an equivalent to Times Square.

The question, however, is whether the diversity and public quality of this space must be destroyed in order to save it. Is inclusion, is difference, necessarily incompatible with safety? What is the source of the loss of confidence that is eroding our historic cosmopolitanism? From whence the idea that in New York it is necessary—or even possible—to remove completely all sources of tension, or even struggles for cultural and political expression in a public space? Of course, a sense of personal security is necessary for a space to function as a public place, but one must have the confidence to weigh, with some delicacy, the legitimate claims of security against the dynamic, even messy elements that make a space public and that impel the process of making public culture.

To say that a space is in some sense contested terrain is not to deny its public character; it is to confirm it. Times Square has been a celebration of and a complicated reconciliation of difference, remaining so today, when it has lost much of its centrality and vitality.

Current proposals to save the theaters and the lights at Times Square are not wrong, but they totally miss the point. They do not grasp the real historical and political stakes at 42nd Street and Broadway. This complex intersection represents an important tradition and is a contemporary symbol for an alternative to the dominant American presumption of sameness. Times Square, in short, symbolizes the difference between New York and those Puritan and Jeffersonian myths that continue to find resonance across the Hudson. Perhaps New York's own myth, to say nothing of its

practice, has never been fully elaborated and achieved, but New York and America would both lose were it casually abandoned. If New York gives in, if New York abandons engagement with difference, who will be left in America to stand against the rising intolerance toward difference, the new provincialism, to use the most gentle of possible epithets?

A theory of society and culture such as I have described does not constitute a politics. But without it, without a symbolic representation of diversity and difference, the much discussed but still unrealized progressive politics of a "rainbow" coalition is an impossibility.

Even if success were achieved in New York, it would still remain uncertain whether New York could make a culture and politics of difference respectable in America. Might New York's myth of difference ever effectively compete with the dominant American myths of sameness? Or must we be always beleaguered and different? □

Notes

[1] Page Smith, *As a City Upon a Hill* (New York, 1966), esp. chap. 3.

[2] Frances FitzGerald, *Cities on a Hill* (New York, 1986). Note the modification of Winthrop in her title. The change makes my point in the fewest possible words.

[3] See the very powerful argument in Christine Leigh Heyrman, *Commerce and Culture* (New York, 1984).

[4] David A. Hollinger, *In the American Province* (Bloomington, 1985), chap. 4.

[5] Ellery Sedgwick to Randolph Bourne, Randolph S. Bourne Papers, Special Collections, Columbia University.

DAYS OF THE DEVELOPERS

Jim Sleeper

BOOM AND BUST WITH ED KOCH

When the American Telephone and Telegraph Company announced on March 26th of this year that it would move 1,000 employees from its new Madison Avenue headquarters to Basking Ridge, New Jersey, the Koch administration's fury was tempered only by its embarrassment. Fury, because A.T.&T. had received $42 million in property tax abatements in exchange for a promise to keep jobs in the city; embarrassment, because no one had taken the trouble to get the promise in writing.

Threatening to revoke the abatements anyway, the mayor convinced the company to limit

A Straight Line

. . . The malefactors held responsible for the mess in Gotham have always been corrupt politicians and newly enriched real estate interests . . . . The charge of speculative and unplanned overbuilding . . . is a constant theme, running from Daniel M. Friedenberg's piece in the 1961 "New York, N.Y." issue of the socialist journal *Dissent* to the current populist campaign against gentrification and new luxury condominiums. Similarly, . . . there is a straight line connecting Percival and Paul Goodman's impassioned plea for [a ban on private autos in Manhattan] in the very same issue of *Dissent* with the now-successful fight against the Westway super-highway project.

. . . All this is merely the story throughout history of the rise of cities and the response to that rise of those who were, or felt themselves to be, dispossessed . . .

. . . The power of New York, contrary to its critics, comes from the brute economic strength they despise. But because of that strength, there is talent here, and the money to back it, to burn. The pity of it all is that the real resources of the city, so much greater than anything in the imagining of its present detractors, could be used to lead with excellence rather than level with mediocrity.

—SAMUEL LIPMAN, in "New York in the Eighties: A Symposium," the *New Criterion*, Summer 1986

its transfers and refrain from renting its building to outsiders before 1994 (when his fourth term would be over). Yet the fracas only reinforced his critics' complaint that the $1.3 billion in property tax breaks given big firms since 1978 have been wasteful, because irrelevant to their choosing Manhattan since at least 1981, when the current real estate boom began. These booms have lives of their own, the critics said, and sensible taxation for sound public purposes won't kill them. Indeed, this one, just now beginning to ebb, would have a longer life ahead had the city collected much of the forgone revenue and spent it on the infrastructure, transit, schools, and housing the firms and their workers need in order to function here. Besides, for all the city's generosity to developers and corporations, A.T.&T.'s decision showed that you can't give any specific company enough to offset whatever other considerations prompt it to leave.

That Koch couldn't or wouldn't see this, grudgingly accepting only the most belated curbs on the giveaways even after mainstream studies supported his critics, reflects something important about his mayoralty that historians of the city will try to explain—its abdication of government's legitimate "police powers" over burgeoning development, and its abandonment of any civic mission broader than what "development" itself might define. The explanation isn't so simple as "corruption by developers," "the trauma of the fiscal crisis," or "the spirit of the times on Wall Street and in the White House," though it is all these and more. Koch's infamous self-absorption is mentioned; others say some kind of personal blackmail is at play. All we can do here is sketch the capitulation in commercial and housing development and allude to it in other areas.

Admittedly, political establishments are reactive; like generals, they're usually fighting the last war. It's especially true of cities, which are run by entrenched, often parochial interests, yet lie open to capital and human migrations that dwarf their limited powers. No matter how loudly Koch claims credit for the recent expansion, its force has surprised him, just as the severity of the economic/fiscal crisis of the mid-1970s surprised his predecessors, themselves the products of an even larger, more precarious boom. "Just as we knew little about the city's economic decline while it was happening, we know less than we should about what's producing this boom," says Bowery Savings Bank chairman and former developer Richard Ravitch, who heads Koch's Charter Revision Commission. Certainly no city government that's gone from being a nearly bankrupt object of national scorn in 1975 to running a $700 million budget "surplus" today, as host to what *Business Week* calls "The New York Colossus," can have done much more than play "catch up" with world forces and trends converging upon it in twelve short years.

It has been a mighty convergence, indeed. Since 1981, roughly forty-five million square feet of new commercial space have been built in Manhattan alone, an increment as large as the *total* space in Boston and San Francisco combined. The city has gained almost 375,000 jobs since 1976 for a total of 3.6 million, a sixteen-year high. Tourism is up from 3.3 million in 1975 to 17.5 million this year. Even the recent 3.4 percent jump in subway ridership, to nearly 3.7 million passengers a day, has confounded the Metropolitan Transit Authority's projection of zero growth, which itself had been thought optimistic after twelve straight years of decline. The world forces behind these developments include enormous foreign investment (the number of foreign banks here has tripled since 1970 to include ninety-four of the world's hundred largest);

massive immigration (around 2.4 million since 1970, helping boost the city's population from a thirty-year low of 7.1 million in 1980 to 7.5 million now); and, riding both tides, the conspicuous consumption of affluent Latin Americans, Italians, and others who are here, they say (as CUNY professor Sidney Shanker reports), because they couldn't wear their fur coats in public in Lima and Rome.

Just as no mere mayor can claim credit for such growth, neither can he be blamed for the consequences of rising oil prices, strong dollars, international drug traffic, the federal deficit, housing and welfare costs, new technologies that disperse investment and employment, and an increasingly self-sufficient exurbia attractive to corporate planners who prefer the simulated vitality of "mall" environments to the real and unpredictable vitality of cities. "If you're really smart and can read the trends, you can move the development process about one percent toward the city's best interest," explains former City Planning Commission vice chairman Martin Gallent. "It's only when the market already *wants* to be somewhere that you can get it there."

And yet, as Gallent would be first to insist, what looks like just "one percent" now can have big consequences later. It's precisely the velocity and, in a new world economy, the *contingency* of the current expansion—which rests less on the city's past advantages of geography, technology, and homegrown wealth than on fickle notions and quick calculations about its "chemistry" and "quality of life"— that make all the more fateful those options a mayor does take at the margins of the great transformation. Koch's decision to abdicate even the modest "clearing house" functions of local government, as well as its broader city-building powers, undercuts both the current boom and the "New York Ascendant" envisioned by his own Commission on the Year 2000.

Policy Defaults

Three signal failures of the Koch administration deserve attention, though this article cannot give them equal space if it is to do minimal justice to any of them:

• *Mismanagement of the Manhattan boom itself.* Koch has said candidly: (a) he doesn't think long-range planning is possible and (b) government should get out of business's way. Three key issues here are tax incentives, which unnecessarily bleed essential service revenues; zoning, or rather, the abandonment of responsible city planning in favor of selling off variances and publicly owned parcels to the highest bidders to replenish the treasury; and wasteful, destructive boondoggles, publicly sponsored, privately driven, like Westway and the Times Square "renewal" project.

In addition, the economic development of the four boroughs outside Manhattan has been mishandled by undue emphasis on capturing a "back-office" spillover from Midtown and Wall Street. With a few exceptions, this is not where the boroughs' promise lies; yet manufacturing and new indigenous small business there are all but ignored, or even pushed out.

• *Failure to accept that the private market can't provide low- and moderate-income housing or prevent homelessness.* Naturally, Koch has bewailed the end of direct federal housing aid and tried to replace it with $4.2 billion in locally generated revenue (from the city's own capital budget, the World Trade Center, Battery Park City, and "Big MAC" surpluses) to rehabilitate city-owned apartments and construct new housing.

But the mayor has failed utterly, out of what can only be described as an ideological commitment to the "free market," to hold the line against immediate causes of homelessness (itself the tip of an iceberg of "doubling up" and dislocation involving hundreds of thousands) and to support the many replicable models of nonprofit, community-based housing development that have emerged across the city. A little recouped tax incentive money would go a long way here. Instead, many successful experiments are all but dying on the vine while the city auctions its foreclosed parcels to the highest (often unqualified) bidders or sells them to upscale developers. Government doesn't so much "get out of the way" as choose between competing approaches to property relations and housing development. Demoralization and incompetence in the city's housing agency reflect the mayoral bias, compounding the crisis.

• *Failure to prepare the work force for investors, and vice-versa: the crisis in race relations and education.* This is beyond the scope of this essay, but it has been sounded in part by the mayor's own Commission on the Year 2000, headed by Board of Education President Robert Wagner, Jr.: however many new jobs the city gets, its predominantly minority youth are inadequately prepared for them. The mediocrity reflects not "leveling" reforms, but profound inequities in resource distribution countenanced by Koch. That the consequent staggering minority youth unemployment fuels violent crime and underground economies only reinforces the deep but seldom discussed racism of corporate planners.

The mayor's misleadership in race relations has squandered the remarkable opportunity he had, as an elected official popular with those corporate planners, to alter their perceptions of the tens of thousands of minority youngsters struggling in good faith to make the most of pathetically limited resources. Some corporations have reached out, only to discover, as did four major banks and New York Telephone this year, that a majority of high school graduates couldn't pass eighth-grade-level exams to qualify for jobs. A few companies have found, however, that developing training programs with high schools pays off because it significantly improves youths' performance as it broadens their horizons. The problem is that Board of Education support has been so poor that Time, Inc. and CBS Magazines have withdrawn their support for school writing programs, while the banks charge—and the Board acknowledges—inadequate follow-through by the schools. That Koch has never seriously joined the battle of corporate perception and commitment is a tragedy of unimaginable dimensions.

II. Whose Boom?

Had AT&T's $42-million tax break failed to keep it in town? That was because the real estate market was so strong, explained Deputy Mayor for Economic Development Alair Townsend. Clearly the company could make more renting out its space at high prevailing rates—

and needed to, after the breakup of its industry.

Officials said much the same on April 29th, when J.C. Penney, the nation's third-largest retailer, announced that it would move 3,800 jobs from Sixth Avenue to Dallas: a boom is a boom, even if those who have to sell out of it include big, venerable firms. Most corporations here "have committed themselves" to Manhattan's economies of agglomeration and "are much less likely than in previous years to move their headquarters out of town," wrote one urban planner in the fall of 1985.

City officials touted this line even when soaring housing costs and collapsing transportation and schools were cited in May and June, as Mobil Oil, United Brands' Chiquita division, Hoechst Celanese, Montgomery Ward, KLM, and TWA announced, in a continuing drum roll, their plans to move 3,800 more jobs from the city. Obviously, *somebody's* able to brave New York's rigors, officials said, else demand for space wouldn't be keeping pace with construction, and we wouldn't be replacing jobs even faster than we lose them—a net gain of roughly 45,000 a year since 1983.

That "somebody," of course, is the burgeoning financial industry and other corporate services from advertising to insurance. Koch managed to time the announcement of a 1,500-job expansion downtown by the Shearson-Lehman Brothers brokerage firm with news of TWA's departure. "When we start losing the industries of the future, we'll start to worry," said an aide. Whereupon The United States Life Insurance Company and Deloitte Haskins and 'Sells, the seventh-largest accounting firm in the country, announced they would take 1,100 jobs to Connecticut and New Jersey. And NBC considered crossing the Hudson.

These tremors prompted Koch to offer new commercial and utility tax aid to firms willing to relocate north of 96th Street or in the other boroughs, which were now declared competitive with Jersey suburbs. Even if that were true in dollars, it missed the point, as did celebration of the strong market and new industries: when firms leave Manhattan's

special environment, it's either to go out of business, as have hundreds of manufacturing firms that needed proximity to competitors, customers, and suppliers but couldn't pay soaring rents; or it's to find someplace clean, convenient, and safe, which the boroughs are not when compared to the suburbs where most corporate decision makers already live. And once cleanliness, convenience, and safety have become more important to a broad range of firms than anything New York has to offer, we're talking about problems that won't be solved by more tax breaks. Either the city has become intolerably filthy, congested, and dangerous, or its economies of agglomeration and other allurements have dimmed for firms whose technologies and priorities are changing.

What City Hall's circumlocutions showed last spring was that little had been done about the deterioration of municipal services, congestion, and crime, to say nothing of city planning itself, which affects all three. The city had been too busy throwing its resources into the boom, as if that would make it continue forever. The city had become as narrowly focused as some of the developers.

Manufacturing Destroyed

Nowhere has this folly been clearer than in the destruction—not just "natural" demise—of the light manufacturing companies, employing from ten to fifty people each, where more than a million New Yorkers, a third of the city's work force, found jobs in the 1950s. As 750,000 such jobs, the mainstays of stable working-class families and neighborhoods, left the city largely for reasons beyond its control, newly arrived blacks and Hispanics filled more than 70 percent of the 300,000 remaining, while others became unemployed.

What isn't beyond the city's control is aggressive protection of the hardy survivors, whose number appears to have stabilized. Yet half-hearted zoning of manufacturing districts has been too cumbersome and seldom backed by enforcement. If white-collar firms and young loft-seeking professionals could pay more per square foot than the ailing manufacturers, why should the city stop them? So argued the developers and the newcomers themselves, noting that many manufacturing spaces were already going begging as printers and garment manufacturers moved to Hackensack or Taiwan.

But City Hall hasn't just accepted these arguments; it has collaborated in urban renewal schemes that obliterate hundreds of firms with ten or fifteen years' life still in them. The ill-fated Lincoln West luxury housing and Times Square "renewal" would have done this. Luxury residential and commercial developments sponsored by the city and the Port Authority on the Brooklyn and Queens waterfronts are directly displacing thousands more manufacturing jobs and pricing out others nearby.

Yet these developments and the new industries they serve aren't as vital to the city's economic and social underpinnings as the smaller firms upon which hundreds of thousands of blacks, Puerto Ricans, and non-English-speaking immigrants depend. It's as if the politicians and developers wanted to "whiten" the complexion of Manhattan and, more broadly, to get rid of the wage-earning poor. Even the city's campaign to capture corporate "back-office" operations for the boroughs—which has met with appropriate success in office parks in Staten Island and Queens and may well revive downtown Brooklyn—misconstrues the true sources of the boroughs' vitality. Ultimately Brooklyn and the Bronx cannot disport themselves as suburbs or gussy themselves up to become Stamford or White Plains. Their strength depends on small and medium-sized businesses founded mostly by the black, Hispanic, and immigrant and first-generation American families who live there.

Undoubtedly, pessimism about the entrepreneurial proclivities of native American blacks and Puerto Ricans in the years before the new immigration eclipsed this truth. Yet it's the new, homegrown firms—not Midtown and the financial district and their back-office spillovers—that will incubate a new middle class—Dominican, Jamaican, Korean, Chinese and Indian; Italian, Polish, Israeli, and Russian (200,000 whites have immigrated to New York

since 1970); and, yes, American blacks and Puerto Ricans.

What the city must do, as State Senator Franz Leichter has been saying for a decade, is shift its tax expenditures away from the big firms and into the basic city services and targeted aid that businesses in relatively low-rent areas like Flushing, Flatbush, and Fordham Road desperately need. Under Koch, too many roads lead to Manhattan, which sends out its young professionals, developers, and tax breaks; City Hall's strategy for the boroughs amounts to preparing them to catch this trickle, which is fine for a few Victorian brownstone neighborhoods and more harmful than helpful to areas beyond.

Five hundred thousand of Brooklyn's 2.3 million people live below the poverty line. The "Metrotech" project, Morgan Stanley's pioneering back-office venture near Brooklyn Heights, and other projects won't need enough mailroom clerks, busboys, and janitors to compensate for neglect of indigenous economic development. Nor will waterfront condos and marinas create enough entry-level jobs to offset those lost from the lumberyards and factories they displace. New York is not Washington, D.C., or even Boston; yet too much is staked on the big corporate service boom, too little on a diversified economy capable of surviving a bust.

Uprooting "Low" Culture

Even if pols and developers want to whiten Manhattan and the waterfront, there is no such silver lining for them in the concomitant expulsion of cultural and other nonprofit institutions that are losing a game they didn't even want to play. On April 10th, the American Cancer Society's executive committee voted to relocate its 300-employee national headquarters out of the city; only a staff revolt has prompted a reconsideration. The national headquarters of the United Church of Christ and the Presbyterian Church announced that they, too, would go, though at this writing the former is reconsidering.

Half a dozen Off- and Off-Off Broadway theater companies, which need Manhattan locations to cross-fertilize and draw audiences, either closed for good or left the city last year, according to New York *Newsday*; for example, the New York Theater Studio quit the Upper West Side for Washington, where it's now the Potomac Theater. Dan Weaks, whose photography graces the cover and several pages of this issue, was forced to move from one Manhattan loft to another and finally to an apartment too small for his work, much of which is in storage, and whose rent forces him to devote most of his energy to commercial work. Colleagues have already decamped to Hoboken.

The plight of nonprofits and artists and the special communities they sustain was underscored backhandedly when news of J.C. Penney's departure prompted Deputy Mayor Townsend to muse, "A year from now we'll still be here, and they'll be waking up in—yuck—Dallas." As it happens, it was Dallas to which H. Ross Perot nearly lured the Museum of the American Indian from Manhattan, an offer he withdrew only because a provision of the museum's charter mandates that it stay in New York. Charging the city with indifference to its pleas for more space, the museum is in court trying to overturn the provision and move to Washington. If it succeeds, warns Senator Daniel Patrick Moynihan, "the city will die a little." It's hard to believe that celebrants of the "New Manhattan" would notice.

City officials and developers planning the entombment of Times Square in a complex of office towers understand that Broadway musicals must be saved, if only as "loss leaders" that soften the big boom's rapacity into something like verve. Other temples of high culture have had the wit to become big corporations themselves, with their own money-making condominium towers and boards of directors that interlock with the investment banking houses. But the city has done nothing to match New Jersey Governor Tom Kean's plans for a performing arts complex that would nurture the little theater companies streaming out of Manhattan.

New York will remain the capital of cultural certification, marketing, and consumption, but its indigenous young white middle-class culture could approach the sterility Townsend attributes to Dallas. That New York has added as much office space since 1980 as there is in all

of Dallas is precisely the problem: it's happening with such speed and indifference to future and past that the cost to the civic culture is registered not just in congestion and displacement, but also in the ascendancy of the "values" of the Big Deal. As the exodus of casualties of the real-estate wars continues, the pyrrhic victors will be left with little more than what Kurt Vonnegut called "the illusion the city gives, to almost anybody, that he must be accomplishing something by talking or eating or drinking or reading a newspaper in such a busy, expensive place." If that's all it's about, why not pay less in Dallas? At least one can raise a family there.

Will the City Bust its Boom?

But let us assume that plenty of great music, Balanchine, and Broadway musicals are sufficient, that playing the real-estate game of musical chairs is bracing. Can one take the new spring in one's step onto the sidewalks of New York? Percival and Paul Goodman, who twenty-five years ago in *Dissent* argued for a ban on private autos in Manhattan, have been vindicated beyond their wildest nightmares. One cannot drive from the Port Authority Bus Terminal at Eighth Avenue to the United Nations at First Avenue in less than forty-five minutes during much of the day. Sidewalks designed for five-story buildings are so crowded that a stroller or someone in a hurry is forced into the gutter. While Midtown office space has jumped 9 percent since 1976, subway ridership there has gone up only 3 percent because people simply can't fit into the stations at rush hour, let alone onto the trains. There isn't enough money to send trains down the tracks two minutes apart, which might relieve the congestion.

Sigurd Grava, a professor of urban planning at Columbia, draws the inevitable conclusion in *New York Affairs*:

> . . . there are reasons to suggest that the free market forces that drive the overall activity are not equipped to address larger urbanization issues. Moreover, by their nature—in stimulating separate actions by individual decision makers in an internally competitive situation—these forces are likely to exacerbate the situation, even to the

detriment of those individuals who profit in the short term. Thus there [is] every justification for government to step in and control the development business with the aim of achieving public objectives and protecting [Midtown] from an aggregation of negative impacts.

Where, then, is the government? The short answer is, trying to play "real estate" with the best of them. If, as nearly every informed observer outside city government agrees, the construction boom would have gone forward after 1981 even without most of the $1.3 billion in tax incentives, then that money would have been better spent planning for the congestion, or lowering the onerous occupancy tax that hits business tenants, not developers. The city could have stoked the boom simply by subordinating its property tax bills to the corporations' or developers' mortgage payments, Richard Ravitch claims; that would have reassured the lenders, who often retard development because they worry that high taxes will preclude loan repayments. Had the city assured the banks that they'd be first in line, the loans would have been made, and, given the boom's success, the taxes would have been collected, too. Naturally developers preferred exemptions. Nothing came of Ravitch's suggestion.

After embarrassing publicity in 1982 by Sydney Schanberg and others about big corporations which, though denied tax breaks, went ahead with construction anyway, the case-by-case decision process, which had led to charges of politicization, was replaced with "as of right," or automatic, grants in specified geographical areas. Then the issue became how area lines were drawn—one of them, running along Union Square East, takes a little jog to accommodate the Zeckendorf Towers' exemption—and whether the geographical approach didn't still give concessions to companies that didn't need them. Finer discriminations would have to be made by an impressively apolitical, professional board under clear guidelines, but no one is sure what those guidelines should be. What is clear is that, long after it was remotely necessary, the Koch administration kept shoveling money into the boom, against those who

issued definitive, damning studies and cried, "Halt!"

The permanent legacy of sunless canyons and paralysis in the streets and subways reflects an even more fundamental default in the planning process under Koch. Simply, he discovered that the statutory "police power" of the zoning resolution, through which a city regulates building densities and heights—and hence light, air, and congestion—can be a money-maker for City Hall. You let the developers exceed permissible densities and heights by 20 percent; they renovate subway stations and build and maintain small public plazas and pedestrian passageways to help accommodate the congestion caused by their extra floors and people.

But the trade-offs are universally agreed, even by city officials, to have been terrible. So automatic is the 20-percent bonus trade-off that developers see it as simply a reward for building, according to city planner Gallent. Yet the city could simply mandate their amenity contributions without even giving them extra floors. The city itself should plan for plazas, parks, broad vistas, and sunlight, using the taxes it could be collecting, instead of dickering over a few shrubs and benches on a building-by-building basis.

A 1982 revision of Midtown zoning largely failed to reverse this abdication of municipal power. Mainly, it shifted the dealing from the East Side—where developer and lender conservatism about "prestige" addresses would have continued shoehorning new buildings into overbuilt places until the area sank into the East River—to the West Side, where, as Gallent warns, "They're now going to do what they shouldn't have done on the East Side in the first place."

A typical embarrassment came at Columbus Circle, where the MTA, which owns the Coliseum site, decided to sell the property to the highest bidding developer. Written right into the specifications for new construction—to get the highest possible bid—was the *requirement* that the developer apply to the city to exceed permissible density by 20 percent (in towers of fifty-eight and sixty-eight stories, as it has turned out) in exchange for renovating the subway station and paying an extra $55 million to the MTA. The winner was Boston Properties, owned by publisher Mortimer Zuckerman, an ambitious newcomer to the New York development scene who for that very reason would have made lavish concessions. The loser is Central Park and the surrounding neighborhood, which will be cast into shadow by a monstrosity which, with its 20 percent bonus, will bring 9,000 more people into and out of the subway station at rush hours. The MTA came away with a cool $455 million for transit; was this really the best way to raise it? We will have fifty years of sunless congestion to ponder that question.

A new "inclusionary zoning" provision does expand the list of bonusable amenities—the things developers give for higher densities—to include low-income housing either in the building or within half a mile of it. Other cities have *made* developers do that *without* granting higher densities—a policy that in Manhattan might have lowered astronomical land prices, as Columbia planning professor Peter Marcuse has noted. Not many developers are expected to choose this option freely. On the Upper West Side, meanwhile, a very professional Community Board 7, led by John Kowal and Sally Goodgold, has helped institute "contextual zoning," which keeps new construction in character with the existing neighborhood's largely admirable play of density and light.

What's sad is that these modest reforms require unbelievable exertion by civic-minded people who have better things to do. They scream, demonstrate, hire consultants, sit up at night crafting political strategy and testimony; then they're baited by apologists for current policy like Rutgers's George Sternlieb; then the Citizens Housing and Planning Council produces an exhaustively documented middle position, which gains modest support from such "enlightened" representatives of the power elite as former City Planning Commission chairman and now developers' lawyer John Zuccotti; and finally, after five or six years and plenty of damage, a tepid reform passes the Board of Estimate. Democracy is controversy, of course, but mayoral vision and initiative could save years—if a mayor more

independent of the developers than Koch were there to provide it.

Need it be said that great boondoggles like Westway and the Times Square "renewal" plan represent the same sorry processes run riot, that they are feeding binges by developers, construction unions, and politicians? Westway has been aptly dubbed "a real-estate development project masquerading as a highway," an awesome plunder of the public treasury and a savaging of public priorities. The great combines hatching these schemes are like herds of urban dinosaurs thrashing about in search of food. It is a wonder that citizens can stop them, and a good question whether mayoral leadership might harness them. "Westway will never be built," vowed candidate Koch in 1977—before he flip-flopped a year later. Plans for reconstruction of Times Square were "Disneyland," "ridiculous," he said—until a new set of actors more politically congenial presented their own version of Gotham.

When it was created in the 1930s under the inspiration of urban visionaries like Lewis Mumford, the City Planning Commission was a powerful fourth branch of government with significant powers over the city budget. Much planning has smacked of elitism and produced its own failures; maybe the original commission was too strong. Today, though, the title of the Zoning Resolution, a book thick with dubious amendments negotiated with greedy developers, should be "Let's Make a Deal." In 1961, when this current zoning framework was passed, Mumford predicted that greed and irrationality would destroy the American city. Can any mayor deflect if not actually mobilize real estate energies toward better ends? Or must he always put the best possible civic face on antisocial adventures? Little in Koch's commercial development policy has given that question a fair test. It is that failure of nerve, as much as the surrender of specific taxing and zoning powers, for which he will be remembered.

III. No Housing Market

In December 1985, the Mayor wrote to thirty-three of the city's major developers, asking how they and the city might construct 10,000 units of housing a year for people making between $15,000 and $48,000—the "moderate" and "middle-income" New Yorkers. The median rental household income in the city is around $12,500—nearly 70 percent of all New York City households are renters—and 27 percent of these tenant households live at or below the poverty line of $10,600. So Koch's letter to the developers didn't even pretend that the market could actually build housing for nearly half the city's population, even with considerable public subsidy or other government support the developers might request.

What the mayor assumed, as do the developers, is that increasing the supply of affordable housing for the middle class will also help the poor. Middle-class people now holding tight to rent-regulated apartments would loosen their grip, and the space would "filter" downward to lower-income people. And, enhancing the lot of the middle class would make the city more attractive to business, which generates taxes and jobs that benefit the poor.

These assumptions are problematic in New York's increasingly corporate economy and high-stakes real estate games. White-collar housing *is* desperately needed, but it's not clear that traditional "filtering" and ladders of upward mobility will work even if such housing is built. Koch's query reflected another problematic assumption—that only profit-maximizing developers can build housing in volume, and that, since they can't build low-income housing without massive subsidies the city doesn't have, there is *no choice* but to concentrate public initiatives on middle-income housing.

Of course the city runs low-income housing programs, from federally subsidized public housing (half a million people in 174,000 units) to "tenant management" and "homesteading" programs in 10,000 city-owned apartments "taken" from landlords who've in fact abandoned them. But the latter are poorly funded, tightly constrained; the city adopted them only because residents had already pioneered them without its permission. Nor has the notion that large, professional nonprofit entities—building

societies, unions, churches, foundations, community organizations—can build or rehab low-income housing in volume ever really sat well with the Koch administration as a matter of policy—or politics.

The nonprofit efforts are suspect because they alter the structure of property relations, taking what had been private, for-profit buildings and land and turning them into (minority) nonprofit coops, often in areas where the (white) market might someday revive. If it does revive, the city can make money selling its foreclosed properties to the high bidders and, thus spurring gentrification, increase its tax base. Or—perish the thought—the low-income cooperators might embrace the market themselves, selling out to reap "unearned" windfalls on the land and subsidies the city gave them.

Never mind the reasons, beyond our scope here, why this is unlikely to happen. City Hall radiates mistrust out of greed; out of an ideological preference for the market (except for low-income cooperators); and out of a political desire to control. Koch is uneasy with low-income housing not run by the real estate fraternity or by government. Which means, given the state of the market and federal funding, that he is not really comfortable with low-income rehab and construction at all. His comments and policies have made this very clear.

So Koch asked his friends in the fraternity what they needed from him to attack the housing crisis at its middle. The developers formed a committee under the aegis of the Real Estate Board of New York (REBNY) and came back with a wish list and a promise. The wish list included abolishing rent regulations, streamlining bureaucratic reviews, revising union rules, building codes, zoning constraints, and more. The promise was a surprise: "Do these things for us," REBNY said, in effect, "and, to show our good faith, we'll put up 3,000 units for people in the income range you mentioned, and take no profit. What's more, we'll do it without public subsidy, just to show how much could be done if only our reasonable reforms were granted."

The project that emerged was "hailed by both developers and the city as a breakthrough," according to the *Times*, "a sign of serious commitment by all parties to clear the economic and administrative obstacles that for years have made it virtually impossible to make a profit by building middle-income housing on a large scale." A first site was selected in the Kingsbridge section of the Bronx (suspiciously close to affluent Riverdale, critics noted), and work was begun on a 1015-unit complex to be called Tibbett Gardens. REBNY president Steven Spinola, formerly president of the city's Public Development Corporation, and developer Fred Rose took overall charge. A mayoral blue-ribbon panel headed by Planning Commission Chairman Herb Sturz began work on the developers' wish list. "Housing for working people," the mayor called the effort.

Abolition of rent regulations was impossible, so the developers declared that the units wouldn't be rentals. No matter; the condos would still be priced for middle-income people. Nor could the city revise its procedures systemically to meet the developers' demand on such short notice; but it donated the land and put up the construction capital, insulating the developers from risk. It also expedited environmental reviews as much as it could, trying to meet the demands for "reform" in at least this one demonstration.

By February 1987, with plans, financing, and reviews complete and construction set to begin, the developers' promise had failed. "A terrible admission of defeat by the real-estate industry," said George Sternlieb, its most consistent apologist. Tibbett Gardens's thirteen buildings and landscaped courtyards would be handsome. But, even with a $25-million city capital subsidy, which will be incorporated into the plan to write down the price of each apartment by $25,000, the cheapest two-bedroom unit will cost $107,000—that's roughly $15,000 down and $1,100 a month for mortgage, maintenance, and carrying.

"How many families making $25,000 a year could afford it?" asked Bob Herbert, a *Daily News* columnist. "The answer is none because the bank wouldn't even grant the loan." Officials conceded that a $44,000 income is the minimum required, with $52,000 more likely. Though the development will loosen the market near Riverdale for people in that range, it

certainly "will not provide a model for bringing the private sector back into housing production," wrote *Times* real-estate columnist Alan Oser. This, even with the city's free land; its assumption of the development risks; its $25 million subsidy, which developers had said they wouldn't need; and the development professionals' own time and services at little or no cost.

There were excuses: soggy ground required concrete pilings; the size of the complex drove up costs. And, "It will take a sea change in . . . zoning and the reduction of the influence of the community boards [the Kingsbridge community opposed the project] to create a market," a developer complained to *Times* reporter Alan Finder, blaming the government. But the developers themselves had selected the site and the size. And Deputy Mayor for Policy and Physical Development Robert Esnard said government had done its part. "More and more of the housing market has disappeared from the private sector's spectrum," he noted. Or, as Sternlieb put it, "the economics of housing, *even if you perfect the process*, defeats the market." [Emphasis added.]

The Tibbett Gardens debacle is important because it telescopes lots of debate. For one thing, it puts the industry's wailing about rent control in perspective. Rent control may indeed be an unfair way to allocate scarce housing, because it's not means-tested. But the claim that removing it would unleash torrents of moderate- and middle-income construction is false. Nor has rent control been the primary cause of housing abandonment; the incomes of New York's renters are so low in comparison to soaring housing costs that even were rent ceilings lifted, profits would not increase sufficiently to make most buildings attractive investments. As it is, landlords in poor neighborhoods have had trouble finding tenants who can afford even controlled rents. And the gap between incomes and housing costs widens every year.

As it does, the bottom half of the rental market sinks out of reach even of the downward "filtering" of housing that projects like Tibbett Gardens are supposed to encourage: even if one thousand households earning $44,000 or more move to Tibbett Gardens, depressing rents in the buildings they leave behind, so that one thousand moderate-income people can replace them and leave still other space vacant, this last group of apartments simply can't be rented more cheaply by a landlord seeking even a modest return.

And because the Koch administration refuses to provide adequate resources to nonprofit community housing groups, preferring (despite recent mayoral claims of a policy change) to sell city-owned parcels to high private bidders and pour millions of dollars into middle-class projects like Tibbett Gardens, the bottom half of the income scale has little relief in sight. Even "low- and moderate-" income units to be constructed with some of the $4.2 billion announced by Koch are rising inexorably in price as the city jiggers with the income eligibility limits: the higher the tenant's income, the less public subsidy, and the more units Koch can construct with the money. The Mayor obsesses about the number of units he's producing—not *what kind*.

As the market leaves more tenants stranded outside its threshold, the homeless shelter and welfare hotel system yawns forbiddingly below. "The only thing that's kept the number of homeless individuals under control is that so many can't abide the city's shelters," Kim Hopper of the Coalition for the Homeless told Tom Robbins and Chester Hartman in the *Village Voice*. The results, Robbins and Hartman observe, are grim—and invisible to more fortunate New Yorkers:

There are 200,000 families, most . . . in substandard dwellings, on the waiting list for public housing;. . . New York City's biggest homeless housing program, as Councilmember Ruth Messinger points out, is one it would rather not talk about: allowing some 50,000 families to illegally double up in the Housing Authority's 174,000 apartments. . . . At least 50,000 families are doubled up in privately owned apartments. And nearly a quarter—437,000—of all city renters spend more than half their income on rent, making them likely candidates for future evictions.

It's not as if nobody saw this coming. For years, countless officials and activists pleaded with Koch to impose a moratorium on rampant upscale market conversions of the Single Room Occupancy (SRO) hotel units that a third of all homeless shelter users list as their last previous address. While Koch diddled, the conversions continued, often with arson and thuggery as the means of eviction. As recently as two years ago, Representative Bill Green told a housing class at New York University that the chief cause of homelessness is the illness of people "deinstitutionalized" en masse from upstate mental hospitals. He didn't mention that many of these people, who could not afford or manage apartments, functioned adequately in SRO hotels. The evictions have driven them over the edge.

In 1982, after nearly 100,000 SRO units had been converted, the state forced the city to withdraw the tax incentives it had been giving the converters. Eventually a moratorium on conversions was imposed. Large nonprofit outfits like the Local Initiatives Support Corporation and developer James Rouse's Enterprise Foundation are giving community-based housing organizations resources to help bring the city's own programs to affordable levels for the target populations.

At best, Koch cooperates with the more impressive of these efforts—he could hardly reject them—when he should be out beating down the foundations' and philanthropists' doors. Time and again, he has had to be confronted with virtual *faits accomplis*—with impeccable work plans, the clout of important men, and the activities of organized thousands of low-income people who've built powerful community organizations or simply ripped the tin seals off empty city-owned buildings and moved in. Instead of reaching out to such people in advance, the mayor writes letters to the real estate fraternity and pours millions into projects for people whose incomes are in the top fifth of the population—incomes, even at $50,000, that are four times the median rental household income.

Why These Defaults?

No one examining the mayor's record can fail to note that his ever-shifting rationalizations for development and housing policies have been as duplicitous as the policies themselves have been inappropriate. Always, the city is dragged kicking and screaming into long overdue reforms of tax concessions, zoning provisions, boondoggles, contracting procedures, housing regulations, sales policies on city-owned properties, and anti-corruption statutes and codes. Always, the administration cites as proof of its prescience earlier reforms that had to be wrung out of it just as painfully at the time. There is no learning curve. For all his volubility and obvious intelligence, Koch will be remembered for derelictions of duty as awesome as Reagan's.

Indeed, there is little in the Reagan administration's disingenuous pronouncements and disinformation that couldn't have been learned from the New York City Department of Housing Preservation and Development or the City Planning Commission. The latter, trying as far back as 1961 to foist an urban renewal scheme on Jane Jacob's West Village, "acted with that stealth and dishonor which is possible only when men move from the highest of motives," as Murray Kempton put it twenty-six years before Oliver North became a man of "honor." Koch hasn't improved on this record. He even has his own equivalent of "national security"—fierce competition from New Jersey—to justify his giveaways to developers. It was only poetic justice when Donald Trump turned those lavish precedents against the mayor to support his own demands for unprecedented tax concessions to keep NBC from crossing the Hudson.

What accounts for these policy defaults and their constant misrepresentations? As in Washington, they do not lack for apologetics of the loftiest sort. New York's capacity for civic and cultural excellence depends on its brute economic strength, we're told; those who would level the city's vast resources to pursue justice and equality would produce only mediocrity and stagnation. These arguments might be diverting if they didn't overlook corruption and suffering so deep that the fruits themselves are poisoned, leaving us only with the cultural "excellence" of the big deal, the fast inside trade, frivolous adornment, high consolation, and, ultimately, the escapism and decadence

whose provision has become such a big business in the city.

What about corruption itself as an explanation for Koch's failures? A *Times* editorial last summer noted that fully half of the $9 million in 1985 campaign gifts to Koch and the other seven members of the powerful Board of Estimate (comptroller, city council president, and five borough presidents) came from 175 donors, most of them real-estate developers and brokerage houses and their law firms, and that, "one way or another, that kind of money inevitably purchases influence."

It certainly influences the borough presidents, most of whom have been characters out of Nast cartoons during Koch's reign and whose support he needs on the Board. Martin Gallent, whom the mayor declined to reappoint to the City Planning Commission because chairman Herbert Sturz asked him not to, recalls that he was always the lone dissenter on misguided ventures in the Bronx, even when principles as sacred as public waterfront access were being violated in the commission's approvals of projects. Finally, he was given to understand that catering to Bronx Democratic party leader Stanley Friedman as broker for Bronx developers was the price Koch paid for support from Friedman's puppet borough president, Stanley Simon, on the Board of Estimate.

One would have thought that Friedman's access to the Parking Violations Bureau was concession enough. But we know now that Koch was either unaware of the plunder or awfully naïve about its value. What he did not underestimate was the county leaders' power over borough presidents—especially when, as in Donald Manes's Queens and Howard Golden's Brooklyn, county leader and borough president are one and the same.

This suggests that the mayor was "corrupted" less by developers' contributions to him directly than by the political impact of their contributions to others. But activists won't soon forget how cleverly the mayor derailed a ten-percent capital gains tax on sales of buildings worth more than $1 million, a tax enacted in July 1981 to help fund the mass transit those buildings' employees and residents use to get to work.

The real estate industry lobbied fiercely, and Koch caved in—artfully: he delayed the tax's starting date till October, prompting an unprecedented rush of 130 big sales in August and September. Then, when few such sales were made once the tax took effect, Koch announced that the measure was "defective" and got Albany to replace it with levies so modest they cut the city's take on a $340 million sale of the American Express building from $18 million to $3 million.

"Corporate turnstile-jumping," transit advocates dubbed the ploy, handing a campaign issue to Koch's 1982 Democratic gubernatorial primary opponent, Mario Cuomo, who pledged to reinstate the levy. "A perfect tax," Cuomo called it, noting that it covered transactions that no one could threaten to heist to New Jersey, and that it funded a transit system upon whose reliability the very value of Manhattan real estate depends.

On another front, journalist Jim Smith contended that City Hall's refusal to help manufacturing jobs survive soaring rents reflected informed scrutiny, not of "natural" market trends, but of the mayor's campaign gifts, which "come overwhelmingly from those who [want] to displace manufacturing with luxury housing or commercial space."

And yet, for all the scandals, the charge that Koch is corrupt remains as unsatisfying as the assumption that he subscribes to lofty conservative notions about urban development. Whatever measure of truth these explanations hold is best assessed in the context of a real estate industry that is bigger than both of them and that is to New York City what Big Oil is to Houston.

The Real Estate Fraternity

Although there have been interesting newcomers in recent years, New York's lenders, developers, builders, brokers, and their lawyers and publicists remain a small world. Other industries and people occupying the buildings may come and go; the real estate fraternity is forever. That is why it makes special claims on local government through its lawyers, campaign gifts, and civic savants. The latter can be found at the Citizens Housing and Planning Council, a venerable developers' and planners' group from which have come many top city housing officials; the Real Estate Board of New York, the industry's lobby, to which many city housing officials go next; the Association for a Better New York, founded in the fiscal crisis by builder Jack Rudin; and half a dozen other organizations, including, in a sense, the *New York Times* editorial board, whose pronouncements on local economic development and housing are written by the developer—friendly Roger Starr, Abe Beame's former housing administrator, and by Herbert Sturz, former Planning Commission chairman.

No matter what coalition elected him, any New York mayor must move in tandem with this remarkable establishment, whose members sift the sites for new industries, classes, and modes of consumption, shaping New Yorkers' housing options and preferences in a speculative process whose tides are swift and unsparing. "The notion that any New Yorker has a right—which is embodied neither in land ownership nor in leasehold tenure—to remain forever in the section of the city in which he currently lives cannot be made consistent with the economics of land and construction," Starr has written, explaining how cosmopolitan "excellence" gets a good, swift spur from the developers.

Unscrupulous speculators are as happy to cash in on self-fulfilling prophecies of devastation as of revitalization, manipulating racial fears or ordering up brutal evictions to accelerate either process. But the industry's leaders, with some Faustian exceptions like Harry Macklowe, don't dirty their hands with such "scavenging," which they find beneath them and in any case less lucrative than deals cut on a main stage cleared by others.

Most of these eminences—the Milsteins, Zeckendorfs, Silversteins, Kaufmans, Steyers, Fishers, Helmsleys, and others—are elderly Jews, a cohort shaken by the Great Depression and the War but buoyed by the possibilities of the New Deal and the unexpected resilience of the postwar boom. Those formative experiences made them liberal Democrats who believe in big growth, big government (big federal subsidies, anyway), even big unions— all sparked to excellence, of course, by capitalist visionaries like themselves.

Predominantly self-made men, they know about breaking with "the old neighborhood," though they keep up their folk-ways in the breakfast room of the Regency Hotel, which has replaced the table at the back of the local delicatessen. Having done well by the welfare state, which in effect capitalizes their ventures and subsidizes their corporate and residential tenants, they feel that, with pluck, persistence, and their own example in view, others can share in the feast. To a remarkable degree, these men's sons have followed in their footsteps—the new Zeckendorf Towers at Union Square are Bill, Jr.'s monument to Bill, Sr.—just as they followed their immigrant sires, who were carpenters, house-painters, glaziers, and small-time developers.

That Ed Koch is one of them in spirit goes almost without saying, though it's likely that these stolid, wealthy family men find him just a bit strange. He is their man not so much because they've "bought" him as because he shares their beliefs (even about rent regulation, which they know he can't assault). Relations range from cordial to courtly; as Sam Freedman noted in a *Times* article on the aberrant feud between Koch and Trump, "developers in New York have traditionally kept their grievances with the city to themselves, or have channeled them through their lawyers." It is because Trump (that pushy WASP) broke the code with public criticisms of the mayor, as much as because his demands are outrageous, that Koch opposed him.

Even then, though, the lines of force have been clear. When Koch's housing commissioner Anthony Gliedman denied a $50-million tax break to the luxury Trump Tower, forcing the developer to win it in court, Trump didn't get mad; he got even by hiring Gliedman away as a vice-president of his organization. In that capacity the former commissioner was sent down to City Hall's Blue Room last spring to monitor his former boss's refusal to grant a 100-percent, twenty-year tax break on the hundred-acre West Side site to which Trump wants to lure NBC. One can only imagine how Koch felt, seeing Gliedman in the back of that room. Here is a power over people and their aspirations that transcends the reach of corruption statutes and conservative urban philosophy.

No one pretends that professional households making $50,000 or even $75,000 a year are accumulating great wealth in New York, or that the city can survive if it drives such people away. Nor should anything in these pages be taken to imply that one city can shoulder the costs of economic redistribution through local housing and economic development programs. None of the objections to city policy raised here rest on such assumptions. Denying gratuitous tax abatements to Smith-Barney or A.T.&T. is not redistributive. Reasserting municipal power over zoning is not redistributive. Helping low-income communities establish themselves in properties the marketplace has abandoned—properties those communities have clung to and often saved—is a revolutionary expropriation only to those content with the parasitical economies of the slums.

Challenging these perverse arrangements and the mythologies that sustain them has become the agenda, not of a few literary radicals with too precious a notion of urban vitality, but of thousands of dedicated New Yorkers who live exposed and vulnerable to one another and to degrading, oppressive conditions. That agenda could be even more broadly and effectively shared under the leadership of a LaGuardia, the predecessor Koch says he most admires.

Perhaps the most candid observation from City Hall in recent years was Deputy Mayor Robert Esnard's to the *Times* on the occasion of the Tibbett Gardens failure: "When the Federal Government pulled the money away from us, there was only us left." But the record of "us"—our city government here in New York—is an intolerable municipal shame and a standing reproof to those who think that chasing big booms is the way to build great cities. It is for losing himself and his administration in that mirage, more than for the corruption scandals or his personal problems or style, that Ed Koch has worn out his welcome. Let us hope we've learned at least that much from his stay. □

To Fulfill New York City's Promise

The June 1987 report of the Commission on the Year 2000 proposes reforms and innovations to enhance New York as "a world city," "a city of neighborhoods," "a city of opportunity," and "a civil city." It is a document far more progressive than the mayoral administration that commissioned it—a discrepancy muted in the report's apolitical, consensus-oriented language, which juxtaposes reforms facing little opposition and already underway (stricter Midtown traffic enforcement) with proposals stoutly resisted by constituencies, interests, and often City Hall itself (committing more city-owned property for low- and moderate-income housing development).

It is in light of that discrepancy that we offer the following "short list" of reforms. They are not original; they are the ones most dependent upon a mayor's "heavy lifting" through vigorous political pressure and sustained public persuasion. On some of these, the governor has an equally important political and educational leadership role to play.

1. *Establish public financing of primary and general election campaigns.* So important has money become in the electoral process that this isn't just a "good government" reform; it is our only chance to free public policy making from the stranglehold of legal bribery. It is also the only way for elected officials to regain the public respect they have lost as players in a bloated, perverse electoral system. Campaigns should cost less (electronic media are publicly licensed and should be made to serve the public); and office-holders shouldn't enjoy perpetual incumbency that rests on huge warchests rather than accountable leadership. Citizens should familiarize themselves with the broader ethics-reform agenda of the New York Public Interest Research Group, 9 Murray Street, New York, N.Y. 10007, (212) 349–6460.

2. *Commit more city-owned property and other resources toward low- and moderate-income housing.* In several large, poor neighborhoods, the city has foreclosed so much property that it controls the market. Too often, it has sold these properties to the highest bidders in hopes of enhancing its tax base, but the ensuing displacement of low-income people saddles the city with new shelter and social service costs that overwhelm the returns. Instead, the city should embrace the changing structure of property relations implicit in the low-income tenant co-oping programs underway in its buildings thanks to community-based, nonprofit housing development corporations, many of which enjoy sophisticated foundation support.

City officials have pressing economic and political reasons to work with private developers to produce middle-income and market-rate housing, but public resources are too easily diverted into those efforts at the expense of low- and moderate-income eligibility and stabilization. Stronger linkages must be established between market-rate development and the production and rehabilitation of low-income housing, as is done effectively in other cities. New Yorkers should familiarize themselves with the agendas of the Association for Neighborhood Housing Development, 236 W. 27th Street, New York, N.Y. 10001, (212) 463–9600.

3. Spectacular recent failures in Board of Education jobs and employment training programs underscore that the system has not kept faith with the energy and commitment of thousands of young, mostly minority New Yorkers—not the other way around. Bureaucratic protectionism too often pits the interests of the system's employees against those of its students and their parents. For example, the Board of Examiners, which certifies teachers' qualifications, is a destructive anachronism that must be abolished in favor of district-based screening procedures that meet certain system-wide minimum standards. The school custodial system is similarly outmoded and subversive of intelligent district-based planning.

The Board of Education itself should be appointed by and accountable to the mayor, subject to the approval of independent, professional screening panels; and principals should be evaluated by visiting accrediting panels composed of professionals and parents independent of the particular school and granted full access to its records and systems. Teachers should be empowered to work together, collegially, to set the content, methodology, and tone of their classroom work. To achieve both excellence and equality of access to educational opportunity, it is not enough just to set high standards; those standards must be pursued in the context of the structural reforms listed here. Finally, as Sol Stern argues in this issue's "Round-Table," these initiatives must be backed by the largest commitment of new resources in the budget—and, indeed, in the city's history. The mayor must build a consensus about the funding of education more powerful—and more credible—than Ronald Reagan's consensus for a huge military buildup. More information is available from the Public Education Association, 39 W. 32nd St., New York, N.Y. 10001, (212) 868–1640.

4. Debate about welfare reform must not be allowed to obscure two basic, urgent initiatives with potentially far-reaching consequences: *increasing the level and availability of the welfare grant and providing day care to all who are eligible and who want it* are matters of economic good sense and simple justice. The city does not set the welfare grant level, but it imposes onerous, often capricious restrictions that force many to live in poverty without benefits. Indeed, 59 percent of New Yorkers living below the poverty line get no benefits. The grant level should be increased by the state to at least poverty line and, potentially, to half the state median income. Employment incentives should, of course, top that.

At least 65,000 families need and are eligible for day care that doesn't exist; increasing its availability would allow more women to work their way off welfare and reduce the pressures that lead to child abuse. No single policy initiative would do more to improve the conditions and economic prospects of poor single-parent households than the provision of universal day care. More information can be obtained from the Welfare Research Institute, 11 Broadway, Room 832, New York, N.Y. 10004, (212) 344–5466.

—J.S.

Ada Louise Huxtable

STUMBLING TOWARD TOMORROW

The Decline and Fall of the New York Vision

Nineteen twenty-nine was a banner year for visions of New York. In the heady atmosphere of the beautiful life and endless tomorrows of that doomed decade, just before the future died, all dreams were possible. In 1929 the architect-delineator Hugh Ferriss published his drawings and descriptions of "The Metropolis of Tomorrow," a crepuscular Elysium of wide-spaced, soaring spires in perfect axial symmetry that managed to combine the aura of the traditional Beaux Arts City Beautiful with futuristic intimations of Le Corbusier's towers-in-a-park. This magnificent Manhattan was rigidly organized into impressive formal "zones" for business, arts, and science, with supertowers marking the intersections of grand avenues. Multilevel pedestrian and vehicular precincts separated people and cars. Faceted, futuristic skyscrapers were bridged by overhead roads and trimmed with airplane platforms. The text detailed the ways in which this ideal New York would increase the convenience, pleasure, and well-being of its inhabitants. Ferriss's vision is high fantasy and high art.

Also in 1929, the *First Regional Plan of New York and Its Environs* appeared—an epochal document produced by the Regional Plan Association that was meant to carry the city and its surrounding territories into the tomorrow of 1965. This was a different kind of vision. It combined a comprehensive survey of the city's and region's conditions and needs with specific short- and long-term recommendations in a series of eight volumes (followed by two more in 1931) for what might be called the beginnings of *realplan* (as in *realpolitik*) in New York. This study stands as a classic exposition of pragmatic concerns placed within a framework of future ideals. It dealt with metropolitan growth, population trends, land values, traffic, transit and transportation, the protection and regulation of buildings and land use through zoning, the role of government, issues of public health and recreation, consideration of neighborhoods and community planning, physical conditions, and public services.

As a vision, and as an actual blueprint for regional development, the First Regional Plan was enormously influential. Among its frequently restated principles was "the promotion of the highest economic uses that are consistent with true social purpose," which included "restraining the actions of owners who obtain profit for themselves to the injury of other owners and the community." Obviously, the Regional Plan Association had its share of dreamers, too.

Nor did the region's planners ignore visions of a more aesthetic nature. They commissioned architects' views of recommended land use improvements with possibilities of urban and artistic grandeur. Two-tier development along Manhattan's rivers was visualized by architect Francis S. Swales—the lower level for commerce, the upper level for drives along which "magnificent dwellings might arise." (It helps to remember how much of the city's waterfront was used for garbage-dumping and slaughtering at the time.) The redoubtable Eric Gugler would have extended and filled the Battery for a plaza with a "lofty monument" meant to be a "magnificent sea gate to the metropolis." ("Magnificence" had obviously not yet gone out of style.)

Model of Trump Television City, proposed for the West Side Rail Yards 1987

Harvey Wiley Corbett showed stacked streets for cars and pedestrians, lined with continuous arcades. "A Terminal over the West Side yards of the New York Central" was presented as "great masses of buildings with mighty arches spanning the cross streets," a megastructure in an inflated Early Park Avenue apartment-house style as notable for its sedate uniformity as for its monumental ambitions. (Television City's proposed bid for grandeur, on the same site, would be pinned on the illusory glory of the tallest building in the world. Corbett's image is not only memorable, but almost spookily postmodernist prescient.) "The drawings tell more than words," the description concluded in some awe.

A 1930 book devoted to the Regional Plan by the author and journalist R.L. Duffus observed that "the art of the builder is making great strides in America . . . if [New York] seizes its natural opportunities [it] may find a whole new architectural language of its own, worthy of its magnitude and prestige." Almost sixty years later, it would seem that all natural and unnatural opportunities have indeed been seized. The architectural language, however, is something else.

Visions have their uses. They also change with the times. The City Beautiful is a lost ideal that inspires nostalgia in the hearts of a fast-culture generation full of fashionable retro-romanticism. But the accepted vision of New York today is of a process as much as of a place: it is a hyperkinetic, creative kind of multiframe supercity video in which chaos and hype are equated with an almost mystical vitality. The city that never sleeps is also the city that never stops. It is essential to this vision that it cannot be completed or fulfilled. And then there is that timeless vision that will not die, brought by those whose names and color change with the years, of the city of opportunity, where the streets are paved with gold. If you consider the price of the land and the profits to be made, which have a certain constancy that transcends boom or bust, that is the one realistic vision that endures.

The vision of Hugh Ferriss, forever co-opted in "artists' renderings" of the "city of the future," and the studies and recommendations of the Regional Plan Association, with their pragmatic ideals and goals, had one important thing in common: both were based on the idea of the physical plan. The physical plan was the product of data, specifications, and projections from which a picture of a place could be made, to show how a city, or its component parts, would appear when the recommendations were carried out. (The "artist's rendering" was always in demand.) Even the most schematic indications were immediately translatable into recognizable reality.

This didactic, concrete prescription built a certain rigidity into the vision. And sometimes

Regional Plan of New York, Francis S. Swales, architect. From the 1929 Regional Plan book: "A terminal over the West Side Yards of the New York Central would have the superb advantage of a riverfront site for a development corresponding in size and importance to Grand Central Station."

the vision owed more to the logic of topography and land use than to local needs and characteristics; planners were surprised to find that it wasn't always what the natives wanted. But what eventually proved to be the Achilles' heel of physical planning and led to a near-universal reaction against planning in general (an upheaval still under way) was the fact that this kind of planning relied on a simplistic, static concept implying—and depending upon—a continuity of conditions during the years between formulation and realization. Neatness and high-mindedness counted. Physical planning was predicated on the idea that both the original assumptions and conclusions, and the form given to them, were unchangingly valid and desirable. (We are watching the fallacy at work in Times Square now—with the Forty-Second Street Redevelopment Plan. Clean-sweep replacement remains popular with politicians in part because it makes for a more predictable bottom line for the developer.)

The Master Plan: End of an Era

The recognition of urban planning and design as a real need, and its rise as an academic discipline in this country in the years before the Second World War, were part and parcel of this physical approach. The physical plan culminated in the all-encompassing prescriptions of the Master Plan. At its best, the Master Plan was conceived in broad, humanistic terms integrated with public and user-friendly needs from governance to quality of life. It was flexible enough to give guidance and coherence to private development while rolling with the urban and economic punches. The new downtown Boston is the result of such a plan made almost thirty years ago, and without a similar set of guidelines to build on its strengths today, many of the perceived virtues will be lost. At its worst, the Master Plan became a dehumanized exercise in bureaucratic map- and picture-making, creating a series of urban fairy tales with mythical happy endings told in four-color overlays destined to gather dust on planners' shelves.

In New York, the rising popularity of the idea of directed growth and the early history of the planning movement was paralleled by the

creation of the New York City Planning Commission as part of charter revision in the 1930s. The charter changes also mandated a master plan. The new agency played a somewhat mysterious role in municipal operations at first; its most clearly and earliest understood function was the use of commission vacancies for political payoffs (immediately) and more complex ethnic-borough-religion-and-gender payoffs (later on).

The commission had one charter-specified function, however, that gave it unusual purpose and power: it was charged with the annual preparation of the city budget. While a good part of this, logically and properly, came from the agencies involved, and another part, inevitably, was vaguely conjured to cover the course, the point of the process was to provide a budget with a broad overview of the city's needs and priorities; charter reformers visualized a Solomon-like role for the planners in which they would adjudicate disputes and guarantee the long view.

The budget charette (and eventually, charade, after New York developed its unique hanky-panky with capital and operating funds in a kind of Ponzi scheme of delayed but inevitable fiscal disaster) took place every year. The master plan was always put off. Such a plan obviously represented a Herculean task requiring sibylline skills and enormous staff time. During the long reign of Robert Moses, who cast a very long shadow and stretched an even longer arm into all of the city's agencies, not surprisingly no one dared suggest a non-Moses master plan.

The New York City Master Plan was finally completed in 1970, in 440,000 words and six handsome volumes, about thirty years late. It was given the ultimate birthing push by government funding programs that required a master plan as a prerequisite for federal grants. It fell as flat as a pancake and has been reviled ever since. It didn't deserve the bad rap; this was quite a remarkable document, whatever its conspicuous faults or omissions. But it was doomed because its timing was fatal; it coincided with an increasing awareness of the complex social base of urban problems that remained untouched by physical improvements, coupled with a rising tide of community

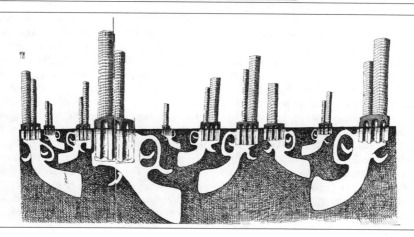

activism. In the intervening years, cities had been split and neighborhoods destroyed by bulldozer urban renewal. People were plan-shy. When New York's communities saw what their planners had wrought for them, there was revolt in all the boroughs.

Ironically, this came on the heels of several years of notable planning achievements in New York that marked a high point of physical planning. A pioneering Urban Design Group had been created to work on projects at the local level, as well as larger public facilities; Offices of Lower Manhattan and Midtown Development had been followed by similar offices meant to deal with onsite problems in other boroughs. They were staffed by some of the best and the brightest young professionals ever attracted to public service, who still believed that the future lay in some other direction than Wall Street. Imagination, inno-vation, involvement—and vision—were in long supply.

If the dreams ran high there were schemes to match. It would have been a good deal less than wonderful, even had it been possible, if all the plans of the 1960s had been carried out—such as raising the land level and narrowing the East River in Lower Manhattan, or building the Piranesian megastructure originally proposed for Battery Park City. But the intellectual and creative drive directly involved with city affairs has not been equaled since; in fact, it no longer

exists. To mistake the miasma, or buzz, or vibes that are constantly cited by the city's boosters as some magic penumbra of innova-tive energy is to confuse the sound effects with constructive creative focus.

It is clear now that New York City's Master Plan marked the end of physical planning and the beginning of another era in municipal policy and practice. By one of those portentous and cataclysmic quirks of fate, it coincided with the advent of the city's fiscal crisis of the 1970s, which made the idea of large-scale planning even more unreal. The perspective drawings of balloon-holding happy families in banner-decked pedestrian plazas against back-drops of sleek new housing and sailboat-flecked harbors joined the topographical maps and transportation networks in the permanent municipal dust. The murmuring on the outer radical fringes about concerns that do not yield to the T-square had entered the academies as a new gospel of social planning, reflecting an increasing trend and backlash everywhere. What had started with the counterculture in the early 1960s, when architecture and planning students had literally taken to the streets, setting up storefront operations in the most troubled areas, had created a new agenda of social planning. (Anyone remember advocacy architecture? And Earth Day?)

Environmental and historic preservation and community input became the watchwords of the newly sensitized. Still smarting from community objections, and without funds, the city turned to the miniplan, to street-corner surgery, and sometimes to cosmetic surgery at that. The ad hoc approach was legitimized. The scale and reach were small. It was New York's near-bankruptcy, however, that brought not only planning, but the city itself, to a grinding, ignominious halt—a catastrophe from which it has never really recovered in terms of its physical plant and services in spite of the return of a much-flaunted prosperity. And it was charter reform, again, that institutionalized the Planning Commission's new and much-weakened position. Responding to this altered planning climate, charter changes of the 1970s established community boards, environmental reviews and ULRP, the Uniform Land Review Process, cumbersome but useful additions that have proved, on balance, to be wise and worthwhile.

Less noticed, but of critical importance, the commission's budget-preparing function was eliminated under the rubric of reform (by now, city-watchers should see "reform" as a red-flag word hoisted by each new generation substituting its own mistakes and bad judgment for the errors of its elders; but hope, and generations, spring eternal). That budgetary function, which dealt with the coordinated needs of the city on all of its interlocking levels, had made the commission much more than a physical planning agency. Back in the hands of the budget bureau, different priorities were inevitably set.

What the Planning Commission was left with was a largely unread, quasi-hypothetical *Statement of Capital Needs*—a document that became another dust catcher. Even if the loss of faith in planning and the power plays among agencies had not been decisive factors, the fiscal malpractice employed by several administrations preceding the debacle eventually made it necessary to give control over all major money matters to a higher authority, the Municipal Assistance Corporation (MAC)—the fiscal policy and planning agency that bailed the city out and set it on the road to financial stability.

Hindsight tells us what went wrong: New York was constantly changing under the planners' feet. Although much valuable infor-

mation was gathered and analyzed, the Master Plan was out of date the moment it was printed. The city had turned out to be a fragile and interdependent, highly unpredictable, fractious, erratically functioning entity far beyond planners' conventional ideas or projections and often in conflict with them. Through trial and error, a better understanding was emerging of the lessons of the past as well as more appropriate goals for the future, an understanding of context and character, of human scale and needs. The comprehensive struggle to physically eradicate urban blight had failed to alleviate the pressures of poverty and deprivation or the growing cataclysm of drugs and despair.

Even with the return of good times, the position, prestige, and strength of the Planning Commission were never regained. The powerful new agencies that arose to shape policies and expedite development have diluted and scattered the commission's authority and control. Some bodies, like the Office of the Deputy Mayor for Finance and Economic Development and the New York City Public Development Corporation, which should be working closely with the Planning Commission, are independent of it; the Public Development Corporation inaugurates huge, controversial projects that raise serious questions of scale, impact, and appropriateness. Prizes of publicly owned land, such as the Coliseum site at Columbus Circle, are handed out by the Metropolitan Transit Authority and the city for purchase or lease on a highest-bid basis. Matters of public policy and the quality of urban design have been routinely left to the developers until the belated appointment of an independent review panel, which operates in a limbo of *droit économique* and *a priori* design unconnected to any planning jurisdiction. In all of this activity, the broad and interrelated concerns of the planning process have been subverted and reduced to revenue-producing operations. Whether this is conscious policy or not, it is real policy, of a most shortsighted and dangerous kind.

But the trouble goes far deeper. The skills and values that planners hold—concerns for the future in more than abstract terms, methods and techniques for guidance, a professional understanding of the factors that control the quality of urban life, a sense of a balanced relationship between that quality and economic growth, the ability to visualize the results of an abstract proposal and to see the reality behind the artist's rendering and the increasingly esoteric legal maneuvers—those skills and values no longer command respect or credibility. With the fall of physical planning, a modern belief system died—the liberal conviction and optimistic faith in a perfectible, or at least predictable, future world.

Giving Away the City

And much more has been lost than faith, which has its natural limitations. The Planning Commission is no longer the proposer of plans and projects, the initiator of ideas and interventions, the agency responsible for evaluation of the multiple effects of massive construction. It functions reactively to the proposals of others, reviewing them only after the developer's horse has left the barn at a fast trot. At least one corporate real estate executive has said that New York gives away not only the store but the farm and the barn. With the leverage of development pressures on the city's side, it calls none of the originating shots except to auction off sites for superprojects that relate to nothing much farther away than the megabuilding next door, usually through no more than the purchase of its air rights. Their connections to the future, beyond tax projections, are tenuous. Their place in the public realm is off the bottom of a nonexistent list.

Most important, the climate in New York is antiplan—not in the ideological sense now in intellectual fashion, but in the most reactionary terms of exploitative economics since Manhattan's proverbial purchase from the Indians. Developers are quick to tell you that they play by the rules and conditions the city sets. But New York is the home of the big real estate leagues and it is easy to tell the pros from the pols.

We have now gone through physical planning, and social planning, and have entered an age of numbers planning. Through attrition and default, the only real planning game left in town is zoning. In 1961, zoning reform (yes,

reform again) turned a faulty, much-amended statute into a revised set of rules meant to correct those faults, which immediately developed faults of their own. When construction boomed again, the dangers of a new kind of permissive, manipulatable zoning became clear. Automatic bonuses given for street amenities, permits and variances as trade-offs for special features, led to unprecedented building size and density. Flagrant overzoning became a visible reality as economic conditions favored the unprecedented abuse of its possibilities. Every major new structure broke the city's existing scale and overpowered its streets. The monstrous became ludicrous when mediocrity (never in short architectural supply) began to come in fancy dress with the advent of postmodernism, in which silly raids on history in the hands of shrewd image-salesmen and their abetting architects raised the ante and the buildings to a sickening scale, turning the merely silly into a remarkably sinister product.

But to those who do numbers planning, these buildings are beautiful. The way one looks at them is as mathematical multiples. You figure the maximum square footage and then calculate the real estate and/or occupancy taxes, business and sales taxes, and all their fiscal spinoffs. Of course, all of this beauty is somewhat offset by the deals that have become the standard lure to the builder or corporate owner—the write-offs and write-downs, the special legislative incentives and exemptions, the subsidies and depreciations, including such items as forgiveness of sales tax on construction materials and special utilities rates. Although we are told that there is much less of this now, the arrangements made have usually reached well into the future, leaving the recipient the clear winner and the city the likely loser in uncharted economic uncertainties. (Who, for example, could have foreseen the extraordinary rise in Manhattan land prices? Who would dare predict anything about the cyclical nature of an increasingly monolithic financial services economy?)

Numbers planning is not real planning in that it does nothing to address the building of a stable economic base beyond the fine art of tax forecasting and financial packaging. The essential elements for such a base are a work force with sufficient education and skills, adequate housing and schools, functioning transportation—all those factors that afford an acceptable (meaning competitive with other places) quality of private and public life. Not everyone is happy to draw sustenance and support just from New York's supercharged, polluted air. One pays an obscenely high price for a way of life that is not much better than jungle warfare.

The city's tacit or open helpfulness in the rise of real estate values (read rising tax base) through zoning that encourages speculators' escalation of those values is beginning to boomerang. When a troubled (or smart) company finds that the value of its Manhattan headquarters is greater than the value of doing business here, it sells and decamps. To attract and keep corporations under New York's "hardship conditions," when the flight alternative is more attractive, quick fiscal fixes are necessary. (The city threatened to sue when AT&T announced plans to sell its headquarters building and move to New Jersey, in spite of the special tax advantages it had received. If the company really means to stay, however, it would be nice if it replaced the dead trees that help make its public plaza one of the more doleful places in town.)

Large and small business departures are accelerating, while the default of giants, like Mobil and J. C. Penney, makes headlines. The Deputy Mayor for Finance and Economic Development, Alair Townsend, a wonderwoman with numbers, juggles employment and industry figures and the pluses and minuses of the ins and outs with impressive skill. She is also a source of some succinctly Big Apple quotes about the tastes and choices of the defectors. How will J. C. Penney feel when it wakes up rich in Dallas instead of poor in New York? "Yuck," she says eloquently. In this bazaar atmosphere of temptations and trade-offs, no one is addressing the deeper and more lasting problems that are immune to defensive accounting.

Felix Rohatyn, the man who headed the fiscal restructuring of New York and who can figure with the best of them, repeatedly urges more constructive policies. He has lashed out at the city's delays in using MAC surpluses for desperately needed housing. Recently he urged that the latest surplus be spent on the public schools. Currently, MAC funds have been earmarked for hiring police and rebuilding the city's neglected infrastructure and some current budget needs. But this is catch-up ball directed at the long-term damage wreaked by the disastrous cuts that started with the fiscal crisis. It is not laying a foundation for the future through the foresighted provision of a continuing base of employment and prosperity. It cannot be called planning of any persuasion.

On to the Twenty-First Century

The report of the Mayor's Commission on the Year 2000, a recently completed municipal think-tank effort with observations that can hardly be called upbeat, has come to the appalling conclusion that New York is no longer the city of opportunity. Some of those wonderful vibes—the ones that are supposed to guarantee that the future is here and you can have it all—have gone out of sync and sour. The idea that the hassle was the prelude to the prize, that living on the edge was a fun challenge in a town where all things were possible, is still part of the "I Love New York" mythology. But today a record 25 percent of the city's population, unemployed or poorly employed, lives below the poverty line. That figure, still rising, is the highest in the city's history. New York's burgeoning prosperity, its aggressive affluence, has not touched one quarter of its people.

The most alarming finding of all is that the city's customary routes to employment and assimilation simply are not working. Skills are required today that the school system does not provide. In the words of Robert Wagner, Jr., who headed the study, New York "no longer offers the same opportunities or absorption in terms of race or poverty" that have long been its traditional pride. The course was to the swift, and for the less swift, at least, the way was still open to the good, or decent, life. The commission has found a city more divided than it ever was before, divided ultimately by class rather than by race, divided by immovable and unyielding barriers. What is gone is the vaunted upward mobility that was a tenet of the

American, and New York, way of life—the ability to move out and up, to become part of the mainstream.

The Commission on the Year 2000 report makes clear the connection between the city's social pathology, educational failures, hardcore economic problems, and a disturbing and uncertain future. Understandably, Mr. Wagner, now president of the Board of Education, has welcomed Felix Rohatyn's call for the use of MAC funds as direct aid to the public schools. Sylvia Deutsch, who heads the Planning Commission, speaks of reestablishing the city's virtually extinct housing pipeline. In the last twenty years, according to her figures, housing production has decreased from 60,000 dwelling units in 1966 to 7,000 units in 1985, and two thirds of those were not affordable homes.

Deutsch is worth watching. A former head of the Board of Standards and Appeals, where she dealt with development, she evidently plans to focus her energy and experience where they can be made to count. This includes zoning review, attention to the neglected outer boroughs, and an attempt to find mechanisms to help the commission function again as a planning unit. She is neither antidevelopment nor inclined to architectural judgment—both proper stances for the Planning Commission—and she does not appear to be about to go toe-to-toe with the Manhattan real estate crowd and their friends at City Hall. Her vision is a practical and sociological one. She is a realist, and so is her program.

What is missing today in New York is the spirit that inspired Hugh Ferriss's vast pictorial idealism and the Regional Plan Association's initial farsighted goals. It does not matter that Ferriss reached unrealistically for the stars or that hindsight makes the First Regional Plan a mixed bag of fulfilled and unfulfilled expectations. It is the reach that is important, the sense of a larger destiny than the bottom line.

No one is perceiving, or parlaying, the opportunities presented by unprecedented development for a comprehensive, coordinated or responsible overview that would put growth in context and in touch with the future. As an example, the West Side corridor to the new convention center was studied in the 1970s by the Office of Midtown Development when the center's location was still under discussion. The point was not to create a blueprint that could never be followed, but to define ways in which inevitable redevelopment could be integrated with desirable connecting tissue and public features to raise the quality and facilities of a related whole. Now that the convention center is completed, activity is accelerating. The rebuilding seems about to proceed as a series of independent actions and patchwork deals in which the city is simply the expediter for construction.

Vision is a remarkable thing. It goes in and out of fashion, like clothes. For Le Corbusier, on his first visit to New York in 1935, the skyscrapers were too small to match the image in his mind. For Henri Matisse, arriving in New York by boat and seeing the skyline with a painter's eye, the same buildings were dematerialized in atmosphere and color—"a sensation of gradation of tones from the base to the top . . . which evaporates in the sky . . . like a mirror of water . . . a ravishing spectacle . . . in a crystalline light." For developers and investors, this shimmering mirage is a money machine. For the rest of the world New York's skyscrapers are still poetry and fantasy. They continue to intimidate and exhilarate in a perennial sky show. But they have ceased to be beacons of hope. □

A CITY DIVIDED

Gus Tyler

A TALE OF THREE CITIES

Upper Economy, Lower—and Under

New York's economy is divided into three parts: upper, lower, and under. The first two—upper and lower—are old hat, retailored now to fit the service economy. The third—the underground economy—has moved from being a pest to being a pestilence. In toto, they compose a complex entity in which disparate parts live in symbiotic embrace.

The concept of a "dual economy" in the United States—an economic ghetto of vast proportions in the midst of a prosperous nation—is neither new nor peculiar to New York. Economists have named the two economies "core" and "periphery," or "primary" and "secondary." In the large, capital-intensive, highly mechanized, oligopolistic industries, earnings have been—and are—high, even for the most unskilled. In the small, labor-intensive, fiercely competitive industries, earnings were—and are—low, even for the more skilled operatives. As is evident from the description—capital-intensive versus labor-intensive—these classifications were conceived in an industrial (manufacturing) society.

Historically, New York City did not fit into this national pattern. The city was never blessed or plagued by the smokestack, as is Pittsburgh with its steel mills, Detroit with its auto assembly plants, or Akron with its tire factories. Although New York has been a great manufacturing center, one of the largest in the nation, its manufacturers operated relatively small plants, turning out light products through labor-intensive production—such as apparel, printed materials, leather goods, plastics, ceramics, furs, paper products.

In still another respect New York has been different from the rest of the nation: it has never been without a sizable service sector. As a crossroad of the world, it has always had hotels, restaurants, department stores, theaters; as a cultural center, performers, galleries, dance and music studios, libraries, museums; as financial pivot of the globe, Wall Street denizens; as an image maker, Madison Avenue; as turf for corporate headquarters, lawyers, accountants, executives, clericals, brokers, security guards, charwomen. New York had a vibrant service sector long before the nation as a whole turned to "services" as primary employer.

But in one respect New York is the same as the rest of the nation: jobs in the goods-producing sector have been in rapid decline while jobs in the service sector have been in rapid ascent. New York is a caricature of the national economy—with similar, but overdrawn, features. The shift from manufacture to services, however, has not meant the end of a "dual economy," either nationally or in New York. The duality has been transferred from those making goods to those rendering services.

At the end of the Second World War, there were more than a million jobs in manufacture in the city. Today, there are less than 400,000. Three out of five manufacturing jobs have been wiped out. Some of these jobs paid well, most did not. But even those that did not were, by and large, better paying than like jobs in other parts of the country. New York was the high-paying end of low-pay industries—largely because of the strength of unions in the needle trades. Women's and misses' outerwear, for instance, showed average earnings of $315 a week in 1984, $8.40 an hour. The same industry, however, that in 1977 employed more than 73,000 now employs 63,700—a steady and continuing loss of above-poverty jobs.

The loss of manufacturing jobs in New York—jobs that were the base of a lower- and middle-middle class—has been more severe than in the rest of the nation. Between 1976 and 1986, the absolute number of jobs in manufacturing in the country actually *increased* from 18.9 million to 19.1 million. (As a percentage of all jobs, manufacture did fall from 23 percent to 19 percent.) In New York City, in the same years, manufacturing jobs nosedived from 535,700 to 394,700, a loss of 141,000 in a decade: more than one job out of every four was wiped out. (As a percentage of jobs in New York, manufacture fell from 16.8 percent to 11 percent.)

The common explanation for New York's loss of manufacture is that its business climate is not congenial to manufacture. In part, that is true. Manufacture requires space, and space in New York is expensive. To avoid the high rents of Manhattan, many manufacturers moved to the other boroughs, where factories became the core of solid neighborhoods—with many walking to work and back and forth to homes for lunch. The collapse of manufacture in these boroughs is a minor social, as well as a major economic, tragedy.

Although it is not possible to discount the local "climate"—high rents, high crime, high taxes—the real reason for the steep drop in New York 'manufacture is the unstated, but understood, policy of Washington that labor-intensive manufacture is a "sunset" industry, that it has no role in America's economic future, and that—in light of the above—it is both necessary and desirable to give this industry away to other countries, especially at times and in ways that will buy the friendship of those countries. Although the United States government has, for many years, had an instrument in hand to regulate the flow of imports in apparel and textiles, Washington has

consciously used the process to promote imports at the expense of American jobs in labor-intensive manufacture.

American manufacturers have joined in the strategy: they contract out their sewing to other countries. Department stores have done likewise: they have foreign makers turn out their wares with the store name stitched in overseas. The great New York banks have silently cheered from the sidelines because they believe that the growth of labor-intensive manufacture in debt-laden countries will earn debtors the necessary American dollars to service their intolerable burden. In the process, New York City—the traditional heart of light manufacture—is hard hit, harder than the rest of the nation.

Statistically, the tragedy of the hundreds of thousands displaced from New York City's manufacture is no problem at all: jobs rose from 3.1 million in 1976 to 3.8 million in 1986. Theoretically, those who lost jobs here got jobs there, since the total number rose. If people were just interchangeable numbers, the equation would balance. But people are not that fungible: they are specific—with given traits, skills, and access or lack thereof to jobs. The factory worker in New York City who averaged $431 a week in 1984—more than $10 an hour—is not likely to find a new job as a computer programmer, stockbroker, or even schoolteacher. He is far more likely to find himself grasping for a straw in that sector of the service economy that barely pays the minimum wage—or to turn to the proliferating underground economy.

Before we leave the manufacturing sector and turn to the service and underground sectors, just a word about high-tech—that touted savior of our economy. Whatever this Messiah is doing elsewhere, he is not doing much for the city. "New data for 1985," reports Samuel Ehrenhalt, commissioner of labor statistics for the New York Metropolitan Area, "show that manufacturing job losses in New York City have extended to the high-tech sector, which has seen a sharper rate of decline than other manufacturing activities. Jobs in high-tech manufacturing industries declined by 23,000 or 27 percent in the eight years ending in March 1985, as against a 22 percent loss in non-high-tech manufacturing." The reason? All our Silicon Valleys have been moving to Asia.

On the other hand, those high-tech industries that provide services—as distinct from the manufacture of high-tech—have grown by 28,000 in the same period. Taking both the making and using of high-tech, the total industry is a wash item, showing about a 1 percent growth. High-tech is not the light at the end of the tunnel for those displaced from manufacture.

In terms of employment, the service sector has offered hope. In 1986, 85 percent of all jobs in the city were in the service sector, up from 81 percent in 1976. In absolute numbers, the service sector rose from 2.5 million jobs in 1976 to 3 million in 1986. New York outdid the nation, where in 1986 75 percent of the jobs were in the service sector; in absolute numbers an increase from 56.8 million to 75.2 million.

This "service sector," like many economic concepts, is not a fact; it is an artifact, an invention of pundits. It includes brain surgeons and the brainless, airline pilots and dishwashers, stockbrokers and stockboys. It includes blue-collar people who wrap and tote; white-collar people who sell, type, file; no-collar people who handle fast food, sweep floors, or see to it that you don't shoplift. It includes law offices with legions of lawyers and their paras as well as mom-and-pop stores, free-lance writers, roofers, thespians, theologians, psychiatrists, and street peddlers.

Nowadays it is fashionable to say that earnings in the service sector are about half the earnings in the manufacturing sector. This statement is more or less correct if we are talking about the "proletariat" in the service sector—the nonprofessional, nontechnical, nonmanagerial person. There are many such "working-class" jobs in New York's service economy. For instance, there are (1984 figures)

Gus Tyler

Redistributing the Wealth

In most discussions of wages in America, only the average earnings of workers are considered. A more realistic approach, however, must differentiate between the wages of workers in mechanized monopoly industries and in wage-oriented competitive industries. It is the workers in these latter industries who pose the problem of indigence even in the midst of an "affluent society" and who make up a major part of that one-fifth of the nation that is still ill-fed, ill-clothed, and ill-housed.

A primary step in relieving the oppressive poverty of this one-fifth of the nation (not confined to the South but all too present in the streets of our greatest metropolis) is to raise the Federal minimum wage and to extend its coverage to the millions of workers who are not included under the present provisions. A national statute would establish a firm base on which to erect a higher wage in areas that offer "external economies" to the manufacturer. Unions could then negotiate more rewarding contracts because the wage differential between union and non-union areas would be offset by the advantages of the metropolitan climate.

A second step is to encourage rather than discourage unionization outside the already well organized areas like New York. Federal (or state) legislation or court actions which hinder union organizing efforts in the generally unorganized sectors of the nation not only keep wage levels low in these sectors but depress wage levels nationally. Lack of unionization in Mississippi or Georgia directly affects earnings in Brooklyn and the Bronx. Actually, the South is merely the most militant and effective spokesman for a "rural" point of view that acts as a nineteenth-century drag on a twentieth-century civilization, as an agrarian weight around the neck of the metropolis.

A third step is to use governmental power to tax the more affluent sector of the society to care for the needs of the less affluent. The 25 percent profit return on original investment not uncommon in steel and autos as contrasted with the one percent profit in garments does not derive from an inherent virtue of metal over fabrics, but from the monopoly character of the former and the competitive character of the latter. The workers in the latter industries suffer although many of them possess skills as great or even greater than those required in the basic industries. If the products created by low-paid workers are vital to our society—such commodities, for example, as food, fibers, wood, tubes, bulbs, transistors, dresses, overalls, shoes, gloves, and diapers—then society has no right to victimize these workers because their industries are competitive and defy automation.

—*Dissent*, Summer 1961 □

119,000 employed in "eating and drinking places" at an average pay of $200 a week— which is, indeed, less than half the going pay in manufacture. The fastest-growing sector of those in low-paying service jobs are engaged in "individual and family services," where the average pay is $174 a week; there are about 50,000 holding such jobs, up from 11,000 in 1977. The average pay for those in the low-wage service sectors that are *expanding* is $251 a week—again, well below manufacturing wages. Among the "expanding industries" in New York—that is, those creating new jobs—there are many that pay poorly.

But then there are many that pay well: stockbrokers and dealers, for instance. Between 1977 and 1984, their number grew from 56,000 to 99,000—an increase of 43,000. And why not? Their average weekly earning was more than a thousand dollars. Of some three dozen "expanding industries" in New York, these security-handlers showed the greatest growth. It figures: a casino society needs croupiers.

Brokers are, of course, only part of a larger universe, commonly bunched under the acronym of FIRE (finance, insurance, real estate). In 1984, average earnings in finance were $711 a week, in professional services (legal, accounting, auditing, engineering, architecture) $587 a week. In the world of FIRE there is a high ratio of professionals, technicians, and managers— about one out of every three as contrasted with one out of five in the rest of the city's economy. In the eight-year period 1977 to 1985, the finance, business, and related professional services showed a gigantic gain of 200,000 jobs with average earnings of $590 a week.

The question that remains is whether the booming service economy creates more well-paying than poor-paying jobs. The answer may be—"both." In a fact-filled speech sponsored by the Council on Economic Education, Commissioner Ehrenhalt grouped the city's expanding industries into three categories: higher earning, intermediate earning, lower earning. In the years from 1977 to 1984, the "lower earning" spawned 151,200 jobs; the

higher earning 135,300 jobs; the intermediate 137,400. On this basis, it might be argued that more bad than good jobs are being generated.

But, points out Ehrenhalt, what is happening in the "expanding" industries is only half the picture; the other half is what goes on in the "declining" industries. The "lower earning" industries lost 85,400 jobs, while the "higher earning" lost only 45,700. So when we net it all out, the higher earning industries are growing much faster (15 percent) than the lower earning industries (7 percent).

These provocative calculations—based on "industries"—still don't tell the whole story. "Industries" are ranked by "average earnings." But, as Herbert Bienstock, former regional commissioner of labor statistics, likes to note: "Behind every average lurks the distribution." Behind the high pay in "finance" lurk the commissions of the broker and the measly pay of the woman at a teller's window. If "averages" were realities, the people of Brunei would be the most prosperous in the world as they claim their statistical share of the sultan's cash and solid gold bathtub. Within the duality of the service sector, with its higher and lower earning industries, lies a further duality within each of these categories.

Consider the range in a category referred to as "professional, technical, and managerial," for instance. The high-sounding titles suggest big bucks. In some half a hundred select occupations in the United States, we find airline pilots and navigators at the top of the list with salaries of $738 a week. They are followed by lawyers and judges with $724. At the bottom of the list are recreation workers who earn $231 a week; just above them are kindergarten and prekindergarten teachers with earnings of $276; and above them are "licensed practical nurses" with $294. (These 1984 figures assume full-time work.)

In sum, the "dual economy" of old continues into the new service society. As in the past, the debate will continue as to whether we are creating more good than bad jobs. Evidence can and will be mustered for both sides. *But the polarized economy—disproportionately large numbers at the extremes—continues.*

In New York City's economy, this polar structure takes on geographic and racial overtones: who gets the better jobs and who is stuck with the crummy jobs? A quick reply would be: the good jobs go to people who do not live in the city and the bad jobs go to racial and ethnic minorities. That statement is, of course, an exaggeration. There are New York City residents who hold better jobs and there are "whites" who hold poorer jobs. Yet the shocking hyperbole points to a painful truth.

In the only data we were able to uncover on who, by and large, gets the better jobs (dug out of the last census in 1980) we found that the annual earnings of nonresidents were double the earnings of residents. Median earnings for all employed in the city were $12,970. The median for those working in the city but living outside was $21,191. If we remove the "outsiders' " earnings from the total, the "insiders' " earnings are less than the overall median yielding, of course, a result that shows commuters earning about twice as much as the natives.

If the number of people living outside the city and working inside it were small, the data would be of little relevance. But the "outsiders" represent more than one out of five working in the city (21 percent). Of the jobs that in 1979 paid $50,000 a year or more, outsiders held more than 60 percent. Clearly, a disproportionate piece of the "upper" polar region is occupied by Dashing Dans and Dotties from Connecticut, New Jersey, Long Island, and Westchester County. In the lower regions, blacks, Hispanics, and women are disproportionately entrapped. *The "dual economy" is doubly dual—racially/ethnically/sexually, as well as economically.*

In a study entitled *Closed Labor Markets*, the Community Service Society of New York (CSS) records "The Underrepresentation of Blacks, Hispanics and Women in New York City's Core Industries and Jobs" (1985). The thrust of the study is that the city's economy is ghettoized. While white males are relatively mobile, black and Hispanic males and females and white females have their fixed places in the economy. The greatest mobility belongs to the most advantaged (white males) and the least mobility to the most disadvantaged (black females).

The "ghettos" are as might be expected. The highest percentage of white males in any one occupation is in the category of salaried managers and administrators; of white females, secretaries; of black males, janitors and cleaners; of black females, nursing aides, etc; of Hispanic males, janitors and cleaners; of Hispanic females, sewing machine operators. The stereotype turns out to be the truth.

Even where there are exceptions, they prove the rule. Where blacks and Hispanics do break into managerial posts, it is commonly due to federal involvement or affirmative-action consent decrees. But even here, the "managerial" posts held by minorities are characterized "generally" by "low pay," notes the CSS study.

The relative mobility that whites have in moving from one industry to another is a distinct advantage in finding jobs. Minorities who are more restricted do not enjoy that luxury. If they find themselves in an industry that is on the decline, they often have no place else to go. And, as Ehrenhalt pointed out, many of the low-paying industries—the turf on which minorities live—are in rapid decline. As a consequence, unemployment among blacks and Hispanics is much higher than among whites—and the gap is likely to grow.

At a time when the unemployment rate for New York City ran at 8.1 percent (1985), the white jobless rate was 7.2, the black 11.5, and the Hispanic 13.4. Roughly, Hispanic unemployment was double that of white, and black unemployment was in between. The results would have been even more lopsided were it not for the growth of government employment in the city. In the last year or two, as job growth has slowed down in the private sector, the slack has been picked up by the public sector, primarily by city government—an area where minorities get a better break than usual.

Distressing as the jobless figures are (New York's overall rate is above the national), they do not really reveal the extent of the problem in terms of societal impact. The overall figures mask the fact that for a vast army of teenagers the world of work is not their world. These are young people (16 to 19 years old) who are actively looking for work but cannot find it. Among white youth, the jobless rate is 22.5 percent and among black youth 47.9 percent—one out of two.

Even this high rate of idleness among youth does not reveal the depth of joblessness, because the official count—as is well known by now—does not include the so-called "discouraged," of whom there are many. "Based on a recent BLS [Bureau of Labor Statistics] study of workers aged 20 and over, with three years on the job in all industries, 271,000 New York State workers were displaced due to plant closings or moves, slack work, or the abolishment of their positions or shifts between January 1979 and January 1984," reports Ehrenhalt. Only about half of these displaced workers had found jobs by January 1984. About one in three remained "unemployed." But about one in five (18 percent) dropped out of the labor force. In a period of five years, about 50,000 people left the world of work.

Although the official unemployment figures conceal the extent of idleness, they do not do so intentionally. There actually are figures published by official sources that do reveal how many people are not at work in the adult population. It is the ratio between the number actually employed and the number of adults in the total population. The *Economic Report of the President*, for instance, regularly carries a table entitled, "Civilian Employment Population Ratio." For 1986, it was 60.7 percent nationally: six out of every ten adults were on a job. It was higher for whites (61.5 percent) and lower for blacks (54.1).

The count for New York is startlingly different. Only 51.6 percent of the adult population is employed in the city as contrasted with the 60.7 percent in the nation. Among blacks it is 50.4 percent and among Hispanics it is 43.4 percent.

Where do the "dropouts" go? If they all left the city or the planet, there would be no problem. But they neither disappear nor die. They live amidst us and—most make a living. But they do so in unorthodox ways, in the wide, wild world of the underground economy.

Much of the underground economy is outrightly illegal, simply criminal: burglary, mugging, trafficking in drugs, shoplifting, arson, hijacking, robbery, pilferage. Much of it is only technically "illegal," because the income is not reported to the IRS. Still another part is dubiously legal, as with those who cheat on social welfare programs. Many if not most

Slave Wages

Why have not compassionate citizens cried out to Congress more loudly to protect our most vulnerable wage earners? Partly, it is due to a stereotype of those working for the minimum. The common perception is that they are few, teenagers, and part of the minority elements who have not yet found their place in the American mainstream. Put vulgarly, they are seen as a handful of stray outsiders. The facts, however, belie the belief. The victims of the descending floor are not few. In 1986, about 6.7 million salaried and hourly workers earned the minimum wage—or less. An additional six million received wages that were just above the minimum . . . from $3.36 an hour to $3.99. . . . This adds up to about 13 percent of wage and salaried employees.

Contrary to the myth, most of those working at the minimum wage are white: three out of four, according to Earl F. Mellon and Steven E. Haughen in a piece on "Hourly paid workers," appearing in the *Monthly Labor Review* (February 1986, p. 25). While it is true that there is a disproportionately high number of blacks who work at the minimum, they are actually only one out of five in that unhappy level. If it were true that most of those employed at the minimum were black, that would be an added reason to lift the minimum, to avoid further polarization of American society along economic and racial lines.

Finally, most of those who work in the minimum world are not teenagers. The largest number—twenty years or older—make up more than two-thirds of those at the minimum. Only 31 percent are teenagers. In short, adults—age 20 or older—make up nearly 70 percent of those earning the minimum. (These were the findings of a Minimum Wage Study Commission in 1981 and prevail in 1986 Current Population Survey statistics.) Twenty-eight percent are the heads of households and another 28 percent are spouses.

Reprinted from the AFL-CIO
American Federationist, March 21, 1987. □

of the families that have dropped out of the formal economy survive and, sometimes, thrive in this "informal" economy.

As with the industrial and more recently the service economy, so too in the underground the law of duality persists. There are the thousands, tens of thousands, of women who stitch, paste, fold, join things with things in their crammed flats, earning whatever the boss will pay them when they tote back their finished work. The earnings may be a dollar an hour or less—without Social Security, unemployment insurance, health coverage. On the same block are teenagers pushing crack or running numbers or peddling hookers whose average earnings compare with those of our stockbrokers and dealers. These are the poles of the underground economy.

There are the stray muggers, hitting the nearest target for some quick cash, living from day to day in the way of the feral beast; then there are the organized criminals, the oligopolists of the underworld, who stake out their turf, make their long-range plans, exact a steady toll from their victims, "tip" the man on the beat. Here, too, are upper and nether reaches of an economy. There is that Turk with his falafel pushcart or that Senegalese peddling his "authentic" works of African "art" on the streets, making just about enough to come back another day; then there are the hijackers and loft-burglars who supply high-class legitimate outfits with stolen goods, wholesale. There is the undocumented worker who waits tables in a diner for what amounts to "tips only" that he or she never reports; and then there is the fixer who is "tipped" with several thousand dollars for his services in getting some public official to okay a contract. There is the lowly employee who pilfers tools, merchandise, paper clips, and personal computers, and then there is the mousy accountant who embezzles a couple of million.

Such an "informal" economy is not peculiar to New York or the United States or to the last quarter of the twentieth century. Crime and black markets are endemic to all civilizations. But in our times, the endemic has become epidemic.

Just about every New Yorker is aware of the underground economy, although he or she rarely thinks of it as such. It goes on right under our nose in the form of street crime, sidewalk vendors, cash deals, prostitution, drug pushers, flea markets, shoplifting, pickpockets, home burglary, loft break-ins. We respond by buying stolen goods when we think it is a bargain, paying in cash when we get a discount, installing burglar alarms and window grates, taking lessons in karate, staying out of the subways, and refusing to walk the streets alone after sundown. But whatever we do, we are aware of the all-pervasive presence of those who make their living outside the law.

In no small measure the growth of the underground economy is due to the rapid decline of jobs in certain traditional low-paying sectors. As Ehrenhalt argues, poorer-paying jobs are not growing as rapidly as better-paying jobs in the city. That means that the people who once filled those marginal slots are now without work altogether. *To stay alive, they invent their own economy—illicit or illegal as it may be.* Historically, the number of vendors has always risen during periods when people could not find a traditional sort of job. Remember the apple sellers of Depression days? Crime has always been a traditional way to redistribute income in times of despair. So it should be no surprise that in New York the "informal economy"—euphemism of academic choice—should be booming.

A second reason is undoubtedly the opportunities for a parasitical way of life in a culture where there is great wealth and it is on display. The money is there for the taking and there are those who will take.

A third reason, applying primarily to those who operate in the "cash" economy—a crime that few consider to be a crime—is the desire to escape taxes. "If the rich don't pay, why should I pay?" Transactions in cash are a plebeian equivalent of the patrician "tax shelter."

For thousands of younger people, the underground economy is the normal lifestyle. They were raised in families and neighborhoods that know how to make it in the shadows. Within these communities the role models are prostitutes and pimps, drug pushers and muggers, bookies and numbers runners. The work is easy though risky; the pay is good and tax free; the entrepreneurial spirit has free rein. The mores of the larger society are a bore and a burden; the school is irrelevant at best and an obstacle at the worst. The way to go is the way of the street—a tried, tested, and approved *modus vivendi*, a counterculture without ideology. Within the city, these inhabitants of the underground economy build their growing city—with its own ethos, ethic, and expanding turf.

How big is this underground economy? Official statistics are of no help. The collectors of data have repeatedly declared that they do not deign to gather such garbage; they exclude the underground from the count of the Gross National Product. They ignore it although thousands of people in the city work in it full time, are active consumers, create goods, render services, accumulate capital, put money in the bank, and cheat the city, state, and federal governments out of taxes. They are not included in any official count because, as one witty economist put it, "Economics deals with goods—not bads."

Intrigued by the challenge—to count the uncountable—I have spent about a dozen years collecting anecdotal evidence, stories, and stray statistics to estimate the size of the underground economy. My tentative conclusion is that, in the United States, it represents about a trillion dollars (1985), or a sum equal to one-third of the Gross National Product.

If ever we get to count the underground operations, we will have to revise all our concepts about the nature of the city's economy. We are apt to find that manufacture is not declining at all; it is merely moving from the factory into the home. In which event, the old duality in manufacture still persists, with a very sizable portion of it paying wages of less than one dollar an hour—with no overtime and no fringes. We will also have to revise our estimates on retail trade to allow for the thousands of sidewalk vendors. We are also likely to discover that we have more millionaires in our midst, fattened on drug sales, gambling, embezzlement, bribery and extortion, than are revealed by the tax returns. We will discover that there is a very real economy, of considerable magnitude, operating outside official ken—even more polarized than the formal economy.

Like the theologic trinity, the three phases of New York's economy are one. The affluent—whether businesses or individuals—provide a market for the service economy. Those who serve in restaurants, cafés, hospitals, homes, offices, beauty parlors, warehouses, department stores at very modest pay make life more comfortable for those they serve. Those who in a past era might have been employed in semi- and unskilled jobs at a livable wage turn to a parasitic existence, preying on the affluent, less affluent, and even the nonaffluent.

Thus does New York come to resemble the kind of society against which Plato warned in *The Republic*: "Wealth and poverty: the one is the parent of luxury and indolence, and the other of meanness and viciousness, and both of discontent." Such a city, said Plato, is really two cities: "one the city of the poor, the other of the rich; these are at war with one another."

New York is such a city today—split racially, ethnically, geographically, and economically. It is a house divided against itself.□

Jim Chapin

WHO RULES NEW YORK TODAY?

The Forging of a New Unity Among the Elites

New York City politics are at a low point. The city that pioneered in municipal unionism, public hospitals, and a university system, the city that seemed to be a "social democratic bastion" in a capitalist nation and a significant factor in establishing the New Deal, is now presided over by a mayor whose public stance, at its worst, alternates between comedian and spokesman for the politics of resentment.

We have had other low points. The 1920s and the 1950s, decades when conservative Republicans administered the nation, were also periods when New York Democrats seemed unchallenged and therefore prone to abuses unchecked by constructive opposition. But in those times at least some opposition forces were visible: radicals, an active press, reform Democrats, the citizens' groups. And Democratic majorities did not mean that there were no opposition parties, as is largely the case today.

At present, liberal critics see New York as a once-liberal city ruled by a new conservative alliance. In this view, the turning point of recent political history was either the fiscal crisis of 1975 or the mayoral election of 1977. Yet a fiscal crisis might just as well have energized our politics as dampened it. As for the 1977 election, the voters were offered a wide array of choices and chose Koch.

Liberals have given two contradictory explanations for Koch's win: the death penalty and deals with the machine. (Later explanations tended to stress the role of money, overlooking the fact that Koch spent the same amount as Bella Abzug and half as much as Mario Cuomo in the runup to the crucial first primary.) The death penalty myth implies an agitated and enraged public, and the "deal with the bosses" a supine, easily led electorate.

But polls taken by the Abzug campaign two weeks before the primary showed that only 19 percent of likely primary voters even knew that Koch was for the death penalty; 11 percent thought he was against it, and 70 percent didn't know his position. What really made Koch's conservative stance popular was his anti-unionism, fueled by the strikes of the Lindsay years and the belief that high wages for city employees were part of the reason for the city's economic crisis.

The second argument—Koch's deal with the bosses—assumes they could deliver votes. They couldn't. A "regular" endorsement is often a handicap, as Koch recognized in asking Brooklyn boss Meade Esposito to soft-pedal his support in public. In Queens Koch won his two 1977 primaries against home-boy Cuomo even though the "regular" organization backed Cuomo; he then lost the county in the general election when the "regulars" finally endorsed him! The crucial fact in all these 1977 elections was the Catholic-Jewish percentage in various boroughs, and the only county where Koch did worse than such a split would suggest was Brooklyn. The crucial endorsements that won the runoff for Koch came from minority leaders like Basil Paterson and Herman Badillo, who became deputy mayors in his administration.

The problem with focusing on the personality of Ed Koch or on the corruption scandal is that it overlooks a more enduring pattern of New York City politics. In fact, there has rarely if ever been an unabashedly "liberal" era in terms of either our voters or our mayors. Defeats of Tammany Hall came from coalitions of left *and* right: conservative Democratic regimes were periodically thrown out by "fusion" "top-bottom" coalitions of patrician reformers and proletarians that look exclusively left-wing only if you cover one eye. Liberal memories of Fiorello LaGuardia focus on the support he received from the American Labor party and his strong pro-union and New Deal policies, but omit his close ties to bankers and such Republican patrons as Samuel Seabury and Robert Moses. Memories of John Lindsay don't acknowledge that his electoral majority in 1965 was largely a traditional Republican vote, and that his narrow win against divided conservative opponents in 1969 came only after tacit agreements with many of the forces he had fought in his first few years. In fact, many of the key figures in the Koch administration come from the Lindsay administration.

The bipartisan incumbent-protection society that has now arisen in the city's electoral politics is a sign of the accommodation reached not only among politicians, but also between major interests that in the past supported opposing politicians. Business, labor, and even (or especially) the media all now support incumbents. (And each other as well.) If the open endorsements by Republicans and Ed Koch of each other are seen as reflecting only Koch's unusual ideology and personality, then the solution would be simple: replace Koch. But then what about the covert mutual support that Senator Al D'Amato and Governor Cuomo rendered each other in 1986? Why was Cuomo's 1982 victory over Lew Lehrman probably aided privately in the voting booth by conservative Republican leaders Warren Anderson, John Calandra, and John Marchi? Why have the two parties cooperated in maintaining the gerrymandering that keeps the State Senate Republican and the State Assembly Democratic? No wonder the 1985 mayoral election and the 1986 state election saw the lowest turnouts in history.

What accounts for this coalescence of political and private interests in the governance of the city?

The recent decline of political life in New York City has several causes, some of them contradictory. People on the left tend to explain it in terms of the feeling (and reality) of the powerlessness of the dissatisfied. People on the right point to the satisfaction of the majority: many citizens are reasonably well off and don't believe that politics is likely to affect their lives in any significant way. Both explanations contain a measure of truth.

Probably most important is the unity of the city's elites since the near-catastrophe of 1975—an arrangement hammered out during the financial crisis by banker Felix Rohatyn, labor leader Victor Gotbaum, and Governor Hugh Carey. Eager at first to avoid a "Hobbesian war of all against all" that seemed likely as a consequence of near-bankruptcy, now they are content with the city's prosperity, limited as that may be to some segments of the population. In the past, progressive elements had opportunities when they were part of broadly based coalitions; now the city has a single unified leadership resulting from a process that incorporates in the same administration both civic reform and "regular" corruption.

This social truce has been reinforced by the media. It is not simply a matter of media support for incumbents and a failure to oppose Things As They Are; it is more a matter of an attitude toward the political process itself. Once, the media reinforced that process; now they denigrate it. Once there were many competing sources of political news, all urging upon the voters the importance of the political process. Now there are relatively few sources of such news, and most of them treat politics with a kind of "objective" contempt. Equally important in recent years has been the power of television to convey negative images to people who would not in earlier years have seen them. As television turns politics into marketing and show, politics becomes another sport, and even political leaders imitate the television commentators by "responding" to events outside their scope. Reagan and Koch comment on their own administrations as if they were outsiders. If you can do nothing real, then politics as show is more liable to express negative attitudes than positive ones.

The result is "power without responsibility," in the famous phrase of Stanley Baldwin. Politics becomes a matter of personality and the ability to keep the media interested. Reagan's geniality is more important than his deplorable ideas. Cuomo fascinates by his (usually failing) struggle with his own bad impulses; Koch by his unabashed glorying in his own hostile ones. Both these men seem obscurely wounded, and therefore fascinate media observers.

Rival Parties

The rule of real estate and the Democratic party was known in the past, but not usually with such dominance. In the New York City of 1900, Protestants were Republican or Fusion voters and Irish Catholics were Democratic. Jews, Germans, and newer immigrants tended to swing between the parties or into protest movements of the center and left. Therefore, anti-Tammany coalitions always bore the stamp of "top-bottom" coalitions, a concept not invented by John Lindsay. And when these coalitions won, it was always the conservative part that defected first.

Since Lindsay's primary defeat by John Marchi in 1969, the newly reconstituted conservative Republican party has ceased to be a competitive force in New York City. In the five elections its line for mayor has averaged 11 percent of the vote, with a high of 15 percent (for Ed Koch!) in 1981. When, in the past, New York City Republicans created a majority by joining with portions of the center and left, in every case pressure from conservative voters was enough to cause them to dismantle the coalition. Today there is no evidence that the conservative Republicans even entertain such a possibility. The irony is that by pushing their party closer to the politics of the rest of the nation, they have destroyed it as a force in New York City.

What of the minor parties? They took their strength from an unusual feature of New York State election law that allowed minor parties to endorse the same candidates as major parties. In almost every other state in the 1890s the major parties joined together to pass anticoali-

tion laws so as to wipe out the Populists (by not allowing joint endorsements of the same candidate). But in New York, where the Populists were weak, such legislation wasn't "necessary." Later, when the Socialists were strong, it was a convenience for the major parties to join together against them. The American Labor party and its fratricidal sibling, the Liberal party, were Jewish liberal parties as against the Catholic Democrats who were not liberal enough; the Conservative party was a Catholic conservative party as against the Protestant Republicans who were not conservative enough. Both lost their *raison d'être* when the major parties were taken over by ideological/ethnic allies: once the open primary was introduced, these parties really began to collapse, since liberals could win in Democratic primaries and conservatives in Republican primaries. By now the Liberal and Conservative parties survive only as organs of patronage and, occasionally, political blackmail.

What of the reform movement in the Democratic party? While some of its members fight on valiantly, most of those elected have become the establishment. The reformers always depended (more than they admitted) on both an ethnic base (Jews fighting Catholic politicians) and on the media. But now, with Jews triumphant in the city and with the media supporting even an Al D'Amato against a Mark Green (something impossible to imagine a decade or two ago), the reformers find themselves all but helpless. And as office holders increasingly are people recently elected as reformers, it becomes harder and harder to get younger activists aroused or involved. Many politicians win elections as independents or reformers and then—somehow—the "regular" organization survives and takes over.

One problem with Democratic reformers is that once elected they seldom face serious opposition again, so that they tend to settle into the habits and pleasures of office. The reformers discover, as well, that their earlier supporters can offer them little help in running the government, while the "regulars" can "fix" things and introduce them to important contacts. (It was this, more than anything else, that "seduced" Ed Koch into his coziness with the machine.) The key to the "regular" organization is that, although not a successful electoral machine, it is a successful governmental operation. Its members are personally agreeable, in many cases knowledgeable; they can help "get things done," in their own way.

Events of the last year or so have begun to alter the perception of the Koch administration from one fixated on race and ideology to one riddled with corruption. (Both of course can be true.) Unfortunately, the exciting discoveries of personal corruption have diverted attention from the real scandal of recent years. Liberals tend mistakenly to attribute the failings of the Koch administration to remnants of the old political system rather than beginnings of a new one. Despite the dramatic developments in the Parking Violations Bureau and the Transportation Department, "machine" penetration of the municipal bureaucracy is more limited under

---

Jo-Ann Mort

Ruth Messinger — Local Issues, Socialist Vision

If Ruth Messinger were in high school instead of on the New York City Council, she would be considered "the most likely to succeed." So said a January 1987 *Daily News* poll. City officials and opinion-makers were asked to rate the thirty-five members of New York's City Council and the Council president. Messinger got the survey's highest overall rating—3.99—leading in every area from intelligence to accessibility and, most impressively for the one New York City Councilmember who belongs to the Democratic Socialists of America, she led in an understanding of city finance.

Messinger, first elected to the City Council in 1977 to represent Manhattan's Upper West Side, has become a national figure, far outreaching her duties as a legislator for a community regarded as Manhattan's most liberal. Even with soaring property values and restaurant mania, the district continues to send her back to the Council with overwhelming support. In her last reelection campaign she beat her opponent by a margin of four to one.

Trained as a professional social worker, Messinger rose to prominence on the West Side through her leadership in local community issues, but especially as an elected member of Community School Board 3. Her three children are all products of New York's public schools.

Originally, she ran as an insurgent community activist against Manhattan's entrenched liberal reformers. Today, ten years later, she is probably the most popular elected official on the West Side.

How did an Upper West Side mother of three, school board activist, and unabashed democratic socialist rise to such prominence in Ed Koch's New York? In many ways, Messinger's plunge into electoral politics resembles that of other women of her generation who realized that their public service could be put to its best use in political office.

"I was raised in a quintessentially liberal Democratic, ADA, *New York Times, Citizens Union Voters' Guide* household," recalls Messinger. "I was very involved in a whole set of issues and movements: the anti-war movement, the women's movement, West Side issues like housing and public education. Through fairly serious Jewish religious training and a familial devotion to social service, I was concerned with people who had less and with government's responsibility to meet their needs."

Messinger joined the Democratic Socialist Organizing Committee (later Democratic Socialists of America, or DSA) shortly after being elected to the Council. She credits her joining to Paul DuBrul, a longtime city activist and urban planner, who spotted Messinger as someone who could combine the concerns of democratic socialism on a local level with more abstract theoretical concerns.

"I don't think my colleagues or constituents are interested in the particular label of democratic socialist," says Messinger about her affiliation. "They're more interested in what it's like to negotiate with me. But I believe that some of the things people find satisfying in dealing with me come from my holding a whole universe of socialist concerns. There's an assumption among some people that being on the left means being dogmatic

Koch than it was under his predecessors. Not the old-line Democratic machine but professionals like Deputy Mayors Nat Leventhal, Bobby Wagner, Jr., Stanley Brezenoff, and Alair Townsend have played major parts in the Koch administration.

The truly serious problem of the Koch years has been the ascendancy of large-scale "honest graft" tied to real estate, and the extent to which that ascendancy is now taken for granted. It is assumed that the public interest can be secured only by trade-offs with private interests that present New Yorkers with impossible policy choices—mammoth boondoggle projects in exchange for desperately needed subway station renovations and the ever-fading promise of an enhanced tax base. The alternative is always assumed to be abandonment of the city.

Koch seems to believe that real estate interests nourished by state capitalism are somehow "entrepreneurs" who represent pri-

---

and inflexible. But I'm highly committed to listening to all sides of an issue and at least making clear where I'm willing to negotiate."

Entering city government toward the end of New York City's fiscal crisis forced Messinger to formulate answers for those who accused her of big spending. "You can't talk about all the things you believe in unless you answer the next round of questions. The trigger that got me involved in how to fund the programs I thought were essential was the issue of tax abatements," she says.

"If you had asked me fifteen years ago what I would work on through the 1980s, I wouldn't have mentioned a sophisticated understanding of taxes, revenue, the hard number side of economic equity; but once you enter that universe, it explains a lot of whose wheels go round for whom."

"Ruth has taken untouchable issues like the J-51 tax abatements and turned them into household words," says DuBrul. The J-51 program, created in 1955 to help finance the upgrading of cold-water flats, actually intensified the gentrification of the Upper West Side, where developers were offered tax abatements and exemptions by the city to rehabilitate their housing stock.

Another issue on which Messinger has focused attention is commercial rent control. Calling small businesspeople the "backbone of neighborhoods," she has built a boroughwide effort to address this problem. Her proposed commercial-rent-control legislation forced Mayor Koch to commission a study even while Messinger continues to advocate regulation.

Answering the inevitable charge that she is anti-development, she describes herself as "an advocate for government's responsibility to devise a long-range plan for growth, employment opportunity, and the relationship between residential and commercial development and city services that support that development." Messinger has been able to draw on a socialist tradition of planned growth in her years in the Council, when it has often seemed she was fighting an uphill battle.

Recently, she achieved new prominence when, early on in the municipal corruption scandals, her office became a refuge for whistle-blowers willing to risk their jobs to expose corruption in the city agencies. Additionally, she was an early proponent of legislation designed to limit the size of campaign contributions.

If Messinger's democratic socialism surfaces visibly in her policy work, so does her feminism. In turn, her feminism is also informed by her socialism. "Women concerned about women in New York City must be concerned with an economic component," she says as she discusses her current thoughts about developing a strategy for adequate day care in the city.

She immediately points out the employment opportunities for women and men in the day care field. Moreover, in a city where forty percent of the children are growing up in households below the poverty line, day care is "clearly a long-term investment," she observes.

Yet, today, the city provides day care for just 18 percent of the children who qualify under income eligibility and 10 percent of the youngsters in welfare hotels. So, asks Messinger, how do you expand day care without the city having to pay either the total cost of the center or the total cost per child? Tax breaks and land use assistance should be used for this financing instead of granting tax breaks to developers for trees in their buildings' lobbies and atriums, she argues. "If we are serious about diversifying economic development in this city, especially in other boroughs, well, then, don't do it without day care."

With a four-person staff and a reserve of more than twenty student interns a semester, Ruth Messinger is daily making at least a part of democratic socialism credible, and affordable, for thousands of New Yorkers. □

vate enterprise. What former Urban Development Corporation head William Stern calls "the commercial party" of law firms, bankers, and construction companies has always existed, but in at least some competition with ideological interests and economic interests. Now, big government and big business stand together on a playing field where no one else seems even to have a voice. The tendency of the Koch administration to let entrepreneurs carry on needed building projects in return for state favors suggests that local government is "progressing" backward to a precapitalist condition: one waits for the salt monopoly or tax farming!

By contrast, the corruption recently uncovered in the "regular" machine organizations is nothing new, except, in a few cases, for its remarkable stupidity—which may itself reflect the greater difficulty the "regulars" have had in gaining access to the rich founts of cash legally available to real estate entrepreneurs. The "regulars" have no access to mayoral judicial patronage, and virtually no access to most of the crucial positions in the city administration. They have been restricted to Transportation, Ports and Terminals, and a few other lucrative but not important spots. Crises in such agencies as the Human Resources Administration reflect the impact of disastrous Reagan cutbacks rather than traditional Tammany-style corruption. After Queens Borough President Manes's suicide, the search for his machine's links to city agencies petered out because there were in fact so few. The "regulars" continue to dominate the City Council (of no great import) and the borough presidencies (important only because of their votes on the Board of Estimate, the city's main policy and appropriations body). If the Board of Estimate is now going to be devalued pursuant to present court orders, the City Council will become an important bastion of "regular" strength, though the mayoralty itself may gain the most power of all.

The dirty little secret of Koch's governance is that in personnel and policy it is hard to distinguish it from what passes for liberalism in its present, extremely shrunken incarnation throughout the Northeast. Electorally Koch comes from the right wing of reform, which can be traced in New York City mayoral primaries from James Scheuer in 1969 to Al Blumenthal in 1973 to Koch in 1977, with its strongest appeal in just those precincts— Riverdale, Brooklyn Heights, Forest Hills, and above all, the East Side of Manhattan—that used to be the bastions of Fusionism and Republicanism. Some liberals have tried to make something of Koch and Cuomo as opposite sides of the Democratic party, but it's not a very big difference in the realm of economic policy. They have supported the same candidates for president; they have supported each other for office except when running against each other.

That is not to say that the rhetorical differences of the two men do not have real-world consequences. Because Koch talks the way he does he is identified as a figure on the right of the Democratic party; because Cuomo talks the way he does he is identified as a figure somewhat to the left. Perhaps the most serious criticism to be made of Koch is that his years as mayor have resulted in such sharply reduced expectations with regard to political life that Cuomo's undistinguished performance as governor can be excused on the grounds that at least he isn't aggravating race problems. It would take a microscope to find a major policy difference between Cuomo and Republican Governor Kean of New Jersey.

I would argue that Koch's "racist" and "conservative" appeals have not been vital to his political success, but that they were self-chosen and probably even somewhat damaging to him. (That Koch seems to have been expressing personal biases rather than engaging in political opportunism makes his behavior even more remarkable.) The conservative white ethnic vote has deserted him every time he really needed it: in his four races against Cuomo in 1977 and 1982. He lost the liberal whites and the minorities not because of his 1977 campaign or even his record in government, but because of his rhetoric after his election. Three of the leading institutions of liberalism in 1978 (New York Americans for Democratic Action, New York State New Democratic Coalition, New York Civil Liberties Union) were led by people who had supported him in 1977, yet he went out of his way to attack them (despite the fact that, for example, he received 92 percent of the New Democratic Coalition's delegate vote in his general election race against Cuomo and played a major role in the 1978 NDC convention's endorsement of Hugh Carey for reelection.)

The same thing happened with the minority vote. It was Koch's decision to break with his deputy mayors (Paterson and Badillo), and to exacerbate relations with the minority community by the things he said. Perhaps this was "no accident," but that such rhetoric was not necessary is suggested by the ability of Cuomo to ignore minorities both in appointments and in policy without creating any serious opposition to himself in New York City.

At present almost all the leading Democrats in office are corporate liberals with an austerity streak. In this sense, they are conservative reformers. From their point of view, popular input on governmental issues should be restricted to such "style" issues as the death penalty and the drinking age, while the basic economic policy—government by and with corporations—continues.

The left in New York had major influence in the past because it could attract allies (with rather different goals) from the top of the society. Right now these allies are missing: there is no serious upper-class opposition, no serious party opposition, and no serious press criticism.

As long as the city economy continues to prosper, no matter how unevenly, and there is no substantive change in national politics, there is little chance of a serious change in the city's direction. The progressive successes of the past reflected times when ethnicity was displaced by working-class unity *coupled with* a conservative elite drive for honest reform. That such a drive can be found among today's yuppies may be doubted.

That is not to say that our mayor is forever. Koch is weakest at the center of the Democratic coalition and stronger as you move away from that center. He is stronger among non-Democrats than Democrats, stronger among all Democrats than among primary voters, and weakest of all among the hard-core primary voters. He is also weakest among the two ends of the Democratic party: for instance in 1982

Cuomo beat him in Staten Island and Manhattan. Conservative ethnic bastions like Howard Beach have never been the core of Koch's support (in fact Howard Beach voted for Cuomo over Koch, by two to one, four times); his base has remained in moderately liberal areas like Forest Hills, among people who quite probably feel equally negative about the white mob that attacked blacks and the blacks who were attacked.

Koch's greatest strength in 1989 as in 1985 will be the divisions among his opponents. The numbers suggest that a black of the type likely to be a candidate in New York City (a regular politician such as Percy Sutton or Denny Farrell, or an "outsider" like Vernon Mason) cannot win the mayoralty, but is likely to prevent another candidate from putting together the actual majority that probably exists against the mayor.

Which brings us to the theory of the inexorable march of the "minority majority." Advocates of this theory point out that in the 1980 census, 48 percent of the city's population was nonwhite (counting Hispanics as nonwhites); to this must be added the continuing population shift, and the probability of an undercount of the minorities. There are, however, a number of weaknesses in the argument. Those who can't be found by census takers are unlikely to be found to vote. Far more minorities are under eighteen, which may be important for the politics of the twenty-first century, but reduces their present impact. Many of them are not citizens. Finally, and most important, there is the sleight of hand by which Korean shopowners in Washington Heights or Cuban doctors in Jackson Heights are assumed to be prospective members of a coalition working for the interests of welfare mothers in Bedford-Stuyvesant. (This is not to say that the new minorities will not affect local elections, just that there is at present no basis to assume a single citywide majority.)

It is also important to note that the once-missing black vote is no longer missing; since the 1981 primary elections, blacks have been steadier primary voters than whites. If votes are to be increased, it is more likely to be from groups other than the blacks. A large black turnout is unlikely to lead to a black mayor soon, for the simple reason that there is a general election. Race remains central to the politics of New York City, but the city will probably remain one of the few great American cities not to have a black mayor by the end of the century, largely because New York's ethnicity will continue to resemble a mosaic rather than the one or two colors that dominate in most big cities.

The most recent ethnic change is going in a different direction: the fastest-growing groups are Russian Jews, Portuguese, Greeks, non-Puerto Rican Hispanics, and Asians. Most of them are well to the right of the older "new groups" of Puerto Ricans and blacks, but hardly to be counted as firm adherents of the national, let alone the local, Republican party. It will perhaps be easier in this environment to recognize that immigrant insurgencies are generally pluralist rather than radical in nature. Some are even regressive.

It has been a characteristic of state and municipal politics that ethnicity has overlapped with class but has been more important than class. This latest ethnic replacement will someday lead to another turnover: in another decade, Jewish office-holders in the city will face the fate they or their predecessors meted out to aging Irish office-holders three decades ago. When such replacements have been carried out against groups with major roles in the intellectual community, the rhetoric of decline and collapse has generally been invoked, as witness the ability of WASP intellectuals around the First World War era to write entire books about the decline of the city.

If one notes that the relations between the private and public sector are more important than the ethnicity of those who hold positions in these sectors, it is possible to see that in New York City these are moving in contradictory directions. On the one hand, public power is now clearly greater than private power, in a way not true in past crises: J. P. Morgan could stop a stock market crisis by himself in 1903, but in 1929 his successors needed federal help; similarly, banks could dictate a solution to a city fiscal crisis in 1933, but by 1975 saving the city required the state and the pension funds. The banks' ability to dictate a solution to the city passed in a few months in 1975, and by 1977 their policy demands could be rebuffed.

Analysts seriously interested in socioeconomic changes must avoid legends. They must remember that left-wing achievements in the past came as part of broader alliances. They must stop mistaking ethnicity for politics; while ethnicity may be more important than class to voting, economics is more important to governing policy than ethnicity. They must stop making heroes and villains: for it hinders the ability to think about the actual sources of support for the present system or, potentially, for serious change.

Koch's politics are as inexorably tied to the 1970s as Lindsay's were to the 1960s. Since modern capitalism is increasingly linked to the operations of the state at all levels, control of the state (or, in this case, of the city) offers a very great prize indeed; but it can be won only by coalitions encompassing instincts and forces many of which may not be on the left. If we are to learn seriously from past coalitions, then alliances with new ethnic groups and "good government" types are both necessary.

If the prosperity of city government continues, it will be impossible to keep self-interested elites together. There will then be battles over the spoils. If, on the other hand, the economy declines, the current consensus will fall apart because more difficult choices than Koch has been willing to make will be forced upon the mayoralty. The callousness of a city in which twenty five-year-old Wall Street bankers making $500,000 a year leave Grand Central Station by stepping over the bodies of the homeless may once more become unacceptable, and a candidate for mayor who can join the interests of disparate groups in a coalition for progressive change will come forward. The agenda for such a mayor will have to be built in the experience of the newest ethnic groups, in the civic associations, and by journalists; these are traditionally the three arenas in New York City in which new political ideas have been put forward. If this happens, then once again the city which is the capital of international finance can also be a center of progressive change. ☐

Nicolaus Mills

HOWARD BEACH— ANATOMY OF A LYNCHING

New York Racism in the 1980s

T he New Park Pizzeria in Howard Beach, Queens, is not a place you go to if you're looking for trouble. It's too small and too neat, and so close to Cross Bay Boulevard, the main street in Howard Beach, that anyone driving by in a car can see in the front windows. Like the Cross Bay Bowling Lanes next door, the New Park Pizzeria is a place where families and teenagers mix comfortably. Go to the New Park Pizzeria on a weekend night, and you're back in the 1950s. Customers come in, eat their pizzas at the wooden picnic tables opposite the counter, then drop their paper plates in the trash barrel by the front door. Only the sounds of airplanes taking off and landing at nearby Kennedy airport remind you that the New Park Pizzeria is not really part of small town America.

The family atmosphere of the New Park Pizzeria is no longer what comes to mind, however. All that changed on the Friday before Christmas 1986, when three black men made the mistake of stopping there for something to eat. Now Howard Beach calls to mind the kind of racial violence that twenty years ago characterized Philadelphia, Mississippi, and Selma, Alabama. The difference is that twenty years ago such racial violence seemed about to end. The deaths of black and white civil rights workers in Philadelphia and Selma were the cause of national outrage, and what followed was the Civil Rights Act of 1964 and the Voting Rights Act of 1965. But no comparable legislation has followed Howard Beach. It has

seemed too much a New York problem to be remedied by a quick fix.

The chain of events that produced the Howard Beach violence began just after midnight on December 20 when three black men walked into the New Park Pizzeria. Their car had broken down, and they were tired and cold after unsuccessfully trying to get a tow. They had walked three and a half miles, and a pizza seemed like a good idea. A few minutes before they had exchanged insults with a carload of teenagers, most of them from nearby John Adams High School, but the incident amounted to no more than name-calling. Unaware that they were in danger, the three black men, Michael Griffith, his stepfather, Cedric Sandiford, and a friend, Timothy Grimes, went on eating their pizzas.

A short while later, a police car, responding to a 911 call that there were three "suspicious" black men in the New Park Pizzeria, stopped by. But the counterman said there was no problem, and the police drove off. It was the last chance Griffith, Sandiford, and Grimes would have to get out of Howard Beach safely. Minutes later the carload of boys they had exchanged insults with returned. The boys had gone back to the birthday party they were attending for help. Now there were twelve of them, and their weapons included a metal baseball bat and a tree limb. When they saw what they were up against, Griffith, Sandiford, and Grimes began running.

Running was the right decision for Timothy Grimes. In the dark he managed to elude his pursuers, and later that night he hitchhiked back to his home in Brooklyn. Griffith and Sandiford were not as lucky. After cutting through a parking lot and zigzagging down side streets, Griffith was chased onto the nearby Belt Parkway. There a car driven by Dominick Blum, a white court officer returning home from a play at Brooklyn College, struck Griffith, killing him instantly. Sandiford, running behind Griffith, was caught by his pursuers before he could reach the Belt Parkway. Badly beaten, he had enough presence of mind to feign unconsciousness, and when his attackers left, he crawled through a hole in a nearby fence and staggered onto the Belt Parkway. There police found him dazed and bleeding.

The death of Griffith and the attack on Sandiford and Grimes could not have come at a worse time. Two decades ago when Mayor John Lindsay walked the New York streets trying to restore order after the 1967 riots, there was a feeling that at least some white politicians cared about what happened to blacks. In the 1960s New York's liberal political establishment prided itself on its opposition to racism. Many of them, including Ed Koch (then a reform congressman from Greenwich Village), even participated in the Southern civil rights movement. But by the 1980s, such concern seemed to have vanished.

Ed Koch may still be a long way from Ronald Reagan on race, but in New York Kochism is often viewed as a local version of Reaganism. "I see him as an instigator of the climate of racial fear in this city," the Reverend Calvin Butts, the executive minister of Harlem's Abyssinian Baptist Church, said earlier this year. During the Koch years life for blacks in New York has been especially rough. Infant mortality among blacks in the city is twice the national average, and during 1985–86, while unemployment for whites in New York dropped from 7.2 to 5.6 percent, it rose by almost a point for blacks. Worst of all, as many blacks see it, has been the feeling that in Ed Koch's New York black life is cheap. Despite his description of the Howard Beach attack as "a modern lynching" and the "worst crime in

the recent history of the city," the mayor has often seemed indifferent to blacks. His closing of Sydenham Hospital in Harlem, his opposition to the appointment of a black chancellor of schools, his resistance to a 1983 investigation into police brutality by the House Subcommittee on Criminal Justice are what blacks remember when they think of Ed Koch, and they see his feelings pervading New York in the 1980s. They note that the men in the white mob that in 1982 killed transit worker Willie Turks outside a bagel shop in the Gravesend section of Brooklyn were never convicted of second-degree murder, and they believe that for the police anything goes when the suspected criminal is black.

In recent years there has been a series of arrests in which a black man or woman was surrounded by the police, then killed in circumstances in which there seemed a clear alternative to lethal force. The victims included Arthur Miller, a popular Bedford-Stuyvesant businessman, who, following a street altercation, died when the police used a choke hold to subdue him; Eleanor Bumpurs, a deranged sixty-six-year-old, shotgunned as she brandished a knife while protesting her eviction from her Bronx apartment; Michael Stewart, who, after being arrested for writing graffiti on a subway, arrived at Bellevue Hospital brain dead; and Nicholas Bartlett, a Harlem street vendor, who was shot to death by eight police officers after he allegedly attacked and injured one of them with a fifteen-inch pipe.

To New York City's black community the violence of Howard Beach came as no surprise. Rather it seemed the culmination of a series of white-on-black encounters that in recent years have become increasingly ugly. The tragedy that Howard Beach represents for New York's nonwhite population, now more than half the city, is not, however, what has transformed the killing of Michael Griffith from a headline into an ongoing story. The media have had little that was new or interesting to say about Howard Beach. Both on television and in papers the principal focus has been on how the legal strategy employed by Alton Maddox and C. Vernon Mason, the attorneys for Sandiford and Grimes, has aroused racial tensions.

The strategy, as both lawyers argue, consists

of trying to get the legal system to work by refusing to cooperate with it. The aim is to showcase the problems blacks have when they come before the courts. When the strategy succeeds, a case that might otherwise get lost in the system is turned into a controversy. The political and legal establishment is then forced to act or publicly defend itself, and the black community in turn is given a cause around which it can organize. The strategy was very successful in the case of Lee Johnson, a black Union Theological Seminary student, who said that he had been dragged from his car in Harlem and beaten by two white policemen. When the mayor, among others, questioned Johnson's story, Mason told Johnson not to testify before a grand jury, and the ensuing controversy set off a chain of events that eventually led the mayor to appoint the city's first black police commissioner, Benjamin Ward. In the Michael Stewart case the noncooperation strategy was far less successful, actually impeding a conviction according to the trial judge. But even in that case, Maddox did not go away empty-handed. Ten days after being criticized in a special counsel's report for his handling of the Stewart incident, the chief of the New York City Transit Authority, John Meehan, resigned.

In the Howard Beach case the noncooperation strategy began three days after the murder of Michael Griffith. In Maddox's view his client, Cedric Sandiford, was being put in the position of a defendant. The night of the murder, Sandiford had been spread-eagled and searched, then, despite his injuries, made to sit in a police car for two hours while his possible involvement in another crime in the area was checked. In the ensuing days stories were given to the press that Sandiford's explanation for what he was doing in Howard Beach did not hold up. For Maddox the climax came when Sandiford, his vision still impaired from the beating, was asked to pick his attackers from a lineup. Maddox advised Sandiford to refuse to show up for the lineup, and when he failed to show, the case was thrown into turmoil. Maddox in turn found more reasons to believe that a "bad-faith" investigation was being conducted by Queens District Attorney John Santucci and the Queens police. Little effort

had been made, Maddox found, to check out witnesses who lived in the area, and the confession of Jon Lester, a key defendant, had not even been videotaped. Most suspicious of all in Maddox's judgment, the car of Dominick Blum had not been impounded on the night of the murder, and there had been no arrest of Blum. "If they don't arrest Blum, there is no point in our being involved," Maddox told the *New York Times*.

At the preliminary hearing in Queens on December 30, the noncooperation strategy appeared to backfire. By this time Vernon Mason had joined the case as attorney for Timothy Grimes, and with both Sandiford and Grimes refusing to testify, there were now no eyewitnesses to identify the attackers. The only charge District Attorney Santucci could make stand was one of reckless endangerment against the three defendants who had already given statements. In the press and in political circles, the pressure on Maddox and Mason to change their tactics began to mount. Harlem Congressman Charles Rangel declared, "I don't see what we gain or what justice gains by not going forward with what we have," and even Manhattan Supreme Court Justice Bruce Wright, arguably the most respected black jurist in the city, joined the critics. "We'll never know what happened unless Maddox brings this witness forward," Wright observed. "It just doesn't make sense to withhold evidence that may shed light on this case."

But Maddox and Mason did not alter their strategy. They continued to insist that John Santucci was not doing his job. Now their emphasis was not simply on Santucci's shortcomings but on the need to replace him. "We cannot say what is going on in Mr. Santucci's mind, but the appearance of justice would seem to mandate a special prosecutor," Alton Maddox insisted. Maddox's complaints, Santucci replied, were "the same old tripe—knock the system, dissolve the police force." As the conflict escalated, it was, however, Santucci who began looking for a way out. At the start of the new year, he coupled a plea to black leaders for cooperation with a statement that his office was considering turning over the case to a Federal prosecutor. Later in January, after calls for Governor Mario Cuomo to appoint a special prosecutor began to build, Santucci told the *City Sun*, a black New York paper, that he would bow out if it would promote better race relations. The following day at a meeting with Governor Cuomo, Santucci restated his willingness to bow out, and the stage was set for a meeting between the governor and the city's black leadership.

The result was a stormy six-hour session on January 13 that ended with Charles "Joe" Hynes, the special prosecutor for the New York City Criminal Justice System, taking over the case. Hynes's appointment was one that Maddox and Mason initially opposed. They wanted someone in no way tied to the state or city government. But the governor refused to budge on this, and when the black leaders present at the conference decided to moderate

their demands, Maddox and Mason dropped their objections. Sandiford and Grimes would, they announced, cooperate with Hynes, and their meetings with him and his staff took place in a very different atmosphere from those with Santucci.

But as Hynes began to develop his case, he did not build it around Sandiford, whose version of events following his beating often contradicted the evidence. Instead, Hynes interviewed the teenagers who had stayed behind at the party. Then his staff did a psychological study of those who had participated in the beating. The result was a much clearer picture of what happened the night of December 20 and a decision to base the prosecution on the testimony of one of the

---

Wesley Brown

Where Pluralism and Paranoia Meet

Nowhere is the meeting between pluralism and paranoia more apparent than on the subway. Despite all our high-minded rhetoric about the marvels of diversity, there is a wariness bordering on extreme caution when straphangers are confronted with the dizzying mix of cultural difference and life circumstances. Maybe it has something to do with being underground? In many ways this subterranean world reflects the irrational in our nature. The fact that riding the subway can summon up our worst fears and long-standing grievances makes understandable the tight facial masks lost in the sounds of a Walkman or locked behind books and newspapers. Everyone stakes out his or her territory with no thought of giving ground. People plant themselves into a spot with the finality of a tombstone. Men, in particular, have a way of encamping themselves in an open-sesame leg spread, with the knobs of their knees pointing out like closed-mouthed cannons.

The Number One Broadway Local cleaves a path through the earth of Manhattan, filling up with and emptying itself of every conceivable grouping of people. Each morning when I take my six-year old son Anthony to school, and later in the afternoon when I pick him up, a sunburst of mostly black and Latin adolescents blazes on and off the subway on

Manhattan's Upper West Side. They flaunt their gorgeous bodies through the cars and show off their agile minds with loud, blunt language that is often offensive. Most of them will probably outgrow this brazen, self-absorbed behavior, which is symptomatic of an American craving for public disclosure of private life and the tendency to confuse freedom of expression with exhibitionism.

The public perception of attempts to draw attention to oneself is largely a matter of style. A man parachuting into Shea Stadium during a game of the World Series is applauded and not automatically viewed as a threat to public safety. However, a display of bravado by a young, indigo-skinned black male, moving through a crowded subway car like a point guard bringing the ball up the court, sporting a haircut that makes the shape of his head resemble a cone of ice-cream, and wearing barge-size sneakers with untied laces thick as egg noodles, is immediately considered a dangerous presence whether he is or not. As I once overheard a transit cop say to a young black man on a subway platform: "It's not what you did. It's your attitude."

I see that same "attitude" being attributed to my own son, who is outspoken, streaking in height as

gang, Robert Riley, who in exchange for cooperation was promised reduced charges.

In this new version of the case, Dominick Blum, the driver of the car that hit Griffith, was no longer a suspect, as Maddox and Mason had declared he should be. Blum's statement as to his whereabouts before the accident and his lack of knowledge of anyone in the Howard Beach gang checked out completely. But those who had begun the fight outside the New Park Pizzeria were now much more deeply implicated in the death of Griffith than before. They had not, as Sandiford's original story indicated, merely chased Griffith, who, after getting away from them, made the mistake of trying to cross the Belt Parkway. They had actually pursued Griffith so closely that in order to escape them he was forced onto the parkway. A similar case had occurred in Boston in 1982, when a white mob chased a black man onto railroad tracks, where he was killed by a train. A Boston district attorney had obtained a second-degree murder conviction, using the "tunnel theory" that the victim had no choice but to risk his life in order to get away. When Howard Beach became news, the same Boston district attorney contacted Santucci's office, and Hynes, after taking over the case, sent three of his staff to Boston to review the tunnel case. Thus, in early February, when Hynes began his presentation to a Queens grand jury, his legal strategy was far different from Santucci's, and he had as his principal witness one of the teenagers responsible for the death of Griffith. This time second-degree murder charges against three ringleaders of the gang were sustained, and

---

though a Masai gene is stalking him, and a high-wire act in his own right. I've already had to fight with teachers and administrators who are quick to judge his spirit as armed and potentially dangerous. I see the outlines of the battles I will have to wage on his behalf, and I'm deeply troubled by segments of this city poised to expect only the worst from black and Latin youth. Is it any wonder that the Bernhard Goetz trial held New Yorkers captive? Whatever opinions people have about whether Goetz was justified in shooting those four black youths, the case touched every nerve where safety and menace intertwine with our conflicting emotions about race.

I walk through the turnstile and onto the platform at the West 59th Street station. A black man is playing an acoustic guitar, mixing classical and popular modes in a manner that makes what he's playing sound both familiar and unlike anything I've ever heard. He is dressed plainly, in a plaid shirt, jeans and sneakers; and there's nothing particularly striking about him except for the mustache that completely smothers his upper lip. He holds the neck of the guitar like it's the hand of a dance partner and presses the wooden torso against his own as though he is comforting a friend. He cocks his head to the left and eavesdrops on the conversation he is having with himself. What he has to say is voiced as a hum that is both throaty and nasal.

Then something occurs that is difficult to explain. I've become much more aware of the pattern of my own breathing. It's as though some pocket of tension has been released, allowing the air keeping me alive to circulate more freely. I sense this in the other twenty or so people standing around me who also seem more involved in their own breathing. The remarkable thing about what is happening is that, separated as we are by the fear of what makes us different, we are joined together by our profound attention to this music. I can't help thinking that if the context of this scene were more overtly political, this black man (or anyone else for that matter) would not be able to command the attention of such a diverse collection of people. It is far more difficult to find the equivalent political gestures that not only speak to us across the borders separating us but also inspire a commitment to improve the quality of life.

But perhaps something just as significant is missing from that assessment, which is more cultural than political. Italo Calvino once said that New York is a city of sadness, binding its inhabitants together by a thread that is continually stretching, "so that at every second the unhappy city contains a happy city unaware of its own existence." Living in New York demands that we become street-smart urban dwellers. Our sophistication in coping with the ways of the city often numbs us to the cruelty in our midst. However, for a brief moment on a subway platform in mid-Manhattan, a black man playing a six-string guitar has helped us find a city within this city of sadness that affirms our common humanity. And although it is fleeting, if we refuse to be bullied into unawareness and fear, finding another city comparable to the one we've just experienced may be only a second away. □

nine others were indicted for lesser crimes, ranging from manslaughter to inciting to riot.

The February 10 indictments produced great relief in the black community. "This is the first step in bringing this case toward some resolution," Harriet Michel, the head of the New York Urban League, observed. "It is a validation of the contention of the lawyers that an extra perspective was needed." Her validation sentiments were echoed by Maddox and Mason. Although the conspiracy Hynes uncovered was not the one the two lawyers initially insisted existed, their tactics had, nonetheless, proved successful. The legal controversy they created had both worked in their clients' favor and exposed shortcomings in the Queens district attorney's office. For Maddox and Mason, there was also the added bonus of Governor Cuomo's involvement in the case. Not only did the governor appoint a new prosecutor, at the end of March he followed up his appointment by proposing legislation designed to stiffen the penalties for bias-related violence in New York State. The governor linked the timing of his civil rights proposals to Howard Beach. "This legislation is a belated and modest response to a blatantly serious disease that affects our society," he announced.

Equally important for Maddox and Mason was the politicizing of the black community that the Howard Beach controversy made possible. A week after the death of Griffith, there was a protest march through Howard Beach, then a larger rally of blacks at Boys and Girls High in Brooklyn, and at the end of January a "Day of Outrage" protest in Manhattan, where demonstrators marched from a midtown hotel for the homeless to the mayor's apartment in Greenwich Village. By comparison with the civil rights demonstrations of the 1960s or even those held recently in Forsyth County, Georgia, the turnout at these events was small; but in a city where in recent years the black community has been politically quiet, the Howard Beach rallies were an important departure. As Brooklyn Assemblyman Roger Green noted, "Meetings on social issues that used to draw ten or twelve people now get one hundred or two hundred. Rallies that once drew two hundred now draw two thousand. Something is happening."

To Maddox and Mason that "something" is a New York civil rights movement. "What you find now is that New York is no different than Birmingham or Alabama or Nashville, and that things that occurred in those cities twenty years ago are being replayed in New York," Maddox, who, like Mason, was born in the rural South, observed. It is a view that puts the two men—with their militancy and legal skills—in the vanguard of black politics in New York in the 1980s, and it also establishes a clear rationale for when the black community should take to the streets. As Mason observed at a press conference the day the Queens grand jury handed down the twelve indictments Hynes asked for, "It was you black people marching and meeting and protesting all over the city who provided the fuel for these indictments."

The indictments that Hynes was able to get have not, however, silenced Maddox's and Mason's critics. Especially among liberals, there has been sharp criticism of the two attorneys. In legal circles the attack on Maddox and Mason has been led by Richard Emery of the New York Civil Liberties Union. "His [Maddox's] methods are sabotage and the pursuit of racial division," Emery told the *National Law Journal*. "He is very big on charges and very short on proof. That's a method we learned to despise during the McCarthy period. I will never work with him again." What Emery and lawyers like him have in mind are the shotgun accusations Maddox and Mason leveled as the Howard Beach case was unfolding. They point to the latters' claims that Dominick Blum was part of the murder gang, that there was a conspiracy by investigators to deny Cedric Sandiford's version of events, and that on the night of December 20 the police drove away from the New Park Pizzeria knowing there was a gang waiting outside it in the parking lot. Each of these accusations threw new doubt on the fairness of Queens officials and advanced Maddox's contention, "There certainly is an official policy in this city never to convict a white person for killing a black person." But as time showed each of these accusations to be untrue, Maddox and Mason made no attempt to retract them. They simply went on to new charges. Maddox's and Mason's critics contend that the two lawyers made it impossible to separate legitimate complaints about DA Santucci and Queens officials from a smear of them.

But it is the political role Maddox and Mason have played outside the courtroom that has drawn the most fire. "I have followed Maddox's career for years, and its most consistent themes have been hidden agendas, self-promotion, and hatred of all law enforcement," columnist Jack Newfield wrote in the liberal *Village Voice*. What Newfield had in mind was the kind of challenge Maddox laid down at the height of the Howard Beach controversy when he told the *City Sun*, "One of the things that you have to understand, as far as the white liberal wing of the civil rights movement is concerned, is that they have a vested interest in controlling what happens in the black community. They refuse to accept the fact that black men and women have brains similar to theirs." Nor is it just the rhetoric of Maddox and Mason that has upset liberals. So too have aspects of the protests Maddox and Mason have helped lead. From the start these have had a separatist thrust. Early demonstrations were coupled with a call for a boycott of white businesses, then of white pizza parlors (on the grounds that the Howard Beach violence began in a white pizza parlor), and at a key rally in Brooklyn, all whites, including white reporters, were barred. Such actions, Maddox's and Mason's critics contend, not only alienate sympathetic whites but foster the illusion that in a city as racially mixed as New York blacks can go it alone.

The debate over the meaning of Howard Beach has thus taken on many of the overtones of the 1960s debate over black power. At that time liberals favored an integrationist strategy that emphasized coalition politics and a black-liberal-labor alliance. Militant nationalists, particularly after Stokely Carmichael became chairman of the Student Nonviolent Coordinating Committee (SNCC), were represented by a black-power strategy that stressed separatism and race consciousness.

For all the similarities between now and then, there is, however, no seeing the response to Howard Beach as a replay of the 1960s. The old roles just don't fit. To be sure, liberal whites have been offended by the broad-brush attacks of Maddox and Mason, but the difficulties that the exodus of whites from SNCC caused the civil rights movement are not happening again as a consequence of Howard Beach. In recent years whites in New York have simply not been deeply involved in black politics, particularly on such basic issues as police brutality. There was no massive outpouring of white anger over the deaths of Michael Stewart and Eleanor Bumpurs or to the closing of Sydenham Hospital. Blacks in turn give no indication that they are, on the whole, anxious to pursue a separatist strategy or that they believe, as one Howard Beach protest sign declared, "New York is Johannesburg." A *Newsday* poll conducted just after Governor Cuomo named a special prosecutor showed that only 19 percent of the blacks surveyed gave Maddox an excellent to good job rating on his handling of Howard Beach, while 52 percent gave him a fair to poor rating. Similarly, the call for a black boycott of white businesses went nowhere, and despite talk of widespread black retaliatory violence, that too has not materialized. There was one vicious black-on-white attack in Queens following Howard Beach, but arrests were quickly made, and the incident never went further.

Is it possible then to see Howard Beach leading to something other than more racial division? The answer to that question will in no small measure depend on what happens when Joe Hynes brings his case to trial, but even a spectacular courtroom victory by Hynes may not be enough. The racial tensions that led to Howard Beach are not about to disappear suddenly. Nor, as Alton Maddox and Vernon Mason have demonstrated, are they about to go unchallenged or unexploited. If Howard Beach proves anything, it is that New York City's vaunted recovery from near bankruptcy has left blacks and whites further apart than ever. In the 1980s blacks and whites in New York don't just find it difficult to act in concert. They are not even sure that a lynching strikes them with equal horror. □

Michael Oreskes

IS IT STILL A UNION TOWN?

Our Divided Labor Movement

When Rupert Murdoch bought the *New York Post* in 1976 he launched his new product with a declaration that New York was "a newspaper town again." The Newspaper Guild, under pressure to grant Murdoch wage and work rule concessions, responded by distributing buttons declaring, "New York: A Union Town Still." The implicit defensiveness of that move—a major union has to remind people that *this* is a union town?—underlines the state of labor in New York. Even here, in one of the cradles of American unionism, there has been both serious erosion and a dramatic shift in the base and nature of union power.

To be sure, the Guild's button emphasized what is still an important truth: for all its economic troubles and internal strife, the labor movement holds a strategic position in the city's life and politics. It is the one institution straddling the great divide of modern New York. More than the church, political parties, or media, the unions, or at least certain of them, bridge divisions of race and class that are the city's crucial social challenge. They are the most significant force with both a presence at the centers of power and strong ties to the city's poor who are clients—welfare recipients, schoolchildren and their parents—or even, in low-wage occupations like health-care attendants, members of unions themselves.

But to say that labor occupies a strategic position is not necessarily to say that it has the strength, unity, or inclination to take advantage of it. It is only to say that whatever labor does will matter beyond its own ranks, influencing whether the city's current divisions will widen or dissolve in the multi-ethnic city of the 1990s.

Two central challenges imperil a construc-

tive response. First, the city is undergoing a wrenching transformation that, overall, has weakened union power: the nonunion sectors of the local economy are booming, while unionized sectors shrink. The exceptions are jobs in local government and construction. Outside these sectors, unions have not only been slow to organize stockbrokers, lawyers, and clerks in the burgeoning financial and corporate service industries; they are even losing some of their grip on such traditional sectors as manufacturing.

Second, the labor movement is riven with factional, ideological and personal strife—so much so that a visitor to several major union leaders in the city finds himself asking whether there is still a labor "movement" at all. When the city's AFL-CIO unions sought a new leader for their Central Labor Council last year, what should have been a debate about the future rang with battle cries from the past; the outcome revealed a left or progressive wing unfocused and divided within itself, and a conservative or right wing relatively more disciplined and unified. One came away with an impression of competing organizations that all just happen to be in the business, as it were, of representing different groups of workers to their particular employers.

No one knows exactly what portion of New York's work force is unionized. Clearly, it is far higher than the 18 percent of the nation's workers who belong to unions. But while the city's economic boom increased the number of stock and commodity brokers by 57,000 in a decade, key segments of the traditionally unionized garment industry declined by almost exactly the same number of jobs. And the overall decline in manufacturing here has been considerably greater than in the nation as a whole. Contrary to a common misconception, the job loss is not just among small, nonunion shops and light industries. "It's massive in dimension and pervasive among manufacturing industries," says Samuel Ehrenhalt, head of the New York office of the Bureau of Labor Statistics. Printing, textiles, and plastics have all been hit hard, as have support industries like trucking and shipping. For the first time in its history, the International Ladies' Garment Workers' Union (ILGWU) has embarked on organizing outside the needle trades, among office workers—a sector where several other unions have already met with considerable frustration. Not only are unionized sectors dwindling as a share of the entire job market; according to Professor Leo Troy of Rutgers University, the nation's leading expert on levels of unionization, union strength within its own traditional sectors is weakening, too.

Troy has not yet issued precise figures, but one doesn't need statistics to see what is happening. Although it would be difficult to build an office tower without the construction trades, it would be just as difficult to find such a new building whose office workers are predominantly unionized. And while electricians, carpenters, masons, and the rest are bloated with contracts on midtown office construction, they seem to feel no great motivation to defend union turf on smaller projects, including renovation work, often undertaken with non-union labor.

Garment manufacturers, meanwhile, haven't fled the city or the nation in recent years as often as they've simply opened nonunion sweatshops in Chinatown or Queens; the proverbial "Taiwan" has come to them, in the form of the greatest wave of immigrants to New York in half a century. That same wave has thus far permitted several new hotels to open in midtown Manhattan without the participation of the Hotel and Restaurant Workers Union. A young waitress at the Novotel Hotel on Broadway explained recently that she felt more in common with her employer than with the union, which she claimed was corrupt. How did she know? "The hotel gives us all the information we need," she said. According to Professor Troy, some employees in growth sectors even view unionization as a threat to their jobs rather than a way to improve wages and protect working conditions—not an attitude one expects of workers in New York.

With the exception of the air traffic controllers at LaGuardia and Kennedy airports, public-employee unions have maintained if not expanded their position of strength. But even here, there have been sea changes. The public-employee unions' role in the 1975 fiscal crisis, which involved accepting wage concessions and committing union pension funds to keep the city from default, has given public-sector unions a special and, to some, ambivalent status and influence as architects of New York's fiscal recovery. To some, particularly rank and filers who don't play tennis with investment bankers or see any dollar benefits, the special relationship is a mistaken accommodation. To others, the partnership is a model for unions in the post-industrial world. "It

gives a link and justification which the rest of the labor movement sorely needs to rebuild its strength," claims Michael Piore, an economics professor at MIT; he says he notes this distinction in "influence" between New York's labor movement and that of the rest of the country whenever he travels. Sellout or shrewd partnership, the new relationship clearly has something to do with the fact that public-employee unions have managed to offset the decline of unionization in manufacturing and commerce in New York. And it accounts for much of the political power that labor retains in the life of the city.

Politics in New York is indeed inseparable from union power, to a degree unknown virtually anywhere else in the country. Unions provide the manpower, a good deal of the brainpower, and even, to a considerable extent, the money in local electoral campaigns.

The weakening of county political organizations has only strengthened the role of union political operations. Mario Cuomo's first Democratic gubernatorial primary victory over Mayor Ed Koch in 1982 and his general-election victory over the much better financed Republican conservative Lew Lehrman were organized largely by labor unions, especially at the field operations level. Fernando Ferrer, who took over as Bronx Borough President after the Bronx Democratic organization scandals, counts among his top advisers the president of one public-employee union and the political director of another. The top political adviser to powerful new State Assembly speaker Mel Miller is the former political

---

Jewel Bellush

Room at the Top: Black Women in District Council 37, AFSCME

For years, one of the most exploited segments in public services had been the nonprofessionals in New York City's hospitals, public schools, and governmental offices. Receiving the lowest pay among municipal workers, they remained primarily outside the organized labor movement, segregated in jobs without status. By the 1960s, they were predominantly black women, working in settings that included hot, crowded kitchens, unpleasant laundries, and large dehumanized hospital wards. Confronting the professionally trained (e.g., doctors, nurses, teachers, school supervisors, and office managers), they often experienced demeaning treatment and menial assignments. Trapped in their jobs, and with little education or training, they constituted the city's public sector underclass. And yet, within the hospital setting, for example, these black women performed the most direct, crucial services.

To organize them was no simple task, with unyielding management opposition, a dispersed hospital system spread over vast areas in the city's five counties, general ignorance about the labor movement, and suspicion as to the ability and determination of unions to provide the channels for resolving their multifaceted problems. It was a slow, tortuous road for those from the American Federation of State, County, and Municipal Employees (AFSCME) who went out to organize.

Directing the field operations among the hospital workers (a key organizing effort for securing DC 37's base of power in the city), was a young, determined, and attractive black woman, Lillian Roberts. She had joined the labor movement as an eighteen-year-old nurse's aide in Chicago in 1946, and was quickly identified as a potential leader by a young Victor Gotbaum when he headed AFSCME in the Windy City. As she would throughout her union career, Roberts quickly attracted workers, gaining their confidence and winning their respect. And she continues to do so as New York State Commissioner of Labor. "I have always seen the union," she repeatedly underscores, "as a protector of working-class rights that transcends all the other things." It was largely through her skillful organizing endeavors that AFSCME built one of the largest union locals in New York and the nation. It was through this local of some 12,000 hospital workers that black women were helped to improve their lives.

Two other larger locals that represented primarily black women were the Clerical/Administrative (1549) and the Schools (372). The former is by far the largest single local of the Council, if not the nation, with over 27,000 members scattered throughout city departments. They include typists, stenographers, telephone operators and various levels of clerks, involving some thirty managers. The Schools local, with some 17,000 who are employed at the Board of Education, is mainly part-time school lunch orderlies, family paraprofessionals, school-crossing guards, and neighborhood workers.

As a result of these new recruits, the power base of DC 37 shifted dramatically by the end of the 1960s from laborers and motor vehicle operators (white, male and of Italian descent) to hospital, school and clerical/administrative workers who were black and female. Here, within this comparatively vibrant union, the impact of the civil rights

director to former AFSCME DC 37 head Victor Gotbaum. Even Mayor Koch, who was elected in part on a "get tough with city workers" platform in 1977, has since found it expedient to ally himself closely to the more conservative uniformed unions (police and fire) and to maintain a truce with the others. Nationally, labor was so concerned with its ebbing power in 1984 that it put aside past practice and became directly involved in Democratic party politics to ensure Walter Mondale's presidential nomination; in New York, unions had been doing that for years.

But "inside influence" in electoral politics has involved compromises, too, as in the frequent decisions of traditionally liberal public-employee unions to support Republican candidates in crucial State Senate races in order to remain on the good side of the Republicans who control the State Senate. Who is co-opting whom? The answers aren't always clear. Unions have used their Senate entrée to improve pensions and, during and since the fiscal crisis, to strengthen the city budget and hence their own chances of winning raises and increased services to the poor. On the other hand, the Republican Senate's resistance to tenant protection, progressive taxation, and ethics reform is well known, and to some activists it has not always been clear that a determined statewide effort couldn't dislodge the Republicans from power.

Strategic power refers to more than electoral influence, however, and even to more than the traditional, if not always legal, capacity to shut down the city through strikes. In New York,

and feminist movements continues to be felt as black women move upward into positions of leadership. Today, some 60 percent of DC 37's membership are black women.

As a union leader, Gotbaum brought to DC 37 a unique social idealism and a rare sensitivity to its multicultural composition. For some sixteen years, his good right hand in the council was Lillian Roberts. Having emerged from a background similar to those of most female members, Roberts understood their personal plight and was aware that they were generally trapped in menial dead-end jobs. Assisted by the head of the council's education department, she launched DC 37's famous career ladder program in the late 1960s. In addition, Roberts pressed those responsible for steward training to encourage black women to participate by providing a program that was concrete and relevant to the job concerns of black women.

When she left in 1981 to head the New York State Department of Labor, Roberts was replaced by Stanley Hill, a black former social worker. Drawn from the ranks, he steadily moved upwards through the channels of leadership from volunteer-activist to local president, and then through the council's divisional structure. Successsor to Gotbaum, who retired in 1987, Hill shares Roberts's concern for black women members.

A second element that has helped black women are the many opportunities provided by the union—its open organization, its democratic spirit of elections, and the varied channels for membership participation. Generally, it is in the local that members with leadership potential display their skills and are identified. Participation in meetings, speaking up and becoming active in committees constitute the grass roots launching pad for a union career.

Behind the union's effectiveness as an expanding influence in decision making is its professionally run Political Action Department. One of its major sources of strength is the large core of black women volunteers. As many as 1,000 of them participate annually and regularly—the two largest constituencies being the Clerical/Administrative and Schools Locals. They attend Political Action Committee meetings and are trained in lobbying and campaign strategies workshops. Over the years, a number of them have moved into staff positions because of the political skills honed in this department.

A third factor serving as an important asset in the development of leadership is the council's broad array of educational and training programs. Black women constitute the bulk of participants in most of the Council's educational programs. Among the offerings that attract them are career opportunities in health, basic skills improvement, high school equivalency and a college education provided at headquarters. In cooperation with Cornell University's School of Industrial and Labor Relations, a specially designed program is offered for women interested in leadership that includes courses in women's studies, labor history, economics and communication skills. Attendance at these programs is exceptionally good with a high passing rate. Bridging the gap between the traditional, academic approaches to credentialism and the practical needs and capacities of the council's working women has required innovative strategies. Small classes and extensive remedial and tutorial assistance bolster its "hands-on" approach which members require. Many come anxious about returning to school and with a fear of failure. Sitting with others, however, who face similar difficulties, bolsters participation and tends to allay uneasiness. Overall, these programs lend a special spirit to the union which encourages members to assume leadership.

Excerpted from SAGE, Vol. III, No. 1 (Spring 1986)   □

another dimension of union power involves labor's ability to mediate between the city's elites and its poor. The United Federation of Teachers (UFT), for example, despite its historic differences with minority champions of "community control" of the public schools, has come, almost by default, to "represent the children," the phrase used by the union's new president, Sandra Feldman. Without question, there is no more potent political force for the public schools than the UFT, and it is not just union propaganda that the organization fills a real void left by the weakness of parent, social service, and minority constituent groups.

That mediation and advocacy role is even clearer in the case of health-care and day-care workers, not only because their clients are poor, but also because their own members are themselves among the working poor—or have achieved security and middle class prospects only because of their unionized jobs. In addition, many public-sector unions are among the most integrated institutions in the city; a number of blacks otherwise stymied in reaching top positions in New York's political and civic life are emerging as heads of important unions.

In recent years perhaps the most important such transition in leadership in the city took place in January 1987, when Victor Gotbaum was replaced by Stanley Hill as executive director of DC 37. Hill, a black man from Queens who had risen through union ranks, instantly became a major figure in New York politics. The Postal Workers Union, Local 1199 of the Health Care Workers Union, and the largest local of the ILGWU are all now headed by blacks.

The intermediary role is imperfect, of course, for the interests of union members are not always identical with the interests of the poor. Indeed, at the conservative end of the labor spectrum, the gap between city workers and poor clients could not be wider than it is between the leadership of the Patrolmen's Benevolent Association (PBA) and black and Hispanic New Yorkers outraged by police misconduct and brutality that they charge is predominantly racially motivated. The head of the PBA has launched strident attacks upon the city's first black police commissioner, Ben-

jamin Ward, and is regarded by minority leaders and, indeed, many minority officers, as hostile to black and Hispanic advancement within police ranks.

It is in times of crisis that leadership matters most, but labor in New York is facing its crises divided by squabbles over job market turf, political access, and personalities. The ILGWU, as already mentioned, is competing with at least half a dozen other unions in the so-far frustrating effort to organize office workers. Three different unions are attempting to organize the growing field of home health-care attendants who care for the ailing and elderly. And when these workers, predominantly black, working-poor women who make only about $4.50 an hour, rallied late last spring in front of City Hall, with the support of both the Reverend Jesse Jackson and New York's John Cardinal O'Connor, to demand higher wages, one of the three unions, the more conservative Service Employees, stayed away because of a dispute with 1199 and an AFSCME (American Federation of State, County and Municipal Employees) district council over tactics and jurisdiction.

Nothing illustrates the political and personal divisions better than the fight last year for control of the city's Central Labor Council, composed of the leaders of all the AFL-CIO unions in the city. For more than a generation, the council had been synonymous with one man, Harry Van Arsdale—curmudgeon, tactician, extraordinary organizer, friend and adviser to several mayors. It was Van Arsdale who had served as a conduit for funneling the resources of private-sector unions into public-sector organizing during the "heroic" years of municipal unionization in the 1950s and 1960s.

It was a symbol of changing times that Mayor Koch was absent from Van Arsdale's funeral at St. Patrick's Cathedral in 1986; it would have been unthinkable for Koch's predecessors to have missed such an occasion. But equally symbolic was the ensuing struggle for succession in the Central Labor Council. Van Arsdale's son Thomas, like his father the head of Local 3 of the electrical workers, took over the council pending an election to fill the job for a full term. He was opposed in that contest by Victor Gotbaum, then retiring from DC 37, the largest municipal workers union.

In the bitter, hard-fought campaign, Gotbaum emerged with a lead of about 5,000 out of 800,000 votes cast by union leaders on the basis of total membership. But a number of Gotbaum's supporters, including locals within his own district council, were disqualified for failing to pay their dues on time, and Van Arsdale was declared the winner in a ruling by AFL-CIO President Lane Kirkland. Gotbaum still contends he should have been ruled the winner. But even if he had been—and many of his own supporters feel he lost fair and square—the election would have revealed a movement almost evenly divided by contending ideologies and personalities.

Gotbaum, for example, says he was denied victory by Kirkland because the latter is a strong supporter of American foreign policy, including aid to the *contras* in Nicaragua, while Gotbaum is just as strong in opposition, and therefore "not the leadership's kind of guy." Gotbaum says he would not have tried to use the council as a platform for foreign policy issues, but he believes his views are an important reason why national labor leaders would not have wanted him in control of the most central of all labor councils.

Van Arsdale insists that he, personally, did not feel that national or world politics was a deciding factor, but then adds, "There can be no doubt there are people in the trade union movement whose first interest is not the trade union movement; whose first interest is not the United States. Their interest is furthering the interest of the Soviet Union. Who they are I don't know, but they're out there. They would like to have control of the city's Central Labor Council to further their interests."

How important was this belief to his supporters? Van Arsdale says that "a small number saw that as the issue and were excited to vote for me." Is he suggesting that a Gotbaum victory would have meant Communist control of the council? "I don't know," he

responds. "There are a lot of people who supported him who are in that category."

What all this makes clear, of course, is not a conspiracy of the sort Van Arsdale perceives, but an ideological and personality-driven cleavage in the city's labor movement. At a time when labor's central challenge in New York is to organize the people who do the grunt work of a changing American capitalism—the back-office workers, secretaries, and tellers—two men vying for leadership have been questioning each other's motives and credentials on foreign policy.

Two footnotes to this leadership struggle cast additional light on internal politics and communications. First, Van Arsdale's supporters, drawn heavily from the more conservative building trades and other private-sector unions, were impressively disciplined; they checked the books every day to make sure their supporters' union dues were paid up. Gotbaum, by contrast, lost because several local unions did not pay their dues properly and were disqualified. Second, one major public-sector union, the UFT, sided with Van Arsdale, part of a legacy of years of distrust of Gotbaum by UFT leaders. After Van Arsdale's victory, a UFT official was named secretary-treasurer of the Central Labor Council.

How much difference the leadership of the Central Labor Council can make in meeting the challenges confronting unions in New York is open to question. The movement needs new organizing strategies to reach a changing work force, and it will need strength that comes not only from top leadership if it is to put those strategies into effect. "There is a labor movement," Sandra Feldman of the teachers union insists. "It needs a lot of pulling together. It's a far cry from what it once was. I think it could be pulled together. It remains to be seen if it will be." With ebbing membership in declining industries in a time of economic trouble, unions often feel forced to defend their own bases against newcomers instead of reaching out to potential new members in other areas. But that decision is not something that affects only union members and their employers. It is one of the pivotal factors shaping New York's political and social life for the next generation. □

John Mollenkopf

THE DECAY OF REFORM

One-Party Politics: New York Style

Throughout U.S. history, periods of rapid social and economic change have led to political realignment, especially under the stimulus of a severe economic downturn. By these lights, realignment should now be taking place in New York politics. All the ingredients are present. Since the 1950s, the white population has become a minority, and economic restructuring has diminished the white working class and weakened its trade unions and regular party organizations. Meanwhile a new black, Hispanic, and female service-sector labor force has arisen, on which organizations like District Council 37 are based. Either the severe recession of the mid-1970s or the current political scandals could well have triggered the formation of a coalition of underrepresented groups to challenge the established order. Challenging coalitions did elect minority mayors in Chicago, Philadelphia, and even Los Angeles. Yet a liberal reform realignment hasn't happened in New York, nor do its prospects seem bright. Why?

The fiscal crisis of the mid-1970s obviously intervened in the city's political development. But the results of this crisis were not a foregone conclusion. They must be explained. In the immediate aftermath of the fiscal crisis, many on the left analyzed it as a direct business intervention into politics. In this view, corporate influence as embodied in the Municipal Assistance Corporation and the Emergency Financial Control Board, the cooptation of public-sector unions by making them the city's new banker, and the 1972 Nixon landslide combined to shift "coalition" politics rightward in New York.

This explanation is only partly convincing.

Certainly, the national political mood and the necessity of local retrenchment demoralized and chastened liberals in New York and provided a field day for those wishing to discredit the Lindsay experiment. But that does not explain the staying power of the conservative coalition erected by Mayor Koch.

For one thing, the post-1977 economic boom has driven the city's tax revenues upward, reduced government's dependence on the private sector, and allowed it to regain its autonomy. The Financial Control Board and the other fiscal oversight mechanisms are now a residual phenomenon, despite the fact that city spending and hiring increases are as rapid as they were in the Lindsay years. For another, the crude picture of business hegemony over politics overstates the cohesion of big business and the ability of businessmen as individuals or a class to get their way in city politics.

The conservative coalition really came to power with the mayor's election in 1977, when the economy was on the upswing and a supportive Democratic president occupied the White House. It was reaffirmed in prosperous times in 1981 and 1985. The Marxist explanation may have captured a powerful truth about a certain moment in the mid-1970s, but it has a hard time explaining the subsequent decade. When all is said and done, a capital strike that decimates a city's economy cannot be used as a precision tool to sculpt day-to-day political developments.

Since the fiscal crisis, a second set of analysts has tried to take this into account by viewing New York's political development in terms of political "inflation" and "deflation." Martin Shefter's *Political Crisis, Fiscal Crisis* makes this case best, but so do Jonathan Rieder's work on Canarsie and Charles V. Hamilton's work on black politics. Shefter argues that too many disparate groups were able to exert a claim on city spending during the Lindsay years, resulting in the political inflation of spending, but not of revenues, which the Lindsay coalition lacked the power to extract to the degree needed. The result was fiscal breakdown.

According to this view, fiscal crisis gave major players in city politics the opportunity, and the tensions of racial transition gave them the incentive, to cut some groups off. The business elite had been alienated by a poor business climate; the white middle class had been alienated by minority political and territorial gains; minority groups had become demobilized and vulnerable by their dependence on soft money city programs. This set the stage for Mayor Koch to organize a conservative accommodation among big business, white-ethnic Catholics, and Jews that could restore fiscal balance under the symbolic banner of disproportionate cuts in programs serving blacks and Hispanics.

Although this analysis coincides better with observed trends in New York City, it, too, faces problems. One concerns the fiscal restraint that business is supposed to have secured from government. City spending and hiring increases have outstripped the growth of the city's economy since 1983. In fact, local government employment was the single most rapidly growing sector of the city's economy over the last year. This suggests that business influence is either less than commonly thought or that the city budget is responding to other, stronger political pulls.

Another problem with the "political inflation" analysis concerns the conservative shift of the white population and the supposed reconciliation of its Jewish and Catholic elements. A close look at the numbers reveals that Jews mobilized at the polls to support Mayor Koch much more than did Catholic ethnics. In the 1985 mayoral primary, white Catholic assembly districts had a lower turnout than black or Hispanic districts. Most of the variation across white districts' support for

Major Owens Asks, *Who's Stealing Your Vote?*

Only You Can Stop Them this Tuesday

On September 23rd, you voted to send Major Owens to Congress by a 2,900-vote margin—a loud and clear 54–46% victory over his opponent.

On Columbus Day Weekend, the defeated Vander Beatty invaded the Brooklyn Board of Elections with 35 members of his ring, including his wife, convicted of 52 felony counts of vote fraud in his behalf in 1974; convicted forger Caspar Yaspar, and others. Thousands of signatures were forged on voter registration cards to make Democratic Congressional Nominee Owens' victory look rigged.

A 1982 Brooklyn political leaflet

Mayor Koch is accounted for by their Jewish population, not their Irish or Italian voters. The mayor is an ethnic politician far more than he is a class or race politician. His electoral success derives not so much from a general polarization between middle-class white ethnics and minorities (Irish and Italian voters have always been more conservative) as from a shift among Jews away from their traditional liberalism.

The sources of this shift are many. Tensions from the 1968 school strike and racial succession in neighborhoods like Flatbush certainly spurred it. In the context of the need to retrench, the mayor's neoconservative populism also pushed it along. But in a deeper sense, success itself may have destroyed the Jewish liberal reform impulse. Before the victories of the reform movement—beginning with the Stevenson and Lehman campaigns and De Sapio's defeat by the Village Independent Democrats—and the Steingut ascendancy in Brooklyn, Jews were still underrepresented in regular Democratic ranks and public office. As a challenging group, they had a strong incentive to link up with other outsiders to make up a reform coalition. The success of reform, however, enabled Jews to dominate the political establishment in four of New York's boroughs. (It is often forgotten that the late Queens Democratic boss Donald Manes started out as a reformer.) And with success, alliances with outsiders became less necessary.

Finally, it is wrong to view blacks and Hispanics as politically inactive and excluded. Although vote totals in black and Hispanic neighborhoods tend to be less than in white neighborhoods, these neighborhoods have more young people and more noncitizens. Controlling for these factors, black and Hispanic turnout in the 1985 primary was actually higher than in neighborhoods with the highest white populations. Contrary to popular wisdom, turnout was highest of all in Hispanic areas, perhaps due to three active Hispanic candidates for the City Council presidency.

Moreover, between 1982 and 1985 the greatest increases in voter registration, reaching 10,000 per assembly district, were registered in majority black and Hispanic districts. Exit polls suggest that about 23 percent of the 1985 mayoral primary electorate was black and 13 percent Hispanic. (Twenty-nine percent was Jewish and 24 percent non-Hispanic Catholic.) Given relatively low turnouts among non-Hispanic Catholics and the impact of voter registration among blacks and Hispanics leading up to the Jessie Jackson candidacy in 1984, Koch was justified in worrying about minority support and spending the bulk of his field operations campaign money in black and Hispanic areas.

This effort was rewarded. Koch won 70 percent of the Hispanic vote and an impressive 37 percent of the black vote, despite a challenge from black assemblyman Denny Farrell. Minority support for the conservative coalition further undermines the simple image of racial polarization. The weakness of blacks and Hispanics in New York City politics thus stems more from division and disorganization than from inactivity and exclusion.

If neither the Marxist nor the political inflation school of analysis fully accounts for why a conservative coalition dominates New York City politics to the exclusion of a liberal reform realignment, what does? For an answer,

we must go below the surface of the reigning neoconservative ethnic populism and ask what it is about the way New York's politics is organized that pushes this style to the fore. What, to borrow Ira Katznelson's phrase, are the "trenches" that shape the battleground of urban politics?

First, New York has a weakly organized, one-party political system. As political scientist V.O. Key noted in his famous study of southern politics, such systems rely on factions rather than parties to articulate political differences. As a result, coalitions are fluid, personality-oriented, and often based on invidious racial, ethnic, or status distinctions. Issues are blotted out. In such an environment, the regular political clubs, despite losing power at the center of New York City politics, can continue to hold sway at the periphery. Mayor Koch has shown himself a master of southern politics, New York style.

In this system, outsiders who wish to make common cause with defecting political insiders have few good ways of organizing themselves. New York City's reform coalitions have always contained disparate elements. Even when victorious, over time their lack of organizational discipline leads to decay. The sheer difficulty of generating even a modest political dialogue among black, Hispanic, and white reformers illustrates the point.

Second, the post-industrial revolution is producing new cleavages in New York City that Mayor Koch has proven better at capitalizing upon than have would-be liberal reformers. The feminization of the labor force, the rise of new service occupations, immigration from the Caribbean and Asia, and geographic shifts have produced tensions that simple white/black or middle class/working class distinctions do not capture. The sad effort of the Coalition for a Just New York in 1985 to find a consensus challenger to Koch revealed splits between blacks and Hispanics, male and female black leaders, and Manhattan and Brooklyn leaders. The numbers of native blacks and Puerto Ricans are stagnant if not declining; population growth comes largely from West Indian and Dominican immigrants, producing conflict over who speaks for blacks and Hispanics. And the most rapidly growing racial minority is neither black nor Hispanic but Asian. Gender differences are also important: most male-dominated occupations are growing slowly or contracting, while female-dominated occupations are expanding. These differences seem to divide and weaken the effort to mount a liberal reform challenge. They also provide the mayor favorable territory for a divide-and-conquer strategy.

Finally, the reform impetus that arose from the civil rights, antiwar, and citizen participation movements of the late 1960s has dissipated. In New York, powerful ideological stimuli are needed to overcome the tendency to factionalism. The late 1960s provided such stimuli. Since then, the symbolic, and in some ways substantive, recognition of black claims, the end of the war, and the growing number of contracts to community-based organizations, caused these ideological appeals to lose their power. Most important, white middle-class reformers got what they wanted and no longer needed moral outrage and an assault on the system. It is no accident that Koch has made more senior political appointments from the ranks of the Lindsay administration and nonprofit organizations than from political clubs.

So the failure of liberal reform in New York City stems not just from government's subordination to the private market or from battles won and lost by various constituent groups, but from the fundamental way political competition is organized—or *systematically disorganized*—in New York City. Mayor Koch has skillfully played on cleavages within constituencies that might support a challenger to him. But these constituencies have been unable to build any organization, or even a forum for discussion, that can cut across the divisions within and between them.

Will these patterns continue? The mayor's strength amid a scandal that would have brought down many of his predecessors suggests that they may. But there is also contrary evidence: the mayor's standing within the corporate elite and middle-class Jewish public opinion may have weakened. He has said he will be elected a fourth and even a fifth time, but long mayoral regimes do tend to decay and lose the capacity to generate new ideas and excitement. Kevin White of Boston illustrates how a reform caravan can end up drawing its wagons in a circle.

Inexorable demographic changes will also have an effect. As the white population continues to age and decline, as minority groups grow into voting age and become citizens, and as new organizations arise to represent such expanding groups as women service workers, the electoral calculus will continue to change. The mobilizing impact of emerging social inequalities cannot be discounted, either.

Most important, if political disorganization lies at the heart of the current conservative ascendancy, then serious efforts to construct new kinds of political organization may be able to overcome it. Organizations that cut across these divisions, such as the public-sector labor unions or the City University, bear a particularly heavy responsibility for the future.

Finally, as the pivotal part of the city's electorate, the middle-class Jewish population must rekindle its commitment to liberal reform. If the politically ascendant issues cause middle-class New Yorkers defensively to protect achievements won, ironically, through past reforms, the future will be bleak for urban liberalism. If, however, the historic bond between Jews and other rising minority groups can once again be forged, then New York's conservatism may be passing. □

CONFLICTS AND CONSTITUENCIES

Philip Kasinitz

THE CITY'S "NEW IMMIGRANTS"

Cultural Snapshots—from Koreans to Caribbeans

New York is, once more, an immigrant town. Not only do the public schools now give instruction in seven languages (eight if you count Mandarin and Cantonese separately), but programs to serve eight additional language groups with instruction primarily in English are now in place. Teachers try to communicate with parents who speak at least a dozen more tongues: an English-as-a-second-language specialist recently asked me if I knew anyone who could translate notes to parents into Tigriña, the language of northern Ethiopia. In Brooklyn one can now take the test to operate an automobile in Russian, and in lower Manhattan my Citibank automatic teller will "speak" to me in Spanish or Chinese. And our law enforcement officials, long wise in the ways of Italian and Jewish gangsters, must now try to make sense of the doings of that small minority of Chinese, Vietnamese, Korean, Colombian, Jamaican, Russian, Israeli, and Nigerian entrepreneurs who choose that time-honored route to the "American Dream."

The 1980 census, even with its alleged undercount of undocumented aliens, found that 24 percent of New York's population were foreign-born. By mid-decade the City Planning Department estimated the city's immigrant population at 30 percent, and it will most likely top one third by 1990. The large majority of these people are recent immigrants, having arrived since the Hart-Celler immigration reform of 1965. The range of cultural diversity among the immigrant groups is probably greater than it has ever been.

What this new diversity means for the civic culture will be a central question in the coming decade. In some ways it is a familiar question. For at least a century and a half, New York has been the port of arrival for large numbers of immigrants and the point of departure for their ambivalently American children. New York's contributions to the nation's high and low culture, as well as its occasional unease with the rest of America, reflect this fact. Even Tocqueville paused in his account of American voluntarism and community to warn that New York was different: the sizable "rabble" of free blacks and immigrants that had formed by the 1830s would, he warned, soon make the city ungovernable, save by force of arms. Friendlier observers have seen New York's immigrant diversity as the key to its vitality and today many look hopefully at the most recent arrivals.

In the pages of *New York* magazine and the *New York Times Magazine*'s quarterly "Worlds of New York" section, the new immigrants are now seen as a continuation of New York's most distinctive tradition; their exotic nature is transformed into something familiar and, particularly in contrast with domestic minorities, reassuring to many middle-class whites. Katherine Davis Fishman, in a recent *New York* feature on the Lower East Side's Seward Park High School, where four fifths of the students come from non-English-speaking homes, sums up the attitude: "The more things change, the more they remain the same."[1]

There is a large element of truth in that. It is impossible to watch the recent explosion in the foreign-language press (New York is now home to four Haitian, three Korean, and several Chinese, Indian, and Russian papers), the fights in the Dominican community over the relative importance of local politics here versus the struggles back home, the academic success of the children of Chinese garment workers, the tentative steps being made by West Indians in Brooklyn Democratic party politics, or the role of recent immigrants in the intellectual life at the City University, without being struck by the resemblance to earlier periods.

Yet nostalgia should not be allowed to obscure reality. The economy of 1987—apart from the resurgence of the sweatshop—is not the economy of 1907. The politics of post-fiscal-crisis New York is not the politics of the early twentieth century. For many recent immigrants, particularly those from the Caribbean, the fact that home is only a low-cost air fare away also makes for different attitudes about home and host countries.

Most important is that the overwhelming majority of New York's recent immigrants are nonwhite. For all of the discrimination that white immigrants have suffered, groups considered to be "white" have long been seen as at least potentially assimilable into American life. The language of white ethnicity, if often tinged with regret for lost ties and traditions, has largely been a language of hope for collective upward mobility. This has not been as true for Hispanics or Asians, to say nothing of the rejection and segregation generally experienced by blacks. Today these immigrants in New York find the meanings of racial categories in flux. Their own diversity further complicates the landscape. As "minorities" become the numerical majority, they are also becoming vastly more diverse internally.

Asian Immigrants

In their journey from "yellow peril" to "model minority," New York's approximately 350,000 Asians have come the furthest in terms of acceptance. Yesterday they were the only racial category to suffer complete exclusion from immigration and were for many years barred from naturalization; today Asian leaders worry that positive stereotypes may cloud reality as much as negative ones did. Teenage pregnancy among Cambodian refugees excites far less concern than among other groups, and when gunfire between Chinese gang members claimed the life of a teenage guest at a New York University dormitory party a few years ago, the incident was quickly forgotten. The conviction that things are "going so well" has probably limited the amount of serious academic study of New York's Asian communities, and most journalistic accounts of the Asian populations of lower Manhattan and Queens seem to end with restaurant reviews.

Yet Asians remain the victims of prejudice and discrimination. Precisely because they have broken down many barriers of structural exclusion, Asians now find themselves the targets of scapegoating in fields where they were not a significant presence a generation ago. Rumors (always officially denied) of exclusionary quotas at elite colleges; complaints that their obsessive hard work is destroying the cultured atmosphere of educational institutions and that they have "taken over" New York's best high schools; attacks on "clannish" small merchants in black and white working-class areas; and the bitter disappointments faced by those merchant's children when they discover that top grades from a top school do not guarantee a top job in corporate America—these kinds of discrimination are more like those faced in the past by white ethnic groups than like systematic racial segregation.

Asian New Yorkers are too diverse to constitute a unified group. They include millionaires fleeing the uncertain future of Hong Kong and the penniless, traumatized survivors of the Cambodian holocaust. Political refugees from Vietnam and Laos have different outlooks than those fleeing poverty in the Philippines. New York institutions reaching out to these communities report widely differing experiences. Despite the legendary insularity of Chinatown, the International Ladies' Garment Workers' Union has made significant inroads in the Chinese garment industry; a union-sponsored day care center and college scholarship program now play an important role in community life. By contrast, in Korean-owned garment factories, kinship ties between employer and employee, as well as barriers of language and distrust of outsiders, have stifled unionization efforts almost completely.

The face of Asian immigration most familiar to New Yorkers has been that of the small business entrepreneur. Hard work, community-based credit-generating mechanisms, and ethnic ties have allowed recent immigrants to virtually monopolize several of the small business sectors: Koreans in the fruit and vegetable trade, Indians in the newsstand business, and, increasingly, Arabs in neighborhood grocery stores. The entrepreneurial skills of these immigrants seem to have catapulted them into the middle class. However, as sociologist Illsoo Kim writes in his fine study of New York's Korean community, *The New Urban Immigrants,* many of these small business people are highly educated professionals for whom entrepreneurial activity is a new—sometimes distasteful but necessary—step toward getting a foothold in the new land. Far from proof of having "made it," the small business is merely a way for newcomers with some capital but little English and no American credentials to make enough money to move into easier lines of work and to educate their children, who will then regain for the family the professional status the parents have lost.[2]

What those who celebrate this process often miss is the psychological toll it takes on the children, particularly if they cannot "achieve" at a level that justifies the parents' sacrifice. Small wonder, then, that some Asian students seem driven, and that they often focus their abundant energies in the certainties of mathematics and the hard sciences. Yet many young Asian New Yorkers are also moving into the more esoteric (and less lucrative) fields of the arts, particularly classical music (look at any recent graduating class at Juilliard!) and, as Kim himself attests, even the social sciences.

On whose terms is this assimilation proceeding? Sociologist Peter Rose, making the now standard comparison between Asians and Jews, maintains that while many Asians have benefited from affirmative action programs, most remain committed to private enterprise rather than power politics or the welfare state as the vehicle of upward mobility, a fact that neoconservatives find particularly admirable. Still, Rose worries that:

> While more and more Asians have come to represent the best of what those who promulgate "Americanization" would like to create . . . they are not and will not be fully assimilated, at least not in the foreseeable future.[3]

That, however, is precisely the point. The celebration of the new immigrants reflects in part a dissatisfaction with the American present: because they are *different* from other Americans, immigrants embody what is best in New York's (if not necessarily in America's) cultural traditions. For all of their entrepreneurial success, they have not yet fallen prey to the "cultural contradictions" of an American capitalism that both requires and erodes non-marketplace engagement. The immigrant, striving and vital, is free of the "American malaise."

This line of argument has an ugly underside. It ignores the real problems many immigrants face and often serves as a not-so-subtle criticism of America's "other" minorities. A South Bronx high school principal recently told me that he welcomed the influx of new Vietnamese and Cambodian students into his otherwise black and Puerto Rican school because, "being a minority group themselves, they serve as a good example that you really can make it if you want to."

"Hispanic" Diversity

Hispanics, the largest of New York's new immigrant populations, generally receive much less favorable press than do Asians. Yet like Asians, "Hispanics" do not really constitute a coherent category at all, much less an "ethnic group." Whether or not common experiences and a common language can bind them into such a group during the next decade will be one of the most interesting political and cultural questions for the New York of tomorrow.

Many, probably most, of New York's nearly two million Hispanics are not, strictly speaking, immigrants at all. Puerto Ricans are U.S.

citizens by birth, and most of them were born right here in New York. For an increasing number of the students in the public school system identified as "Hispanic," English is their first language; many are third- and even fourth-generation "New Yoricans."

The largest segment of New York's Hispanic population, Puerto Ricans are also the poorest and, according to Angelo Falcón of the Institute for Puerto Rican Policy Studies, the most likely to see themselves as a racial minority akin to blacks, rather than as an ethnic group analogous to the descendants of European immigrants.[4] In addition, the social bases of Puerto Rican ethnic identity may well be eroding. Over the years, Puerto Ricans have lost most of their geographical enclaves to urban renewal, arson, abandonment and, most recently, gentrification. This has cost the community many of its more distinctive institutions as well as its political power bases. Yet Puerto Ricans remain a distinct and remarkably unassimilated population in New York despite their long history here.

The ambivalence with which New York's "native" Hispanics and the new immigrants view each other is reflected in the recent evolution of that grand old New York tradition, the ethnic parade. In the 1950s there was an "Hispanic Parade." Although the overwhelming majority of the participants were Puerto Rican, the European elements of Hispanic culture were emphasized and floats representing various Latin American nations and Spain were prominently displayed. In the early 1960s the parade split into an exclusively Puerto Rican parade and a general "Hispanic" event. The former grew into a massive political display; the latter soon died from lack of interest. Then, in the early 1980s, two more parades were added. The Dominican community undertook its own event in Washington Heights and the annual "Hispanic" parade was revived. Like the earlier "Hispanic" event, this Columbus Day parade emphasizes things Spanish, yet unlike its predecessor, its organization is dominated by South American immigrants, with few Puerto Ricans involved.[5]

Estimates of New York's Dominican population now range from 300,000 to 600,000, the variance due to the large number of undocu-

mented residents. Like Puerto Ricans, Dominicans are concentrated in blue-collar employment and as such have borne the brunt of the recent economic transformation of New York. Not surprisingly, they are poorer than other major immigrant groups: their median family income in 1980 was only $9,681. Living principally in upper Manhattan, Dominicans are the largest single nationality group among the post-1965 immigrants in the city. Hampered by poverty and often yearning to return home, they have only recently begun to make any inroads into the city's political life.[6] Where this predominantly dark-skinned group will align itself vis-à-vis New York's black and Hispanic leadership has yet to be seen. The dismal economic situation in the Dominican Republic means that many long-time activists are now resigning themselves to staying in the U.S. and are slowly beginning to participate in U.S. politics.

The Hispanic population also includes Cuban, Colombian, Argentine, and other Latin American immigrants, here for a variety of political and economic reasons. Concentrated in Queens, these groups are pulled politically in various directions. Maintaining their distinctiveness from other Hispanics may mean higher status in the eyes of whites. In fact, for Hispanic as for black immigrants, the pressure for social status discourages intraracial assimilation and encourages ethnic separation. On the other hand, alignment with these larger groups could bring significant political clout. Whether the new Latin immigrants maintain their national identities, or make "Hispanic" a self-conscious group rather than a mere demographer's category, will depend, in large part, on the extent to which they share common institutions.

Foreign-Born Blacks

Perhaps the least visible of all of the new immigrant groups, New York's growing foreign-born black population, has undergone the greatest transformation in diaspora. Numbering at least 500,000 (twice that much if the most liberal estimates of the undocumented population are to be believed), these immigrants from

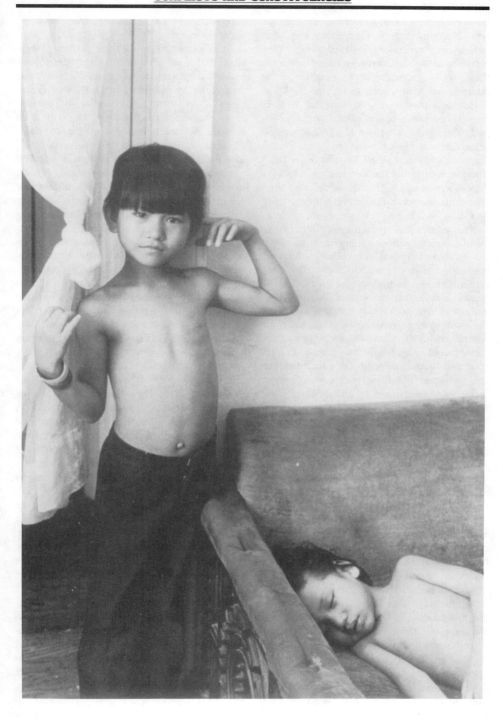

the West Indies, Haiti, and increasingly Africa, hail from historically interrelated but often insular and generally small countries. New York has brought them together, and as a result the city is increasingly the center of an international Afro-Caribbean culture.

How do they relate to the native black population? West Indians often share a feeling of kinship with American blacks and express resentment at being used by conservative academics like economist Thomas Sowell as a living refutation of the devastating effects of American racism. At the same time they represent distinct cultural and political traditions. In the last several years some West Indian leaders have complained bitterly that Afro-American politicians take them too much for granted. Economically, black immigrants have done relatively well in New York; their median income is higher than that of native blacks, although far lower than that of Asians and native whites. Yet this progress seems less the result of entrepreneurial activity (as Sowell would have it) than of high labor-force participation, particularly by women. For the most part these immigrants are concentrated in the low-wage but rapidly expanding service sector, especially in nursing, clerical work, and child care.[7]

European Groups

Finally, there are at least 200,000 recent immigrants from Europe in New York today, the largest number of whom are Russian Jews and Southern Italians. They have revitalized many older white ethnic communities, and have founded their own enclaves. They are as varied as the nations they come from—Greece, Poland, Ireland, Great Britain, Albania— although high rates of self-employment are common across the board. There is also a new European undocumented-immigrant population, perhaps the least-known immigrant group in the city today. Generally entering the country on tourist visas, these young people fill many of the underpaid service positions in Manhattan's chic restaurants, bars, and boutiques, where white faces and "cultured"

accents may add the requisite touch of atmosphere.

In examining the role these groups play in New York, we should not forget the importance of immigrant communities for their home countries. Perhaps even more than in earlier times, New York today teems with exiles, critics, reformers, and students who will go on to shape the future of nations around the world. Corazon Aquino received her college education in Riverdale. The New York Haitian press, long the main voice of the opposition, played a major role in the overthrow of the Duvalier regime. Maurice Bishop frequently said that the most important Grenadian constituency was in Brooklyn, and several long-time Brooklynites held positions in his government, while others have been important sources of financial support for the party that eventually replaced it. On the island of St. Vincent, anthropologist Linda Basch notes, New York community leaders frequently return home to work for candidates in national elections; and fund raising in New York has played a part in every Colombian and Dominican presidential campaign in recent years.[8]

Immigrant New Yorkers also affect the economic life of their home countries. One anthropologist studying three communities in the Dominican Republic estimates that one third of all families there receive money from relatives in New York.[9] Such remittances account for at least 10 percent of that nation's foreign exchange earnings.[10] In smaller nations the role of remittances is even greater. In 1976 the U.S. State Department estimated that the number of people from tiny Belize working in the U.S., mostly in New York, was larger than the entire Belizean labor force, and that money they sent home exceeded the earnings from sugar exports, Belize's other major source of foreign exchange.[11]

New York is also a contributor to the popular culture of the immigrants' home countries. Major Taiwanese entertainers now travel frequently between Taipei and Queens, and one of the most popular Merengue bands in Latin America is based in the northern New Jersey suburbs. The Mighty Sparrow, Trinidad's leading calypso singer, now records exclusively in Brooklyn. In this way the immigrant communities serve as bridges between their homelands and New York, bridges across which money, political ideology, and both high and popular culture flow both ways.

What does the presence of these newcomers mean to the city as a whole? For one thing, it has widened the cultural gap between New York and the rest of the United States. More than earlier immigrant waves, the post-1965 immigration is not really a national phenomenon. New immigrants are concentrated in a few metropolitan areas and nowhere does the range of different nationalities equal that of New York. Some groups, such as Dominicans and West Indians, are overwhelmingly concentrated here. Others are found elsewhere in small numbers, but New York's size permits the sort of critical mass needed for self-conscious ethnic communities.

It is true that in the two other cities most affected by the latest "new" immigration, Miami and Los Angeles, an even higher percentage of the populace is foreign-born. More than one journalist has suggested that "LAX" airport is the new Ellis Island. But in Los Angeles, with the predominance of what Michael Walzer has termed "single-minded" uses of public space, the composition of the population means less for the civic culture. In an automotive, decentralized, sprawling city with a minimum of public life, contacts between natives and immigrants and among immigrants themselves are kept to a minimum.

In New York, by contrast, we cannot help but rub shoulders with the newcomers, and they must rub shoulders with each other. This is not necessarily because New Yorkers are more tolerant, but because the physical conditions of daily life make it impossible to avoid. Yet it is in this rubbing of shoulders that the true vitality of New York lies. Cities, Louis Wirth observed half a century ago, are the natural breeding ground of hybrids, and New York remains the kind of city he had in mind.

It is not hermetically sealed "urban villages," no matter how appealing that idea of community is, that make New York such a creative place. It is the fact that what villages there are constantly intersect and chafe against each other. Their inhabitants are brought together in the schools and the universities, in

the parks and the nightclubs, in the subways and the streets, and (although as a socialist it has taken me some time to come to grips with this fact) in the marketplace. In these intersections, new possibilities are created and new syntheses are born.

We are not always aware of these developments, because they often take place in what to the outsider may seem unified ethnic communities. Yet just as Jews on the Lower East Side brought together dozens of distinct European strains to create a New York Jewish world, so today's immigrants are reworking bits and pieces of their diverse backgrounds into new cultural identities. As Paule Marshall has recently written, a walk along Brooklyn's Fulton Street today brings one in contact with

> . . . the sights and sounds, colors, smells, and textures of the entire Caribbean archipelago . . . Fulton Street today is the aroma of our kitchen long ago . . . it's the sound of reggae and calypso and ska and the newest rage, soca, erupting from a hundred speakers outside the record stores. It's Rastas with their hennaed dreadlocks and the impassioned political debates of the rum shops back home brought out onto the street corners. It's Jamaican meat patties . . . and fast food pulori, a Trinidadian East Indian pancake doused in pepper sauce . . . Fulton Street is Haitian Creole heard amid any number of highly inventive, musically accented versions of English. And it's faces, an endless procession of faces that are mostly black — for these are Mother Africa's children — but with noticeable admixtures here and there of Europe, India and China. . . .[12]

Thus, what at first seems the preservation of something old is in fact the creation of something quite new; built on Caribbean elements to be sure, but brought together in a new and unique way. Several years ago the Mighty Sparrow summed it up in a calypso which became a theme for the Labor Day Carnival celebration on Eastern Parkway:

> You can be from St. Cleo or John John
> In New York, all that done
> They don't have to know who is who
> New York equalize you!

This coming together is as filled with

creative possibilities for West Indians today as it was for immigrants in the early years of the century. Already New York is the world center for Caribbean music, theater, and intellectual life, as institutions such as the City University of New York Caribbean Studies Association and its new journal, *Cimarron*, strive to bring together the various strains of West Indian culture with Hispanic, Caribbean, and Afro-American elements.

Caribbean immigrants, with their insular histories and their huge numbers in New York today, may present an extreme case. But similar fusions are happening elsewhere. "Hispanics," a synthetic category if ever there was one, are sowing the seeds of a corporate identity despite their deep internal divisions. In New York, common interests and common media are bringing together people previously (to borrow an old quip) divided by a common language. Asians, of course, do not even share that, and only time will tell whether "Asian" will ever become a meaningful category to those within it.

Fusion across these broad categories is, of course, even more problematic. One institution that has tried to bring together Hispanic, West Indian, Afro-American, and African cultural actors is the Caribbean Cultural Center, whose lectures, concerts, exhibitions, and conferences all put forward a self-consciously pan-ethnic vision based on the shared West African roots of the groups in question. "We are the majority culture in this city," asserts Center director Marta Moreno Vega, and she would be right if her broad concept of "we" were shared by more people. Interestingly, although her constituency is, for the most part, intellectuals, it is in popular music that this fusion has taken place most successfully and actually reaches a mass audience. The mixing of folk elements from throughout the world is today's most distinctive "New York" sound: a sound that has started to spill out of the nightclubs and into the more rarefied world of the theater, as evidenced in the recent work of Lee Breuer and Bob Telson.

When it comes to political action, however, such unity is much harder to find. The Cultural Center's annual festival has little trouble selling out large halls with four concerts that feature eclectic mixtures of Puerto Rican, Brazilian, West Indian, Dominican, and Afro-American performers. Yet in 1985, when it sought to add a panel discussion on political empowerment to the series of events, the panelists far outnumbered the audience.[13]

The unspoken truth that lies behind the calls for nonwhite unity in New York today is that relations between native blacks and immigrants, including black immigrants, while increasingly robust in the cultural realm, are often badly strained in the political one. The inability of the Afro-American leadership to make even minimal concessions to their potential coalition partners, Hispanics and Caribbean blacks as well as progressive whites, destroyed their chances of making a credible challenge to Mayor Koch in 1985. Demographics dictate that in the future coalition will be even more important, yet for many reasons it may be difficult to achieve.

Immigrant and black interests have often been in conflict in this country, but the current immigration has sharpened these tensions. Such conflicts are perhaps inevitable. Blacks frequently complain that Korean merchants won't hire blacks in their own neighborhoods and drain capital from the area. The Koreans respond that they have revitalized dying commercial strips with incredibly hard work and, for the most part, family labor, which if paid in hourly salaries would not come to minimum, much less union wages. The problem is that both are right. When blacks see hard-won gains of political struggle, such as affirmative action, going to benefit recent immigrants, they have every reason to be angry—although how much of this is due to immigrant guile and how much to administrative subversion is not entirely clear. It is also true that new immigrants are pulled into the midst of the American dilemma almost immediately on arrival. Soviet émigrés had scarcely begun to settle in Brooklyn before they were being referred to as the "last white hope" by the area's real estate dealers, and some Asians seem to pick up American racial attitudes so quickly that one is reminded of a very bitter routine by Richard Pryor about Vietnamese refugees at citizenship class being taught the proper pronunciation of the word "nigger."

For Hispanic and black immigrants who make up the majority of the new New Yorkers, relations with native blacks are deeply ambivalent, and matters are not helped when scholars use the relative gains of dark-skinned immigrants to point up the alleged failures of native blacks and native ("New Yorican") Hispanics. For many such immigrants, the question of where they will fit in the city's racial division of power will depend largely on circumstances and on leadership. Many share the middle-class aspirations of most of the city's whites and blacks, and when these aspirations are merged with ethnic pride, many may indeed turn their backs on the underclass and head for the suburbs, psychologically if not physically. But issues such as police brutality and the racial attack in Howard Beach (whose victims were all West Indian immigrants) may serve to pull together people of color across ethnic lines. Finally, there is the possibility of a coalition-building politics that brings together native blacks, immigrants, and native whites around local issues. That may sound hopelessly idealistic, but organizations such as East

Brooklyn Churches have, in a modest way, made considerable progress in that direction.

At its best, New York has historically shown the potential for a public life that emphasizes equality without requiring conformity. It is a model of politics in which diversity is welcome and perhaps even rewarded. This ideal has seldom been achieved in practice, particularly where nonwhite people are concerned. It also contains the danger that the various component parts will seal themselves off in opposition to the whole, the results of which might, at best, be something akin to Los Angeles and, at worst, Beirut. Still the idea of different people coming together in the public sphere is a central part of the city's cultural history.

Whether the newcomers will embrace such a politics remains to be seen. It is deeply disturbing that the public schools, once an arena that brought various groups together, may be losing this function, as many immigrants, like many natives, establish private

schools along ethnic lines. On a practical level, one can hardly blame them. Yet this does not bode well for the future of the civic culture. On the other hand, the City University continues to play a vital part in the intellectual life of immigrants. For all of CUNY's problems, it remains as good a model of a pluralist institution as we have.

In an increasingly privatized city, diversity may matter less than it once did. Yet despite more private schools, more automobiles, and a more individualistic culture, New York continues to have a vibrant public realm compared to most American cities. In the context of this public life the haphazard bringing together of people from everywhere in the world cannot help but be a creative force. This was true fifty years ago, and for the most part it continues to be true today. If that isn't what New York is about, what is? □

Notes

[1] Katherine Davis Fishman, "American High," *New York*, March 2, 1987, p. 78.

[2] Illsoo Kim, *The New Urban Immigrants* (Princeton, NJ: Princeton University Press, 1981).

[3] Peter I. Rose, "Asian Americans: From Pariahs to Paragons" in Nathan Glazer ed., *Clamor at the Gates* (San Francisco: Institute for Contemporary Studies, 1985).

[4] Angelo Falcón, *Black and Latino Politics in New York City: Race and Ethnicity in a Changing Urban Context* (NY: Institute for Puerto Rican Policy Studies, Inc., 1985).

[5] For a more detailed description of these events, see Philip Kasinitz and Judith Freidenberg-Herbstein, "Caribbean Cultural Celebrations in New York City: The Puerto Rican Parade and the West Indian Carnival" in Constance Sutton and Elsa Chaney eds., *Caribbean Life in New York City: Social and Cultural Dimensions* (New York: Center for Migration Studies, 1987).

[6] Eugenia Georges, "New Immigrants and the Political Process: Dominicans in New York." Occasional Paper No. 45, New York University Center for Latin American and Caribbean Studies, April 1984.

[7] See Philip Kasinitz, "New York's West Indian Community," in *New York Affairs*, Spring 1987.

[8] Linda Basch, "The Politics of Caribbeanization: Vincentians and Grenadians in New York City," in Sutton and Chaney, *op. cit.*

[9] Sheri Grasmuck, "The Impact of Emigration on National Development." Occasional Paper No. 33, New York University Center for Latin American and Caribbean Studies, June 1982.

[10] Ernest Preeg, "Migration and Development in Hispaniola" in Robert Pastor ed., *Migration and Development in the Caribbean* (Boulder, Colo.: Westview, 1985).

[11] Quoted in Robert Pastor, "Introduction: The Policy Challenge," in Pastor, *op. cit.*

[12] Paule Marshall, "The Rising Islanders of Bed-Stuy," *New York Times Magazine*, "The Worlds of New York," November 3, 1985.

[13] In March of 1987 the Center held another conference on the issue of minority empowerment, with significantly better results.

NEW IMMIGRANTS IN NEW YORK CITY

A Photography Contest and Exhibition

Grouped together here and placed throughout this section are some of the winning entries to the contest, sponsored by *Dissent* and the Long Island University Honors Program. Entries were accepted and judged separately from professional and nonprofessional photographers.

The full exhibition of the winning entries will open on November 17, 1987 at the Salena Gallery, Long Island University Brooklyn Campus, on Flatbush Avenue opposite the DeKalb Avenue Station (D, R, N, B, M) in conjunction with an all-day conference, "Justice for All: Inequality and the Politics of Hunger," at which copies of this issue of *Dissent* will be on sale. (For further information, call (718) 403–1049, 1058.)

Dissent wishes to thank the four distinguished documentary photographers who served as judges: Jerry Dantzic, Abigail Heyman, Arthur Leipsig, and Walter Rosenblum. Our thanks to Jan Rosenberg, who conceived the contest, and to David Williams and Bernice Braid of L.I.U., who organized and administered it with her.

Contest winners are:

Professional Single Images

1. Paul Calhoun, "Atlantic Hotel—Chinatown, N.Y., 1982," p. 508
2. Krystyna Baker, "Pani Maria," p. 509
3. Anders Goldfarb, untitled, p. 510

Professional Essays

1. Paul Calhoun, Chinese-American working men in New York, p. 511

2. Corky Lee, Asian-Americans in New York City, p. 513
3. Mel Rosenthal, Refugees from Indo-China in New York, p. 512

Non-Professional Single Images

1. E. Ira McCrudden, "Latino Families Swimming—Coney Island," p. 514
2. Ernesto Urdaneto, "Mi Padre," p. 515
3. Rebecca Anne Zilenziger, "Abuela," p. 517

Non-Professional Essays

1. Leah Melnick, "Cambodian Refugees in the Bronx: Adaptation and Change in an Ethnic Community," p. 516
2. Maya Berman, untitled, p. 518
3. Virginia Joffe, "Benjamin Ginzburg, Sunday Afternoon Dinner at His Grandparents' Apartment, Brighton Beach" (Photo not available at press time).

Honorable Mention

1. Paul Calhoun, "Chinatown, New York, 1984," Professional
2. Paul Calhoun, "Mrs. Chin—Grandchildren, Canal Street Store, 1984," p. 496
3. Eddie Wexler, "Little Italy," Professional
4. Eddie Wexler, "Delores"
5. Arvind Garg, "New Immigrant from Africa Making a Living in NYC 14th Street at Union Square, 1986," Non-Professional
6. Eve Heller, "Morning Sweep," Non-Professional
7. E. Ira McCrudden, "Polish Immigrant Swimming—Coney Island," Non-Professional □

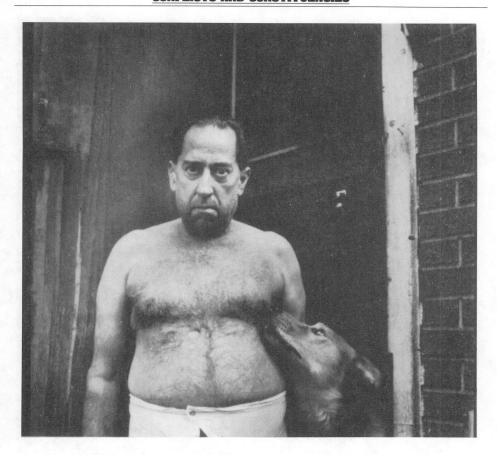

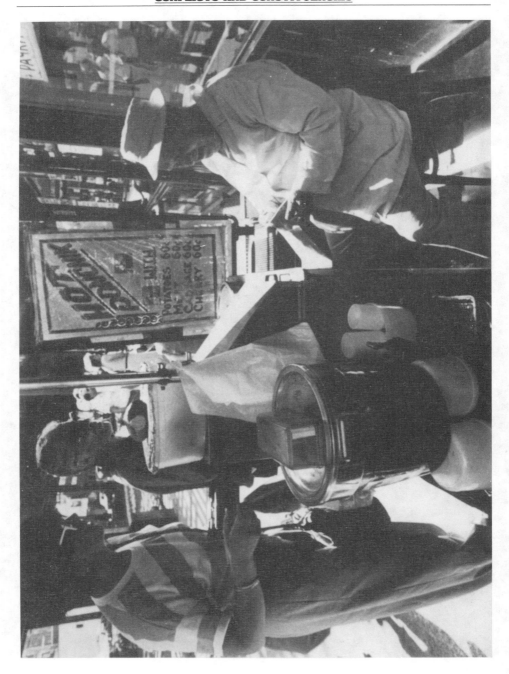

Roger Waldinger

MINORITIES & IMMIGRANTS— STRUGGLE IN THE JOB MARKETS

The commonly told tale about post-industrial New York is that of two cities, of white elites and minority poor, of advanced services and a crumbling manufacturing base. The conventional explanation for the ills of the minority poor is equally simple: they lack the skills that today's employers want.

But there is a problem with this story: over a million nonwhite newcomers, often low in skills, rarely speaking English, lacking credentials, are doing reasonably well, particularly in comparison with native blacks and Hispanics. Indeed, many of the immigrants seem to move quickly into the middle class, or at least its lower reaches. And the explanations for this divergence are not simple at all.

Through the Factory's Revolving Door

Though the shift from goods to services in New York has driven the number of easy-entry jobs down, recent immigrants still start where their predecessors began: at the bottom. They inherit the low-status, insecure jobs that native New Yorkers are no longer willing to do. Nowhere is this transition clearer than in the city's quintessential immigrant trade: the garment industry.

When the bottom fell out of the market for New York's garment industry in the 1970s, hourly earnings dropped relative to those in the rest of the city's already depressed manufacturing sector; working conditions—never good to begin with—got worse; and seasonality became more pronounced, producing a small weekly paycheck. Consequently, native workers real-ized, as one employer put it, that "they can get more doing something else" and they dropped out of the industry's labor supply. By 1980, just over a third of the industry's production workers were white—a drop of almost fifty percent since 1970—and most of these workers were on the far side of their careers.

Replacements came from a familiar source: immigration from abroad. In contrast to the natives, to whom a garment shop is far worse than an office or hospital job, the immigrants came "hoping to find any job, it didn't matter . . . as long as it was a job." The turnover of workers—high even in bad times—meant that employers were always looking to add a new hand. The industry had already adapted to Puerto Rican workers with supervisors who were bilingual or could at least mediate between Spanish-speaking workers and non-Hispanic employers; hence there was an infrastructure ready to absorb new cohorts of Latino immigrants, the largest group of whom came from the Dominican Republic.

Informal networks helped newcomers find jobs where other immigrants were already employed: three quarters of a group of Hispanic immigrants I interviewed found their first job through connections with relatives or friends. Finally, some arrivals started out by working in a factory owned by a fellow (or sister) immigrant garment capitalist. Thus, by 1980, newcomers from the Third World made up almost half of New York's needle trades proletariat. The consensus among garment employers: "If there were no immigrants, the needle trades would be out of New York."

But why did immigrants—and not native blacks or Hispanics—take over these entry-level jobs? Several factors seem to be involved. Like many low-wage manufacturing industries, garments suffers the stigma of being an "immigrant trade." One factory owner told me:

> I find that whereas there are fewer blacks in the factory, the office staff has become black and Puerto Rican. This has been the normal progression: the parents work in the factories, and the kids look for white-collar jobs. In the office we get young Hispanics and blacks who are second generation and have never set foot in a factory.

Moreover, the extraordinary outflow of whites from New York during the 1970s opened up opportunities in the services and the white-collar sector; hence job choices widened and most of the alternatives available to moderately skilled native blacks or Hispanics were preferable to working on a punching press or sewing machine.

But even in entry-level employment markets that carry no immigrant stigma, newcomers often have an edge over blacks: the strength of their informal networks. "Connections" are particularly important for job-finding in small business industries where there are few defined career ladders or bridges from one firm to the next. The legal immigration system actually reinforces these ties since it rations entries on the basis of family connections to U.S. citizens and residents. This link between settlers and newcomers never seemed to provide as strong a tie between black southern migrants and northern settlers. And the growth of black female-headed families provides another negative—the "missing uncle" factor, George Sternlieb calls it—since close relatives are especially important in finding good jobs.

Discrimination also comes into the picture. Studying immigrants and blacks in New York's restaurant industry, Thomas Bailey found that many owners would recruit immigrants but were loath to hire blacks in the "front of the house" where contact with customers is high. The portals to the remaining skilled jobs also essentially remain closed: though the number of apprentices in New York's construction trades has doubled since 1980, the proportion of minority apprentices has actually gone down. Finally, the importance of the ethnic network as a source of labor gives recruiting a strong exclusionary bias; because immigrants going into business often hire their compatriots, native blacks find themselves shut out of many jobs.

Enterprising Immigrants

The passing of an older generation of Jewish, Italian, and Irish entrepreneurs whose own children have no wish to succeed them in small business has left space, even in declining industries like garments, for new immigrant contractors, now mainly Chinese, but also other Asians, Dominicans, and Greeks. In similar fashion Koreans took over small retailing from Jewish or Italian owners who were just too old, tired, and scared of crime to keep on minding their stores.

Why do the newcomers gravitate toward business? In some cases, they bring traditions of self-employment or skills that give them an edge in some particular business line: Greeks from the province of Kastoria, where a traditional apprenticeship in fur-making is common, have entered the fur trade; Israelis are in diamonds, a traditional Jewish business centered in New York, Tel Aviv, and Antwerp; and Indians from Gujarat, renowned for their prowess in trading, arrive to extend the family business. But for many immigrants, it is neither a love affair with a business nor a preference for being one's own boss that leads them into the petty bourgeoisie, but the quest for profit as a compensation for professional frustration: though highly educated, many immigrants arrive speaking little English and lacking the licenses and certifications needed to enter the fields for which they have trained. "This kind of hardship is for the first generation only," says a Korean fishstore owner who had been a teacher in Seoul.

But the crucial factor is that opportunity beckons: there is considerable demand for the particular services that immigrant business owners offer. Immigrants have their own special consumer tastes, not just the old staples like foodstuffs or newspapers, but also foreign-language videos and electrical goods with current adapters for use back home. The business of adaptation itself is also a thriving one: the immigrant travel agent, accountant, lawyer trades on the offer of confidentiality, trust, and a more personal way of doing business. And finally, the immigrant boss has good access to cheap, reliable labor in his family and the larger immigrant network: neighbors, acquaintances from back home, "friends of friends." Thus, a common pattern is for new arrivals from the Dominican Republic to seek work in a garment shop owned by a compatriot; many shops are filled with workers from the same hometown.

Working for the State

The mythology of ethnic business is that immigrants do well because they have a special knack for turning a dollar. The reality is that immigrants are more willing to take their chances on what are often bad bets. In the small-business field, where the mortality of new firms is appallingly high, the key is the *rate* at which new businesses start up. And the immigrant self-employment rate is high; in 1980, almost 13 percent of foreign-born male adults were working for themselves, and among groups like Koreans, Chinese, Indians, or Greeks the proportion was considerably higher. By contrast, just over 3½ percent of native black males were self-employed in 1980 and among native Hispanics the self-employment rate was almost as low.

Fully one third of New York's native blacks employed in 1980 were working in the public sector, according to the census—a considerable net gain in jobs over the figures for 1970, even though the public sector has declined. In a sense, this, too, is a story of ethnic succession. Though the fiscal crisis pared down municipal payrolls, jobs were mainly shed through attrition, not layoffs: most of those who retired were civil servants high in seniority—who, as it happened, were mainly white. Fiscal stringency also led to lower wages and reduced fringes, which in turn lowered the public sector's attractiveness to whites. Thus, minorities increased their share of the public-sector jobs when municipal employment was shrinking; they did still better once hiring resumed

and city government payrolls began to swell. In 1985, 42 percent of New York City's employees were nonwhite, as were 52 percent of the workers hired by the city that year.

In the public sector, blacks have found their surest route to stable, well-paying employment as well as their best chances to get ahead. Not only are New York's native blacks overrepresented in government jobs, but the proportion of government managers who are black is twice as high as in the private sector. Moreover, public-sector positions are also effective vehicles for movement into higher social class. A recent study of high-level civil servants in one city agency found that blacks in these ranks tended to be of working- or lower-class origins and were far less likely to come from middle-class families than their white counterparts.

Ethnic Division of Labor

And so, the conventional "tale of two cities" account of New York's postindustrial transition can be misleading. What we've witnessed is an extended game of ethnic musical chairs, in which positions as well as players have changed, and in which differences among minorities stand out almost as sharply as those between whites and nonwhites. Immigrants have settled into small business, especially retailing and manufacturing, while native blacks have lost ground there; but the latter are gaining in the public sector, which does not loom large in the immigrant employment picture.

But the story's complexity shouldn't eclipse its elements of suffering and conflict. Immigrant competition and structural change have hit New York's minority poor like a double whammy: poorer blacks and Hispanics are mismatched for work in the advanced services that increasingly replace goods production; and they lack the strong kinship and self-help networks that give immigrants the edge in the small firms and competitive industries that continue to offer low-skilled employment. Moreover, immigrant success has cut into the market for firms where native minorities do find work: New York doesn't have more McDonald's restaurants because its immigrant restaurants compete on price. Even the immigrant mom-and-pop store has returned to give the supermarkets—employers of minority youth—a run for their money.

This divvying up of the economic turf has made confrontation among minorities an increasingly important fact of life in New York. In the public sector, competition between Puerto Ricans and blacks often breaks out into the open, with Hispanics charging that they have not gained full benefit from the many equal-employment opportunity programs of the past two decades. In the marketplace, ethnic strife also erupts, as between black neighborhood residents and Korean entrepreneurs who have replaced Jews as the most visible merchants there. Dominican garment factory-owners complain that "the Chinese are killing business for us," while Colombian storeowners in Queens worry that the explosion of Indian and Korean businesses will push them out of their neighborhoods.

And so the economic story of the latest immigrants ends with a surprising twist. New York's newcomers are mainly nonwhite; but they are living and working under conditions that are different—and often separate—from those that established, minority residents know. Although it's too soon to say what these contrasts fully portend, one thing is sure: the ethnic division of labor is the crucible out of which new—and unpredictable—forms of ethnic identity will emerge. □

Martin Kilson

THE WEAKNESS OF BLACK POLITICS

Cursed by Factions and Feuds

Since the 1950s the politics of New York blacks has been characterized by weakness and factional division. Compared with the political gains of blacks in cities like Atlanta, Chicago, Philadelphia, Cleveland, and Detroit, black politics in New York is marked by low influence and a marginal presence.[1] Several features of black New York's politics demonstrate this weak political incorporation: (1) the failure to elect a black mayor, to mount a serious black mayoral challenge, or to play a decisive role in a successful mayoral coalition; (2) the absence of a viable black presence in New York City's dominant decision-making bodies; and (3) a faction-ridden black leadership.

Yet other aspects of black New York's political position do not by themselves indicate weakness. Twenty-five percent of the city's population is black, and blacks have seven of the thirty-five city council seats (20 percent). There is one black borough president, David Dinkins, for Manhattan, who was elected in 1985. Dinkins sits on the eight-member Board of Estimate, a mayor-dominated body that decides on the city's contracts, appropriations, land use, and other such matters. One key agency head is black, Benjamin Ward, commissioner of police. State and national officials elected out of New York City are also part of black New York's political profile; these include four of fourteen congressional seats (27 percent), 13 of 60 state assembly seats (21 percent), and four of twenty-five state senate seats (16 percent).

It would not seem unreasonable to expect that this range of office-holding by 25 percent of the city's population could be translated into

a strong level of coming together for *common* purposes, that is, for political incorporation. Why hasn't that happened? There are two interrelated reasons:

1. Ethnic parochialism, sometimes racism, among white politicians. In calling for "neopluralism" as a way to overcome the weak political status of New York blacks, political scientist Martin Shefter envisions a white "mayor who practices the politics of bargaining and conciliation, rather than the politics of [ethnic or racial] denunciation. . . ."[2]

2. An absence of cohesion in the black leadership or political "class," riddled as it is with factions and feuding.

Weak Pluralistic Dynamics

Though it is often assumed that New York politics offers blacks a substantial range of political access—accessible parties, cosmopolitan or liberal politicians, at the very least conciliatory politicians, etc.—this assumption seems less valid on closer scrutiny. In the 1950s–1960s period, under the Wagner and Lindsay administrations, when blacks were just beginning to penetrate the decision-making hierarchy (e.g., Hulan Jack became the first black borough president, in Manhattan, in 1953, and J. Raymond Jones gained the New York County Democratic leadership in 1964–1967), New York's pluralistic political atmosphere was conveyed mainly through the posture of the mayors, not the actual behavior of the mediating agencies that formed New York. The powerful builder-bureaucrat, Robert Moses, treated Hulan Jack as a token figure, viewing him contemptuously as "the puppet borough president of Manhattan."

From the 1950s into the 1970s, New York's political posture toward blacks showed a gap between the city's liberal and cosmopolitan image and its racially tight-fisted power structures. Angelo Falcon, a keen analyst of New York's ethnic politics, had this discrepancy in mind when observing recently that "New York, more so than many other cities, has been able to postpone confronting the issue of minority political empowerment. . . . *Minority politics is not something that is simply defined internally, but develops within a broader context that plays a critical role.*"[3] (Emphasis added.) This "broader context" is what I refer to as a city's pluralistic dynamics.

In the 1950s and 1960s, a major factor in New York's weak pluralistic dynamics was the failure of the Republican party to compete for black support in any meaningful way, even as it was reaching out to Italians and Jews, traditionally Democratic ethnic groups. The lack of viable competition caused blacks to be locked into the Democratic party, which in turn exploited this cul-de-sac, stifling black political growth.[4]

Comparative analysts of ethnic group politics—Robert Dahl, Edgar Litt, L. Raymond Wolfinger, and others—have shown that weak pluralistic dynamics, in the form of ethnically exclusive parties, will usually thwart an ethnic group's politicization. Theodore Lowi has hypothesized that "leaders of new ethnic minorities making claims for recognition and representation . . . are likely to find that their most effective claims are on the minority party," which in New York means the Republicans. Lowi found that whenever the Republicans won out over traditionally dominant Democrats, this coincided with "periods of influx of new ethnic minorities to the top."[5]

But this new political-inclusionary cycle, as we might call it, was short-circuited for New York blacks. The minority party did not reach to black newcomers to provide them with a moderate or strong alternative. Herein lies the weakness of black New York politics.

Whatever the sins of the Republicans, the Democratic party shares major blame for New York's weak pluralistic dynamics vis-à-vis blacks. For one thing, the Democrats take for granted the one-party cul-de-sac; they cultivate black support on terms grossly unfavorable to black political needs and interests.

This Democratic party behavior is typically reinforced by "backlashing" black initiatives for greater clout or independence. An early instance of this occurred in 1939, when black Democrats, led by J. Raymond Jones, sought leadership of the patronage-rich, 95 percent-black Nineteenth Assembly District. Tammany Hall squashed this initiative, but for only three years. In 1941, LaGuardia's strongly pluralist mayoralty successfully backed a black district leader.

Yet in the post-war era backlashing by the Democratic organization was common, especially in Brooklyn during the late 1960s and into the 1970s. In the early 1970s Major Owens formed the Central Brooklyn Mobilization for Political Action and Albert Vann the Vannguard Independent Democratic Association. Though heavily opposed, or backlashed, by Democratic boss Meade Esposito's organization—led by black client-politicians like Samuel Wright, a state assembly member later convicted of fraud—these independent political thrusts survived, eventually sending Vann to the state assembly and Owens to Congress.

The Koch mayoralty—1978 to the present—fashioned another backlashing posture for the white power structures. In his first administration, Koch appointed a black as Deputy Mayor for Labor Relations—an important job in view of the large black city labor force—and supported an increase of blacks in professional or managerial city jobs. He also appointed as Deputy Mayor for Policy a presumptive ally of blacks, Herman Badillo, a leading Puerto Rican politician.

Yet what Koch giveth with the left hand, he taketh with the right. Throughout his administrations Koch innovated a unique form of what I call backlashing toward blacks, not simply on behalf of a boss-ruled organization but tinged with racist-like undertones. "The mayor's rhetoric during his first term," observes Martin

Shefter, "was especially feisty on racial issues, contributing to his popularity among the city's white ethnic groups. . . ." Shefter elaborates:

> . . . Mayor Koch did several things that caused his relations with black political leaders to deteriorate. In contrast to his predecessors, Mayor Koch did not select his black appointees from among the city's black political establishment, nor did he clear his selections with that leadership group, and this they denounced as an "act of political contempt." Second, the mayor reorganized the city's poverty program, evoking even louder protests from black political leaders and activists. . . . Third, the mayor proposed closing some municipal hospitals in black neighborhoods, and for this he was charged with being willing to sacrifice black lives for the sake of balancing the city's budget. . . . Black politicians responded with such fury to the behavior of the Koch administration because these actions withdrew concessions that black politicians had extracted from previous administrations. . . .[6]

In dealing with blacks, the typical New York white power group (or politician) frequently circumvents the politically tested and viable sectors of the black community and its leadership, and instead deals with a marginal leadership sector composed essentially of client-politicians—untested newcomers, flamboyant self-starters, etc. The power structure thereby creates within the black community a faction beholden to it.

A decade ago Charles Hamilton noted that while liberal institutions like federal agencies and foundations offer funds for black neighborhood and community development, these funds actually distort systemic and authoritative political structuring. According to Hamilton,

> this facilitates building relationships and ties vertically—up and out—not horizontally, throughout the community—and, thus, the fragmentation. They [the federally-funded leaders] see no need to come together for collective, community-wide action . . . maintaining their own individualized contacts with their external "angels."[7]

This fragmentation of black political life is propelled by external interests often hostile to a strong black political incorporation. This politics reigned supreme among New York black politicians throughout the 1960s and 1970s, as Percy Sutton's political career demonstrates. In the Lindsay administrations, which broadened somewhat the range of pluralistic forces, such a fragmented politics receded to some extent. But the successor regimes of Abraham Beame and Edward Koch refurbished this politics—for example, Koch's appointment of a black maverick newcomer, Haskell Ward, to his first cabinet. And when such a political maverick's tenure expires, the political-incorporation spin-off for the black community is marginal. This situation is what Joyce Gelb refers to when she writes:

> The [elected] Negro politicians who . . . can maintain constant channels of communication to both a broad-based and relatively stable group of constituents, continue to be overlooked by white political leaders. . . .[8]

This sort of politics reached a high point in the 1960s and 1970s for a very good reason. It was in this period that black New York was gaining the *potential* to bid for parity in political incorporation. This potential appeared, however, precisely at the point when several white ethnic groups—especially Italians and Jews—were overcoming the longstanding hegemonic pretensions of the Irish in New York politics. A politics of fragmentation toward blacks helped Italian and Jewish politicians to consolidate their positions, without contending with black empowerment.

Why do black politicians acquiesce in this situation? Because they lack an alternative or the capacity to effect one. Black New York politicians distrust their own capacity to achieve political unity comparable to what has evolved in Chicago, Atlanta, Philadelphia, and Detroit. Gelb found that unity among black politicians in New York comes "only when a black politician is attacked with what is perceived as racial intent." Black New York's politics are very much like the classic case described by V. O. Key under conditions of one-party rule in Southern states—conditions that foster factionalism, feuding, and a politics of personality.[9]

Joyce Gelb explains the rivalries in black

New York politics in terms of mobility barriers. The racist limits on black entry into entrepreneurial and professional roles creates an oversupply of persons seeking mobility through politics. This demand/supply imbalance—too many professionally trained blacks chasing too few opportunities—leads to a crude fend-for-yourself outlook. Thus Gelb observes that "frustration occurs when success appears elusive. . . . Because there is no one institutional channel to power . . . aspirants will take their chances when support is offered by a dissident faction or pressure group." This frustration, in turn, enables black politicians to justify "an unwillingness to defer personal political gratification in the name of unspecified community goals."

Two Politicians Confront Divisive Politics

Basic to black New York's divisive politics is a self-serving ethos, the opposite of the other-serving rhetoric common among black politicians. Reversing this situation has eluded even such skillful black politicians as J. Raymond Jones and Percy Sutton. Jones attempted such a reversal in the late 1950s. His political style is best revealed by contrasting him with Adam Clayton Powell, New York's first black congressional representative, elected in 1944. Powell was a self-made politician, based in the "personalistic" structure of his church, employing symbolic and ritualistic political materials (racial militancy, flamboyant rhetoric) to mobilize black support. J. Raymond Jones was a machine politician, employing party resources (patronage, organizational loyalty) to achieve political influence.

For one-dimensional politicization, the quick-fire and cathartic politics used by Powell had a certain value, as suggested by Powell's emergence in the ethnically-safe twentieth congressional district in 1944.[10] But when seeking a strong incorporation into the decisive political structures of New York City, the sure-fire method of J. Raymond Jones (known as "The Fox") was required. A crisis in Powell's often quarrelsome status in the Democratic party in 1956 provided J. Raymond Jones the opportunity for an authoritative structuring of local

black politics, unifying and disciplining diverse political ranks.

Largely for short-run political benefits, Powell broke ranks with the Democratic organization and backed Eisenhower in the 1956 campaign, causing the Democratic organization to seek Powell's expulsion. Jones, though in keen competition with Powell for control in Harlem, doubted that Democratic leader Carmine DeSapio could defeat Powell in Harlem. Jones organized other black leaders to back Powell and succeeded in thwarting Powell's expulsion. He immediately translated this victory into an authoritative structuring of black New York's politics.

But the feuding that defines the politics of black New York prevailed. Instead of following the lead of Jones, the other politicians reverted "to the old competition," as Kenneth Clark observed. They were unwilling to undergo the political equivalent of a baptism-of-fire, the authoritative disciplining and structuring in the hands of a politically tested leader. Why this fear of political structuring among black politicians? Clark's explanation remains one of the best:

> An important reason might be that some of these leaders suspected Jones of trying to build his own political empire at their expense. The irony is that their suspicions of him left them in the same kind of predicament of dependence on white leadership. Jones had failed to calculate the tremendous power of past patterns of ghetto deprivation that expressed themselves in suspicion and rivalry.[11]

The legacy of Jones's failure persists to this day, and it even hindered his consolidating his own position in the Democratic organization. In 1961 Jones brilliantly executed an independent petition to save the second-term mayoral nomination of Mayor Robert Wagner, whom DeSapio (the head of Tammany) sought to discard for a hand-picked candidate. In return, Wagner sought Jones's elevation to New York County Democratic leader, but failed. White attorney Edward Costikyan got the post. Three years later, in the fall of 1964, Wagner again sought to reward Jones with the Democratic leadership post, and this time succeeded.

But Jones was not himself part of a

well-structured political mechanism capable of pyramiding posts and powers into a strong political incorporation. Thus Jones's tenure as Tammany boss was brief. Ousted in 1967, his political career was finished.

The Experience of Percy Sutton

While Jones's political career was winding down in the late 1960s—along with that of Adam Clayton Powell, replaced in Congress by Charles Rangel—black New York politics had already experienced the formative stage of political incorporation. This breakthrough from a longstanding position of weakness was facilitated by two progressive forces during the 1960s: (1) federal policies and programs generated by the civil rights movement that helped move blacks from a marginal to incorporation status; and (2) the election of two strong pluralist mayors, Robert Wagner and John Lindsay, who supported political accommodation to black New York.

By the late 1960s, a main concern of black New York was the quality of its political incorporation—whether it would be weak or strong, would remain cyclical or achieve stability. Although the difference can be measured in terms of the number and proportion of elected and policy-managing officials, a more crucial indicator is the presence of skilled and astute politicians capable of simultaneously maximizing both the intra-ethnic (black) and systemic (white) sources of political clout.

A new black political leader now came forward, Percy Sutton. But Sutton failed to effect a strong political inclusion of black New York. Perhaps the major reason was his overdependence on a client approach to politics: he so shaped his politics around his political brokers—especially Tammany head Frank Rossetti—that his own ethnic organization flagged. This imbalance between the power broker and ethnic organizer persisted throughout Sutton's career, creating what I call a kind of client-political incorporation.

The politics of client-incorporation enables politically skillful leaders to carve out a power niche for *themselves*, but not for their constituency. This power niche produces sizable personal clout for black leaders, as well as

some wealth and business opportunities. But it seldom facilitates effective political incorporation for blacks in general.

Indeed, black client-politicians exercise their clout within closely circumscribed limits set by their white brokers. This makes uncertain the black politician's ability to advance his own power. Especially is this true with regard to pyramiding successive political offices, such as mayor, county party boss, state party boss, governor, U.S. senator, and onward. This process is fulfilled when it becomes transferable from one cohort of black politicians to another or, what amounts to the same thing, to uniting with allies, such as Hispanics, women, even white ethnic politicians. Precisely Sutton's failure to effect such pyramiding closed out his political career.

Sutton's political rise was a sign of his skill as a political opportunist. In the early 1960s, he anchored himself between the competing (even feuding) Democratic camps—the Tammany Hall regulars and the Democratic reformers.[12] The opportunist in Sutton prevailed over whatever there was of the political visionary. When a choice had to be made, Sutton backed the Tammany regulars more often than not.

His first major opportunity to influence New York politics as a client-politician came in 1967 during a contest for the county Democratic leadership. Tammany Hall regular Frank Rossetti was opposed by West Side Democratic reformer Ronnie Eldridge, an ally of Senator Robert Kennedy. Harlem Democratic regulars held the balance of power between the warring Democratic camps. Sutton, the best organized of the rather poorly organized black politicians, chose Rossetti, who, in fact, prevailed.

For the next decade Sutton's alliance with the New York Democratic leader consolidated his position in New York politics. He functioned as a district leader, a high-profile client ally of Rossetti, and the only black member of the powerful Board of Estimate by virtue of being Manhattan borough president. But Sutton never functioned as an instrument for the effective political incorporation of a broad black constituency.

The costs of preferring a politics of client incorporation never fazed Sutton. Impressed by his own reelection as borough president in 1969 and again in 1973, Sutton assumed that New York politics was now ready for a major bid at political pyramiding—his own elevation to the mayoralty. Sutton announced his candidacy in 1977, hoping the Democratic organization would fall into line behind him. He had many I.O.Us with Democratic regulars, especially Abe Beame, an important Rossetti protegé whom Sutton had helped to elect mayor in 1973. In return, Beame had promised to appoint large numbers of blacks to important positions in his administration. In addition, there was a tacit understanding that Beame would back Sutton for mayor in 1977.

But most of the Democratic regulars did not honor their I.O.Us. Tammany, moreover, did not prevail on Beame to keep his promise to step down for Sutton; instead, Beame ran for reelection, claiming that charges of financial maladministration required him to clear his political name. Beame eventually lost the primary to the man who would become New York's second Jewish mayor, Ed Koch.

This double-cross stunned Sutton, who nonetheless mounted a campaign—an experience equally traumatic. For it seems Sutton expected the Democratic leaders and their media allies to assist him, as the first black mayoral candidate, in overcoming the ethnocentric or racist perceptions of white Democratic voters.

Nothing of the sort happened. Sutton faced "the most disheartening, deprecating, disabling experience I have ever had." He had expected, rather naively, that the transethnic aspect of his client-politician operations would automatically translate into a public image of him as a cross-racial, not merely a black, politician. "For the first time," explains Sutton, a very fair-skinned black, "I experienced articles in newspapers . . . addressing my constituency as being only black. Now when you are set aside like that and you are trying to raise money, that is an awful burden to bear. . . . I was rather unprepared for the isolation of me as a candidate on the grounds of race."[13]

After a lackluster primary campaign, Sutton finished fifth in a field of seven, gaining just over 50 percent of the black vote and hardly any support from whites. Sutton's client-alliance politics came to an abrupt and bitter halt. Black New York, still faction-riddled, took a long time to regain the Manhattan borough presidency—until 1985, when City Clerk David Dinkins was elected after several attempts. An easier succession to this post by a black would have almost certainly occurred had Sutton translated his "personalistic" political clout into an instrument for the political organization of blacks.

Sutton lacked a sense of the interconnectedness between black politicians' power and the empowerment of their constituency. Throughout the 1970s Sutton nurtured his multimillion-dollar business endeavors in the communication industry (radio, television, newspapers)—his class payoffs, in short—while so neglecting an effective political structuring among blacks that he was unable to make Mayor Beame keep his promise on major black political appointments. And when black factionalism enabled Beame to renege on appointing Sutton's protegé, Wilbert Tatum—a newspaper owner—as New York's first black deputy mayor, Sutton lacked the political tenacity to squash such factionalism.

The Factionalism Continues

Black New York politics has gone down its faction-ridden roadway in the 1980s. No black politician with the requisite skill and astuteness has yet emerged to impose a unifying political framework over highly localized politicians and factions to consolidate black New York's electoral potential.

The black electoral potential in New York is, in fact, pathetically underdeveloped compared to that in other cities. By the mid-1980s only 56 percent of eligible blacks in New York were registered, while in Chicago black registration was 70 percent. Furthermore, black politicians' control over the black vote is extremely weak. In the 1985 mayoral primary, Koch won 38 percent of the black vote—nearly as much as the 40 percent won by black state assemblymember Herman "Denny" Farrell.

Furthermore, the political process by which Farrell emerged as the minority mayoral candidate reveals the persistence of pathological factionalism and feuding in black New York politics. Black politicians formed the Coalition for a Just New York as a mechanism for presenting a unified front in the 1985 mayoral campaign; but no such unity was forthcoming. The Coalition's effort was marred by extraordinary factionalism, pitting Manhattan politicians against Brooklyn politicians and blacks against Hispanics. Black/Hispanic feuding in the campaign was particularly pathetic. Insofar as they constitute 20 percent of the population and 13 percent of the Democratic mayoral electorate (compared to 25 percent and 23 percent respectively for blacks), Hispanics would seem to be a natural electoral ally for black politicians. But the sway of factionalism and personalism among black politicians has blinded them to this possibility.

Even though it was apparent that no black candidate of mayoral stature and vote-getting potential was available for the 1985 campaign, the coalition of black politicians refused to back the candidacy of the leading Hispanic politician, Herman Badillo. Instead, Farrell, a politician of minor skills and less than stellar leadership, got the nod from the Coalition for a Just New York.

There is still some political hope for blacks in New York. The emergence of new black politicians outside Manhattan is one sign. Black politics in Brooklyn is different from the faction-riddled and personalistic tradition of Harlem. It was, in fact, a Brooklyn black politician, Albert Vann, who tried to bridge the black/Hispanic cleavage during the 1985 campaign. Vann supported Badillo, partly out of a clear grasp of the logic of coalition politics that he and Major Owens have experimented with successfully since the early 1970s in Brooklyn. Vann also had a personal reason for backing Badillo—his campaign for the borough presidency of Brooklyn in which he needed a sizable Hispanic vote. Vann lost the race to incumbent Howard Golden—gaining 60 percent of the black vote but only 28 percent of Hispanics—but he did surface as the first major black politician to support a major Hispanic politician. Other black politicians favoring

coalitions have emerged in the Bronx and Queens—for example, Reverend Floyd Flake, a newly elected member of Congress. Black New York's hope for greater political effectiveness lies, in good part, with these politicians.□

Notes

[1] For comparisons of groups in terms of political incorporation, see Rufus Browning, Dale Marshall, David Tabb, *Protest Is Not Enough: The Struggle of Blacks and Hispanics for Equality in Urban Politics* (Berkeley: University of California Press, 1984).

[2] Martin Shefter, *Political Crisis-Fiscal Crisis: The Collapse and Revival of New York City* (New York: Basic Books, 1985), pp. 209–211.

[3] Angelo Falcon, *Black and Latino Politics in New York City* (New York: Institute for Puerto Rican Policy, 1985), pp. 21–22.

[4] Joyce Gelb, *Black Republicans in New York: A Minority Group in a Minority Party* (Unpublished manuscript, 1970).

[5] Theodore Lowi, "Functionalism in Political Science: The Case of Innovation in Party Systems," *American Political Science Review* (September, 1963), pp. 576–577.

[6] Shefter, *Political Crisis-Fiscal Crisis*, pp. 178–180.

[7] Charles Hamilton, "Public Policy and Some Political Consequences," in Marguerite Ross-Barnett and James Hefner, eds., *Public Policy for the Black Community* (Port Washington: 1975), p. 245.

[8] Joyce Gelb, "Blacks, Blocs and Ballots: The Relevance of Party Politics to the Negro," *Polity* (September, 1970), p. 311.

[9] V. O. Key, *Southern Politics in State and Nation* (New York: Knopf, 1949).

[10] See Martin Kilson, "The Militant as Politician: Adam Clayton Powell, Jr.," in John Hope Franklin and August Meier, eds., *Black Leaders of the Twentieth Century* (Urbana: University of Illinois Press, 1982).

[11] Kenneth Clark, *Dark Ghetto: Dilemmas of Social Power* (New York: Harpers, 1967), pp. 159–160.

[12] See James Q. Wilson, *The Amateur Democrat* (Chicago: University of Chicago Press, 1962). Data on Sutton's career are based in part on Douglas Schoen, *Report on Harlem Politics 1967–1972* (Unpublished study, January 1973).

[13] Michael Oreskes, "Blacks in New York: The Anguish of Political Failure," the *New York Times* (March 31, 1987).

Interview with David Jones

THE LOT OF BLACK PROFESSIONALS

"Meritocracy" Proves Elusive in New York

At a conference on "leadership succession" in New York late in 1985, I was struck by the remarks of David Jones, then executive director of the city's Youth Bureau, now head of one of the city's oldest nonprofit social service agencies, the Community Service Society. Jones mentioned in passing, but not casually, that several bright young black lawyers he'd known in some of the city's most powerful law firms during the mid-1970s had committed suicide and/or suffered mental breakdown, at least in part because of the ambiguity surrounding their failures to succeed as first-rate lawyers, much less become full partners in their firms.

When I talked to Jones at the Community Service Society in January 1987, he described the recruitment of capable young blacks as "window dressing" by firms that still block black advancement to positions of real leadership.

We worry about the plight of the two thirds of the black population battling poverty and social disintegration, but Jones's account makes clear that all is not well among that other third. Moreover, he argues, the two phenomena are related: precisely because blacks plucked for Ivy League scholarships and dazzling career paths tend to be overly trusting of pure meritocracy and so avoid forging links to a political power base "back in the community," they remain highly vulnerable to racism as individuals, even as they deprive the black community of a more sophisticated leadership.

In cities like Atlanta and Chicago, where, Jones notes, there has been a better relationship between black elites and masses, not only has there been stronger black political power, but blacks in the private sector, too, have more often managed to rid themselves of some of the tortuous ambiguities that bedeviled the young law associates he describes.

—JIM SLEEPER

Dissent: Tell us a little about the history of the black middle class in New York.

Jones: It goes back many generations, even before the Civil War. It emerged because of the separate black economy that was a consequence of discrimination—black lawyers, doctors, undertakers, ministers, and other professionals served the black community and weren't allowed access to the larger white society. Because my father [Thomas Russell Jones] was a lawyer and state assemblyman and later a judge, I grew up as a middle-class black in Bedford-Stuyvesant and remember "Jack and Jill" and other social organizations, as well as the church-related groups that formed the core of black middle class society. I saw fine homes, a genteel setting, but one also more integrated with the black working class.

That was really the first of three stages in black middle-class evolution—the providing of professional services directly to the black community. Second, between the world wars, another element of the black middle class emerged, based on academic degrees and the arts, in enclaves like Greenwich Village;

whites often glamorized creative blacks growing out of the Harlem Renaissance and coming downtown.

Then, out of the civil rights movement, there emerged not just black political leaders, but leaders in the unions and the private sector, people coming up not necessarily through the "right schools" or contacts but through their own wits and talents.

My own was a very insulated environment. I don't really recall, growing up in the 1950s in Bedford-Stuyvesant, very much prejudice, other than what you saw in the press. I knew that you didn't go up to a white policeman for help. I remember driving down to Maryland with my family and being refused service. But because of the close neighborhood ties you had a fair amount of protection.

For most of us, ironically, that started to crumble when we became involved in the civil rights movement. Even before that, my sister and I were sent out to private school in Manhattan. After being in P.S. 138 until the third grade, I couldn't read. The school had more substitute teachers than any other. So I was taken out and put in Brooklyn Friends— which made it clear to my father that they had done him a great favor—and then in Elizabeth Irwin in the Village. There were very few blacks there; though none of us knew it, Angela Davis had come through two or three years earlier.

Dissent: How were you accepted by your schoolmates?

Jones: You had no sense of overt discrimination. These were sons and daughters of liberals, though I remember that when my class graduated in 1966, and I was class president and a black girl was the only National Merit scholar, admitted to Radcliffe, suddenly some parents were irritated. It was obvious from their comments that it was all right to bring in tokens for "uplift," but when we got the things everyone else wanted for their children. . . . I still remember some sharp comments that went around, though that wasn't universal, by any means.

And we were also isolated from the black community—

Dissent: You were going home to Bedford-Stuyvesant at night. . . .

Jones: Sure, but there was clearly a disjunction. What kept my attention focused back there was my father's running for elective office and his founding the Bedford-Stuyvesant Restoration Corporation, having his first meetings with Robert Kennedy. But I was drifting away from the young people I'd grown up with. I was set on going to college. I never considered a black college. I was recruited by Wesleyan, which was making a determined effort to get blacks.

There, I was shoved up against it, a predominantly white campus but a sizable minority of black students—they've maintained it at 15 percent black and Hispanic. So we had a critical mass, and we were being radicalized by what was going on outside—Martin Luther King. I had already heard King speak. I'd been arrested at Downstate Medical Center, which had refused to integrate its construction, and at that demonstration I'd talked with Malcolm X. All these things were swirling around, and in a way it was moving you, making your decisions for you.

I joined a black student group called Ujamaa—"the black family"—that covered the ideological spectrum. Everything was in flux. There were some incidents with guns, flirtations with the Black Panthers. I was on the student judiciary board and got one of the young black men off who was alleged to have had a pistol in his room; he's now a lawyer, very conservative. I just went to a reunion of black professionals who'd gone to Wesleyan: there were sixty people, black men and women, just from the N.Y. area, who had thrived, at least in part, because they received a first-class college education that demanded first-class work, without the kind of racial chauvinism that lets minorities just get by— only to fail when they confront the harsh realities of competition and racism in this city.

Dissent: How did you feel at that time about your parents' middle-class generation—that they'd laid a foundation, or "sold out" to whites?

Jones: It was mixed. Everyone was looking at externals on campus—how you wore your hair, whether you associated with whites mostly or were involved in black causes. It was felt that you couldn't have it both ways, though many of us did. There were those who became involved in black studies, others in conventional studies. Cliques developed. I became an intern for Senator Robert Kennedy, a contact that was developed because I attended all the early meetings with my father in the development of the Bedford-Stuyvesant Restoration Corporation. But we were all pretty radicalized; the rhetoric got pretty intense on campus.

There was an enormous amount of arrogance; we were the chosen, our training would make everything possible. A lot of anger, but an enormous amount of excitement. The demonstrations brought results, the colleges were receptive. . . . But there wasn't much reaching back into the black community, partly because of our physical isolation. I did some tutoring in Middletown, which has a sizable black population. But it was felt that we were the vanguard, we were going to be the new leadership.

When I went to Yale Law School in 1970, there was a major push by educational institutions to increase black admissions. But by 1973–74, there was a sudden drop in interest. The attrition rate was enormous, they were kicking black kids out all over the place, and interest in civil rights among the faculty did a 180-degree turn. I remember when I was a first-year student, Ralph Winter, now a prominent federal judge, then a professor, confronted a group of black students protesting drops in black adminission, lack of black faculty, and the curriculum; the administration was saying, "No way," and admissions of blacks dropped off very fast.

Dissent: What did that say to you?

Jones: It didn't say enough. Somehow we didn't see that this would carry through after law school; if anything, we thought, in our least admirable moments, well, this will diminish the [black] competition, we'll be particularly special. Activism declined as a result. The notion was, they've let in too many unqualified people, but since we're here and doing fine, we must be the exceptions. It was a fundamental misperception.

Dissent: Why?

Jones: Well, there was all this talk about our being important players in society, the leadership group of the country. I think our mistake really began by sitting in an elite circle talking just as cogently as our classmates and competing well with them, and saying, okay, I'm going to become a full member of the establishment. We failed to see that something might intervene. We didn't see that from day one white students were making connections with law professors that would lead to the *Law Review* and to clerkships. Almost no black knew why one should spend time networking. All we knew was that our relatives oohed and aahed over us.

And we *were* getting recruited by law firms, so there was no reason to see our mistake. We didn't see these as entry-level jobs that would go nowhere. We thought, boy, they're coming to us because they see us as among the next leaders of their firms and the nation. If we put in the hours and do well, that'll happen. If no blacks made partner before us, that was because *we* were so much brighter.

The point is that there was almost no sense of having to reach back into and rely on any kind of black constituency. If anything, the notion of any "constituency" outside whatever partner we were going to link up with was alien.

Dissent: Yet you had in you that undercurrent, that experience of activism. . . .

Jones: Not so much in law school, where the self-selection curbs that; and besides, the civil rights movement was losing steam. I had worked with Robert Kennedy in the Senate, I had run part of his Connecticut campaign in the 1968 presidential race. So I already knew I could be part of the political establishment. Then the senator died, and my connections began to fade. . . .

Dissent: But you must have met some white liberals who were genuinely committed to your assumptions about leadership.

Jones: Fritz [F.A.O.] Schwartz, Jr. [recently New York City Corporation Counsel] recruited me to Cravath, Swaine and Moore, got me to come on as a summer associate, yes. We saw the liberal attitude of the firms and took this as an access point. And some few of us did get through [to partner], more so outside New York City: in Washington, Atlanta, Chicago, because there were constituencies they could lean on. Partly this isn't a racial issue. It's the problem of reaching for the brass ring—a lot of very bright people are competing. But some had an edge, a kind of support system that we didn't recognize as coming into play. We had a naïve assumption that we were entering a pure meritocracy *and* that we would move in these circles comfortably enough to make fast friends and move forward. I didn't really notice that, because of the senator's death and the decline in the Bedford-Stuyvesant Restoration, my edge was growing dull.

Dissent: So your disillusionment with this notion of meritocracy plus the slight edge of contacts through a constituency was gradual?

Jones: I certainly didn't see it at first. Summer associates—black or white—were treated royally at Cravath. I think it began to emerge when I looked at the treatment the older black associates were getting at firms throughout the city. I spent a year as a law clerk to Judge [Constance Baker] Motley in the federal courts, and when I came back in 1975, it wasn't so much the assignments I was getting—I wasn't on the IBM case, which was probably an early indication of the problem, though I was on Time, Inc., Shell Oil—but the comments I got about my campaign leaves. I was in the Carter campaign in New York and

when I came back, while all the reviews were right, there were comments like, "Oh, you're not really committed to us"—this from a partner, who said it laughingly. Already at that point there were several black associates who'd been passed over, and one of them had had real trouble and ultimately committed suicide.

My turning point came when a senior black woman who was a litigator told me that after six or seven years she was told she ought to go to the U.S. Attorney's office for what was described as "more seasoning as a litigator." She was a very articulate, talented young woman who had been friendly with a managing partner, which I never was—I had gotten into some problems with some partners over what I perceived as racial remarks, and I certainly had never played tennis with a managing partner. So I was very concerned when I saw what happened to her.

I was getting nervous. I was being very well paid, but watching the signs all around me; I was four years in at the time. There was very little new recruitment of black associates. The assignments were nice enough, but you began to understand how you couldn't afford to make a mistake, while your white compatriots were getting patted on the back after each mistake and told, "I did the same thing when I was a young lawyer." If a black made a mistake, it was always, "A-*ha*, we always knew there was too much affirmative action."

There was a moment of truth that viscerally we were coming to recognize, and you began to wonder what you would do if you were passed over, since the firm had a policy of "up or out." There was no black partner at this point. There were seven of us blacks, and my forte was litigation, so I was looking around for something else when, because of my work with the Carter campaign, [Deputy Mayor] Haskell Ward called me up and said, "Mayor Koch is looking for a special adviser," and I said, "Sure," and I took the job.

Dissent: Were you having discussions with other black associates about what to do if passed over?

Jones: No, there wasn't much of a network at that point. People were very reticent, because talking about it is a sign you might think you're not going to make it. Also, you're in such a rarefied group that everyone still thought they were going to do it. Again, most people were not relying on any constituency other than their "godfather." I realized I didn't have enough of a support base here.

Dissent: And you knew of others who flipped out?

Jones: Yes. I was pretty insulated because of my past activities in politics; I had a sense of options. But I began to see there was a weakness here that had larger, "political" elements: "This isn't just you, Jones." Some of the others at firms throughout the city were coming up against it, a feeling, "Oh my god, I've failed."

Dissent: Does the experience of past discrimination factor into it—a feeling that the issue is discrimination, not personal failure?

Jones: I had been pretty abstracted about that. I remembered stories my father had told me about being in the South, people drawing guns on him in the Army. I finally got my own lesson while up in Maine on a college spring break, fishing on a roadside. I got hit on the side of the head and backed up against a bridge abutment by some mill workers. I got beaten up and I called the police, and they laughed. I'd been called names, but never assaulted, so that changed my perspective. I think I would've taken a completely different direction without that assault, because suddenly the stories my father had told me made more than just intellectual sense. They took on a tangible impact, especially because I hadn't been bothering anyone, not even talking to anybody.

I survived, but there's the perception that you can't get away, and that it's just when you forget that that you're most vulnerable. I took it to heart. It's shaped how I've seen things since.

Dissent: How does one balance staying in the community for support with pursuing a professional career?

Jones: It can be done. The Harlem guys have done it better than Brooklyn. I can't help but feel that there's a generation of highly trained blacks who could've brought about real power-sharing in New York and gotten just what they wanted by doing that. The only time I was ever recruited actively was when Harold Washing-

ton was elected in Chicago, and the firm said flat out: "We want you to work in our municipal bond financing department in Chicago." Suddenly people had to pay attention if you were any good.

What I've been preaching and trying to tell young black professionals is, this isn't morality or civil rights, this is whether you're ever really gonna hold the keys to the boardroom. Failure to have a base of some sort with clout means you won't move, no matter how many cocktails you have with the managing director. You need a real core of support, even if it's not direct, even it it's just a sense that, Oh, brother, we could work on the next municipal bond financing if we had a black mayor!

And that's what we didn't realize, that you need to have some sort of institutional power base even if you aren't personally connected to it. I still have trouble convincing people of this. Many young lawyers listen to me like I'm from Mars.

I think a black professional leadership group is essential, though not the whole story. Jesse Jackson reaches the grassroots population that I can't even come near. He can start to move a whole mass of people who are angry, who have nowhere to go. But ultimately you also have to have a group that can exercise some control, not only in the political sector but also in the economy of the city.

Dissent: What's your reaction to black professionals who respond favorably to Louis Farrakhan?

Jones: I see that as embitterment. Even though they may not act on it, I think anyone black who gets to be my age, 38, has a lot of bitterness. I've been relatively successful in my career, but I get angry when I think of my father, because I think there's no question that in a different kind of society he would have been tremendously and productively powerful, not only for blacks but for the city and nation.

Dissent: Can you tread the line between wanting to be racially immersed, building power, and becoming so immersed that it tends to separatism?

Jones: In my angrier moments I understood the sources of lot of the rhetoric. There's no way to tell people to understand both sides.

You see guys like [California Assembly Speaker] Willie Brown who've managed to work it out. [Manhattan Borough President] David Dinkins has worked it out. At the same time, though, Brooklyn seems to have edged into a backwater. Except when issues like Howard Beach flare up, and everyone gets dragged along.

Dissent: If your own cohort had stayed more with the community, they would've been able to come forward during times like this and have more leverage . . .

Jones: Yes. The professional cadre could have achieved the career objectives they wanted by reaching back. Even the idea of contributing to a black political campaign is very recent; for the first time you see people who write out $5,000 checks. We didn't want to do it at first; it was considered that you might be looking too black. Even now, we still have too many who want to hang back.

It's a question of how long it takes. Each passing year you lose more and more young people. You see it here at the Community Service Society as we examine statistics on public education and college enrollment, fewer and fewer minority people are getting through with a first-class education. Fewer people are capable, more are demanding remediation and support. As the base contracts, it becomes more difficult to mobilize different groups. To kids who drop out of Boys and Girls High School, the demagogues make perfect sense, when they listen at all, as opposed to a guy who's got a job and a house and kids in school. The problem now is that there's really no established leadership committed to pursuing their professional careers *and* to reaching back into the community at the same time. I and some of my age group have to be part of the effort to change the situation to link black professionals back to the communities from which they came. □

Xavier F. Totti

THE MAKING OF A LATINO ETHNIC IDENTITY

The Latino press and Latino leaders claim that their group may well be the political movement of the 1980s. Estimates show that by the year 2005 those classified by the census as Hispanics will outnumber blacks to become the largest minority in the United States—politically, socially, and culturally—a demographic event of great significance. Within the group there are visions of a golden epoch where "now that we have the numbers" it will be easy to achieve greater political representation and national prominence: to become, in the words of the League of United Latin American Citizens (LULAC) president, Ruben Bonilla, "a truly visible political force." The bold ones even envision transforming the United States into a bilingual nation.

This prospect has not escaped the attention of the media and of prominent politicians. Some, like California's ex-senator S. I. Hayakawa, already see the specter of a linguistically divided nation in which a large percentage of its citizens, with ties to nations south of the border, will demand that Spanish be made the official second language in the states where they predominate. Others, like Colorado's governor Richard Lamm, believing that the national spirit is fragmenting, and fearing a problem similar to that of Canada with Quebec, want action at the highest levels of the federal bureaucracy. Pluralists, on the other hand, many of them in New York, argue on behalf of this "different" migrant group and view the traditional three-generation European pattern of assimilation as the product of a different era. Using the Afro-American experience as example, and bilingualism as a model, they question the integrative character of American society and the processes through which assimilation was presumably achieved. The cultural pluralists would expand the conventional boundaries in defining who and what are Americans.

Although there are millions of citizens who identify or are identified as Latinos, the existence of an organized Latino ethnicity can be questioned.[1] In many cases the assertion that a Hispanic ethnic culture exists is prompted by self-interest, fear, or, for administrative reasons, by the state.

We can see, however, a common Latino identity emerging in the United States. It is being haltingly erected by those who cross their "individual group boundaries and seek solidarity in a wider Latino unity."[2]

But why is it that such a group has not fully emerged and made its social and political weight felt in the United States? The Latino presence is superficially strong in North America. Business and advertising recognize the importance of the Latino market. Most major corporations have devised special ad campaigns to capture what they consider the fastest-growing consumer segment in the country. Even the ultra-"American" (and anti-union) Coors Brewery has declared the 1980s the "Decade of the Hispanic." But to explain the lateness of the group's political and social assertion, we must first describe the constituent parts of the whole, stressing their dissimilarities, in order to clarify the processes that foster the emergence of a Latino ethnicity.

Uneven processes in history, nationality, and migration account for the differences in the four components of the group: Mexican Americans or Chicanos, Puerto Ricans, Cuban Americans, and the new migrants from other countries in Latin America (who mostly entered after the new immigration laws of 1965). The first three are the dominant groups, each having settled in a different part of the country and established for other Latinos patterns of settlement and relations with the dominant society where they predominate.

Of the three groups, the most numerous nationally, though the least prominent in New York, are the Mexican Americans, or Chicanos, some 8.7 million, or 60 percent of the 14.6 million officially counted Latinos in 1980. Chicanos are also the oldest Latino population in the United States because the Southwest and Texas were once part of Spain, and then of Mexico. Following the Mexican-American War of 1846, Chicanos moved rapidly from majority to minority status, suffering progressive pauperization through the loss of land, pressed into *barrios,* and victimized by segregationist policies.

The black civil rights movement of the late 1950s and early 1960s showed Chicanos the value of massive organizing for gaining equality. With the end of the *bracero* program, agricultural workers were able to organize for better conditions. Cesar Chavez's United Farm Workers' (UFW) organizing efforts in California, and the land struggles of Reies Tijerina in New Mexico, combined standard organizing efforts and traditional cultural symbols, which attracted a wide spectrum of Mexican Americans. By the middle 1960s, Chicanos were aggressively asserting their separateness in a variety of organizations (grassroots or *barrio,* professional and university student organizations) and demanding a place within the general society.

The second-largest Latino group, 15 percent or two million and dominant among New York Hispanics, is made up of mainland Puerto Ricans. The main outlines of their situation are familiar to most other New Yorkers: U.S. citizens by birth, Puerto Ricans do not encounter the migration and quota system that affects all other migrants; indeed, moving from Puerto Rico to the mainland is like any other internal move within the United States. The massive migration of Puerto Ricans to the mainland began with the government's effort to industrialize the island during the late 1940s. Development schemes included encouragement to leave; migration was seen as both a social safety valve and an economic asset. Encouraged also by the availability of cheap air fares due to the surplus of airplanes after World War II (Puerto Ricans are the first airborne migrants in history), the Puerto Rican population on the mainland quadrupled between 1940 and 1950, and tripled again by 1960.

Puerto Rican political organization and ethnic identity in the United States was late developing. The legal status of Puerto Ricans, which facilitated their migration to the mainland, created a shifting population constantly going back and forth for personal and other reasons. The unresolved political status of Puerto Rico also encourages direct interest in its politics and affairs. Candidates for public office there campaign in New York for the support of those who might return to Puerto Rico at election time. The establishment by the Commonwealth of Puerto Rico of an office in New York interfered with the development of a local cadre of leaders. When New York politicians were confronted with a community problem, they consulted the representatives of the Commonwealth government instead of going to the *barrios.* Finally, the Democratic party, a white ethnic working-class party in the Northeast, showed no interest in organizing poor Puerto Ricans. Reform movements within the Democratic party, basically middle class with middle-class agendas, also showed little interest. But the black civil rights movement and the maturing of the Chicano movement served as an inspiration in the development of Puerto Rican political organization and identity. Another push to organize came from the Great Society federal antipoverty programs, which bypassed the local political machines and encouraged local leadership. However, unlike politically conscious Mexican Americans, who adopted the name Chicanos to announce their Mexicano identity, mainland

Puerto Ricans still are in disagreement over how to view themselves—whether and how different they are from their relatives back on the island. Most do not accept the proposed term "Neorican."

Cuban Americans, the third-largest group, add up to 800,000, or 5 percent of the total official Latino population. Cuban Americans entered the U.S. heavily with the official status of refugees following the Cuban Revolution of 1959. The class origin of most of these refugees differed markedly from that of other Latinos; most migrants from revolutionary Cuba came from the upper and middle classes (the bourgeoisie, the traditional middle class, and the "new" middle class). Many arrived in the United States with considerable capital. Many more of their leaders migrated with them than with the other groups; covert federal aid to overthrow the Cuban government gave Cuban exile leadership, old and new, a source of patronage.

By the late 1960s, when efforts to overthrow the revolution had failed, Cubans more or less began to settle in for a permanent exile and, especially in South Florida, entered the political arena. In the New York metropolitan area, Cubans are heavily concentrated in northern New Jersey towns and, to a lesser degree, in upper Manhattan and Queens. As is to be expected from refugees of "socialist" revolutions, Cubans are politically conservative (most belong to or vote for the Republican party) and also exhibit the highest conversion rates to U.S. citizenship of all Latino migrants.

Group Identity

Given these different and disparate migratory processes, what, then, unites Latinos? How do they constitute a group? I believe two things serve to induce the formation of the Latino ethnic identity. One, of course, is the perceived shared cultural background in contrast to the larger American culture, with the Spanish language at the center. The other is the structural position of most Latinos within American society, and, as its consequence, their relationship to the state apparatus and politics.

The shared cultural background, even if it is a superficial construct that leaves out the heterogeneous nature of the groups, has a tremendous force in identifying Latinos across national boundaries. That background, nurtured in common values, is constantly reinforced in the mass media, both in the U.S. Latino press and in that of the separate countries of origin.[3] The notion is further solidified by the immediate, traditional presence of the "colossus from the North" in the life of Latin America. The Spanish language serves as more than a *lingua franca* among the groups; it is the most visible and immediate mark of their shared distinction from the rest of the society. The language is also a *living* force since, unlike other migrants in the United States, Latinos are followed by a powerful and complex system of Spanish-language mass media. Today the Spanish-language media in the United States include sixty-five newspapers, sixty-five magazines, sixty-seven television stations, and 430 radio stations. Two television groups, Spanish International Network (SIN) and Netspan, are able to transmit coast to coast. Furthermore, most major Latino television markets have at least two competing Spanish-language stations.

The maintenance of Spanish and the ideal of bilingualism and formal bilingual education are, as recent surveys indicate, immutable tenets of identity for most Latinos.[4] In 1980 eight out of ten Hispanics interviewed in the New York metropolitan area favored formal bilingual education. A nationwide survey found, irrespective of national origin and length of residence in the U.S., that bilingualism was the personal goal of most. Compared to previous surveys, there was "no sign of increased commitment to mastery of English at the possible expense of Spanish; the commitment to Spanish is stronger if anything."[5] In ordinary everyday discourse, even among fully bilingual or English-dominant Latinos, Spanish continues to preserve a special notion of self. Like Guarani among bilingual Paraguayans, it's the voice of the soul; uttering a few words of Spanish signifies a separation from the dominant culture and a symbolic unity. The force of Spanish among Latinos, in intraethnic and interethnic encounters, lies in its ability to compress many contradictory symbols in the search for power, reflecting exclusivity, nostalgia, and/or respect among speakers.

Especially important in the processes of creating a new ethnic identity are those occasions when shared "culture" leaves the remembrances of the old country and is used to adapt to and describe life in the present environment. Among migrants and their descendants, these are the creative moments of forging new interpretations and future traditions. Within the process of Latino ethnic formation, the music of composer-singer Rubén Blades and the poetry of Tato Laviera are examples of the use of expressive culture in forging a new unity based on common traditions and a present similarity within the new polity. Blades, the most popular Latino singer of the moment, sings to a unified Latino group in America, composed of those from the "south," of a different color, of a strange tongue, united by both a common origin and their present situation in the United States. For Blades, those situations are generally the products of exploitation, discrimination, and poverty (both here and in Latin America). In the song *Siembra*, he urges Latinos to use their *conciencia*, in this case their identity and pride, to improve their situation. He warns assimilated Latinos of the pitfalls in their quest for the American dream; the song *Plástico* categorizes those who unequivocally assimilate into the complacent middle class as shallow, "plastic" individuals preoccupied with the latest fashions and willing to mortgage their future in the name of "social status." Both *Siembra* and *Plástico* urge Latinos to unite and through education, hard work, and the inner strength of the group create their own better future.

Like Blades, Tato Laviera also speaks of and about a new environment. Laviera's work is bilingual, parts in Spanish, parts in English. He is looking for a new medium of expression to describe the current situation. It is no longer the poetry of "salvation in the tropics from this alien society" (of concrete jungles). In his latest book, *AmeRican Folklore*,[6] Laviera moves out from his "Neorican" and New York ghetto reality to reach the deeper cultural roots that unite groups, as in the poem *"Vaya Carnal."* The *carnal*, or full brother, is the street Chicano, whom the street "Neorican" has discovered as his brother. Their brotherhood emanates from a similar past and a common popular street culture. Laviera ends the poem calling both himself and his *carnal "chicano-riqueños,"* hoping that this unity will create a future *totalmente nuestro* (totally ours).

As expressed by both Blades and Laviera the uncertainties lie not between assimilation and the maintenance of the traditional culture, they do not present two or more static, all-or-nothing cultures, but interaction and creativity within new situations. They speak of poor, working-class and street Latinos who are forging a new consciousness out of their shared past and present condition.

Political Life

But we will better understand the unity of the Latinos when looking at their structural similarities within American society and at their relations to the state. It is in this sphere that they unite to organize politically. Latinos in general, Cuban Americans being the exception, occupy the lower rungs of American society and suffer job discrimination due to the ethnic segmentation of the work force. It is in dealing with state programs like affirmative action, the welfare system, the criminal justice system, the schools, and the electoral system that Latinos become homogenized, both from above and from below. They began to organize politically as the American state began to tackle problems of racial and social inequality in response to the black civil rights movement. In that sense, in their relations with the state, Latinos differ markedly from previous ethnic groups. When they entered the wider American scene in large numbers, they were able to benefit from the New Deal and Great Society agendas. Organizing for collective action to demand rights and benefits from the state became one of the ways they could mobilize their shared cultural values and gain recognition as an entity.

At first, most organizing was sectarian, within "national" lines. Thus Puerto Ricans in New York City at the beginning of the civil rights movement separated from other Latinos, most of whom were not citizens and could not vote, establishing their own parade as a symbol of their political aspirations and their strength. Politicians, who previously catered to the Spanish-speaking population, began to address most Latino problems in terms of the Puerto Rican population. Federal program funds and student scholarships were distributed only to Puerto Ricans.

Such organizing along national lines began to change significantly in the 1970s, as the "new migrants" began to accept their permanence and interest in the local political process, and as the state began to manage its minorities (and the funds destined for them) across intra-Hispanic divisions. The emergence of a wider Latino identity and the birth of organizations promoting their political and social enfranchisement began with their daily interactions in the neighborhoods of New York or Chicago, or any other city where two or more Latino groups interact.

Manhattan's Upper West Side, for example, had been a working-class Irish and middle-class Jewish neighborhood, until, in the late 1960s, large numbers of working-class Puerto Ricans and then Dominicans moved in. Today it serves as home to the largest Dominican population in New York City; like most multi-ethnic neighborhoods, it is spatially segregated.

Dominicans began migrating to the United States in large numbers after the 1965 change in the immigration laws. The change also coincided with the American invasion of the island and the establishment of the repressive Balaguer government. One of the first acts of the Balaguer regime was to dismantle the local popular organizations that had flourished under the social democratic regime of Juan Bosch. Those *barrio* leaders who could escape migrated and eventually, looking for jobs, found their way to New York City.

Once here they took control of most Dominican voluntary associations and clubs, and founded branches of the Dominican opposition parties. All their activities centered on Dominican politics, human rights violations, and the defeat of the Balaguer government. At the same time, taking advantage of the open-admissions policy of the City University of New York, many became professionals. When in 1978 the social democratic party, the *Partido Revolucionario Dominicano* (PRD), triumphed, a massive homecoming of Dominicans ensued. To their surprise, however, there was no place for them back home: the economy was in shambles, with Gulf & Western controlling virtually all activity; political cadres who had stayed were occupying the bureaucratic posts; and their professions brought little economic remuneration.

Members of this group, with a long tradition of political activism and a strong internationalist ideology centered in the Dominican Republic, now realized that their only place was in New York, where they now began to organize and seek alliances with Puerto Rican leaders at the local level. Puerto Ricans in the middle 1970s were experiencing a series of stunning defeats in the city's political arena. Their defeat over the control of a community school board, in a district where they were the absolute majority, left them searching for new solutions to the problems of ethnic politics in New York.

In their alliances, Dominicans and Puerto Ricans founded a series of organizations (most prominent among them the Latino Urban Political Association [LUPA] designed to wrest control from the Jewish minority of the district. Focusing on the fact that all of the dilapidated and overcrowded schools were in the Latino section of the neighborhood, they organized and in 1986 gained control of the community school board. Also in coalition with the Puerto Ricans (and with the crucial help of Puerto Rican lawyers and citywide elected officials), Dominican voters registered for the Community Development Agency elections (CDA controls the municipal allocation of antipoverty funds into communities). Their slate, a mixture of Puerto Ricans and Dominicans, fell one vote short in 1984 of gaining control.

Today, while Dominicans and Puerto Ricans still have their separate social clubs, and some continue to follow the politics "back home," new political organizations and alliances, springing out of their similar structural position in New York society, are forging a new unity. The community and its problems are not seen as temporary or for others to solve, but as part and parcel of their condition as Latino ethnics in their "home" environment. In Chicago, Puerto Ricans and Chicanos have built similar political alliances.

Personal Ties

While political activism and cultural expressions within a shared North American context signal the birth of the Latino group, another critical factor is found at a more intimate level, in intermarriage. Data on Latino intermarriage in New York City show that while 46 percent of Puerto Rican marriages, 55 percent of Dominican marriages, and 62 percent of South American marriages are exogamous, these were not marriages with Anglos but between Latinos of different nationalities. Most Puerto Ricans who married outside their group married Dominicans or other Latinos; the same was true (and to a greater degree) for the smaller Latino groups. Intermarriage, arising out of social and economic intimacy, coupled with the strong sense of a common Latino past and the pressure from the larger society, will ensure for the next generation a stronger sense of the new identity.

Although efforts to unify different Hispanic nationalities as Latinos could fail, it is important to notice that unification is still a new phenomenon, emerging from diverse political, social, and cultural contexts. The Latinos' structural similarity within American society, the changes in state policies towards the poor and the minorities, the present threat to the once-popular pluralist ideology, the dispersal of the different Latino groups from their traditional areas, the impact of Latino mass media on the identity of the group, the patterns of intermarriage among certain Latino groups, and the realization among many that their stay in the United States might be permanent, generate a new impetus to form a collective consciousness.

I am not saying, as it would have been easy to say, that ethnic groups are simply interest groups seeking resources in and from the state. If that were the case, it would have been impossible for Puerto Ricans and Dominicans in New York, or Chicanos and Puerto Ricans in Chicago, to unite under a new consciousness, or for the poetry of Laviera and the songs of Blades to gain popularity, or for the high rates of Latino intermarriage to exist. Their organizational and/or creative efforts would have excluded each other. Instead, under internal and external pressures, guided by both elites and intellectuals with new visions, these groups are rearranging their symbols to emphasize their commonality as an increasingly powerful Latino people. □

Notes

[1] The term Hispanic excludes racial and cultural differences found within the group. Etymologically, Hispanic evokes Spaniards or their descendants. Latino (from Latin American) is a more inclusive denomination accounting for those who come from, or descend from, a specific geographical area where the Spanish and Portuguese legacy is dominant but not exclusive. It recognizes the presence and importance of nonwhite populations and cultures (Amerindian and African) in the forging of the new group.

[2] Felix Padilla, *Latino Ethnic Consciousness: The Case of Mexican Americans and Puerto Ricans in Chicago* (Notre Dame: University of Notre Dame Press, 1985).

[3] The idea of unity among the different republics (the Colombian Federation of Bolivar) is a common theme in the socialization process and in the press. Because of the small national markets, Latin American media, especially film and television, constantly present themes that will attract viewers from all republics. Artists and sport teams from the different countries constantly tour the region borrowing personnel and themes from each other.

[4] Jesus Ranguel, "Survey Finds Hispanic Groups More Unified," *New York Times*, September 8, 1984, p. 22; Pamela G. Hollie, "Courting the Hispanic Market," *New York Times,* December 26, 1983, p. D1; David Vidal, "Study Shows Hispanic Residents in Favor of Bilingual Way of Life," *New York Times,* May 13, 1980, p. 1.

[5] Ranguel, *op.cit.*, p. 22.

[6] Tato Laviera, *AmeRican Folklore* (n.p.: Arte Público, 1984).

Deborah Meier

GOOD SCHOOLS ARE STILL POSSIBLE

But Teachers Must Be Freed from System "Mandates"

I came to New York City in the fall of 1966, and began teaching in Central Harlem a few months later. Within the next two years the schools were embroiled in two strikes. Parents were organized and vocal; teachers believed their recently won powers to be threatened; the city was divided by race and class. And yet there was a lively sense that the old system was done for: change of some sort was on the agenda. Decentralization, pedagogical innovations, parent control, teacher empowerment, accountability, public access, increased state and federal monies. These were the slogans of the day.

At their worst, the city's schools were never bad in quite the way the public imagined. My friends used to marvel that I had the "courage" to teach in a Harlem public school. They imagined schools disorderly and chaotic, filled with violence, knives flashing. Such things could be seen from time to time, but most of us taught in moderately orderly schools, with generally benign, even at times overly docile, though uninterested, children. It was tension rather than actual violence that wore down most school people. Our working conditions were often intolerable, but in ways that seemed either hard to explain or trivial to outsiders.

The real issues that concerned us were rarely noticed by the press, the politicians, the parent organizations, the school boards, or even by our own teachers' union. Instead, ersatz issues were endlessly addressed, and they exhausted us. Violent children and low reading scores were the symbols everyone agreed to talk about; these made for drama and slogans but little understanding.

Absence of respect for the people who made up the roster of school life—parents, kids, teachers, principals—was what was really driving us crazy. Schools reflected this in many ways—mostly trivial, cumulatively devastating. Inventively humiliating procedures began the moment one applied for a job, as one wandered down the Central Board corridors of 110 Livingston Street hoping not to get scolded as one tried to untangle endless Catch-22s. The headline battles ignored the participants' experiences and their perceived complaints. The conversations that teachers, and parents as well, held among themselves remained private, as though even they thought them unworthy of exposure, of "serious" people's concern. There was the state of the school toilets as well as the required daily lesson plans, the time-clock and the endless interruptions.

We were never the carriers of our own stories. We never trusted our own voices. Reforms came, but we didn't make them. They were invented by people far removed from schools—by "experts." And somehow teachers were never considered experts. Such reforms bypassed the kind of school-by-school changes, both small and structurally radical, that teachers and parents might have been able to suggest—changes that, however slow, could have made a powerful difference.

Fundamental school-based reform has been the major casualty of the post-1960s reforms. By the early 1970s both teachers and parents, the new actors of the 1960s, had retreated to their more familiar postures. Parents withdrew to their workplaces and teachers once again closed their doors hoping only to be left alone. The "experts" rushed in. Every time a fault was found, a system-wide solution was offered. And only those changes that could be translated into system-wide, replicable programs seemed worth discussing. If it couldn't be marketed on a grand scale, it was hardly worth exploring. The kind of detailed specificity that teachers could offer seemed a mere nuisance to the policy makers.

And so the proposed solutions led teachers to be treated like interchangeable parts. A rule that made sense in one setting had to cover all settings. Every apparently good protest gave birth to a new mandate, a new piece of legislation, a new contractual clause, a new pedagogical or curriculum prescription. And with every "reform" we encountered new nightmares.

Let me be specific.

Our concern for improved literacy (sparked by the exposure of low test scores) created a mammoth drive to improve test scores. Improved test scores, alas, are best achieved by ignoring real reading activity. School libraries were gradually closed and the librarians eliminated in favor of remedial teachers and remedial reading "labs" filled with expensive prepackaged kits and reading programs rather than real books. Federal funds earmarked for libraries were now spent on "software"—filmstrips and computer programs. District reading coordinators focused on finding the "best" reading system and training teachers to "operate" it, rather than on understanding how children learn to read and the value of being literate. As the curriculum began to imitate the tests, the test-coaching programs became school norms. Children rarely met books intended to be read from front to back. Paragraphs replaced chapters; predictable multiple-choice questions replaced conversation about books. Reading scores went up; literacy collapsed.

There were exceptions. Many good teachers kept doing what they knew was right, and brave principals plugged ahead at educating kids (they would coach for the tests at the last moment, hoping that their scores would not fall hopelessly behind their neighboring "competitors"). A few decentralized districts used newly won local control to unleash talent, to support teachers and principals with ideas, to encourage parent/teacher collaboration. But they did so amid a system that was becoming increasingly test-driven, prepackaged, and bureaucratized.

And then, in the mid-1970s, the schools experienced a major trauma—equal in impact to the late 1960s battles for community control. The city laid off more than 15,000 teachers in response to its financial crisis. A stunning blow—though, as critics noted, no one in the mammoth Central Board offices was laid off.

The impact of this layoff has been virtually undiscussed. In a highly personal profession, the sudden disappearance of so many people, and the attendant reassignment of thousands of others, caused pain and then a kind of numbing. Although it's true that money alone won't buy change, the idea that a system can both ruthlessly cut back on its teaching staff and make educational breakthroughs is absurd. Teachers' salaries were frozen during this period of steady inflation. Class sizes went up, support for the remaining teachers was cut, and school principals were hopelessly mired in new administrative tasks.

There was no one to lead an effective fight to save our schools. The United Federation of Teachers (UFT—the American Federation of Teachers local) tried to assume this role. From the 1950s to mid-1960s the UFT had pioneered a whole array of proposed structural reforms. But the community control fight had both undercut the union's educational position and split apart the city's pro-education coalition. Under attack from all its usual allies for not minding its own business—traditional bread-and-butter demands—the UFT had accepted the more modest posture of factory-style adversarialism. This had not won it friends either. Nor, in face of layoffs, was factory-style militancy useful. In turn, the union's inability to avert such massive layoffs, had an impact on teacher self-confidence, as it did on organized parent groups, who saw years of work destroyed overnight. New York's racial minorities had already lost their 1960s enthusiasm and militancy, and were suffering the first stages of official "benign neglect." They too were largely silent. There was no fight left in anyone.

We were back to business-as-usual, but one legacy of the 1960s remained. No one could now publicly acknowledge that "some children" might be less "teachable" than others. This powerful critical idea was, however, translated, as usual, into a simple-minded mandate. All must now score above-grade (however ludicrous such an idea might be statistically)—regardless of race, color, or social class (although class was rarely mentioned). And, as the social problems of families increased, so did the school's burdens—even though the accepted view of the school's role remained strictly "cognitive." Cognitive got translated into "measurable," which led back to test scores.

In this disheartening atmosphere I found a haven in a maverick school district, where a charismatic young superintendent, Anthony Alvarado, supported by the East Harlem political establishment, was unleashing a mini-wave of real reform. He called upon teachers to make their own local revolution. Within ten years District 4 established twenty small alternative schools led by innovative teacher-directors. As these twenty were gradually established, they sparked change also in the now less-populated neighborhood schools. Although not all the changes were educationally first-rate, they provided opportunities for teachers and children and a welcome feeling of optimism. Alvarado argued, cajoled, manipulated. He attracted talent, he made schooling seem an adventure. He never downplayed professionalism, didn't knock teachers, avoided looking for villains. He didn't mandate one universal top-down system for improvement. He was a maverick who enjoyed mavericks, and he gave many of them a chance to explore—without pressure for quick results or an eye on the media. In fact, he kept things quiet for us, and thrived on minimal confrontations with the outside world. He was also rare in his calm expectation that he would be with us for a long time. (Few of the city's thirty-two district superintendents have lasted more than a few years.)

During those ten years we lived in a protected world, doing our work—steadily and sturdily. Five teachers and I founded Central Park East (CPE) in the fall of 1974 as a progressive school at a time when everyone claimed such an "open" style was dead. We began a second school (CPE II) in 1979 and a third (River East) in 1982. In 1986, under Alvarado's successor, Carlos M. Medina, we opened a secondary school, thus providing East Harlem with a progressive educational institution for youngsters all the way through high school.

During this same period, the city got a new chancellor, Frank Macchiarola. He took an opposite tack. Macchiarola handled politicians, corporations, foundations, and news reporters marvelously well. He promised big changes—always system-wide. We had grown accustomed to federal and state accountability schemes attached to various funded programs, but Macchiarola promised a new citywide accountability system. Teachers were the workers, Macchiarola boasted, and students the products. Our products should roll off our assembly line classrooms in uniformly proper condition—with plenty of inspections along the way. In reality, the new systems were mainly more of the same: more tests, more officially sponsored coaching, plus undisguised warnings that test scores better go up.

By hook or crook, most of us complied. It was pretty straightforward, and only seemed "crooked" to those who remembered that good assessment devices should not be taught to or coached for. (Any more than an eye exam—which loses value if examinees are "too well" prepared.) In fact, in the "old days" such test-specific coaching had been rigorously prohibited.

Since we now used exactly the same reading tests every year from grades 2–8, teaching to the test was fairly easy. Many schools did virtually nothing but test practice from January through April. With no new ideas, larger class sizes and the same old teachers, the city's scores experienced a remarkable and steady rise. (By 1986 most New York elementary school students were scoring above average!)

Yet no one in the city's high schools praised us for sending them better readers. In fact, things got worse in the high schools. By the mid 1980s a majority of black and Hispanic youngsters were dropping out without diplomas. But Macchiarola managed the news well enough to keep this data out of the public eye until after he departed in the spring of 1983.

At the same time, new regulations for special educational services for the handicapped were creating an ever larger and more expensive bureaucracy, requiring lots of testing and record keeping to stay in legal compliance. Over 10 percent of the city's pupils were soon labeled "handicapped"—nearly 120,000 children! Thousands of social workers, psychologists, and educational evaluators (former teachers) were hired, not to remediate, not to assist teachers, parents or kids, but simply to screen—to test, assess and prescribe. At the end of expensive (but shoddy, by average professional standards) evaluation processes, children were neatly labeled, and specific written school goals set:

"Given ten two-digit addition examples, the student will use concrete materials to solve eight correctly"; or "given teacher supervision, praise and positive reinforcement, the student will attend to difficult assignments for five minutes, three times out of four, as recorded by teacher." (Taken from the Division's Manual)

A vast statewide law (called Chapter 53) mandating assessment of all new students for possible handicapping or gifted conditions was instituted in 1980. Thus another vast bureaucracy started testing five- and six-year olds. Finding the results of the first assessment unpalatable (30 percent were found "handicapped" and 2 percent "gifted") Macchiarola allegedly asked for new scoring norms. The result was that children entering kindergarten now had a better chance of scoring "gifted" (30 percent) and very little chance of being labeled "handicapped." Not a bad strategy, since we have few resources available to do anything about handicapped kindergarteners (a child has to be two years behind in reading to qualify for special education monies). Besides, everyone liked being called "gifted." The proliferation of "gifted" kindergarten classes was one result of this screening program. Meanwhile, a straightforward professionally administered hearing and vision exam for every entering student remains a utopian goal in our medically sophisticated city.

From the mid-1970s to the early 1980s, little happened except more window-dressing. A demoralized staff teaching larger classes on smaller paychecks gave the city its rising test scores. It did so both to "look good" and because the pressure on kids to get better scores increased. Macchiarola's other innovation was the institution of two "gates" at fourth and seventh grades through which students scoring in the bottom 25th percentile could not pass. Inflated scores kept the number of holdovers to manageable proportions, but otherwise the only effect of these "gates" was to increase the number of students entering high school as adults—beyond the school-leaving age.

The good press Macchiarola's reforms received made their spread inevitable. Why not a citywide elementary science test? A social studies test? And by 1983 the N.Y. State Board of Regents got on the accountability bandwagon, instituting one of the most detailed and far-reaching top-down educational packages in the nation. This new plan spelled out a statewide curriculum, complete with grade-by-grade testing mechanisms, from kindergarten through twelfth grade, for every accredited school—public, independent or parochial—in the state.

By a mere stroke of a pen, it solved the most complex educational issues. By regulation there was now a plan uniform for all, more "rigorous" and more detailed than former state guidelines and general graduation requirements. It promised equity and quality if students and teachers did their jobs as they were told.

Unlike the high schools, which the Regents curriculum had long controlled, the elementary schools had had room for considerable diversity. The Central Board for years had encouraged individualized instruction, matching curriculum to the child, and pedagogical innovation. Even though this rhetoric was not backed by structural support, at least it gave schools and teachers some elbow room. Some interesting high school innovations had also sprung up, offering alternate approaches to providing adolescents—particularly those most "at risk"—with academic skills. During Macchiarola's tenure as chancellor it was precisely this elbow room that had steadily been invaded.

So while New York City's Board voiced opposition to the state mandates, it had, in fact, already begun to practice what the state was preaching.

All of this was occurring at a time when the employment prospects for New York's "at risk" students—always grim—had reached new lows. A social and political climate hardly friendly to poor minority families left these vulnerable young people with little hope. Even a high school diploma began to seem an unlikely dream. Still, there was no protest.

The union did voice objections, but it had limited clout. Its 1960s militancy had depended on the capacity to strike. Since most of those directly hurt by a strike were constituents of little political importance, and state penalties on strikers severe, the UFT had abandoned its old style of militancy. New York City's students were no longer a cross-section of its voting population. In 1964 over half the students were white. Twenty years later only 23 percent were white and 60 percent were poor enough to qualify for federal food subsidies. The union now depended on its members' electoral muscle, and on alliances with other powerful groups. It had to worry, also, about its public image. Gradually the union's leadership began to address issues with an eye to that broader public. This made it more flexible about traditional union issues, but it was now in a bind about exposing those deteriorating working conditions that it had no effective way of dealing with. It was now dependent on what "others" thought, not just on what teachers found credible. And these "others" were often corporations, business coalitions, and powerful public figures. Many of these "others" appreciated the union's new statesmanship, but they also wanted quick and measurable "results"—something to show for their support of public education.

Overworked teachers and principals, who never had much authorized autonomy anyway, were too overwhelmed with new city and state regulations to find the heart and energy to fight them off. They ignored some, followed others, were cynical about most. Macchiarola had provided a more friendly press; there was a kind of peace between the union and the world,

and the state would now tell us what to do. At least we couldn't be blamed if it went wrong.

Then, for a brief moment in the spring of 1984, there was a flowering of hope and possibility. The mayor and the Board of Education had been forced to select a most unlikely successor to the retiring Macchiarola.

Mayor Koch's choice was Robert Wagner, a respected insider's politician. Wagner is, of course, white. Two minority candidates were also included in the final list of nominees: Tom Minter, a well-credentialed black educator then working at the Central Board, and Anthony Alvarado, superintendent of East Harlem's District 4. The three ran a lively public campaign. Although Alvarado captured interest everywhere, it seemed a foregone conclusion that Wagner would get the job. But the state commissioner, Gordon Amsbach, vetoed Wagner on the technical grounds that he had insufficient teaching experience. Consternation! Disbelief! What to do next? There was talk of starting a new search. But as a *New York Times* editorial noted in response to black and Hispanic outrage, doing so would expose the previous search as a charade. Alvarado was appointed chancellor of the public schools.

Alvarado, who rose from teacher to principal to district superintendent before he was 30, was now positioned to make history in American education. A sense of excitement stirred parent groups and the teachers' union. Within eight months, however, his promising career was tangled in an investigation of possible corruption and misuse of funds. Most of the charges were minor and some merely exposed standard system practices, but the very number of them seemed suspicious. His responses were evasive; media and public alarm grew; Alvarado resigned. The only educational legacy of his brief tenure was the creation of all-day kindergartens.

The board then selected Nathan Quinones as chancellor. Formerly head of the high school division (the only part of the system incontrovertibly still under Central control), he had the additional advantage of being Hispanic, thus averting any accusations that Alvarado's fall might have had racial implications. Quinones was a safe choice. (Ed. note: As we went to press Quinones had just announced that he was taking early retirement.)

The agenda stemming from the chancellor's office has slowed. Neither bottom-up nor bold top-down initiatives were Quinones's style. Nor did he enjoy the public/media "stature" of either Macchiarola or Alvarado. Reducing dropouts, truancy, and absenteeism were his stated major goals—a little each year. These are also the latest federal and state targets. New reports, time lines, and task forces are in place. The state and city have set up teams to "help" schools write plans for how they will improve—higher test scores and lower absentee figures. Lower class size in the early grades is probably Quinones's most important initiative. A subtle campaign to recentralize the city's schools is probably the most dangerous, although it's not clear who is initiating this one.

As I stare at the piles of memos and forms that confront me as a school principal, the job appears somewhere between a joke and an impossibility. The staff and I are directed instantly to implement new programs to resolve current social crises, to use the latest research on teaching, to tighten supervision, increase consultation, and to report back in detail on all the above. There are pages of new rules and regulations to study: the Regents plan alone would take a few months to make sense of. Responding to it would take a lifetime. Meanwhile, finding the funds to buy paper, repair our single rented typewriter, fix a computer, or tune the piano requires most of my time and imagination.

It's even harder this year. Money to run our school is always tight—an adventure in ingenuity and making do. Now an innovative UFT-sponsored plan to create workplace democracy has created instead schoolwide chaos. Previously principals received a lump sum (approximately $10–15 per student for the school year) to spend on all non-textbook needs. This year, the Central Board directed that teachers receive $200 each to order their own supplies. Sounds good! They were given an abbreviated catalogue, two weeks to complete their orders and no time for schoolwide

consultation. Nor was anyone told that the $200 was not in addition to, but largely in place of, routinely available funds. The result: classrooms have gained some well-deserved extras but we have all lost the critical basics: paper, pencils, duplicating fluid, stamps, etc. Once again, a centrally imposed solution defeats an essentially sound idea.

Meanwhile the building in which we work is falling apart. Radiators leak, toilets back up, doors have no locks, windows are broken, fluorescent lights don't work because they need ballasts (which I am not allowed to go out and buy), desks are gouged with graffiti, and because we have too few chairs we have to carry them from classroom to classroom. The payroll secretary has more power over teachers than I do—she can dock their salaries and generally harass them if they are late, or forget to punch out, or are sick without a doctor's note. The custodial engineer is the boss of the building, and can prohibit teachers from coming in early or staying late, or dropping by on off days.

Any halfway decent camp sets aside more time for collective planning for a two-month summer recreation program than teachers are provided to plan a ten-month educational program. We are ordered to stick to "cognitive" (academic) goals, but our students still come to us with the exponential weight of unsolved economic and social family crises. We are ordered to give every child an hour's homework nightly—exact numbers of minutes per child per grade are centrally dictated—and expected to also read, assess, and comment on each. All in one twenty-four hour day. We spend more time and energy making sure that no one who doesn't deserve it gets a free or reduced price school lunch than we do on making the lunchroom a decent place. In a system that refers to the midday meal as a "feeding program" (in England, it is called "dinner"), it is clear that the people doing the "feeding" and those being "fed" are not valued too highly.

Prestigious commissions—like Carnegie and Holmes—speak, at last, of the need to improve the status of teaching, of giving the people who must implement programs the power to design them. And they are right. But they often miss the significance of the details that stand in our way. The struggle is not only over weighty academic rights, but also these seemingly small and petty ones. Reform must address both. But it won't until teachers get more actively involved in the reform movement.

One pioneering county in Florida is planning to rename teachers "executives." But the teachers I know do not object to being called "teachers"; it is teaching that they want to get back to! They resent the time spent "managing," scrounging, making do, not the time spent "teaching." Serious, rooted change cannot happen unless the knowledge of those who do the job is tapped. To make this possible requires support, time—and patience. Patience above all. Mandates only seem efficient because they can at least make claim to "quick cures," in time for the next election. But when we speak of educating for democratic citizenship, rather than job training, patience is at the heart. Perseverance, reflection, flexibility, intelligence . . . but also patience. Schools will not become educationally successful by deadlines and mandates. The only kind of mandates that could help would be of quite a different order. Can mandates be designed that support school-based initiative, inquiry, and decision making? Could we mandate that schools provide teachers with time to talk and plan together? Or that schools be required to make

their beliefs and practices public? For a starter maybe we could mandate that employers give parents time off to visit school.*

School people don't insist on working in a vacuum, "doing their own thing." They want to be "exposed." The more "exposure" the better—so that schooling becomes visible in many ways, not just through numbers and statistics. Formal schooling, after all, occupies at least a dozen of our most impressionable years, and we are involved again as parents when our children go to school. Nearly half a lifetime; years that have enormous influence on public habits, values, and competencies. Hardly an insignificant topic for public discussion. This kind of attention might produce lots of criticism, not just applause. But while teachers (including me) might not always like informed criticism, we would acknowledge more of it, and it could thus lead to real discourse. Strangling schools with red tape and system-wide mandates—big ones or little ones—is what is truly inefficient. Until those who make decisions, including "the public," can see the specific local connections between policy and practice, we will not make the breakthroughs that our rhetoric demands. There just isn't a faster route. □

* A report on the kind of structural change being proposed here appears in an interview in the Spring 1987 issue of the *American Educator*, "Shared Decision Making at the School Site," based on an AFT-backed plan in Hammond, Indiana.

Maxine Phillips

WILL WE SAVE THE CHILDREN?

New York City as Child Abuser

Mayor Koch's face stared out from the bus poster. "I want you to have my children," the caption read, part of a stepped-up campaign to recruit badly needed foster homes. After six years of the Koch administration, its brazenness should not have shocked. Still, it did, for the photo and slogan underscored the callousness with which successive city and state administrations have treated the needs of New York City's abused and neglected children.

"This problem didn't start with Ed Koch or Mario Cuomo," says Richard Murphy, coordinator of the Neighborhood Family Services Coalition, but they have let it continue. Noting that the mayor prides himself on a combative "leadership style," Murphy believes that Koch has "made it easier for people to look away" from what is perceived as mostly a problem of the poor (read: blacks and Hispanics).

In fall 1986 the Coalition issued a comprehensive report on child abuse and neglect in New York City, *The Continuing Crisis*, which faulted forty years of official "political management/damage control" (and could have gone back a lot further).[1] The report spelled out specific steps, some expensive, others not, that could alleviate the suffering of the 60,000 children reported to be abused or neglected each year. It stated that its sponsors would know they had failed if another blue-ribbon panel were appointed as a result. That hasn't happened. Media publicity about the latest child-abuse "crisis," the coalition work of Murphy and others, and city efforts to cut case loads, hire new staff, increase foster-care reimbursements, and coordinate protective and preventive services—plus lawsuits now pending in the courts—promise some relief.

The question remains: Why is it so hard for us to care for one of the most vulnerable populations in our city?

A hundred and thirty years ago thousands of homeless children, mostly offspring of immigrants, roamed New York streets, hawking newspapers or begging, stealing, prostituting themselves. They were seen as criminals and near-criminals who might yet be saved by industriousness and exposure to a different environment. They could be saved by being sent to the frontier to work on farms and be cared for (read: indentured in many cases) by country folk who would offer wholesome homes. The first "Orphan Train" left New York in 1854, and until this exploitation of unpaid labor became an issue, good-hearted New Yorkers thought they were doing the right thing by contributing to this cause.

Orphanages and adoption efforts were primarily for children whose parents were dead. Although there had been instances, even in colonial times, of public concern about abuse of children living in their own homes, the landmark case that sparked reform in that area took place in New York in 1874. A church worker, horrified by the brutal beatings suffered by a child forever to be known in the textbooks as Mary Ellen, persuaded the American Society for the Prevention of Cruelty to Animals to bring charges against the stepmother and father. At the time there were no organizations devoted to protecting children or statutes under which to prosecute abuse of children. Understanding of neglect came later.

Only within the past twenty-five years has child abuse per se become a public policy issue. The watershed date was 1962, when Dr.

Henry C. Kempe and four other physicians published "The Battered Child Syndrome" in the *Journal of the American Medical Association*. Since 1946, when advances in diagnostic radiology allowed doctors to see both old and current fractures, there had been speculation that some children's recurring injuries were not accidental. The article made clear what many doctors had refused to face—that some parents repeatedly beat and injured their children. As a result, a national law was passed requiring physicians to report suspected abuse. States enacted legislation requiring other professionals to report; forerunners of the twenty-four-hour child-abuse hotline and state child-abuse registry were born. Today in New York State, police officers, teachers, and social workers as well as health professionals are legally obliged to report suspected abuse and neglect. Neighbors are also encouraged to do so.

Thus most articles on the subject speak of the dramatic rise in *reporting* rather than actual incidence, because no one can guess whether there is more or less child abuse now than twenty or thirty years ago. What has changed is our awareness of the problem.*

Early efforts to deal with abuse involved removing the child from the home. By the mid-1970s the emphasis had shifted to keeping children in the home, working with parents, and providing increased training and reimbursement for foster parents. New York State passed the Child Protective Services Act in 1973 and the Child Welfare Reform Act of 1979, which called for preventive services to keep children in their own homes and cut down on foster care. The issues were identified at a time of economic growth and liberal social policy, but the legislation was passed as the country entered a period of economic recession and political conservatism.

The ways to prevent most child abuse and neglect are known, but they are costly. Day care, homemaker service, counseling, financial aid, quality foster care are in short supply. "Politicians always take the cheap way out," says child welfare researcher Mary Ann Jones, whose study on preventive services was used to help gain passage of the 1979 Child Welfare Reform Act.[3] "It's been easy to pass legislation for mandatory reporting, but now that everyone's neighbor can turn them in, the system is swamped." She points out that the more people report suspected abuse and neglect, the lower the percentage of "indicated," or well-founded cases. About one in every two cases reported by a professional turns out to be valid. About one in three from neighbors and other people is "indicated." Every charge must be checked out within twenty-four hours, and Child Protective Services appears to do heroic work in meeting that goal.* But checking out complaints is frequently the end rather than the beginning. "Child Protective Services used to be a service," Jones complains. "Now it's an investigative apparatus." Too many cases, she charges, end with the notation, "Indicated. Case closed." In fact, a sampling by the state of a Special Services for Children office in Brooklyn showed that 40 percent of the families in which abuse or neglect was found were not referred to services. What happens to those families? No one knows until and unless they turn up again with a dead child or such life-threatening problems that drastic action is

---

* Most works on child abuse trace a dismal history of officially and privately sanctioned behavior toward children that would now be considered abuse. These actions were thought to be common in times when public floggings, torture, and maiming of adults were legal punishments. Yet in a recent book, historian John Demos argues that it is the stresses of modern life that have led to this problem. He quotes Robert B. Edgerton: "Child abuse . . . has become a serious social problem in the United States and in some other industrialized societies, yet it occurs infrequently or not at all in many of the world's [non-industrialized] societies."[2]

* There is no doubt that ex-spouses or disgruntled neighbors use the hotlines for harassment. But not all unfounded calls are malicious. There are several explanations for the discrepancies. A study by Giovannoni and Becerra on definitions of child abuse—which presented case vignettes to groups of doctors, social workers, police officers, and lawyers, then to groups of white, black, and Hispanic laypeople—found that laypeople were much more likely to consider situations serious than were professionals.[4] Whites were least likely to consider situations serious. There is also the possibility that untrained protective-services workers are not always able to detect abusive situations. In 1985 the turnover rate for protective-services workers in Manhattan was 89 percent, giving them hardly enough time in which to learn the nuances of difficult and highly emotionally charged situations.

taken. And what of the professionals and laypeople who have made reports? Although confidentiality is supposedly guaranteed, families often know who reported them, and professionals frequently find that any hope they had of influencing the family has disappeared in suspicion, even as the conditions remain unchanged.

No one who looks at the situation believes that better city services would mean no abused and neglected children. Pressures of poverty, overcrowding and homelessness, lack of education, substance abuse, mental illness, unemployment, and societal tolerance of violence against children won't be wiped out by bigger appropriations from Albany or City Hall. But in its response to the manifestations of these ills, doesn't society have an obligation to act more decisively against abuse of children?

The child welfare system has always been overwhelmed, but today two of the most striking factors that keep us from fulfilling that obligation are class prejudice and racism. Despite repeated findings that abuse cuts across all racial and class lines, public perception is that it is a problem of the lower classes and minorities.*

"It may sound very cold to say this," a black man with a background in social work recently told the *Village Voice*, "but I wish we had a good number of white kids beaten to death and abused almost to death. Then maybe the mayor would pay more attention . . . ." Says Dick Murphy: "There's a feeling at City Hall that there's a portion of kids who can't make it. . . . There's no will to solve the problem."

Murphy sometimes thinks that as a caseworker in the welfare department under John Lindsay he had more power than he does now as executive director of a voluntary agency. "There was a feeling then that you could change things." But the 1960s and the hopes of the civil rights movement that fueled its reform movements are far away. Few now speak of alliances between clients and workers.

Instead, public reaction ranges from a punitive one that would break up families to a not-so-benign neglect based on an "appreciation" of "cultural differences." When I told friends I was working on this article I often found two reactions: (1) Why do they let so many children go back to dangerous homes? and (2) You have to be careful about your middle-class bias. There are cultural differences in raising children that look like abuse to us but aren't to other people. Translations: those people are either "animals" or sick and their children will be better off without them; and poor people and ethnic and racial minorities are more violent, but that's the way they are, and we shouldn't intervene.

The answer to the first question can be summed up in the old adage "blood is thicker than water." Ask any abused child whether he wants to stay with his parents or go elsewhere, and the answer will be to stay with the parents. Courts will often go with the child's wishes against the recommendations of protective-services personnel, especially since the actual services available are so minimal. In addition, it is extremely difficult to predict which situation will turn into a death-dealing one. Parents who cannot care for their children need help to be able to do so.

The second statement is more troubling, for no sweeping generalization can be made about any one group of people. In their study, Giovannoni and Becerra found that even though laypeople rated *all* examples as more serious than did professionals, they tended to rate physical injury as relatively less serious. Blacks, for instance, were more concerned about matters relating to protection and supervision of children and failure to fulfill general parenting responsibilities while Hispanics showed particular concern over matters of physical injury, sexual abuse, and drug and alcohol abuse. The authors warn: "Cultural differences in the use of corporal punishment cannot justifiably be translated into evidence of

---

* Although poor people and minorities are overrepresented statistically, it can be argued that they are more likely to come to the attention of public authorities than middle- and upper-class child abusers. A doctor told one researcher that a child seen in a public hospital emergency room was five times more likely to be reported than a child with the same injury seen by a private doctor. A nationwide study of family violence found that the factors having the strongest bearing on family violence were age, income, and employment. Families earning more than $20,000 had a rate of violence half that of families earning under $5,999.[5]

cultural differences in the acceptance of 'child abuse.' "

Parents who fear that their children will become involved in a drug culture if left to run in the streets restrict their movements, perhaps beating them if they stay out too late. A Puerto Rican mother tells of hitting her seventeen-year-old daughter when the youngster returned home at 3 A.M. To this mother, the well-publicized mores of the Upper East Side, where children of rich parents stay out all night bar hopping, seem neglectful and dangerous. This mother runs a greater chance, though, of ending up in the abuse-allegation network than any of those parents who have no idea where their children are.

None of the lay groups in the study had any trouble identifying situations involving sexual abuse, extreme physical abuse, and lack of supervision as very serious. The challenge for the state is not to ignore what are widely accepted as abuse situations, but to intervene effectively and to respond to what the community sees as abuse and neglect.

Class prejudice and racism can be openly acknowledged as barriers to helping children. The second reason for our failure to aid children is a more subtle cultural one having to do with how we view them and how we were viewed when we ourselves were children.

Agamemnon may have been punished for it, but he believed he had the right to sacrifice Iphigenia; Abraham could have killed Isaac with no legal repercussions. Only quite recently has anyone questioned the idea of children as property. We remain hesitant about interfering in the parent-child relationship. The dominant culture accepts the idea of physical punishment of children, and so, say Giovannoni and Becerra, "In a very real sense all parents are at risk of some time crossing the threshold into 'child abuse.' " In a sense, many of us *have* been abused, and it is that experience of helplessness and anger that shapes much of our ability to respond to children. Most of us grew up subjected to either emotional or physical violence or very much aware that we could be. This was not perhaps of the severity we associate with "real" abuse, but as Alice Miller points out in *For Your Own Good: Hidden Cruelty in Child-Rearing and the Roots of Violence*, the costs are high.[6] We are both immobilized by our own unacknowledged rage and impotence, and caught up in a cultural web of complicity that supports that violence, drawing very fuzzy lines between "strict disciplinarians" and "child abusers."

The emotional effects of child abuse are well-documented—the children who grow up to take out their rage on society and on their own children or turn it inward in self-destructive ways. What is less well-documented, but follows, is that all of us who as children were physically coerced carry that rage and fear. It may not be as great as that experienced by more brutalized people, but it is there and it immobilizes us. A hint of this occurs in accounts of physicians who refused to acknowledge and report cases of abuse when they saw them. "Potentially severe ambivalence may be generated from the professionals' dual identification, with both the abused child and the abusing parent," say Giovannoni and Becerra. I would argue that the hidden memories of being small and powerless cause us to turn away from the problems of these children. Few people ever take out their rage on the authority figure who humiliated them, says Miller. Instead, the grown-up child takes it out on someone smaller.

That there has been such a major shift in attitudes regarding abuse indicates that massive public education could change our perceptions of children. Within recent memory wife-beating was not considered criminal. The women's movement changed that, and although spouse abuse still exists, social tolerance for it is diminishing. Social mores regarding children could also be changed.

But what can be done immediately? If poverty makes abuse more likely, then easing financial strains is a major remedy. David Tobis of Welfare Research, Inc., notes that fewer than 60 percent of eligible individuals in New York receive welfare. Thirty thousand mothers and children are inappropriately terminated from the welfare rolls every month, even though their financial status has not changed. Day care, expanded homemaker services, better trained and paid staff—all would help alleviate child abuse and neglect. They all cost money. Asked what a "pie-in-the-sky" budget to attack the problem would be, Dick Murphy notes that it's possible that this could be done for $1 billion. No one expects that.

His organization has assembled a coalition that is pressing for short-term goals:

• $5 million to upgrade salaries in the public and private sectors and introduce a differential between master's-degree and bachelor-degree social workers as an incentive for workers to seek more training;

• Better utilization of Special Services for Children's informational systems in order to clear cases more quickly;

• A 75-percent state reimbursement formula for financing preventive and protective services so as to eliminate the current incentive to label client needs in artificial ways tied to a bogus reimbursement formula.

The major long-term goal is to organize preventive, protective, and foster-care services as a "continuum of care" so that children do not get lost in the system.

Where would the money come from? An alternative budget drawn up by the City Project describes a need in 1987–88 for an additional $48 million to provide early intervention, increased staff salaries, increased child-care and homemaker services, neighborhood centers to service high-risk families and children, etc. [7] It's too late to use the tax giveback from this year, but the *Alterbudget* recommends such actions as extending mortgage-recording and real-property transfer taxes to cover cooperative apartments. Currently owners of cooperative apartments have not been subject to these taxes. Closing this loophole would result in an additional $60 million. The *Alterbudget* lists several other taxes or giveaways that could be tightened. The money is there. The will is not.

Between the time this article was written and when it appears in print, twenty-five or thirty children will have died of abuse or neglect in New York. *Their* pain will have ended. We can still do something about the thousands who remain.

Notes

[1] Brenda McGowan, Jeanne A. Bertrand, Amy Kohn, Anne S. Lombard, *The Continuing Crisis: A Report on New York City's Response to Families Requiring Protective and Preventive Services* (New York: Neighborhood Family Services Coalition, 1986).

[2] John Demos, *Past, Present, and Personal: The Family and the Life Course in American History* (New York and Oxford: Oxford University Press, 1986).

[3] Mary Ann Jones, *A Second Chance for Families: Evaluation of a Program to Reduce Foster Care* (New York: Child Welfare League of America, 1976).

[4] Jeanne M. Giovannoni and Rosina M. Becerra, *Defining Child Abuse* (New York: The Free Press, 1979).

[5] Murray A. Straus, Richard J. Gelles, and Suzanne K. Steinmetz, *Behind Closed Doors: Violence in the American Family* (New York: Anchor Press/Doubleday, 1980).

[6] Alice Miller, *For Your Own Good: Hidden Cruelty in Child-Rearing and the Roots of Violence* (New York: Farrar Straus & Giroux, 1983).

[7] *Alterbudget Agenda: Revenue and Expenditure Priorities for the New York City Budget 1987–1988* (New York: The City Project, 1986).

Theresa Funiciello

NEW YORK'S "WORK-NOT-WELFARE" PROGRAM

Governor Cuomo caught the attention of the social welfare world last year with the announcement of a jobs program he called "Work-not-Welfare." (Welfare here refers to Aid to Families With Dependent Children, AFDC, 94 percent of whose recipients in New York are single mothers and their children.) Cuomo's phrase was taken up quickly by state legislators and welfare professionals uncomfortable with "workfare," the term coined by William Safire for Richard Nixon and scorned for that reason by Democrats even when they've embraced a version of the idea through WIN (Work Incentive Program), the federally mandated program to help recipients become "self-supporting."

News of "Work-not-Welfare" leaked months before its actual announcement. Many in "the business" tried to stalk it down. Would it really offer a new approach to the income dilemma of many of New York's poor? Or was it just another way of punishing the wretched? Specifics were elusive. Calls to the state's Department of Social Services and the city's Human Resources Administration (whose own programs were said to be models for Cuomo's) yielded minimal results. Where was the paper? If there really was a new plan, there should have been reams of analyses and charts. Shortly after a *Village Voice* article suggested there really was no plan, the state issued a brief description of this latest effort to rescue the mothers of small children from what some

seem to think is the debauchery of child-rearing, if not from poverty.

Like the storybook emperor, "Work-not-Welfare" was stark naked. It bore a remarkable resemblance to WIN, which had been around since the late 1960s. In fact, a pamphlet published in 1969 by the National Welfare Rights Organization (NWRO) describing WIN anticipated virtually all the elements of the new state proposal. WIN had mandated welfare recipients in single-parent families with no children under six years of age to "register" for job training or actual jobs, few of which ever materialized. The WIN program is widely agreed to have failed; by 1977, the city's Human Resources Administration was unable to demonstrate more than a 7-percent placement rate of welfare mothers into jobs. Yet the new "Work-not-Welfare" program differed from WIN only in that it called for more aggressive placement efforts using the same self-contradictory and ineffective mechanisms as WIN, all in the name of making sure that welfare recipients "work." The single real programmatic difference in the Work-not-Welfare plan is a provision for recipients to "work off" their welfare checks—the essence of workfare.

After some scrutiny of the proposal, the legislature voted it down. Some lawmakers felt it was too costly; others saw in it the discriminatory targeting of minorities to even deader dead ends than before; still others rejected its weak day-care provisions. Through some budgetary sorcery, though, Cuomo managed to allocate enough money to generate the usual flurry of contracts with public and private agencies. The direct service providers, profit making and nonprofit alike, lined up for the dole. The studiers and program monitors got theirs, mostly from foundations. And New York's contribution to a national hysteria over welfare and work got under way. Again.

Like WIN, the new plan includes almost every conceivable training and work "experience" option—the beauty schools and business institutes, the literacy and job skills training programs, the general equivalency degree for high school dropouts. The lure for local welfare administrators is additional state dollars for welfare departments to try every conceivable way to get people off welfare and into jobs—in short, every effort to save welfare families from the dread disease, Dependency, by introducing them to the work ethic.

So why be cynical? Conceptually, providing training and work experience to people in need has undeniable appeal. The problem with the "Work-not-Welfare" effort, like its predecessors, is twofold: it fudges the question of where enough minimally decent jobs will be found; and, by targeting AFDC mothers across the board as the subjects of dependency, even though most of them already leave the rolls within two years, it inappropriately targets (and stigmatizes) some people, while leaving too many others out of any serious effort to promote employment and the work ethic.

Why is this so?

First clue: Beware of Messengers Bearing Gifts. One ought to be suspicious, in the current political climate, anytime significant sums of money are spent on new projects specifically designed to benefit welfare recipients. If the programs are so good, why are only welfare recipients "eligible" for them? There are thousands of unemployed and poorly employed people who would form long lines to sign up for a program they believed would benefit them. The government could even give priority to welfare recipients without excluding these others. For example, why aren't widows with small children, living on Social Security,

either pushed into these programs or at least allowed voluntary entrance? Surely they receive more national sympathy than welfare families, even though they cost more per capita in transfer payments and are intrinsically in the same position as most welfare families. Why don't we offer these, our bereaved sisters, the same opportunity to escape dependency? Does national ill will single out welfare recipients for a program that is in fact more punitive than helpful?

Second clue: The Silly Facts They Overlooked. The majority of the jobs created since 1980 pay the minimum wage, less than the poverty level for a family. *For the first time in decades in New York State, there are more poor people with employment income than "on welfare."* Though fewer as a percentage, wage-earning poor people increased in numbers faster during the 1980s than the welfare poor did. Of all single mothers in the city, 62.8 percent live below the poverty line. When they're employed outside the home, they earn 47 cents for every dollar earned by men. Most jobs available to them not only pay little to begin with, but the ladder of opportunity associated with them is barely a footstool. And, of course, there is an effective 100-percent tax on their earnings: generally speaking, for every dollar they earn beyond certain minimal work-related expenses, they lose a dollar in welfare benefits. When combined with food stamp and Medicaid losses, this means the family is usually worse off in a "job" than on welfare in financial terms.

Any employment program that proceeds without altering these basic economic realities has some other purpose than helping families in need. That purpose, of course, is to "inculcate the work ethic." But since most people work outside the home to better themselves financially, the workfare concept is the worst possible introduction to what "everyone else" is doing, even if we accept prevailing definitions of "work," about which more below.

Third clue: Limiting Aspirations. Although there are dozens of variations to choose from within the "Work-not-Welfare" plan, the recipients are most commonly steered into punitive, meaningless "workfare" slots. Participants are assigned tasks in various agencies for just enough hours to work off their welfare checks; they are prohibited from making even a dollar more, even if they're willing to work more hours. They get no vacation or sick time, no typical fringe benefits—a reflection, perhaps, of the fact that they may not be assigned work performed by "real" workers in the first place, and so are not being trained for "real" jobs. And the rate of sanctions (punishments consisting of serious reductions in welfare checks for 90 days or more) is high, as participants predictably treat these parodies of "opportunity" with the lack of enthusiasm they deserve. In the training programs other than workfare, the outlook is almost as grim. If a mother dares aspire to become a teacher, nurse practitioner, or MBA—"unapproved" programs—the essentials, like child care and carfare, are denied.

Fourth clue: If Bureaucracy Can't Run the Low Hurdles, Why Try the High? The city's Human Resources Administration, which administers the local "Work-not-Welfare" program, has been rocked by scandal in recent years; among commissioners and deputies there is a rapid turnover amid charges of incompetence and worse. How could an organization so wounded, overwhelmed, and barely functioning even before the plan was announced, be expected to implement a program for approximately 100,000 AFDC recipients considered "employable" and their approximately 200,000 children?

At their best, similar programs across the country studied by the Manpower Development Research Corporation show an abysmal "success" rate—one to seven percent more job placements than for control groups of welfare mothers who receive no special "training." Indeed, what the New York bureaucracy seems to do best is save money by cutting off welfare to the 25 percent of the city's AFDC "Work-not-Welfare" participants who are sanctioned for real or perceived transgressions: a mother of a two-year-old who volunteers for the program in order to "better" herself (only mothers with no children under the age of six are required to participate) and then decides, as many have, that it offers nothing, finds her benefits cut if she tries to withdraw. The welfare department argues that once a nonmandatory recipient volunteers, she has relinquished her right to automatic exemption based on the age of her youngest child. Unlike the rest of us who vote with our feet when confronted with inadequate services, the welfare mother becomes the indentured servant of the service-providing bureaucracy.

But the ultimate contradiction behind the program is that jobs with adequate wages simply don't exist beyond the training. What we have is a state-administered game of musical jobs. When the music stops, some poor persons are left without jobs while some others have them. Then we play it again, reshuffling to obscure the inability of our system of resource distribution to take in all the players. It was recognition of this failure that prompted the development of AFDC in the first place.

What is lost in the travesty that is poverty politics today is the central concern of the AFDC program: "the best interest of the child." Is it really in the child's best interest to be packed off to arbitrary day-care arrangements so Mommy can go off to a job that puts no more bread on the table than before? Yes, if one assumes that those who would rather stay home are lazy and that the program puts its participants on the road to better earnings in the foreseeable future. Absent that kind of opportunity, we have every right to question the basic definition of "work" against which mothers who remain homemakers are judged so severely.

Webster defines work as "physical or mental effort exerted to do or make something; purposeful activity; labor, toil." Our society's definition, however, is much narrower, in that work is considered to be only that effort for which one is paid a wage. A black woman hired as a nanny for an upper-class white family is a "worker"; as a mother struggling under adverse conditions to raise her own children on welfare, she is a parasite on society. Oddly enough, most jobs available to welfare mothers are variations of the work they do at home; they are caught in a definitional contradiction and an ideological trap reinforced by the familiar stereotypes about women who spend their nights making babies and their days watching television.

I have been a welfare mother and have worked with thousands of others. The only generalization that has any merit is that welfare mothers are much like the rest of society: all different. Most are off welfare within two years, independent of any work program. That many workfare advocates would impose the program on all recipients with children older than *three* suggests that stereotypes about lazy recipients and the dignity of wage labor alone have replaced serious concern about providing more real jobs and broadening our understanding of work, not to mention the "best interest of the child."

The women's movement has reminded us that women's labor in the home has economic and social value. The point obviously isn't that we should shove women back into the home whether or not they want to be there, but that we should extend the battle cry for "choice" from the *reproductive* sphere to the *productive* sphere. Ultimately, the state is incapable of making the best decision for masses of individual women; the only people who can and should make that decision are those who must live with the results.

Whatever our ideals vis-à-vis wage labor, it is questionable whether our economic system (which isn't likely to change in this century or the next) is capable of producing decent jobs with adequate pay and affordable, quality child care for all who need them unless there is some obvious need within the system itself: during World War II, when women were "needed," throngs of them were brought into the labor market at high wages and offered remarkably innovative child care options. As soon as the "need" was removed, the women and their kids were pushed out. So while we might wish

the political economy would provide more genuine opportunities, it is pure folly to demand that it do so, and for welfare recipients at that, in the absence of some unusual national crisis. We can hold on to our hopes for better jobs, but we ought not to stop there. As long as poor women's need for income is abandoned by both the right and the left at the altar of imaginary jobs, they will have little hope of attaining either. We need to expand the acceptable definitions of work and socially productive activity. Only then can we pay for it through government transfers, untarnished by the bigotry that surrounds AFDC. As the Social Security system amply demonstrates, it is relatively simple to send income to people. In the absence of other means of distributing resources, it may be simply the best solution for those left out of the "job standard." Until such time as a universal system of income security is real for all Americans, we need at least to separate the administration of AFDC from the work programs so that the latter do not substitute threats for opportunities.

A number of other capitalist countries such as Sweden and the Netherlands have quite successfully established universal income security, irrespective of one's relationship to the waged labor market. Some countries, in fact, recognizing the injustice inherent in labeling women's work in the home unproductive, are making serious efforts to include women's unpaid labor in the Gross National Product as part of a broader effort to look beyond jobs alone as the means of resource distribution. Until our society manages to reexamine itself at that level, women will continue to occupy the lowest positions and serve as the political pawns of opportunists and bureaucrats like those who play the empty game of "Work-not-Welfare" in New York. □

Anthony Borden

AIDS CRISIS

The Sorrow of the City

A gay man unflinchingly attends to his lover having seizures even though he knows that his own developing symptoms of AIDS may hold the same agony for him. A priest visits a homebound man with AIDS-related dementia who, convinced there is a disembodied spirit inhabiting his house, leads the father to every room, to bless them. A playwright details with excruciating immediacy how a man with AIDS becomes profoundly isolated though he is not left to die alone, reminding us that so many others surely are. And a member of the People With AIDS Coalition—somehow apologetic—puts off an interview yet again because he is feeling too weak. These are the sad and heroic stories of our city now. And every week, up to 100 of them come to a close.

That is, literally, not the half of it. In a city so recently famous for incidents of racially motivated violence, the terror spreads another way: up to 55 percent of all cases of AIDS here have struck blacks and Latinos, predominantly through intravenous drug use, passing from there to mothers and children (ninety percent of all children with AIDS are black or Latino). These groups do not have the political cohesion that gays have shown, and, particularly for Latinos who have contracted the HIV (human immuno-deficiency virus) virus through sex, the disease can be a harsh stigma even within their own community. As the crisis has mounted, the percentage of minority cases has risen, up six points from a few years ago. Dr. Rafael Tavares of Columbia-Presbyterian Medical Center believes that by 1991, when there will be up to 50,000 new cases in the country each year, 65 percent of those will be people of color.

Fifty thousand. By what mental arithmetic can one comprehend such a figure? The number of fans who pack Yankee Stadium for an important game. The number of American dead in the entire Vietnam War. That number every year.

The president has finally, feebly spoken out on AIDS. And New York City is at last considering the conversion of a hospital into an AIDS center (though it is unlikely to be available soon). At least there is a measure of public consciousness, thanks largely to the gay community, but an overwhelming ignorance remains. And no medical breakthrough could ever redeem the shameful, tardy response. By June 30 the city had recorded 10,601 cases—the highest by far in the country—and an estimated 500,000 were infected with the virus, including perhaps half the gay community. Nevertheless, the imaginative deficiency responsible for the delay persists. Particularly for politicians, but also for many straight people and for the mainstream (and even left) press, there is an inability to see AIDS as our illness. Most of the pious calls to check the spread of the disease before it reaches the "general population" are clear admissions that gays, people of color, drug users, are not generally considered part of "our" population.

As the available educational materials often stress, AIDS does not discriminate. Thus this crisis only bears out society's discrimination. AIDS is indeed a badge, not of deviancy, but of inequality. Our crisis of health may become a crisis of democracy.

This political and civic danger threatens New

York as much as anywhere. Although the sorrow of the city lies in its social tensions, it has an amazing cohesion all the same; the fine line between communal and confrontational impulses gives New York its real edge. Yet where we have the divisions white/black, rich/poor, male/female, the AIDS crisis has added one more destabilizing split: HIV negative/HIV positive. "What do we do then?" a lawyer asked, referring to mandatory testing. "Make the infected wear a yellow star?"

Although New York's response to AIDS has been leagues ahead of Washington's, the city has not proposed as comprehensive a plan as San Francisco. Edward Koch seems not to realize his moral obligation to show the world how to deal with AIDS, but he misses a pragmatic consideration too. Is New York destined to be seen as the center for AIDS care or only for AIDS infection? The answer to this question will determine whether the city can remain a home for so many kinds of people. Can it continue to provide opportunity and social liberation, or will it become instead a place to fear?

In spite of the stakes, Koch blunders badly, often parroting the reigning political nonsense. The Reagan administration is fixated on mandatory testing; Governor Cuomo wants criminal penalties for anyone who knowingly passes on the HIV virus. And Koch, capping a streak of unhelpful proposals, suggested testing all foreigners entering the city—for pleasure or business—regardless of how long they plan to stay. What greater absurdity will he have put forward in the time it takes for this article to go to press?

These proposals are not supported by medical authorities and only detract from—and even undermine—the real work of education, health care, and research. As much as any public official, Koch has contributed to this sideshow by subscribing to the false dichotomy between medical imperatives and civil rights. Fear is used the way exaggerated claims of national security are: to justify inhumane public policy. This reasoning allows Koch to imply that unappealing proposals are forced on us by extreme conditions. Conditions are extreme, but professional prescription calls for the opposite of such proposals.

The course of AIDS from first infection to development of frank symptoms to death can be up to fifteen years. And medical science has only vague statistical impressions to suggest how many people might have AIDS-related complex (ARC) or how many of those might go on to develope AIDS. The rights of those infected—from health care to housing to an untagged, unstigmatized life—must be pursued with as much vigor as the scientific research.

Koch's grandstanding aside, the city has initiated a number of progressive programs. There is an AIDS antidiscrimination unit in the Commission on Human Rights, and over the next year the Health Department will distribute one million condoms in bars, massage parlors, and porn theaters. But bureaucratic lethargy and the politicians' rhetoric of the Other have led to murderous results.

Proposals to make syringes available over the counter so that addicts will not have to share needles have been blocked at the state level. And a five-year city plan covering health care and education, to be administered by a central AIDS office, was seriously weakened during budget negotiations. Overall AIDS-related spending for the current fiscal year will reach $115 million, but that figure is deceptive, since 85 percent of it is mandated spending, particularly for health care. Still, the discretionary funds were substantially increased from last year, although wrongheadedly: while the allocation for voluntary testing and for tracking the infection tripled, that for education and counseling only doubled. This inverted sense of priorities can only be deadly, since testing without counseling is useless, while education alone can save lives.

Official squeamishness and outright disdain for public education are also reflected in the few public-service announcements that have been posted. Early efforts focused on straight women, while a more recent campaign has preached sexual abstinence to teenagers. These messages might complement a broadly directed educational strategy, but they appear in a context of severe neglect of the groups most at risk. When Koch reaches for the profound with his statement, "The only safe sex is no sex," he only sounds profoundly out of touch.

Koch *is* in touch with a politics that sees the crisis as the end of the sexual/social liberation efforts of the past two decades. For much of the argument over AIDS policy is a continuation of the ridiculous "debate" over morals and sexual behavior that the right has thrust on us. And with the intensified moralistic rhetoric comes an invigorated squadron of sex police always ready to keep us from confronting the disease. In response to a letter from Phyllis Schlafly, Jack Kemp and Bob Dole withdrew their sponsorship of a banquet honoring the surgeon general because his programs for AIDS education are too "soft" on homosexuality and sex generally. Under pressure from conservative religious forces, Koch follows with his abstinence campaign.

With official policy drawing such lines in the sexual battleground, private-sector homophobia is nurtured. At a time when the gay community is in shock, humbled, and endangered, it finds itself also under social siege. Although many religious groups from all denominations have taken a leading role in AIDS work, within the Catholic Church the ranks have closed. John J. McNeill, a Jesuit, has been ousted from his order because of his outspoken support of gays. The Bishop of Brooklyn rescinded permission for the gay Catholic group Dignity to hold mass in a church in the diocese. A priest who visits people with AIDS tried to convene a workshop at a meeting of clerics and found that no one would attend. Reported antigay violence doubled in 1986 over the 1985 level, much of it linked to the "AIDS backlash." Intolerance has become even more generally acceptable. As one gay man in the city told me, "I'm afraid of dying of AIDS, but I'm also afraid of surviving."

Most will never realize the extent of AIDS fear and discrimination, but already a vast number of people in the city have lost friends, colleagues. The death of so many young men and women in particular will have a devastating effect on the city's professional corps. In the arts that loss will be made up only in the smallest way by the morbid but intense inspiration the crisis has given to writers, painters, and others. But these aesthetic memorials, or the more private, personal ones, may not be sufficient to purge the tremendous weight of sadness that builds day by day. How does a city express its grief? When will the public period of mourning begin?

Encouraging conclusions are hard to come by when the best odds are for a vaccine in ten years or more and Senator John Danforth wonders publicly about the wisdom of wasting federal funds on the terminally ill "simply to make [them] feel better." It is true that this crisis could bankrupt any public coffer; each case of frank AIDS requires between $50,000 and $100,000. The costs in public welfare and social services are incalculable. But such figures should serve to remind officials that money held back now will in a few years be needed many times over, for far less hopeful purposes. No one has understood this better than the numerous private groups in the city, whose efforts to educate the public and tend to people with AIDS have been the most organized and inspiring. The Gay Men's Health Crisis, founded in 1981, lobbies, raises funds, and has assembled an army of 1,500 volunteers to provide support and home care for an equal number of people with AIDS. Bailey House, in the West Village, cares for homeless people with AIDS. And the People With AIDS Coalition gives advice and friendship in a dark time.

The existence of these groups allows for the hope that a social and sexual retrenchment is not inevitable. As the gay community has matured in the past few years, so the idea of sexual liberation may also mature, bringing with it a more truly open dialogue on sexuality at familial, social, and political levels. It is only through such an openness that we will ever conquer AIDS. And the quick, tireless response of many people in the city shows that humane coalitions can be formed. □

Jan Rosenberg

PARK SLOPE: NOTES ON A MIDDLE-CLASS "UTOPIA"

A familiar story, playing itself out in city after city: skyrocketing housing costs send upscale urban dwellers looking for new areas to "pioneer" (some would say invade) and to reshape to their taste. In Manhattan, it has transformed areas once filled with machine shops and printing plants into the luxury lofts and art spaces of Soho, Noho, and TriBeCa. And across the East River, similar changes march through Boerum Hill, Carroll Gardens, Cobble Hill, and particularly Park Slope—the "brownstone" neighborhoods ringing downtown Brooklyn.

Stroll through Park Slope on a warm Saturday night, past young middle-class crowds patronizing a cornucopia of chic new restaurants offering the latest in trendy cuisine: sushi, Tex-Mex, "continental," five types of Chinese, Thai, and various gourmet take-out shops. A lone shoemaker hangs on, but for a dime store or bodega where you can still get an ice cream sandwich for under a dollar, you have to literally go down the Slope, an avenue or two away. Interspersed among the restaurants are numerous real estate offices and nearly as many "new wave" florists (there's almost a florist a block in the heart of the Slope's Seventh Avenue). New craft shops display expensive, elegant *objets*. Completing the ambience are those emblems of yuppiedom, Benetton's, a nearly-completed D'Agostino's, and a recently arrived "closet designer." (Those from Wall Street who specialize in restructuring corporations can now hire someone to restructure their closets, though some spouses have been known to view this as a

hostile takeover.) These Saturday-night sidewalks are filled with well-dressed, well-coiffed people in their twenties, thirties, and forties (hardly any are beyond their forties). A tennis pro from Sheepshead Bay, accountants and teachers from Bensonhurst, are drawn to the shops, the people, the élan of Park Slope, where they encounter the full range of young professionals priced out of the Village and the Upper West Side, searching for an affordable "outer borough" alternative. The atmosphere is thick with style and expectation; this is a place to be, and to be seen. This is *New York Magazine*'s Park Slope.

But there are other Park Slopes flourishing, in ways less familiar, less commercial. One is the Park Slope of neighborhood day-care centers and nursery schools, of after-school programs and Little League, of PS 321 and JHS 51, of religious institutions, nearly moribund only a few years ago, revitalized by the in-migration of families since the early 1970s. This child-centered, family-oriented Park Slope, anchored in its own institutions, has its own landmarks and symbols: the area around "the monument" at Ninth Street and Prospect Park West on Saturday spring mornings is one of these. Awash in a maroon and yellow sea of St. Saviour's and St. Francis's baseball uniforms, elementary school kids (mostly boys, despite some organizers' best efforts) embody the neighborhood's vitality and—since many if not most are not Catholic—its ecumenical spirit. The kids, drawn from public, private, and

159

parochial schools, wait at the monument for their teams to assemble and games to begin.

A six year-old boy worries about his orthodox Jewish neighbors seeing him in his St. Saviour's uniform, and dons a yarmulke to offset his St. Saviour's shirt before visiting them on the Sabbath after his game. The priests ask the non-Catholic parents and children in the league to participate in and respect their preseason service, now nearly purged of specifically Catholic references. Congregation Beth Elohim (the Garfield Temple) also typifies the neighborhood. Faced with dwindling membership and bleak prospects in 1970, its former grandeur faded, temple members had the good sense and good luck to create one of the early neighborhood nursery schools. Its early-childhood programs helped revitalize the temple, drawing Jewish families into (or back into) Jewish institutional life. The churches and synagogues have made themselves centers of many family-oriented activities, from sports to preschool and after-school programs, potluck dinners and weekend retreats, that knit together some of the baby boomers with children.

Parking is nearly impossible ("double Park Slope," my older son calls it) as I zoom up on a Saturday morning to drop off my child for his nine o'clock game. I pull away quickly to park and get back before the first inning, thinking of my friend, Fred I., the envy of the "silent majority": while most of us quietly grumble that our weeks are dominated by Little League (in our own case, practices on Wednesday, Thursday, and Friday afternoons and "official games" all day Saturday), Fred courageously manages to sneak off to his country house with his brood in tow every weekend.

It's a cold, drizzly Saturday in April and the parade to officially open the neighborhood baseball season is about to begin. Hundreds of kids and their parents huddle together by team, waiting to march up Union Street and over to "the monument." Mayor Koch is going to inaugurate the newly renovated playing fields near Prospect Park's new concert area and playground at Ninth Street, only a stone's throw from the beautifully restored Picnic House and Tennis House—all of which border

the Park Slope side of Prospect Park. The southern and eastern sides of the park, bordered by predominantly black neighborhoods, seem a distant land. The park serves as more of a barrier than a meeting ground between white upper-middle-class and black and Hispanic Brooklyn. Connections between private neighborhood gentrification and the careful restoration of once-treasured, then-deteriorated public space suggest themselves to even the most casual visitor. But for even the most apolitical of Slopers, there is nagging doubt that their good fortune can endure in a Brooklyn increasingly overwhelmed by an underclass as cut off from prosperity as they are connected.

The 1950s and 1960s brought hard times to urban neighborhoods all over the country; Park Slope was no exception. This middle-class family neighborhood was losing out to newer, more promising suburban areas. Clashes between rival Hispanic and Italian gangs made the area inhospitable to the middle class. The park block residents of Third Street, always one of the Slope's most beautiful and desirable blocks (and Sidney Hook's home through the 1940s and 1950s) organized the Park Slope Betterment Committee to promote the neighborhood's revival. They pressured the banks to give mortgages and held meetings to advise prospective neighbors on buying and remodeling homes.

A trickle of newcomers, led by artists seeking affordable housing and studio space, flowed into the Slope. One early "pioneer," a writer-editor who moved to Park Slope with her artist husband in 1968, left Manhattan for the Slope's beautiful, ample space, and affordable homes. A *New York Times* article had trumpeted the neighborhood's virtues: its distinguished architecture and undervalued homes, its beautiful park, and the nearby presence of other artists. The couple bought a prime park block house, though it was occupied by numerous tenants and the neighborhood was still redlined by the banks, and converted it from a rooming house to a triplex for themselves and a floor-through rental. The single-room occupants they displaced have long since been forgotten by the current owners and their neighbors. Built in the 1890s as a one-family house with ample room for servants, the brownstone adapted quite readily to the changed circumstances of middle-class families in the 1970s.

Like artists, 1960s radicals were another important trickle in the early 1970s migration stream. They, too, were drawn by the affordable space, the park, and the presence of others like themselves. Veterans of the antiwar, civil rights, and feminist movements quickly found each other in, and drew each other to, this budding urban community.

Many came in couples, expecting to settle in and eventually to have and raise their children here. Not surprisingly, these 1960s veterans remain central to community politics in Park Slope. Over the years, personal, community, and political interests have converged around issues of housing and education.

Early antiredlining campaigns were organized by people experienced with bankers' power to make and break neighborhoods. Ready but unable to buy houses in Park Slope, a neighborhood the banks did not yet believe in, activists successfully challenged the then-standard diversion of neighborhood resources to finance suburban and Sunbelt development.

Ironically (but predictably) the end of redlining sped up the gentrification, which was soon to work against middle-class housing/investment opportunities. By the mid-1980s, despite considerable expansion of gentrified Park Slope's boundaries, only highly paid professionals, bankers and the like (and those lucky enough to have queued up on time), could afford to own a home in Park Slope.

School politics reflect the neighborhood's concentration of leftists and liberals. Several leading elementary schools have adopted the "Peace Curriculum"; the Community School Board has committed its resources to establishing an "alternative school" similar to the ones in Manhattan's District 4 founded by Deborah Meier.

To the middle class among a generation wary of suburbia's soured promise, places like Park Slope came to be seen as a contemporary alternative, the chance to build a family-centered urban life that is distinctly not suburban. The mix of people in public institutions, the subway rides to and from "the City," the architecture, the shared public grandeur of a partially restored Prospect Park—these eddies against the tide of privatization are reminders that one has embraced a post-suburban dream of a vital, complex, dynamic urban life. □

THE CULTURE OF THE CITY

Paul Berman

THE FACE OF DOWNTOWN

Strokes for a Portrait

Every place and time has a representative personality. For downtown New York in the period just ending—the New York of Soho and the East Village, middle 1980s—the representative personality is a certain type of bohemian, similar to other bohemians we have known, but with distinctive traits. No single art work has managed to evoke this personality in all its characteristics. We do not have a Henry Murger, no *Scènes de la vie de l'avenue A,* not yet, anyway. Nonetheless there are portraits. I point to one called *The Birth of the Poet*.

The Birth of the Poet was a spectacular theatrical failure of 1986 at the Brooklyn Academy of Music. It was a collaboration by Richard Foreman (staging), Kathy Acker (book), David Salle (scenery), and Peter Gordon (music), which made it something of a World Series for at least one branch of the downtown avant garde. The collaborators described their work as an opera. Of course it wasn't an opera, since the music played a minor role. Nor was it exactly a drama, since the book served mainly as one more object for the actors and creators to get weird about.

It was, though, a scandal. A modest-looking young woman stood on stage declaiming preposterous fantasies and reveries. A fantasy about ancient Rome, a revery about sex. A fantasy about New York after the Bomb, another revery about sex—all with Foreman's characteristic crowds and giant human props thundering across the stage, and wispy sounds wafting from the musicians, and enormous dogs painted by Salle gazing stupidly from the backdrop. And though today is, as should have been noticed, the Age of S/M (go to the movies

and you come home black and blue), the tendency of this woman's sex fantasies to involve her getting knocked around outraged the audience, which fled up the aisles and out to the grimy streets, on the grounds of, Better the outside of Brooklyn than the inside of Kathy Acker's head.

That was impressive. Anyone can bore an audience, and *The Birth of the Poet* did its share of that; but to drive people out the door is nearly impossible today, given ticket prices. And not only did *The Birth of the Poet* manage to shock, it also—so I thought—depicted. For there on stage was a certain kind of self-obsessed character, a modest personality in the grip of grandiose fantasies, a radical, a fraud (let's face it: the kind of person who doodles all over the page and calls it an opera), a bore, a person of fitful originality. I'm afraid that *The Birth of the Poet,* being a fiasco, didn't present this personality in a fully rounded way. But in the year since then, Acker has published *Don Quixote,* a novel, Foreman has won an Obie for *Film is Evil, Radio is Good,* Salle has exhibited his dogs and other works at the Whitney, sundry plays and films by other people sharing some of the same ideas have appeared. And drawing from these various productions a trait here, a feature there, it's possible to assemble a fuller portrait, the way that police artists piece together portraits of murderers from the memories of unreliable witnesses. The composite drawing is a little cartoonish, too crudely penciled, and like all composites looks stiff and unlifelike. Yet a face emerges. I detect eight traits:

1. The representative personality of downtown New York is someone who feels divorced from actual experience.

Actual experience may exist and from time to time may get the upper hand; but the downtown personality has trouble identifying this experience or knowing how to respond. That's because the downtowner is a prisoner of culture. He (or she) gazes in the direction of real life, and it is movies, plays, books, and pop music that gaze back. He is trapped in a windowless room of these things. Life is reduced to a cultural reference. You can see this in a poker-faced, witty film like Jim Jarmusch's *Down by Law*, where the characters stumble around a bayou swamp in which every leaf and vine evokes the movies.

2. The downtown personality resents this situation. He feels that his own incapacities aren't the cause of his predicament. Modern culture—especially popular culture—is the cause.

This particular resentment derives from the 1960s. For the idea that visible reality is a deception, that culture is a tool of manipulation, that the obvious world is essentially delusion—this idea was the foundation stone of all the great original radical thinkers of the 1960s. Herbert Marcuse expressed the idea philosophically in *One-Dimensional Man*. Noam Chomsky expressed it politically in his early

essays on liberal ideology. Roland Barthes applied a parallel notion to the study of popular culture. The message was: What you see when you look at the world should enrage you, and the less obvious the reasons for rage, the angrier you should feel. The smallest-seeming fact reeks with meanings that someone has created in order to manipulate you. True reality can only be found by seeing through the deception, by unmasking the culture that surrounds us.

Now, the political consequences of perceiving the world as a vast deception manipulated by elites turned out to be unfortunate for the movements that relied on this branch of radical thought. The idea left no room for common sense, since common sense presupposes that reality is obvious. Political movements that lack common sense have short lives. As a cultural insight, however, the idea hasn't ceased to prosper, for instance in the field of literary theory, where the lack of common sense is generally regarded as no drawback. Likewise in the streets of downtown. And with this background in mind, the downtown resentment can be specified.

It is not an aimless resentment, nor an inward-turning one. It isn't sullen, like the resentments of the 1950s. The resentment felt by the downtown personality is a form of cerebral radicalism and it expresses itself as a program for liberation. The downtowner wants to emancipate himself and everyone else from the deceptions of the imprisoning culture. He wants to smash the golden calf. Richard Foreman actually wheels a golden calf on stage in *Film is Evil, Radio is Good*, in case you

don't get the point. "Here's an idea of my own invention," Foreman's character says while pulling a plug. "De-hypnotize the brain."

3. The resentment felt by the downtown personality is not, however, a straightforward feeling.

To begin with, the downtowner seems to love the popular culture that he resents. Mention *Leave it to Beaver* or early rock and roll, and the radical downtowner will weep real tears—or fake tears, who knows? It's impossible to say. The downtowner relishes making arcane distinctions between popular culture that is beneficent and popular culture that is not, e.g., *Film is Evil, Radio is Good*. But the distinctions aren't meant to be taken too seriously. David Salle attaches a Santa Clause sticker to one of his canvases, covers another painting with cartoon alligators, and there's no way to know what he means by this. He may be snickering at the popular culture, he may be snickering at high art. The downtown sensibility requires exactly that ambiguity.

4. The downtowner is also amused by his own predicament as a prisoner of culture.

He's not interested in searching out the "authentic," the way his predecessors of twenty-five years ago were. He prefers instead to laugh at himself in a self-ironic manner. Therefore his characteristic gesture is comedic, controlled, not hilarious; relentless, not zany. Humor makes the downtown personality looser and better-spirited than his grim cultural

analysis might suggest. But because he does have such an analysis, the humor necessarily takes the form of ridiculous or ironic commentaries on the culture.

Thus the style that Acker calls "plagiaristic," but which could better be called "vandalistic," along the lines of improving Mona Lisa. In Acker's case, vandalism means doing Don Quixote *without* the mustache—as a woman out adventuring. In the real *Don Quixote*, the mad knight comes across a crowd of people on the road including two Benedictine friars, whom he mistakes for evil enchanters and attacks with his lance. In *Don Quixote* by Acker, Quixote the woman goes on the road reflecting on how much she likes sex.

> Don Quixote decided that the only thing's to be happy. Since the sole reason she ever went out of her house was to fuck, she decided that to be happy's to fuck. She was riding her horse along, in order to find sex that wouldn't hurt too much. At this point she saw three to four hundred men. "My God," she said . . . "Here come the friars."
>
> "Please beat us up. We belong to the order of St. Benedictine."

And so forth, relentlessly. You have to laugh. The late Charles Ludlam was a genius at this sort of thing.

5. The downtowner has dissolved into sexual confusion.

Acker's Quixote is a woman in love with a female dog who looks like a boy and was in love with a feminine man who was able to respond because the female dog is boyish. Of

course this is an international and not merely a downtown New York trait. Plays by Caryll Churchill, the English playwright, offer something similar. I quote a description by Enrique Fernández in the *Village Voice* of a recent Spanish film made by Pedro Almodovar: "In the film, Carmen Maura plays a man who's had a transsexual operation and, due to an unhappy love affair with his/her father, has given up men to have a lesbian (I guess) relationship with a woman, who is played by a famous Madrid transvestite."

Very likely the downtowner has also become obsessed with some kind of sexual quirk, for instance getting slapped (the Benedictines), or tying up little boys (Albert Inauratto's last play, *Coming of Age in Soho*). Even without a sexual quirk, the quality of obsession is central to the downtown personality. New Music may be said to offer the higher-consciousness version of same, where obsessive droning is the main idea. Take me out of myself! is the downtowner's cry. It should be mentioned that the only kind of sexual excess not explored by the downtown scene is conventional male over-enthusiasm. Every era has its own taboos.

The berserker sexual aspect of the downtown personality dates, of course, from the pre-AIDS period. In William Hoffman's play *As Is*, the characters remember how they *used* to be crazed sexual adventurers, and loved it; but history has moved on.

6. Filled with these (pre-AIDS) sexual and other obsessions and confusions, ironic and disillusioned about the wall of culture that imprisons him, the downtowner can't help feeling frustrated, vulnerable, and disappointed.

The downtowner suspects that passionate feelings and ways of living exist—but not in our time, in any case not for him, due to the false culture that he understands too well. Therefore the downtowner—especially the downtown woman and the downtown homosexual—hides, but only halfway, a hot, romantic interior beneath a cool, critical, rueful exterior.

The gap between internal heat and external cold is another source of downtown irony and humor. The downtown personality is a thwarted

personality, and the more thwart, the more wry. "In those days of yore," writes Acker, "a man loved a woman who loved him. And vice versa. Not like today." The attitude is visible in David Lynch's *Blue Velvet*, which shows passionate love, but only by first establishing an absurd environment and absurd sexual obsession, so that any time you think the film is taking the sexual passion seriously, you are made to recall that all is in fact a straight-faced send-up. This isn't for real, folks! Strong emotion can be seen only in the lens of an absurd telescope. That's how it is with the downtown personality.

7. The downtowner has an ambivalent relation to intellect.

It could hardly be otherwise. The downtown personality is dominated by ironic bemusement and obsession, and of all mental states, bemusement and obsession least allow for intelligence. The bemused brain is pretty much empty; the obsessed brain is otherwise occupied. That doesn't leave much space. On the other hand, the downtowner's impulse to unmask things and ridicule the dominant culture is largely an intellectual inspiration. So there is a conflict. The downtowner veers from absolute intellectual modesty and renunciation to the most grandiose intellectual posturing. At its worst this produces the numerous pretentious passages in Foreman or Acker. Foreman frankly doesn't mind writing pretentious passages or even lapsing into nonsense. "Understand—it ALWAYS makes sense. Sense *can't* be avoided. If it first seems to be non-sense, wait: roots will reveal themselves." ("Notes on the Process of Making It.") Sometimes the roots never do reveal themselves, of course. With Acker I always feel I'm in a weird, witty revery, then have been rudely transported to a graduate student lounge where some pompous bore is expounding theories about post-deconstructionism.

8. Mostly the downtowner exists in a state of disorientation. That is the aimed-for result, not always achieved, of the ambivalent attitude toward intellect.

An example, if I can reach back to the last decade and a slightly different era, is the avant-garde masterpiece by Robert Wilson and Philip Glass, *Einstein on the Beach*, another opera, in which events on stage and in the orchestra pit are so cool, monotonous, obsessive, and original, that your mind goes into idle, and like all idle things, gets into trouble. You begin to wonder, what is this strange monotony about? Is it about God? The End of the World? The suspicion that you're seeing something Awesomely Grand accounts for the power of *Einstein on the Beach*; but you are not, in fact, seeing anything Awesomely Grand, nor anything definable at all, and you suspect this, too. Hence your disorientation. You haven't the slightest idea what's going on, and you find yourself struck by your own confusion.

The back-and-forth between intellectual emptiness and the suspicion that something large and important is being said generates the interesting quality in David Salle. He paints a gigantic woman's hip and thigh, and hangs a real-life umbrella in front, and the viewer is thrown into a tizzy of interpretation. Why the hip and thigh? Why the umbrella? The obvious truth is that Salle has painted a hip and thigh out of appreciation for female beauty, then has occupied himself with finding other objects that are visually related to produce a theme and variations. Salle is merely doing what art teachers do in art school, getting the students to paint a series of spheres, a series of cones, and so forth, with no value placed on one cone as opposed to another. There's no intellectual content at all. He's painted these objects so flippantly, yet with so much air of importance, you can hardly believe your eyes.

Arthur Danto, in explaining why he doesn't much care for Salle, says: "The work appears to situate itself beyond good and evil, hence outside the sphere of critical discourse altogether, so that such snarls as Oh yeah? So what? Says who? Who cares? What difference does it make? Fuck off! are all the response I would anticipate to my questions and objections." But that's Salle's achievement. Looking at his paintings, you can't help posing Big Questions, to which come back dismissive answers in the vernacular. It puts you off balance.

Being off balance makes the true downtowner feel more at ease, because off balance is how he feels inside.

How to evaluate the art of downtown is, in the end, partly a matter of who you are. The sense of being removed from real life, combined with self-absorption, mixed resentment and sentimentality for the dominant culture, a flip anti-intellectualism that turns into grandiosity at the drop of a hat, all this combined with the hokum that in every era accompanies the avant garde—these traits aren't necessarily perfect for producing great works. Anyone with a love for theater could have appreciated Charles Ludlam, but I dread what most readers will think when they pick up *Don Quixote*. Is it meant to be read, they will ask. (Well, just picked through, in my opinion.)

But what do we want from an avant garde? Let us say that the avant garde doesn't have to write the "news that stays news," that it's enough merely to write the news, if there is any. In the streets of lower New York in the middle 1980s, there is, in fact, some news. The news is that people are actually like that. □

Brian Morton

THE BANKER'S RED SUSPENDERS

Looking at Yuppie Anti-Yuppie Magazines
(*Manhattan, inc.* and *Spy*)

One morning on Broadway I saw a black man approach three young white men. The white men wore business suits; the black man was wrapped in a blanket. As he approached them he put out his hand. But before he could ask for anything, one of the young men thrust *his* palm out and shouted, "Spare a quarter, buddy?" His companions brayed with laughter. The three of them seemed so delighted I thought they were about to burst into song.

As they sauntered down the street, I watched them with a kind of envy. These were three happy men.

When I was asked to write about two of New York's new "yuppie magazines," I was pleased. I thought it would give me a chance to strike a blow at those three morons. But as I spent some time with the magazines, I found that I'd been wrong. These magazines—*Manhattan, inc.* and *Spy*—were not intended for those men, but for a different kind of person entirely. Still, I decided to begin with the picture of those men anyway—because I want the thought of them to be present as an index to the moral atmosphere of the times. What kind of person has felt most at home in the United States during the past decade? The kind of person who can look a homeless man in the eye and laugh at him.

The two magazines I'm going to write about are produced by people with much more decent impulses. What is interesting, and sad, is the degree to which even people of more decent impulses are infected by the spirit of the age. *Manhattan, inc.*, which made its debut in September 1984, has been described by its owner as "a mix of *Forbes*, *People*, and *M*."

Although it does contain a bit of straight business reporting, the heart of it is found in its profiles of prominent figures in the business world of New York.

At their worst, these profiles are pieces of fawning idiocy. When *Manhattan, inc.* wrote about the developer Gerald Guterman, whose chief distinction is a remarkable record of tenant harassment, it concentrated on his . . . art collection.

But most of the profiles aim for a different tone, a tone of lighthearted irreverence. How many business magazines would conclude a profile of a prominent investment banker and his wife by quoting a Marxist scholar's condemnation of class oppression? *Manhattan, inc.* did; and touches like this give it a certain charm.

The April 1986 issue featured an article on Felix and Elizabeth Rohatyn, "society dissidents." The Rohatyns talked about how disturbed they are by the extremes of wealth and poverty in New York. Felix concluded darkly that "something is wrong with the system."

The article ended like this:

As I left the Rohatyns and took a cab down Park Avenue, I was trying to recall something I'd read recently about the rich. . . . When I got home to my Bleecker Street sublet, I found what I'd been looking for. It was in the collected essays of Christopher Hill, the Oxford historian.

"The rich were getting richer, and the poor poorer," Hill writes of the decades preceding the Puritan Revolution. "It may well be that Sir Thomas More was right to see all commonwealths as conspiracies of the rich to oppress the poor. . . ."

If this is true, then perhaps Felix is a bit naive. There's nothing "wrong with the system." The system works, alas, just the way it's always been meant to work.

The writer to whom we owe these reflections is Ron Rosenbaum, one of *Manhattan, inc.*'s contributing editors. Rosenbaum is the sharpest and funniest of the magazine's regular writers; he sets its tone.

A former reporter for the *Village Voice*, Rosenbaum is not an admirer of the business world. In the introduction to *Manhattan Passions*, a collection of his pieces from *Manhattan, inc.*, Rosenbaum confesses that he has developed a "Bad Attitude" towards this milieu, in which people "wipe the margarita foam from their lips and tell you that they'd discovered that the truly important thing for their personal growth at this point in their lives was to make a huge pile of money."

Rosenbaum's interviewing style is similar to the old "rope-a-dope" technique with which Muhammad Ali took the heavyweight title from George Foreman. Ali leaned against the ropes and let Foreman batter him for seven rounds, and when Foreman was completely spent, Ali knocked him out with a couple of quick combinations. Rosenbaum lets his subjects babble on for as long as they like, then dispatches them in a swift concluding paragraph.

After Malcolm Forbes has gone on complacently about his own liberal-mindedness, his essentially spiritual nature, Rosenbaum baits him by making a rude comment about the Reagan administration's war on Nicaragua— and Forbes throws him out of the house.

His profile of Roy Cohn ends more poignantly. After Cohn has boasted about himself for fifteen pages or so, Rosenbaum tells us that he senses social acceptance hasn't made Cohn happy He suspects that Cohn misses the days when he was an outsider, perpetually doing battle against powerful insiders like his arch-foe Robert Kennedy. Rosenbaum comments that Cohn

> misses the old days, misses the thrill of combat.
> Probably even misses Bobby Kennedy.
> As I leave the four o'clock dimness of Le Cirque and all these tales of the way the world

really works, it suddenly occurs to me: I miss Bobby, too.

Clearly, *Manhattan, inc.* is not a magazine for the three men I saw on the street. Those fellows don't miss Bobby, they sure as hell don't know who Christopher Hill is, and whether or not they happen to know which side the president is making war on in Nicaragua, they think it's a great little war just the same.

Manhattan, inc. is for people who are yuppies by default. It's aimed at a young, hip audience of people who see through the hypocrisies of the business world even as they want to make their way in it. The ideal *Manhattan, inc.* reader enjoys the challenges of business, but doesn't take it all that seriously— sees it as a sort of game. If the times were different, he or she might be doing something more public-spirited. A friend of mine who reads the magazine says he enjoys it both because it tells him what's going on in the business world, and because it views business as "basically pretty silly." I think this captures the nature of its appeal.

The first few times I thumbed through *Manhattan, inc.*, I was pleasantly surprised by its irreverence. I wouldn't have guessed that a magazine that views business as "basically pretty silly" could find an audience today.

But the longer one reads *Manhattan, inc.*, the less a tender view of it seems justified. Its criticisms of business are never incisive, never anything but waggish; it's a sort of good-humored court jester to the business world.

I'm not faulting the magazine for refusing to strike moralistic antibusiness poses. I *am* faulting it for a lack of intelligence. In one of his articles Rosenbaum treats us to a brief digression on Balzac, who examined Parisian society with the dispassionate eye of a "physicist" and left us with an incomparable record of his age. The implication is that Rosenbaum would like to be a Balzac of New York. And if *Manhattan, inc.* anatomized the business world of New York with a hint of the intelligence that Balzac applied to Paris, it would be doing us all a service, no matter what its political attitude. But it doesn't.

Rosenbaum's profile of Donald Trump is a case in point. Trump is a man obsessed: the problem of nuclear weapons proliferation, as he puts it, "drives me crazy," and he wishes the government would realize that if it wants to work out an arms control agreement with the Soviet Union, it should turn to a tested deal-maker like himself. Trump comes off looking like a self-infatuated fool, but . . . that's it. There's no discussion of what Trump's development projects have done to New York—of how people like Trump and the forces they represent have transformed the city. To portray Trump as a jerk may seem bold for a moment; but the portrayal is merely personal and therefore toothless.

Balzac loved megalomaniacs, so he probably would have loved Trump. But if he'd put Trump in a novel, I can't imagine that he would have told his story in isolation. He might have told it alongside the story of someone who's never met Trump, but whose life has been touched by him nevertheless. Someone like that man I saw wearing a blanket on Broadway, for instance—a victim of the "Manhattan passion" for grandiose development. The great physicist of society never forgot that wealth and poverty are part of the same equation.

On the rare occasions when *Manhattan, inc.* deals with someone who does battle with Trump and his kind, the results are instructive. A profile of City Councilmember Ruth Messinger in the May 1985 issue described her as a "poker-faced woman with a loud, flat voice," and, though praising her intelligence and her work habits. wrote her off in the end as a relic of the New Left, "ferociously tenacious" but incapable of compromise and incapable therefore of bringing about constructive change. Her "fighting stance" is "unlikely to lead to higher office," nor is it likely "to unseat developers from their place in the city's power structure." The last line of the article is this: "Politicians come and go, but real estate is forever." This is the complacent cynicism of one who's seen through the money-worshipping business world, but who believes that those who try to fight it are doomed and ridiculous.

For a youngish audience that's gone into business not out of conviction, but simply from a lack of alternatives, *Manhattan, inc.* may be the most effective cheerleader that business could have. Business is only a game, it tells us—but it's the only game worth playing.

It's nice that *Manhattan, inc.* misses Bobby . . . but who *was* Bobby anyway? Even if we set aside the role he played during his brother's administration—the hawkishness on Vietnam, the plot to kill Castro, the timidity on civil rights—even at his best, what was he? To miss Bobby is to miss an era when social reform was sexy; when you could have a social conscience and be an insider too.

It's easy to "miss Bobby." To stick your neck out when the times are inhospitable and risk being described as a "poker-faced woman with a loud, flat voice"—that's a little harder.

As I write, *Manhattan, inc.* is in the news. Several of its editors resigned after an argument with its owner, D. H. Lipson, over one of Rosenbaum's articles. Suggesting that the recent insider-trading scandals had revealed the hollowness of the yuppie dream, Rosenbaum had proposed a reeducation camp for "as-yet unindicted investment bankers," in which they would have to learn how to tell the difference "between the peace symbol and the Mercedes hood ornament," how to dress in something other than red suspenders and yellow ties, etc. According to the *New York Times*, Lipson was displeased that Rosenbaum "poked fun at men who wear red suspenders. Several [of the magazine's] writers said that as they understood it, Mr. Lipson was upset because his son wears red suspenders. . . ."

This little tiff will earn the departing editorial staff a reputation for boldness, but it's characteristic that it resulted from an article that made fun of the way investment bankers *dress*.*

Uptown Swagger

Spy, the "New York Monthly," is a humor magazine that's been around since October 1986. A blurb from a West Coast magazine, *Equator*, gives a good sense of what *Spy* is about. Quoting one of *Spy*'s editors to the effect that "most magazines long ago gave up

---

* Rosenbaum has since resigned as well. A pity. He may not be the modern Balzac, but he was the only reason to read *Manhattan inc.*

the notion of the adversarial reporter," *Equator* goes on:

> *Spy* tries the crimes of image, lifestyle and journalism. . . . *Spy* is a *People* magazine from hell: still celebrities, but "served up in a different dish." While other magazines applaud celebrities' successes and fabulous lifestyles, *Spy* gloats happily over their failures and idiocies.

At its best, *Spy* is very funny. I particularly liked its list of the ten most embarrassing New Yorkers, which included Donald Trump, Alfonse D'Amato, Midge Decter, George Steinbrenner, and Geraldine Ferraro. An article on Caroline Kennedy's husband, "Renaissance Man" Ed Schlossberg, featured charts comparing him with Arnold Schwarzenegger (another Kennedy husband), and Leonardo da Vinci (another Renaissance man). The March 1987 issue came with a map of Reagan's body ("Hands: These are frequently seen pointing at the ears while Reagan walks to or from a helicopter—a gesture that says, Gee, fellas, I'd love to answer your questions, but I can't hear you 'cause of the noise from that darn chopper.").

Several of *Spy*'s regular columns are especially enjoyable. Michèle Bennet, *Spy*'s "reviewer of reviewers," makes fools of reviewers like John Simon of *New York* and David Edelstein of the *Village Voice*—simply by quoting them. Another column provides space for letters to the editor of the *New Yorker*. One such letter asked why the *New Yorker* has never published a list of its staff members . . . and *Spy* responded with a complete *New Yorker* masthead. This prompted a thank-you note from an anonymous *New Yorker* writer, because "most of us had to admit that we didn't know exactly what our co-workers did for a living."

The first few issues of *Spy* featured interviews with television journalists by *Spy*'s nineteen-year-old "cub reporter," who specializes in throwing people off balance with idiotic questions. An interview with WCBS-TV anchorman Rolland Smith featured this exchange:

> *Spy*: What is—what is dialectical materialism?
>
> Smith: I have no idea. What . . . I mean, what . . . where are you going with this? I mean, what I don't understand . . . why? Your asking me

what dialectical materialism is in relationship to my job as a local broadcast journalist in New York, uh, is like, uh, putting Oral Roberts in the Mayo Clinic.

I don't know about you, but I find this pretty funny.

But *Spy*'s limitations are obvious. Despite its editor's brave talk about "adversarial journalism," it's hard to say just what *Spy* thinks its adversary is. Some of the fatuous "stars" of New York life are ridiculed relentlessly in its pages; others appear, as friends, on its cover. *Spy* is very much a part of the milieu it mocks.

There's a stifling air of the trust fund about much of *Spy*. A typical feature, commenting on how difficult it is to find a bathroom in New York, contains maps of the Ivy League Clubs of New York, advising you that if you are well-dressed and have an air of belonging, you can walk in and use their bathrooms. The humor here contained a touch of smugness: instructions on how to sneak into the Harvard Club from someone who doesn't need to.

In an article in the March 1987 issue two of its editors refer to *Spy* as an "upstart" magazine. The dictionary defines an upstart as a parvenu; but when you call yourself an upstart, you mean that you hope your elders think you a little bit brash. This is the ethos of *Spy*: not rebellious, just slightly impudent. *Spy* is the young upstart who will pull a few pranks to embarrass Daddy's club—like publishing a map of it so that outsiders will use its bathroom—but who knows quite well that he'll sit on the board of directors someday.

An article making fun of game shows (how bold!) tells us that "the pleasure this kind of show affords is the right to scorn the masses," who are described as "brainless." If any political attitude can be teased out of *Spy*'s repertoire of put-downs, it's a yearning for an aristocracy of the witty and intelligent. But *Spy* never bothers to look very closely into its own idea of intelligence—which accounts for the one truly ugly thing about it: its occasional touches of racism. The poor of New York, many of whom are black or Hispanic, are of course not "intelligent" in *Spy*'s sense of the word. So on the rare occasions when *Spy* chooses to notice the poor or minorities, it is usually to comment on how ill-bred they are.

Some examples of this are mild enough. A satirical exam for prospective token clerks in the New York City subway system belabored the idea that token clerks are stupid and rude; it had the tone of someone complaining about the difficulty of finding good help. An article on "famous nobodies"—people from Harlem who happen to have the same names as various celebrities—expected us to be amused by the fact that Barbara Walters of 138th Street thinks the other Barbara Walters works for NBC. "Barbara Walters, however, works at ABC," comments Spy, a little charmed by the touching ignorance of the lower orders. The article never explained why a teacher named Barbara Walters is less of a somebody than the Barbara Walters who makes millions by putting fatuous questions, in a tone of breathy sincerity, to the same fatuous celebrities Spy mocks.

Far uglier was an article on the mixture of Spanish and English spoken by Newyoricans—Puerto Ricans living in New York. This informed us that the "sweaty, slangy derivations" of this dialect, which sound "disagreeably like someone talking with his mouth full," are the result of decades of "mongrelizing in Puerto Rico and Manhattan," and betray "incompetence in both languages." A Columbia University professor, visiting from Spain, is brought forward to condemn the dialect; but just as hilarious as the linguistic incompetence of Newyoricans, apparently, is the linguistic *competence* of people who speak a language other than English. The professor, we're told, "talked in the elegant, self-conscious fashion of his Castilian dialect, all z's and soft c's blurring into a lisp." His speech is rendered in this way: "I am no elititht. The Newyorican can speak whatever he wanth."

This sensibility is the very reverse of cosmopolitan, and it severely limits Spy's appreciation of New York. Spy never praises the city for its diversity, but rather for qualities like its "uptown swagger." Spy, at times, *is* a magazine for those three men I saw on the street.

Particularly interesting are Spy's running jokes about the *New Yorker*. Spy introduced its *New Yorker* letters column this way: "A cartoon makes you laugh, but you have no way of singing the artist's praises properly. There's a Notes and Comment that doesn't concern nuclear holocaust *or* Nicaragua—right there, you *see* it—but there's no place for you to crow about it. You wish the magazine would let Elizabeth Drew write much, *much* longer pieces—and yet where can you make the case?"

This is funny enough . . . but think about that second item. Nuclear holocaust or Nicaragua. The *New Yorker*'s political commentary has all the well-known vices: that ponderous overearnestness; that *faux naïf* style, in which everything must be spelled out at interminable length. But in its own way, the *New Yorker* is more daring than Spy will ever be. After José Napoleón Duarte was elected president of El Salvador in 1984, and the mainstream media were shuddering with joy about this triumph of democracy, only two magazines, to my knowledge, were willing to mention such facts as that voters had to put their ballots into transparent boxes, while observers from the military looked on. One was the *Covert Action Information Bulletin*, which has a circulation of about ten; the other was the *New Yorker*.

During the Solidarity period in Poland, the *New Yorker* covered the movement attentively, and took care to stress the point that the Polish opposition was not simply demanding what we have here, in the West. The *New Yorker* stressed that Solidarity's program pointed toward a society more civilized than any yet seen, in which political and economic democracy are joined with a system of reciprocal aid. It's true that these pieces were written in that drowsy *New Yorker* style—with a pen dipped in Valium—but they were far more radical than anything that will ever appear in Spy. They were radical because they were thoughtful. Because they weren't focused on personalities. Because they came from a sensibility that isn't satisfied with being a *People* magazine from hell.

Both Spy and *Manhattan, inc.* ("a mix of *Forbes*, *People*, and *M.*") reflect the growing empeoplement of American culture. I don't know if we're more stupid than we used to be, but we're stupid in a new way. The social world has grown so complex that novelists and literary theorists worry that it can no longer be portrayed through stories about representative figures. But in the mind of mainstream America, life is simpler than ever: there's no event that can't be reduced to the dimension of "personalities." From "Saturday Night Live" to *Vanity Fair* to "Sixty Minutes," gossip about celebrities has taken the place of satire, culture, news. Both *Spy* and *Manhattan, inc.* pride themselves on rocking the boat, but they too confine themselves to the superficial level of personalities. A *People* magazine from hell is finally only a *People* magazine.

If I were a casual reader of these two magazines, I'd probably like them more than I do. They're witty, well-written, they have an anti-establishment flavor. I'd probably think of them as hopeful signs that the values of Reaganism never wholly triumphed.

But taking them in in one big dose, having to *think* about them for this article, has put me in an irritable mood. I'm tired of reading about power lunches.

In an essay in *Mother Jones* last year, Barbara Ehrenreich lamented the disappearance of Bohemia, of a "genuine money-hating counterculture to counter the dominant money culture." These magazines make the implicit claim that Bohemia has migrated to a spot *within* the dominant money culture. You can dedicate your life to the quest for a whopping salary, but if you keep an ironic distance from it all, if you remember that it's only a game, then you've beaten the system.

Well, maybe you have. But *Manhattan, inc.*'s reference to Balzac puts me in mind of an earlier attempt to lay siege to society over power lunches. In *Père Goriot*, Eugène de Rastignac, a young man from the provinces, comes to Paris, and witnesses there every variety of hypocrisy and betrayal. At the end of the book he makes a vow:

> Eugène, now wholly alone, took a few steps to gain the highest point in the cemetery, and looked out on Paris winding its length along the two banks of the Seine. . . . His eyes were fixed . . . on the region of that high society in which he had sought to make his way. . . . He gave utterance to these portentous words: "Between us the battle is joined henceforward."
>
> And as a first act in challenge of Society, Eugène went to dine with the Baroness de Nucingen.

In Balzac's later volumes, Rastignac is often glimpsed from afar. He has become wealthy and polished, a cynical master of the social rituals of Paris. He has become a scoundrel. □

Juan Flores

RAPPIN', WRITIN,' & BREAKIN'

Word has it that Machito, the father of Latin jazz who died in early 1984 at 75, was learning how to breakdance. The great Cuban bandleader, who since the 1940s had performed with the likes of Dizzy Gillespie and Charlie Parker and stood at the juncture of Caribbean and Afro-American musical traditions, must surely have recognized an exciting new stage in the dual heritage he had made his own. For break and rap rhythms, with all their absorption of intervening and adjoining styles, remain grounded in African musical expression. They are further testimony to the shared cultural life of African-descended peoples in New York City, which for the past generation, at least, has centered on the interaction of Puerto Ricans and blacks.

The proximity of the two groups is perhaps more striking today than ever before, especially among teenage youth. Aside from some studies of language convergence, the voluminous literature on U.S. ethnic relations includes no sustained treatment of the interaction between Puerto Ricans and blacks. Perhaps the "pop" ascendancy of hip-hop, which stems directly

from that interaction, will provide a needed impetus.

The intellectual antecedents go back even before Machito's beginnings to the early 1900s, when the first contingents of Puerto Ricans began arriving in New York. They were mostly artisans, with a high level of political education, and many were black. Though Cubans and other Spanish speakers were their most immediate coworkers, black Americans were already a significant presence in their neighborhoods and workplaces. One of these very early arrivals was Arturo Alfonso Schomburg, who came to New York in the late nineteenth century. Unbeknown to many, he was Puerto Rican, and in fact dedicated the first period of his emigrant life to the Cuban and Puerto Rican struggle against Spanish colonialism. Early on in this century he moved up to Harlem, there to become one of the foremost scholars of the African diaspora. His contribution has been memorialized in Harlem's Schomburg Center for the Study of Black Culture.

Another black Puerto Rican pioneer, who came to New York in 1917, was Jesus Colon. A long-time journalist and revolutionary activist, Colon in his literary sketches and political campaigns stressed the common historical and cultural experience of Puerto Ricans and blacks. Writing in the 1940s and 1950s, he was the first Puerto Rican author to publish a book in English, and the first to describe in psychological detail his experience of American racism.

An early admirer of Jésus Colón was the Puerto Rican novelist Piri Thomas, and here we draw closer to the contemporary world of hip-hop. Thomas's novel *Down These Mean Streets*, published in 1967, is a work in the autobiographical manner of *Native Son* and *Manchild in the Promised Land* that probes intensely the complex and not always harmonious relations among black and Puerto Rican youth in New York. Here, in scenes set in the 1950s, we witness a young Puerto Rican saying the dozens and hanging out with his black friends; from them he learns that, according to the color code operative in the U.S., he is black and had better start liking it.

With such hints of a longer historical trajectory in mind, it is to this period of the late 1950s and the 1960s that the origins of present-day hip-hop must be traced. In the spectacular surface of Broadway and Hollywood, one thinks of *West Side Story* and *Blackboard Jungle*, the scene of gang wars, drugs, and juvenile delinquency. A more circumspect account, though, would recall that these years saw the dawning of the second-generation black and Puerto Rican communities

in New York; it was the time when the first offspring of both mass migrations, many of them born and raised in New York, were settling into their new situation. They comprised, and still today comprise, the two largest nonwhite groups in the city. They came from southern, largely rural backgrounds; they lived in the same or bordering neighborhoods, attended the same schools, and together occupy the most deprived and vulnerable place in the economic and cultural hierarchy: they are the reserve of the reserve.

Small wonder, then, that young blacks and Puerto Ricans started liking the same kinds of music, doing the same dances, playing the same games, and dressing and talking alike. Their common experience of racist exclusion and social distance from their white-ethnic peers drew them even closer together. In groping for a new idiom, young blacks and Puerto Ricans discarded rural trappings and nostalgic "down home" references, but retained the African rhythmic base and improvisational, participatory qualities of their inherited cultures. In so doing, black and Caribbean peoples came to recognize the complementarity of what seemed to be diverse origins.

One such early intersection of the popular cultures was evident in rhythm-and-blues music of the late 1950s. Although both Fats Domino and Bo Diddley had already infused Latin and Caribbean beats into their influential rock-and-roll sounds, New York was really the site of direct black and Puerto Rican musical interaction. There several street-based groups, like the

Harptones and the Vocaleers, combined black and Latin members, as did the hugely successful Frankie Lymon and the Teenagers. The music itself was basically black rock and roll, but with a good deal of mambo and other Afro-Caribbean features blended in. The same is true of the boogaloo craze of a decade later, though in this case it was mostly Latin musicians like Pete Rodriguez, Joe Cuba and Joe Bataan who were responsible, and the Latin influence was even stronger.

Of course this is only to mention the music that came to be recorded, the studio version of what thousands of young Puerto Ricans and blacks were singing in the streets, schoolyards, and hallways. Starting in the late 1950s and extending through the 1960s, doo-wop or harmonizing prevailed in the same neighborhoods that later gave rise to rap music. Despite obvious differences in style, and the accompaniment of rap rhymes by ingeniously manipulated sound systems, harmonizing clearly prefigures rap musical practice in significant ways. And like rap, doo-wop was a form of black urban music that was accessible to young Latin musicians, as a recent recording of Totico y Sus Rumberos singing "What's Your Name" illustrates. It's a "doo-wop rhumba," and as Totico and his group recall, it fits perfectly.

By the late 1960s the political implications of this cultural interaction were becoming more evident. The civil rights movement and the black liberation struggle sparked the organization of the Young Lords Party. The cultural affirmation following from the work of the Lords and the Panthers needs to be emphasized, since the assertion of racial pride and black and Puerto Rican rights inform the social stance of hip-hop. It is no accident that today's rappers and breakers adore James Brown, whose unforgettable "Say It Loud, I'm Black and I'm Proud" has resonated ever since the late 1960s.

Around this time, too, black and Puerto Rican poets began to join forces: Felipe Luciano, later a leader of the Young Lords, was one of the original Last Poets, and Victor Hernandez Cruz was with the Third World Revelationists. The reliance of "Nuyorican" writing and public readings on the language and cadences of black poetry was evident then, and is still strong today in poets like Louis Reyes Rivera and Sandra María Esteves. As with the popular music, black forms of verbal expression lent themselves perfectly to articulation of Nuyorican experience, and are enriched by the inclusion of Spanish and bilingual usages.

Graffiti-writing also began to become widespread in those years of the early 1970s, and I would associate this movement of naming and identifying with the assertive political tenor of the times. Despite the decidedly personal and turf-oriented cast of early graffiti, the political and social context of this practice should not be overlooked. The same is true when considering the later development, when writing moved to the subways and iconography became a public art form. Though the represented content often derives from cartoons and television commercials, those samples of mass culture take on a transformed meaning when posted in defiance of established rules.

Most of the New York graffitists have been black and Puerto Rican youth, and whatever becomes of graffiti in its commercial and elite transmutations, the movement is part of the ongoing cultural convergence of those communities. So, too, is breakdancing, the first recognizable signs of which also appeared as far back as the early 1970s. This may seem surprising, since the more spectacular features of the current style —floor rocking and electric boogie—are indeed phenomena of the past few years. But some experienced breakers, like Dennis Vazquez (the original Rubber Band Man), often hark back to the days of "up-rock," danced to James Brown's "Sex Machine" and Jimmy Castor's "Just Begun," as the initial innovation in popular dance style. Still part of break routines, up-rock was first danced as an alternative to violent street fighting. This social function of breaking as a surrogate for destructive and self-destructive physical confrontation has remained. It is also one of the links between the contemporary North American style and Brazilian *capoeira*, another African-based dance bearing striking similarities to breakdance and initiated over three centuries ago as a response to slavery.

Such, then, are but a few of the many forerunners and early manifestations of the triple-form style called hip-hop, which is not to say that rap, graffiti and breakdancing are not qualitatively new modes of cultural practice. On the contrary, the innovations brought to each area of popular expression are substantial indeed. Gaining a sense of historical background is mainly important in counteracting the sense of miracle attached to these phenomena as they are represented in the dominant, mediated culture, which portrays these practices and stylistic novelties as though they sprang up suddenly out of thin air. Rather, all aspects of hip-hop belong to the ongoing traditions of black and Puerto Rican experience, and to their convergence and cross-fertilization in the New York setting.

For example, there is some ground for emphasizing the impetus lent by Puerto Ricans to the origins of breaking. The speedy footwork, elaborate upper-body movement and daring dips in up-rock rested on a formative background in rhumba and guaguanco, and was to some extent also anticipated by the Latin hustle. It is indicative that the Rock Steady Crew, the most accomplished of the many breakdance groups, is composed almost entirely of Puerto Ricans. Input from other sources having more to do with Afro-American experience has been duly noted—such as martial arts, the jitterbug, tap dancing, and African social dance. And the performance styles of James Brown and Frankie Lymon were of course key models. But, I'll say with all necessary caution, the impulse toward a radical change in the physical center of gravity in popular dance and toward a "break" in the formalizations of couple dancing seems to follow largely from developments in Latin dance styles.

With rap music, of course, the relative contributions are the opposite. Rap belongs squarely in the blues-derived tradition of black vocals and relies upon rich verbal dexterity in English. Here the cultural confluence consists of Puerto Ricans joining in the extension of Afro-American styles. But the distinctive Puerto Rican dimension is not absent here

either. Recital of decimas and aguinaldos in the Puerto Rican folk tradition involved methods of improvisation and alternation much like those typical of rap performance, while the tongue-twisting (*trabalengua*) style of some plena singing is an even more direct antecedent. More important, perhaps, just as with doo-wop and rhumba, there is a fascinating "fit" between Puerto Rican "clave" and characteristic rap rhythms. One of the Puerto Rican rappers, Rubie Dee (Rubén García), who started off in street music as a conguero and a lover of salsa, illustrated this congruence to me, and he was convincing. Dee, the Puerto Rican emcee from the Fantastic Five, even raps occasionally in Spanish, and is appreciated as a valuable component of the rap repertoire. His brother Orlando has composed bilingual, "Spanglish" rhymes for the Funky Four, which indicates how close rap is to the contemporary Nuyorican experience.

Determining the relative ethnic sources of subway graffiti is the most complicated of all, partly because the first subway writer to attract media attention was Taki, who is Greek-American, and because some of the best subway artists are youths of Italian and other national origins. There is clearly an important working-class basis to the graffiti movement that should not be overlooked. Nevertheless, a majority of the practitioners are black and Puerto Rican, and graffiti experts like Henry Chalfant and Manny Kirchheimer agree that most of the early styles originated with the Puerto Ricans. Graig Castleman in his book *Getting Up* indicates a similar view, though he does not speculate as to reasons and rightly argues against the futile attempt to treat it as an exclusively Puerto Rican movement.

But I think Herbert Kohl had good reason to center his discussion of the graffiti impulse on Johnny Rodríguez, the young Puerto Rican who went to him for reading lessons and from whom he came to learn so much about naming and public identity. Felipe Luciano would associate the vitality of the pictorial medium with the Puerto Ricans' remote Taino legacy, and call to mind the Chicano mural and "placa" movement as a parallel indigenous experience. More pertinent, in my view, is the Nuyorican preoccupation with language in its semantic and graphic aspects, and the need to manifest a sense of idiosyncratic presence in the face of imposed anonymity. Norman Mailer captured this motivation well in his 1974 essay "The Faith of Graffiti": "Your presence is on their presence, your alias hangs on their scene. There is a pleasurable sense of depth to the elusiveness of meaning."

Mailer was accurate, too, in pointing out that it is also a matter of color and ecological aesthetics. Another pioneer of the Puerto Rican migration, the poet Juan Avilés, told me recently that when he first came to New York in the 1920s you could always tell where the Puerto Ricans lived because they were the only ones to put plants in their windows. Similarly, Mailer seems to have been thinking of the Puerto Ricans when he described graffiti art as "a movement which began as the expression of tropical peoples living in a monotonous, iron-gray and dull brown brick environment, surrounded by asphalt, concrete and clangor." Graffiti for Mailer, and he might as well have been anticipating the whole hip-hop ensemble, "erupted biologically as though to save the sensuous flesh of their inheritance from a macadamization of the psyche, save the blank city wall of their unfed brain by painting the wall over with the giant trees and pretty plants of a tropical rain-forest."

Precisely because of its grounding in black and Puerto Rican street culture, hip-hop harbors a radical universal appeal. Despite the momentous hype with which the dominant commercial culture would doom it to quick oblivion, that appeal promises to carry and to flourish. □

Ellen Levy

INDIVIDUALS AND AUTONOMISTS

1970s Group Theater, 1980s Performance Art

*H*ow in my illness I see something. . . .
And how it comes to me that I am a rep-
resentation. The way I suspect that I'm not well
represented. That I'm not well.

This complaint was aired by the Mabou Mines theater collective in its *Red Horse Animation*, first performed at the Guggenheim Museum in 1970. It casually links a problem of art to a problem of democracy. Once America became overwhelmingly dependent on the mass media, both our political representatives and our dramatic representations began to seem alien to us, although a full sense of their estrangement may come to us only in moments of doubt. The political movements of the 1960s seemed to counter the expressive power of the media in their own mass terms, but also proved to be too easily assimilable by the media. There ensued, for those who made this observation, a moment of doubt as to whether we could in fact realize democratic ideals within the mass modes. At that moment, the fact that theater is a non-mass art took on a new relevance for some of its students, trained in the collectivist ideals and improvisatory theater practices of the 1960s, and immersed in the anomalous street culture of Manhattan, where the most valued performances are the least reproducible ones.

They became members of various group theaters, who produced a rich and confident body of work in New York in the 1970s. Group theaters tended to have corporate names—e.g., Mabou Mines, the Wooster Group, the Ridiculous Theatrical Company, the Talking Band— with more or less explicit charters that ceded decision making to all the members, and original repertories whose style and content drew on the peculiar characters of, and relations among, the members. The groups' collaborative process was time-consuming, and its products anything but commercial; but in the 1970s more grants became available to experimental artists, and in Manhattan rehearsal and performance space was still affordable. Even so, that process, and the complexity and refinement of its products, were the groups' chief luxuries; the biggest grants barely covered several salaries, and the group ethos restrained members from becoming stars. The Reagan 1980s brought cuts in arts funding and skyrocketing New York rents that finished some of the groups and left others struggling to survive.

The vacuum they left in avant-garde theater was then filled by a new breed of solo performers who call themselves "performance artists." Just as the collective image of the groups reflected their audiences' still-cherished commitment to social experiment, the performance artists' stance of go-it-alone appeals to those self-seekers of the 1980s who want to believe there is something radical about their individualism.

Observers of the small world of New York avant-garde theater seldom make much distinction between performance artists and the remaining group theaters. Some multipurpose "performance spaces," like the Kitchen, the Performing Garage, and La Mama, host both (the groups also play more traditional theaters, while performance artists often work nightclubs). They compete for the same grants and perform at each other's benefits. The two styles came together in the career of Spalding Gray, whose autobiographical monologues established a genre of performance art. Gray joined Richard Schechner's Performance Group in 1970, quit in 1975 to co-found the Wooster Group, then in 1986 quit it to pursue the solo career he had begun as a sideline in 1979. Gray's success—in the last few years he's had two best-selling books, talk-show appearances, and a feature film accompanied by a publicity blitz—serves both as a measure of performance art's growing popularity, and as a contrast to the group theaters' complete failure to attract the attention of the media. Still, Gray and his audiences assume that he brings with him the anti-establishment cachet of the milieu from which he emerged when he plugs his movie on the David Letterman show or muses on his success in the pages of *Rolling Stone*.

Part of that cachet derives from the term "performance art" itself, which has one meaning in theory but two in practice. The term was coined in the 1960s to describe a variety of acts staged by visual artists who were concerned less with entertaining than with registering a protest against art marketers whose hunger for durable objects increased with their skill at manipulating the objects' prices. Projects as different as those of Chris Burden (a masochist who specialized in putting himself in danger of getting electrocuted, shot, suffocated, etc.) and Nam June Paik (basically a Dadaist who updated the style by incorporating video and other technology in his performances) were alike mainly in their failure to appreciate in cash value at the same rate as paintings and sculptures. These gestures of protest were nonetheless worked out entirely within the terms of current art-history debate. By accepting its terms, performance art ultimately confirmed the art world's power; and in return the art world allotted spaces and funds to performance art, sometimes extending these to performers from the dance, theater, or music worlds. Some group theaters used the margin occupied by performance art as a temporary refuge for work that commercial theaters were not yet ready to accept (Mabou Mines, for instance, graduated from museums to a long association with the Public Theater). Certain other performers had an affinity for solo work

that drove them from the group-dominated 1970s theater scene into the art world, where their theatrical instincts set them apart from the visual artists (who, having defined performance art as anticommercial, had a stake in keeping it so).

Laurie Anderson, the first successful (recordings, videos, movies) entertainer/performance artist, acquired her art world credentials in the 1970s, then went on to build her reputation as an entertainer in the clubs and theaters that became her springboard to media prominence in the 1980s. By that time, in downtown New York, theater and nightclub owners needed low-overhead entertainment, and theater audiences were no longer opposed to the idea of a star system. Still, no one likes to abandon ideals outright.

Although in the art world the label of "performance art" is still a token of relative integrity, in the entertainment world it has started to stick to any solo act that smacks of the outré. Whereas both group theater and the earlier kind of performance art expressed resistance to the culture market, the later strain of performance art presents itself as a "new, improved" variant of commodities already on the market.

Performance artists usually write, and often direct, their own acts; unlike movie or television stars, they seem to control their means of production. But then, so do vaudeville acts, pop stars, and, especially, stand-up comedians—who take a more defensive stance toward their audience than other types of solo act (think of Don Rickles's insults, or Joan Rivers's preemptive self-deprecation) and appear naked of props or accompaniment. (This brand of naked individualism has had a recent surge in popularity, spawning the publicist's proverb, "Comedy is the rock and roll of the 1980s.")

Not coincidentally, performance artists tend to model their acts on those of vaudevillians (Bill Irwin), pop stars (Laurie Anderson), and, especially, stand-up comedians (Eric Bogosian, Ann Magnuson, and Spalding Gray, among others). They appropriate familiar forms in the name of parody or *hommage* and in the interest of efficient packaging ("performance art" has itself become a publicist's handle, while "group theater" is my provisional name for a movement never marketed as such).

In our "self-directed" society, images of autonomy are so familiar as to seem inevitable; and these images fit into the promotional machinery already firmly in place. Performance artists simply accept the "inevitable." Why bother to construct images when you can find them ready-made?

Images of cooperation are harder to come by. The group theaters' models for community are often makeshifts, unelaborated but suggestive, like the bare frame of a house that keeps reappearing in the Wooster Group's plays. In *Route 1 & 9* (1981), the actors assemble the house while blindfolded by taped-over sunglasses, so that their close cooperation is seen to be not just desirable but necessary. This straightforward image rests at the center point of a play that otherwise offers no direct answer to the question of how we might imagine and construct new communities. The notion of a coherent body politic is hedged with quotation marks in *Route 1 & 9*'s first part, which consists of a videotape, played on monitors hung over the performance space, of the group's re-creation of an Encyclopedia Britannica film on how to read *Our Town*. Later in the play, as the performers below evoke a community torn apart by near-demonic forces, excerpts from *Our Town* reappear on the monitors. This time the quotation marks restore a pathos we had almost forgotten how to read into *Our Town*, after seeing so many productions that treated its small-town values as if it were our unchanging reality rather than a fading myth of lost paradise. Along with the play's meaning, *Route 1 & 9* retrieves the memory of those productions, of the school and community theaters where so many of us acquired our first theatergoing habits—of an experience and a text we had almost forgotten we had in common, because they fall outside the power of mass culture.

In other plays of the Wooster Group, *Long Day's Journey Into Night, The Crucible,* and *The Cocktail Party* are also presented in

reconditioned fragments as pieces of the common knowledge of our culture. The group's indirect route to a possible social future thus lies through part of our shared past, leading back from American theater history to fragmentary memories of community—not the media community of interchangeable consumers, but the communities represented in concentrated form at civic gatherings, which audience and performers alike attend so as to feel their character tested and confirmed by the strains of relation. The mass media can only simulate (in laugh tracks or fireside chats) the living presence of others. But theater can actually reproduce that sense of presence, although contemporary theater more often tries to simulate the alienating effects of the media (e.g., Neil Simon's sitcomlike one-liners and the cinematic special effects of Trevor Nunn and Andrew Lloyd Webber spectaculars like *Cats* and *Starlight Express*). The group theaters, however, in turning away from mass culture chose to resume what Clement Green-

berg identified as the modernist artist's proper task, "the use of the characteristic methods of a discipline to criticize the discipline itself—not in order to subvert it, but to entrench it more firmly in its area of competence." Much as Greenberg's modernist painter emphasized painting's flatness, the quality distinguishing it not only from sculpture but also from inherently illusionistic media like film and photography, so the groups drew attention to theater's *liveness*, the volatile quality of the relationship between the members of the audience and their "representatives" onstage, which sets theater apart from inherently alienating media like films and television.

The groups first tested the principle of full democratic representation under the lab conditions of rehearsal. They continued to value the principle even as they endured the agonies of trying to put it into practice. As Mabou Mines's Lee Breuer noted in a recent interview, "the power struggle under the surface" of collaborative groups often tore them apart after "a half-life of about five years." Mabou Mines, however, is still together after seventeen years, which Breuer depicts as stormy but ultimately rewarding: "Now it's a true ensemble—the first thinking ensemble." In a 1960s ensemble like the Living Theater, group impulse was exalted over individual will, but the 1970s ensembles felt that the truest expression of group impulse would allow (if just barely) for the greatest possible measure of individual will.

Some groups had votes and called meetings; but, aware that their forte was art, not government, they relied chiefly on a common language to mediate the clash of wills. What most group members had in common were extended 1960s picaresque educations in theater, in the course of which they absorbed a wide variety of texts and techniques. As a result, the style they forged was a virtuoso blend of techniques, and their texts often quoted the Western theater canon as if it were a privileged language. When Andrei Serban and Elizabeth Swados translated Aeschylus into an invented language for their group piece *Fragments of a Trilogy*, or Charles Ludlam and the

Ridiculous Theatrical Company rendered *Camille* as a drag tour-de-force, they drew their audiences into the work of recognizing quotations, and thereby into their project of recovering theater as a cultural *lingua franca*. The groups also peppered this theater language with the icons and styles of pop culture, both to reclaim them as parts of live speech, and to remind themselves and their audiences of mass culture's capacity for absorbing and alienating us from our means of direct experience.

In the shadow of mass culture, then, the groups and their audiences kept returning to the theater to relearn the language of direct experience. The audience of Mabou Mines's *The Lost Ones*, adapted by Lee Breuer from a Beckett novel, were crowded into a miniature amphitheater with binoculars scattered on its steps. They needed the binoculars to accommodate themselves to a second shift in scale effected when an actor, David Warrilow, opened a small case to reveal another amphitheater in which he placed tiny figures, who, he explained at length, were the disinherited, the not-us. So far the audience was reminded that art distances; and that they were accustomed to viewing the "lost ones" as if through glass; but a blackout was followed by a third shift in scale as Warrilow appeared, suddenly naked, on the steps. He was at once a giant figure, the poor, bare, forked animal, and unmistakably one of us. *The Lost Ones* taught its audience how to see others (as Emerson says) as if they were real, as well as to see themselves not just as perceivers of, but as participants in, a common experience. The play's images imply that the lesson can't be reproduced on a mass scale. Common sense adds that so small an audience requires subsidy. And finally, the subtext of group work, the tissue of relations between members, makes their productions seem especially fragile next to the hardy products of mass culture. *The Lost Ones* had to be taken out of repertory when David Warrilow left Mabou Mines.

The groups shared a belief that figures could not be separated from their social ground. This brand of individualism is thereby strongly at odds with that of performance artists, who style themselves outsiders (hence Eric Bogosian's gallery of addicts and killers, or Karen Finley's compulsive taboo-breaking). Mass culture, however, is all "outside," since it denies the existence of any specific social context that might impede the reduction of individuals to those depersonalized consumers and replaceable stars who keep filling roles predetermined for them by the entertainment industry. Those who obligingly enter on the task of self-making apart from any social context often find themselves (like *Psycho*'s Norman in the archetypically American isolation of the Bates Motel) developing borderline personalities. The main character in Mabou Mines's *A Prelude to Death in Venice* (1979) details the process: "I go into myself. I become self-involved. I try to be self-effacing. But that's self-defeating. I indulge in self-recrimination. But all that does is make me more self-centered" — and so on—until he ends up "beside myself . . . I'm on the edge. I'm on the edge of being a *self-made,* man." Since the character is represented by a bunraku puppet, he is in fact beside himself, dependent for his every move on an onstage puppeteer, actor Bill Raymond,

who plays both his double and his agent, "Bill Morris." The would-be self-maker represses his conscious sense of dependence on others, only to feel it return as the sense of being manipulated by outside forces.

The individualism of the group theaters was formed in the context of a permanent struggle between dependence and independence, cooperation and individuation. From that perspective, the isolation of the "autonomist" looks like an escapist fantasy. But performance artists take this fantasy for a fact, and they focus on it with an intensity that sets them apart from the mainstream types they might otherwise resemble. Whereas mainstream entertainers employ conventions that smooth the transitions between bits of material, performance artists draw attention to the gaps in their stories, which they see as the necessary consequence of their isolation from others who might fill them in. The only big picture they can form is that of the paranoid: since none of it fits together, it must all fit together. In his monologue *Swimming to Cambodia*, Spalding

Gray cites a series of carefully disconnected facts about the American invasion and internal politics of Cambodia, but still finds himself at a loss to explain the reign of the Khmer Rouge. He finally resorts to his own theory of "an invisible cloud of evil that circles the world and lands at random in Germany, Cambodia, possibly Iran and Beirut, maybe even America." This theory is the fruit of a political education that began with Gray's participation in the film *The Killing Fields* (when he confessed his ignorance of politics in an audition, the director's response was "Perfect! We're looking for the American ambassador's aide") and later ended in a monologue. In the monologue as in the movie, our view of historical process is restricted to the few glimpses we can get through the eyes of certain star personalities. Their dominating presence tempts us to infer that the remainder of history (everything that can't be seen through the star's mask) must be "invisible"—that is, unknowable by the isolate personalities in the audience of whom the star is only a magnification.

When Gray's own try at personifying history breaks down in the worst sort of abstraction, he pauses, then reverts to the sort of personal anecdote he tells best. He met a man once; and the man turns out to be none other than history with a human face, not so much Gray's magnification as his distorted (because previously repressed) reflection. This Navy man he met in the no-context of a train's lounge car was, like Gray, a hedonist, a globe-hopper, a solitary. But whereas Gray believes that sex, drugs, and travel broaden the mind, and isolation fosters a healthy skepticism, his acquaintance has carried self-seeking to its logical conclusions: self-alienation—"I wouldn't mind watching her get fucked by a guy once" is his one thought about his wife—and isolation, which has bred in him a delusive identification with state power. Delusive but dangerous, since this anti-Gray is literally connected to history, chained for five hours a day to a button that activates a nuclear warhead. Gray's studious detachment (he calls himself "the perceiver") leaves him helpless in

a confrontation with his opposite number. "I don't know what my platform was—I mean, he was standing for all of America and I was just concerned for myself at that point. I really felt as if I were looking my death in the face."

Yet Gray the perceiver stands for "all of America" quite as much as the button-pusher. Both value their isolation (which they would call independence) and imagine that the best way to preserve that isolation is to defer, when in doubt, to the fully worked-out platform of the powers that be. The moment Gray almost realizes how much his isolation costs is the most powerful in *Swimming to Cambodia*. But the monologue leaves this anecdote behind as Gray becomes more and more fascinated with the way "the camera eroticizes the space" around certain individuals, and so seems to lift them out of history. He ends the film and part I of the stage and book versions of *Swimming to Cambodia* with a new theory: "I suddenly thought I knew what it was that killed Marilyn Monroe." This sudden conversion to star worship comes late in the career of a man who said he had given up on professional acting partly because he "couldn't stand all the waiting while that big, indifferent machine made up its so-called mind."

In the 1970s, the group theater scene offered a disgruntled actor like Gray the chance to achieve genuine independence from the entertainment industry. In the 1980s, Gray and a generation of performers too young to have had his chances have rerouted the impulses of that avant-garde back into the channels of consumption. In an interview, Laurie Anderson tried to talk around the fact that by doing the job herself she had simply saved the machine the trouble of packaging another commodity.

> My idea with making things like records satisfied me because as a performance artist I produce no real physical objects. And a record . . . it's skinny, it's small, and it's cheap, and it's exactly the piece and everybody gets exactly the same thing, and it's *affordable* . . . I like the idea, also, of using a system like a large record company to do it.

The group theaters knew that consumer capitalism was not just one of those user-friendly systems now becoming widely available to the non-pro. It is a big machine, one which is, moreover, designed to make relationships unreadable. The groups therefore took relationships as their text and re-taught themselves and their audiences how to *read*, casually linking the practice of their art with the practice of democracy in the process. They would admit that the model communities they built on the system's shrinking margin were small-scale and fragile, not in the manner of someone confessing a weakness, but of someone imparting a difficult truth about democratic ideals. □

MEMORIES AND IMPRESSIONS

Paula Fox

CIVIL SOCIETY

Moments of Vividness & Promise

I was born in New York City, and I have lived in or around it for a good part of my life. Some neighborhoods, although altered nearly beyond recognition, are still charged for me with the emotions of past events—at least, during those moments when I pass through them.

For what seemed one hundred years, I paid rent to landlords for wildly differing lodgings in various sections of the city. I was always trying to find a way to get out of it during that time, a time when I imagined that if I could only find the right place, the difficulties of life would vanish.

The first time I recall glimpsing New York as a whole was from the deck of a Hudson River Dayliner when I was four or five years old. But I must have found the view of Riverside Drive and its towers oppressive, for I remember I soon returned to a spot near a railing from which I could stare down at the heads of the musicians of a band sitting, two decks below, on camp chairs, playing "Hail, Columbia!" for the pleasure of the passengers. Seventeen years later, a year after the end of the Second World War, I saw the city again—from the outside—as I stood on the deck of a partly reconverted Liberty ship on which I was going to Europe. I didn't look at it for long that time either. I was getting away at last!

By then, I had come to know New York well, the way you know a city when you've had jobs in it—most of them pretty awful—that keep you more or less fed, and out of the weather. No matter what the circumstances, I always found the city hard to live in. But there were moments of vividness and promise, even of glamour. It is startling to recollect them. Cesare Pavese wrote in his diary, "Real amazement comes from memory . . ."

People, some of them now names on headstones, were walking around the city in the days of my youth, and you might run into them in all sorts of places. I met Duke Ellington on a flight of marble stairs leading down from an exhibit by the painter Stuart Davis. I heard Huddie (Leadbelly) Ledbetter play on his guitar and sing *The Midnight Special* at a party in Greenwich Village for a cause I've forgotten. In a jazz club on 52nd Street that was called, I think, Kelly's Stable, Billie Holiday turned to me from the bar as I was passing her and asked me—"Darlin', would you mind?"—to pick up her fur coat, which had fallen to the floor behind her bar stool. Later that same evening, the club doors were shut and I was among a few people who stayed inside, sitting around a table, listening to her sing far into the night. I was taken to the Savoy Ballroom in Harlem where I watched dancers bend and circle and hurl their partners through the air and, miraculously, catch them, to the music of two bands led by Cootie Williams and Lucky Millendar, and then was, myself, drawn into the dance, wondering when the floor would give way then not caring whether it did or not. From Charles Street, where I had an apartment for a while, I could walk a couple of blocks to a bar on Seventh Avenue and hear Art Tatum play the piano all evening for the price of a glass of beer.

One evening I went to Lewisohn Stadium to hear Paul Robeson sing. Planes flew overhead, searchlights played against the sky. Quite suddenly, Robeson walked out onto the stage in a blue suit. He was so splendid, so exalted to listen to, to look at, that the audience itself, I among them, seemed to feel an answering exaltation.

I met him twice after that concert, once in California during the run of *Othello*, and a second time in New York City a few weeks after I had come home from Europe.

Memory always seems to begin in the middle of some story. I had a friend who was a friend of Robeson's. Robeson was spending time with his son, Pauli, who had come to the city from his prep school, somewhere to the north. I recall the four of us in a taxi, but not where we had met before catching it. We were going to a nightclub, Café Society Uptown, to hear a French *chanteuse*, Lucienne Boyer. There was conversation, but I don't recollect saying a word though I must have done so for I remember Robeson looking at me and speaking, smiling. I stole a glance at his hands. Someone had told me that when he played on the Rutgers football team, his own teammates had deliberately trodden on his hands during practice sessions.

The doorman of the club, and the maître d'hôtel who hurried toward us through a shadowed foyer, both recognized Robeson, at whose request we were taken to small room with a balcony that overlooked the main space of the café. Lucienne Boyer was singing in French as we sat down. She stood in a shower of light in a gold dress. She sang a few songs in English; one of them was *The Man I Love*. Robeson hummed along with her, filling the balcony with the indescribable plangency of his voice though it was inaudible to the people sitting below. He whispered to me suddenly to sing, too. I quavered out a few lines then fell silent, overwhelmed at the idea of singing with Paul Robeson. Well—almost singing.

Afterwards, we all went to Grand Central where Pauli was to take a train back to his school. It must have been nearly midnight. In those days, centers of commerce, office districts, even railroad stations, were often deserted at such an hour. As we walked down the wide stairs, our footsteps echoed throughout the vast reaches of the station where not even a late traveler could be seen hurrying to a last train home. The four of us could have been alone.

Then, from every corner of the station, silently flying toward us like swallows, came the station porters in their red hats, converging on Robeson and his son as they reached the bottom step. He stood among them for several moments, talking and listening, laughing at something, once, that one of the porters said to him. That is the place where my memory ends, Robeson on a step, laughing, his head thrown back, his son standing next to him, one of the porters suddenly gesturing toward a platform entrance as though Pauli's train was about to leave and they must run now to catch it.

I see the past differently as I grow older, and so, in a sense, the past changes. I once thought it was the high emotional tone of that evening that made it so memorable for me, its drama. Now I wonder if I did not feel some immense consolatory quality in Robeson's presence that I may have seen reflected on the faces of the porters. I don't really know. But recently I came upon something from the *Book of Common Prayer*: "Thanks be to the Lord: for he has showed me marvellous great kindness in a strong city." I had been thinking about what to write for this magazine, and as I read the word "city" I recalled all at once that evening.

There isn't much social kindness—certainly not civility—in New York anymore. It isn't a "strong" city; it's weakened by greed and waste and the shameless inequities that are their result. The triumphant stupidities, the material preoccupations and fashions of many of its inhabitants appear to me to belong to a world devised in its entirety by Dostoevski's Smerdyakov.

One day recently, I got off the subway from Brooklyn where I now live, and walked through a long passage beneath Fifth Avenue. Against the walls, I counted eleven people, some black, some white, two of them women, lying down or sitting slouched over on sections of dusty cardboard. It was early morning; a number of people were on their way to work, briefcases and bags swinging at their sides. As they passed the fallen on their cardboard pallets, their faces were utterly vacant. Many of them were heavily perfumed, and what struck me was that men and women alike were wearing the same very strong scent. Even so, it couldn't expunge the stench and reek of urine, of the unwashed and undernourished flesh of the people who sought shelter in the passage.

I recognized that scent; it had been sprayed on me as I walked through a department store by one of those clerks with an atomizer who spring at one like a tomcat. I believe its name is *Poison*. □

Michael Harrington

WHEN ED KOCH WAS STILL A LIBERAL

Memories of a Man and His Times

I cannot give the precise date when I first met Ed Koch. Encountering this unassuming if enthusiastic man, I had no idea that he was going to play a major role in the political history of New York City. Koch was a young lawyer who had been, quite briefly, a member of the Tamawa Club, the stronghold of the "regular" Democrats in the South Village ("Little Italy") led by boss Carmine De Sapio. That hardly seemed a port of entry for an aspiring young Jewish politician. One election night, Stephanie Gervis, the *Village Voice* reporter whom I later married, was sent up to Tamawa and I went with her. We were asked to leave rather quickly—the *Voice* was a center of the anti-DeSapio movement—but not before we took in a room in which the women sat in chairs along the walls while the men milled around the center, and the ethnicity was as unmistakable as at Our Lady of Pompeii on Bleecker and Carmine Streets.

That ethnic description has to do with a fact, not with a prejudice. At the time we made our brief visit to Tamawa, Stephanie and I were living together just down from Our Lady of Pompeii in the heart of the Italian South Village. Our neighbors were easygoing and tolerant. We were not, then, unsympathetic to the ethnics who thronged the Tamawa Club that night. The simple reality was, however, that Tamawa was as Italian as the Democratic party of my youth in St. Louis was Irish. And Village Independent Democrats (VID), like the entire Manhattan left of that period, was heavily Jewish. So it was that Ed Koch rather quickly found his way up to the VID loft on Sheridan Square.

I simplify. When Sarah Schoenkopf (later Kovner) took her place at the Democratic State Committee,

there were eleven reformers out of some three hundred members. That little band included WASPs of considerable wealth and family, like Marietta Tree, as well as Jewish reformers like Sarah. Indeed, the progressive wing of the New York Democrats was then something of an alliance between wealthy patrician reformers on the Averell Harriman model, and liberal "upstarts," usually Jewish. I had some reservations about the politics of these reformers, not least because I had never participated in the cult of Adlai Stevenson in 1952. The reformers had proclaimed him the first real egghead in American politics and all but idolized him. I thought of Stevenson as an aloof aristocrat who was really not at home in the party of the American working class, and as a Churchillian conservative who would have made a marvelous Tory candidate for prime minister—which in the United States put him on the left.

When I got to know Ed Koch, he was in the process of becoming the VID's candidate for district leader (male). He had the look of a diffident, somewhat lovable *schlemiel* and was utterly lacking in the overweening self-confidence he acquired as mayor. I liked him immediately, particularly when I discovered that the retiring, modest manner concealed a political maverick. There was a split in the reform movement between the purists and those who understood that they had to become politicians—a new and different kind, to be sure, but politicians nevertheless. At the VID, for instance, there were members who didn't want to get involved in the struggle over naming judges on the grounds that the whole process should be taken out of politics (they rarely specified how that could be achieved). Koch was in the realist camp and would make funny, but acid, comments about his coworkers who were utterly dedicated to losing.

By a not surprising dialectic, once I had decided to enter the unprincipled precincts of the Democratic party it never occurred to me to be opposed to compromise. How could one be pure in an institution that was unprincipled on principle? My radicalism made me something of a realist, which may be why I found Koch's witty cynicism quite congenial.

Koch as a Liberal

This is not to say that he was simply a disappointed apprentice from Tamawa who had made his way to the VID for opportunistic reasons and therefore took the side of *realpolitik*. He was then a deeply committed and gutsy liberal. In 1964 he had gone to Mississippi in a summer that saw three civil rights workers (one black, two Jewish) murdered. That he was quite visible and quite Jewish was not something to endear him to the racists of Mississippi. In 1965 he had staked, and almost lost, his political career when he broke ranks and endorsed John Lindsay for mayor. Stephanie remembers him mulling over that decision in the *Village Voice* office, talking about it with Dan Wolfe, the then editor of the *Voice* who was his mentor. Koch, she remembers, was extremely nervous and very much aware of the danger of what he was doing.

There were those who wanted to purge the handful of liberal Democratic office holders that made the same courageous switch, but Koch survived his principled decision. Later, when he ran for Lindsay's old congressional seat, Lindsay endorsed the Republican candidate against him, an act that Koch bitterly resented. And rightly so.

Even in those early days, Koch was working out a position that turned out to be shrewd politics but pitted him against many in the VID. There was more than a little of the Town-Gown relationship between Tamawa and VID: the working Italian-Americans who lived in tenements, as against the college-educated, mainly Jewish reformers. I don't want to romanticize Little Italy. When Howard Moody, the pastor of Judson Memorial Church on Washington Square—officially a Baptist and United Church of Christ institution, which probably had more atheists, gays, lesbians, and political radicals than any other church in New York—tried to involve some of the leaders of the Italian community in an antidrug program, they resented his Protestant poaching and told him that their youth were not in any danger. A little later, a young man died from an overdose in a doorway just across from Our Lady of Pompeii.

There can be no doubt that the hostility of the Italian-Americans to the interracial scene in Washington Square was partly motivated by racist attitudes. But Ed Koch understood— rightly, I think—that racism was not the whole story. The traditionalist Villagers who lived in the tenements along MacDougal Street—a central artery of the Bohemian Village—were hardly being racist when they complained that they were kept up late at night by the floating party on the streets below. Koch was one of the first of the reformers to reach out to the Italians, to listen to their complaints, and even try to do something about them. That was innovative, intelligent, and, it turned out, good politics as well.

All of which made me admire Ed Koch as well as like him personally. Still, if truth be told, with each of his triumphs Stephanie and I were convinced that it would be his last. When he did defeat De Sapio, we thought he had had his moment—but then he went on to the City Council. That, we thought, would be the climax of a career that had already carried this maverick yet unprepossessing man to unimagined heights. The next thing I knew, Ed asked me to chair his citizens' committee when he ran for Congress. I agreed. Once more I thought Koch had set his sights too high. He won again, of course.

It was at this point that I began to give him advice he carefully ignored. Why not, I said to him, become a ten- or twelve- term member of the House? Pick a committee which is important to you, become its chairman, and help shape the legislative agenda of the nation. But what Ed Koch wanted, above all else, was to be mayor of New York City. This improbable politician would sit in a Village bar (but drink very little) and tell me how he wanted to be like Fiorello LaGuardia. I knew, of course, that that was an utter impossibility.

In the mid-1960s mayoralty campaigns were still in the future. Congressmember Koch had been one of the first politicians to oppose the Vietnam War. At one of the huge Washington mobilizations at which he spoke, someone who came after him began to denounce Israel as a puppet of American imperialism. Koch recounted with gusto how he, a dignitary on this occasion, had rushed toward the podium and yelled "Fuck you!" at the speaker. I liked that quality in Koch and I shared his support of Israel, an attitude that was sometimes controversial in the rarefied precincts of the reform movement.

That maverick spirit was also quite visible during one of the worst moments in New York politics: the school strike in 1968. I have to go a long way around in describing that event, but doing so will identify some of the factors that led to Ed Koch's dramatic political shift in the 1970s.

John Lindsay, elected mayor in 1965 with Koch's support, had decentralized the public school system, creating local and elected district boards of education. In the Ocean Hill-Brownsville section, a black ghetto in Brooklyn, a bitter dispute occurred. Several white teachers were summarily removed by the local, predominantly black school board and sent back to the central office for reassignment to another district. The union challenged that action on grounds of due process, a challenge I approved. But that move was seen by blacks and a majority of Manhattan reformers as an authoritarian, even racist, policy. A bitter struggle followed, which was part tragedy—a conflict between two rights—and part an ugly farce pitting a superficial utopianism against an insensitive emphasis upon formal rights. I found myself in the middle, agreeing with the union on the specific issue, sympathetic to the local black school board and yet suspicious of some absurd claims made on its behalf.

Not a few of the black activists and reformers believed that decentralization was a gate to the educational millennium. If only the local community could control its own institutions, the children would miraculously increase their reading, and other academic, skills. But, I argued in the debates of that time, shrewd conservatives like William F. Buckley, Jr., and Barry Goldwater were perfectly willing to let poor blacks have community control of their ghettos in Brooklyn and Manhattan so long as rich whites had community control of Park Avenue and Wall Street. In the name of a romantic exaltation of the "power of the people," many advocates of a decentralist panacea had forgotten about the power of class structures. White teachers—Jewish white teachers, for there was sometimes more than a hint of anti-Semitism in the dispute—were *the* cause of educational backwardness among so many of the

poor. Give authority to a local school board, and leave every other social determinant in its unjust place, and all would be well.

Al Shanker, president of the United Federation of Teachers, tended to treat the issue as if it were a simple collective-bargaining dispute. He routinely talked on television about the contract, but ignored the fact that the actions of many in the black community were a desperate *cri de coeur* over the fate of children. The utopianism of the local militants was more a product of the social agony of their daily lives than of the shallow theories they sometimes espoused. I supported the union, yet I was all but torn in two by my profound sympathies with those on the other side who, I thought, were morally right, legally wrong, and very ill-advised by theorists from outside their community.

I was then quite friendly with Al Shanker. The first time I met him, in 1964 or 1965, we had together visited a New Jersey grape importer urging him to honor Cesar Chavez's boycott of nonunion grapes from California, and he had gone on to play a major role in supporting that struggle of poor—and mainly minority—workers. Around the same time, there was a united front of the United Federation of Teachers and the militant black community in a boycott of a school system in which inferior education of the poor and shabby treatment of the teachers alike. When Shanker was jailed in a union dispute in 1965 he received a check from Martin Luther King, Jr., to help pay his costs (and shrewdly framed it rather than cash it). Shanker was later to move toward neoconservatism, like certain others of my comrades of that period. But in 1968, I was unaware that such reversals were soon to take place.

My wife suggested that I try to persuade Al to articulate the union position as a commitment to the children rather than as a case for the sanctity of the contract.

I went to the Gramercy Park Hotel, where

Shanker was staying for the duration of the dispute, and was admitted to his room by an armed guard (given the virulence of the dispute, that was not a sign of paranoia). The local board, I said to Al, was presenting its case in terms of the children, and he was talking only about union rights. He was, I continued, committed to the children, too, and should make clear that the union's position was not based on mere legalism.

The insistence on tenure rights, I suggested, should be thought of as a means to attain quality education for all, particularly for minority youth. Al was extremely receptive to my message and told me that he would take it to heart. The next night, or so it seemed to me, he was back to talking about the contract.

The progressive community was deeply divided. There were reform Democrats who broke into public schools and tried to keep them open despite the strike—an action the entire left would have denounced as "scabbing" only a few years before. There were also some anti-Semitic leaflets passed out in Brooklyn. At the same time, the cause of the black community school district was clearly one that commanded moral solidarity on the part of anyone committed to civil rights. And that was true even though the claims for the educational gains to be made through decentralization were obviously extreme. (To his credit, Kenneth Clark, an articulate champion of the local board, later candidly said that he had been wrong in claiming that decentralization would have an enormous educational impact.)

This 1968 confrontation was to prefigure the split in the liberal-labor-black movement which was a precondition of Republican presidential victories. It was also one of the reasons why Ed Koch was to change so much in the 1970s.

Dissonant Notes

It was during those years that I went with Koch, then running for Congress, to a meeting of the upper-middle-class left in a comfortable Manhattan apartment. Koch's position was suitably unclassifiable and, I think, quite genuine. He was, he said, opposed to the strike on the grounds that it was a violation of the state law that denied public employees the right to walk off the job. That satisfied those who were, for whatever reason, against the strike. But, Koch continued, he supported the union's basic demand with regard to the teachers who had been summarily removed. That sat well with the union and its backers. One could argue that this was a calculated exercise in political opportunism, but I don't think so now and didn't then. I did not agree with him—I thought the state

antistrike law an abomination—yet I found his strange attitude totally consistent with his maverick personality. It was, I thought (and think), of a piece with his simultaneous anticommunism and opposition to the Vietnam War.

In any case, I continued to regard Ed as part of my own world and, as late as the summer of 1974, he endorsed my candidacy for delegate to the Democratic Mid-Term Convention. But by then there were some significant intimations that a change was under way.

In 1973, Koch began testing the waters for a mayoral candidacy. He asked Stephanie and me to invite a few friends over to our place in the West Village. Ed arrived with a small retinue from his congressional staff. One of those present was Norman Dorsen, a professor at New York University Law School and a major figure in the American Civil Liberties Union. There soon broke out a sharp conflict between Dorsen, me, and Stephanie on one side, and Ed Koch on the other.

T his was not too long after a furious dispute about a proposed public housing project in the middle- and upper-middle-class area of Forest Hills. The actual proposal, I felt, was ill-conceived: a huge high-rise project in the midst of houses and apartments built to a much more human scale. But is was quite clear that a good part of the opposition to the Forest Hills scheme was based not on objections to a flawed plan, but on a racist hostility to any public housing that would bring blacks into the neighborhood. The liberal position—to build the project, but scaled down, so that it would fit into the area—was defended by a young Italian-American lawyer from Queens named Mario Cuomo. The opponents of the project engaged in strident, and almost openly racist, rhetoric. And Koch took their side.

That evening in our apartment on Perry Street, Ed talked about the need for a social-environmental impact statement whenever public housing was proposed. Strongly challenged by Norman Dorsen and me, he went so far as to argue that blacks really wanted to stay in their own neighborhoods, that they didn't want to mix with whites (many of whom, in the case of Forest Hills, were Jewish). I was appalled. Still, the debate was civil, though sharp. As the evening came to an end, Stephanie said—and I agreed completely—"Ed, don't give up your principles as a tactic in a mayoral campaign you can't even win." We were right on the first, moral count; but in 1977, history was to prove us wrong in our prediction. Ed's switch was indeed one of the reasons he became mayor of New York.

Forest Hills, a turning point for both Koch and the

liberal Jewish community, was in some ways a continuation of the civil war that had started within the left during the Teachers' strike of 1968. It took a while for me to realize that Ed Koch's attitude on Forest Hills was not an isolated exercise but a deliberate political move. In 1975 and 1976, as he geared up for a serious run for the mayoralty in 1977, he moved to the right on a whole series of issues. He began to emphasize his support for capital punishment, a position totally irrelevant to the office of mayor but having a lot to do with the feelings of the white, middle-class electorate in New York. So it was that in the 1977 race I found myself backing Bella Abzug against Ed Koch. And therein lies a story.

Bella and Ed

My early relations with Bella were a disaster but by the mid-1970s I had changed my mind about her. My original hostility had much to do with style—but also with a historic association of style and substance. Bella's manner was, and is, legendary in American politics: forceful, aggressive, sometimes (particularly in the 1960s and early 1970s) strident and even downright nasty. She was no doubt regularly victimized by a double standard: qualities deemed abrasive in a woman are often celebrated in a man.

When I first encountered Bella, I interpreted her style as an expression of a leftist tradition of high-minded viciousness, an ugly inheritance from Karl Marx's dyspeptic attitude toward all opponents. Bella had been a left Zionist as a college student and had learned her lesson all too well. I sensed a certain anti-anticommunism in her attitudes, a political position that was often expressed vituperatively. My reaction to Bella, then, was historical and political as well as personal.

Indeed, in the 1960s, one of the bonds between Ed Koch and me was a shared antipathy to Bella's manner as well as some questions about her views on the Middle East. But after the 1972 election, I became aware that she was one of the hardest-working, most effective members of Congress. A friend of mine, Steve Silbiger, then an aide to Representative Steve Solarz of Brooklyn, began to tell me, from an insider's vantage point, that she was a very serious liberal who, unlike some of her more mannerly colleagues, did an enormous amount of effective work. So my attitude began to change. At the same time, her attitudes toward both Soviet injustice and the defense of Israel, whatever they may once have been, were now similar to my own. When she ran against Daniel Moynihan for the Senate nomination in 1976, I was enthusiastic about her candidacy. It was not just that she would begin to integrate the Senate, the most sexist institution in American politics, but also that I thought she had a capacity to be a great senator. I still think I was right.

And so by 1977, my old friend, Ed Koch, had moved to the right and was running for mayor in a spirit that, I thought, appealed to some of the worst racist and anti-union emotions in the city, and I was a supporter of Bella Abzug, toward whom I had once been somewhat antagonistic. Still, I was not going to forget personal links even though political relations had changed. So I called up John LoCicero, an organizational lieutenant for Ed, and had coffee with him. I still liked Ed, I explained, but I now disagreed with him on some fundamental issues and could not support him for mayor. I asked LoCicero to inform Koch that my backing for Bella was not a personal matter but the result of deeply held political convictions.

Later, after Ed was elected, a friend of mine who had stuck with him told me that he had been quite angry that I had not, despite our differences, backed him. But even then there were still some strange twists left in our relationship.

In the primary, Koch had come in first, but he had to win a runoff race against Mario Cuomo. By that time, Stephanie and I were living on Mercer Street, a few short blocks from Ed's apartment on Washington Place. One night we ran into him as we emerged from an Italian restaurant. Stephanie spoke with considerable emotion, telling him she wanted to vote for him for old time's sake, but that some of his positions made it difficult to do so. She mentioned his attitude toward minorities and the unions and said, among other things, that he had to promise to talk with Victor Gotbaum, the leading public-employees trade unionist in town. Ed agreed and, after he won the runoff and was assured of victory, was as good as his word. Ed, his campaign adviser Dave Garth, Vic Gotbaum, and Stephanie and I had dinner together at Charley O's, a favorite Koch hangout.

There were two striking aspects of that dinner. One was that Koch told Gotbaum that, even as mayor-elect, he found it all but impossible to discover what the city finances really were (at this point, New York City was still in a deep fiscal crisis). And second, although Dave Garth was friendly and open, it was a new development in American politics that the leader of the largest city in the nation would, when meeting with the municipality's most powerful trade unionist, bring his media adviser along.

A year later—a year of bitter acrimony between Koch and Gotbaum—Stephanie and I were asked to dinner at the Gotbaums' as part of a kind of peace effort on both sides. Ed Koch and a few others were there; but it was a small affair and everything began on a pleasant, low key.

Early on I took Ed aside and talked with him about Ruth Messinger, a member of the City Council whom he was crudely attacking as a pro-Communist. And that brings me to the person who is, in many ways, the heroine of this story.

A Reformer Who Stayed That Way

I'm not sure exactly when I met Ruth. She was an activist on the West Side of Manhattan, one of those strange enclaves in which the left was the dominant political power. That meant, among other things, that it was the scene of titanic rhetorical battles over nuances of antiwar or antiracist and antisexist politics that would have been bewildering, not just to the Midwest but to Queens and Brooklyn as well. Ruth had managed to build a constituency and yet maintain a high seriousness about political and social issues.

One of her most trusted advisers was Paul DuBrul, who had joined the socialist movement when he was a student at Hunter College in the early 1960s. Ruth shared our politics and joined the Democratic Socialist Organizing Committee (DSOC).

Over the years, Ruth had done her homework, becoming an effective politician and then City Council member. Reformers—and it is not a sin peculiar to them—had a tendency to lofty generalizations, passionate opinions, and slipshod data. Ruth remained true to her basic principles, but she had learned to relate them to reality better than anyone I know. At the same time, she had been more giving of her time and commitment to DSOC (and later to Democratic Socialists of America—DSA) than any of our members in elected public life. And now Koch was red-baiting her.

I had often talked, privately and publicly, with Ruth on questions concerning freedom, democracy, and the Soviet sphere, and she was as horrified by violations of civil rights there as I. And her trusted confidant, Paul DuBrul, was implacably critical of the very foundation of the antidemocratic Communist regimes. He and Ruth, and the rest of us, were also opponents of America's militarist response to Communist wrongs, and proponents of disarmament and peace. Now Koch, who had seemed to have that very same mix of attitudes when he opposed

American intervention in Vietnam, was turning on Ruth in a scandalous way.

So I told him at the Gotbaums' what I said to him in a letter: that he was profoundly wrong about Ruth. He was, alas, noncommittal and his hostility to her continues to this day.

Have I then merely confirmed one of the oldest clichés of American politics? Was Ed Koch somewhat radical as a powerless young man, who then became smart and unprincipled as he got older and as serious power beckoned? I don't think so.

Why or Did Koch Change?

No doubt, life plays a conservatizing role with most of us. Those blinding, all-encompassing radical certitudes that sometimes are the epiphanies of youth no longer seem so dazzling. Complexities and shadows come into view. And yes, the actual exercise of power, or even its mere imminence, is often a reason for second thoughts.

But there are at least two basic objections to turning such insights into anything like a complete account of social realty. First, if individuals change in this fashion, the world does not. It may well be that younger people, fired with the passion to do something about poverty and war and injustice, become more conformist when they grow old. But that is sad since poverty and war and injustice do not disappear just because aging radicals are less willing to fight them.

And second, the cynical thesis operates imperfectly. That my worldview is more complicated than it was when I became a socialist at the age of twenty is obvious. But I have remained a socialist. And if Ed Koch changed, Ruth Messinger did not. One cannot deal with these matters on the basis of a few scraps of *realpolitik*.

Why did the process of conservatization become so much more pronounced in the 1970s and 1980s? One cannot account for that simply on the basis of individual life cycles. It is necessary to look at the social and historical context.

Ed Koch was, after all, not the only Jewish antiwar liberal who moved to the right. He was part of a social trend affecting many people like him, which is one of the reasons why I reject the simplistic notion that he simply "sold out." Norman Podhoretz, the editor of *Commentary* who happily printed my articles in the 1960s and then moved even further to the right than Koch in the 1970s and 1980s gained neither office nor money by his transformation. The explanation of Koch's conversion as a mere "sellout" misses trends much larger than the alleged opportunism of a single politician.

There was, after all, a general tendency within the Jewish left to turn from socialism or liberalism to neoconservatism. Koch was not an intellectual, yet he was certainly affected by the intellectual trends in the Jewish community. But since there were non-Jews who made the same transition—one thinks, for instance, of the Catholic writer Michael Novak who, as a peace activist, considered himself well to my left and then wound up far to my right— why insist upon the Jewish dimension of Koch's transformation?

Because the issue of Israel played an important role in it—not simply for him, but for a whole stratum of Jews in his generation. With the rise of the New Left in the 1960s, there was a simplistic trend to think of the Palestine Liberation Organization (PLO) as just another movement of national liberation that all progressives should support. Since the PLO was locked in struggle with Israel, that meant, it was illogically reasoned, that Israel must be a part of the imperialist system. That the Israelis themselves represented an earlier national liberation movement and that their conflict with the PLO was a counterposition of two legitimate rights was an idea too sophisticated for some of the youthful activists of the 1960s.

There were similar problems within the United States. During the terrible fight over school decentralization in New York in 1968, there were anti-Semitic leaflets and speeches from the side of those who saw themselves as pitted against a Jewish-led union. That some blacks were driven to such racism by the impossible conditions they had to confront in their daily lives makes it easier to explain even if it provides no reason for condoning what they said. The upper-middle- or even upper-class whites whose salon radicalism ignored, or even justified, that anti-Semitism in 1968 were intellectually wrong and morally reprehensible in a much less ambiguous sense than those whom they defended.

Koch was often rightly critical of the superficial and purist leftism in the early reform movement. He and people like him understandably turned their backs on the mistakes of their onetime friends and then wrongly embraced the principles of their onetime enemies.

In 1980, Koch, by then mayor of New York, made it quite clear that he regarded voting for Ronald Reagan as a decent thing to do. Like many others, he was responding to the crisis of liberalism when he moved to the right. There was a heady atmosphere in New York during the first term of John Lindsay. There was an alliance between an educated and privileged left and an impoverished, mainly black, mass. The go-go years were in full swing and it seemed that an endlessly growing GNP would finance permanent social experimentation. In point of fact, the experiments were much more moderate than the rhetoric. But then the weather changed. When the American economy was internationalized in an unprecedented fashion, when productivity dropped, when new jobs were primarily low paid and unorganized, and so on, many liberals came to agree with Richard Nixon.

The 1960s, Nixon had said in an enormously influential interview the day after his landslide reelection in 1972, had "thrown money at problems." That, as I have demonstrated at book length in *The New American Poverty* and *The Next Left*, was simply not true. The New York City crisis was not a result of the overcommitment of John Lindsay and other liberals. It was the consequence of massive national and international trends. Nixon's simplistic argument did not call for new attempts at innovation in a period when many people were politically tired, and was therefore quite popular. It was not just Ed Koch who embraced such notions. The Democratic Party did too.

Am I saying that Ed Koch was totally unconcerned with the political advantages that accrued to him personally when he shifted toward the right? Not at all. He was not simply the plaything of economic and intellectual trends, but neither was he the pure product of opportunism. He was, very much like the rest of us, a complex man. He did indeed become much too friendly with the real estate interests that built a Manhattan designed for the rich and trendy. That, I think, was his most grievous fault. And it was sad that a man of Koch's personal honesty should have been unaware of the corruption of some of his political allies.

I still think that, in another period, his self-interest and his very real idealism could have yielded a different outcome. But his evolution was not dictated by fate, as Ruth Messinger proves. As she matured, she became more serious, more effective, in her basic commitment.

There was a meeting at the New School in the fall of 1986. A group of German politicians and journalists were visiting the United States, and they talked with some New Yorkers, including city bureaucrats, Ruth Messinger, and me. At one point, a spokesperson for the city launched into a description of all the things that had been done for the homeless. Ruth got up to point out that these things had been achieved under a court order, and proceeded to analyze the complicity of New York in creating homelessness, with precise references to laws and policies. She was as radical as when I first met her years ago and she had deepened her values by making them more informed than ever before.

The case of Ed Koch can be cited by superficial cynics. But the party of hope has Ruth Messinger.□

Morris Dickstein

NEIGHBORHOODS

I was doing some research at the Library of Congress, going through crime films of the 1940s for an article on that distinctive American genre, the *film noir*. This was still the era of the great studios, which could simulate virtually anything on the back lot. But a few producers set out to find authentic locations to give these films a documentary look. I was only a few minutes into Mark Hellinger's famous 1948 movie *The Naked City* when I began to feel like Proust munching on the madeleine. These crowded streets of the Lower East Side, with their grimy tenements and narrow sidewalks, their tiny candy stores, pushcart peddlers, and slope-backed cars, gave me back some vivid images from my childhood. Here was Columbia Street, where my father grew up and his brothers lived; wide Delancey Street, with its grand movie palace and innumerable lanes of traffic leading onto the Williamsburg Bridge on which the film's brilliant climactic chase takes place. Here was the city itself as it appeared in the 1940s, the real protagonist of the movie, with Mark Hellinger on the sound track saying, "There are eight million stories in the naked city." Mine was one of them.

I thought I had long since put the Lower East Side behind me. Like so many Jewish families, my parents had gotten out: moved to Queens in 1949, when I was nine, to open a small business, just when mom-and-pop stores had pretty much had their day. Feeling isolated among lower-middle-class Irish and Italians in Flushing, my folks kept up the umbilical tie to the old neighborhood, which had the only good bakeries and delicatessens, the only real synagogues and yeshivas, the best bargains, and so on. My own ties grew frayed and were eventually forgotten, buried beneath an Ivy League demeanor and a not wholly convincing new personality as an intellectual and a citizen of the world. I belonged to the culture of the West, not the parochialism of the ghetto.

By the end of the 1960s this universalism seemed a trifle hollow, even within the cosmopolitan literary culture of the Upper West Side. The protest movements of the 1960s had encouraged people to "do their own thing," and this lent impetus to a growing pluralism. After a long period of amnesia, I somehow remembered where I came from.

So one day I found myself driving a good friend around the streets of the Lower East Side, which I hadn't seen for ten years or more. Everything looked smaller than I remembered, as if isolated under glass, but charged with a strong emotional current. I was in a keyed-up and sentimental mood, and as we passed the house on Henry Street where I had spent my first decade, I turned and beamed, as if this were Mecca and Medina rolled into one. My friend was silent for a long time, then said haltingly, "But . . . this is a . . . slum." I felt crushed under the weight of a sociological category I had never previously considered.

I suppose the house *was* a slum, though I remembered it as a clean building, a cut above its surroundings, with stable, hard-working tenants, most of whom held down blue-collar jobs. The building was a walk-up with four three-room apartments on each floor. Young couples with young children were squeezed into many of them, hungry for light and air.

I could recall seeing much worse when I was growing up: dark, dingy apartments with bathtubs in the kitchen and toilets off the hall. And there were no doubt worse things I never saw: rat-infested tenements that survived from the days when Mike Gold addressed the "workers' Revolution" as the "true Messiah" that would "destroy the East Side . . . and build there a garden for the human spirit." Why then did this "slum," long since taken over by Hispanics and then Chinese, look beautiful to me? The answer is bound up, I think, not only in nostalgia for one's formative years but in the role neighborhoods play in the life of a city like New York.

As Jane Jacobs showed long ago, people in New York identify less with the city than with their own neighborhood. I myself have passed through every corner of New York, but my life has always been mediated by the neighborhoods I've lived in: the Lower East Side in the 1940s; Flushing, Queens—where my parents still live—in the 1950s; and the Upper West Side since the 1960s. Perhaps I can call upon some of my own memories to shed some light on the patterns of neighborhood life in New York since 1940.

The Lower East Side as I remember it was a small world, remarkably self-contained though far from homogeneous. Was there anything that couldn't be bought within a five-block radius? Everything seemed close by. The yeshiva my parents sent me to, in part to keep me away from the neighborhood riffraff, was only a block away, while the one my even more religious cousins went to was around the corner on East Broadway. Even our little block on Henry Street seemed like a complete unit of its own. There was a druggist at one corner who freely dispensed medical advice, offering first aid to children with scrapes and bruises, minor infections, and sties or cinders in their eyes, and there was a small grocery on another corner that supplied us with dark, thick-crusted pumpernickel and bottles of milk that had a generous head of cream.

I suppose nearly everyone was Jewish in 131 and 133 Henry Street but there were no other orthodox families, though the block was dotted with small first-floor synagogues where Jews from different East European towns prayed separately, as they would eventually be buried in different sections of the cemetery. At the end of the block, where Henry met Rutgers Street, there was a large Catholic church which was as mysterious and fascinating to the Jews as a Gothic castle; we speculated endlessly

about what went on in the small adjoining residence where two ancient nuns kept house for one or two elderly priests who had been on this block forever.

I remember the block best as an intricate playground: the wide space in front of our building that was perfect for sidewalk games, the tall stoops further down the block that provided hiding places for secret clubs and crude sexual exploration, the punchball and stickball games in the middle of the street, and the huge rock-candy formations of piled-up snow that survived for months after a big snowfall like the 1947 blizzard. And I vividly recall the lights and music and dancing as the street was closed off for block parties when the war ended and the soldiers were welcomed back.

The borders of the neighborhood were sharply defined, especially for a child. Years afterward it surprised me to learn that I had grown up only three or four blocks from South Street and the river, only a few blocks from the beginning of Chinatown and not much further from Little Italy, and virtually in the shadow of the Manhattan Bridge, which crossed Henry Street further down like a immense viaduct of gigantic steel girders—all alien territory to my parents and off limits to me as a child.

Instead, our neighborhood stretched east towards the East River Drive—where we piously discarded our sins (symbolized by stale bread crumbs) on the first day of the Jewish New Year—and north past Seward Park towards Grand Street, Delancey Street, and Houston Street, though the Avenue B bus also connected us to the shopping around Union Square. These were the furthest reaches of the world I remember. The chief landmarks on this terrain were the cramped apartments of aunts and uncles, where boisterous cousins in families larger than mine made life much more exciting that it was at home. The rest of Manhattan was a vast mystery, except for the route of our favorite excursion—to Rockefeller Center, where we could get tickets to radio shows, make faces at ourselves on a television monitor, have lunch (meatless) at the Automat, and walk up Fifth Avenue to the Central Park Zoo. When I grew a little older I would scurry with friends across the walkway of the Williamsburg Bridge to set foot on that mysterious continent, "Brooklyn," with all the wonderment of Balboa facing the Pacific or Admiral Peary at the North Pole.

How shall I describe the shock and excitement of moving from this busy little immigrant enclave, neither fully American nor European, to a distant neighborhood where there were no tall buildings or subways and so few Jews that the (Conservative) synagogue could barely get ten of them together on a

Friday night? For fear that I might forget who I was, my parents kept me going to the yeshiva on Henry Street, which added nearly three hours of travel to a school day that already stretched from nine to six, including Sundays. Despite these sweatshop hours, to which I never dreamed of objecting, the subways I learned to use so well became precious keys to freedom, links to magical city events like baseball games, museum exhibitions, and stage plays with live actors who delivered risqué lines to "sophisticated" audiences.

I also found time to explore Flushing, hardly part of New York at all but essentially a small American city of the 1920s. Even today, people in Flushing still talk about "going to the city" or "going to New York" when they mean Manhattan. Going to New York wasn't really necessary, since there was very little that couldn't be had in the great shopping hubs around Main Street (which nowadays is heavily middle-class Chinese), Northern Boulevard, and, in a pinch, Jamaica, which had yet to begin its own slide into becoming a neglected black slum. Here in Flushing I encountered my first Jew-baiting, when a friend was razzed, pummeled, and wrestled to the ground by some tough kids from his class at the local public school.

Here I encountered the classic American mix of prewar frame houses, closely packed together, newer brick row houses, each with a small front and back yard, and shopping blocks of one- or two-story buildings that held small businesses, including my father's dry-goods store. North of Northern Boulevard were larger white-collar homes with beautifully landscaped lawns—a touch of suburbia that always made me envious.

Near Main Street, where the subway ended, small apartment houses full of commuters sprang up during the 1950s and 1960s, but further out, where we lived, a network of separate little communities was linked by an expanding car culture that belonged to Long Island, not to the city.

Though Flushing couldn't supply its people with too many good jobs, it was anything but a bedroom community surrounded by shopping centers. It had its own college, where much later, to my infinite surprise, I returned to teach, its own hospitals, department stores, libraries, garage mechanics, movie theaters, and business districts, including some light industry. What it didn't have, to a family that had moved out from the Lower East Side, was any decent bread or cake, or any of our noisy Jewish uncles and cousins, who felt vaguely that they were in the country on the rare occasions they visited us. Flushing had a well-established, lower-middle-class population: people who owned their own homes,

breathed better air, saw greenery every day, and, if they could afford it, bought small summer cottages further out on Long Island where they could really get away from city life.

Despite the pastoral amenities of life in Queens, including fine parks in nearly all directions, I was bored and alienated by the life we had. I took to spending more and more time in the public libraries, where I devoured everything I could lay my hands on, and at the local synagogue, where I chanted the weekly Torah portion, organized the junior services, joined the Boy Scouts, won a teenage checkers championship, and even preached a sermon now and then. Though it seemed to some, but not to me, that I might end up a rabbi, I was only hungry for culture, secular or religious, another Carol Kennicott, struggling against the limits of my own benighted Main Street.

Only in retrospect did I come to appreciate a small-scale neighborhood where people of modest means could live decently. But for now Flushing was a soulless wasteland to me: I hated being a young intellectual in a business-driven community, hated living just above my parents' store on the only commercial block in the vicinity. Eventually, college and graduate school became my way out; teaching and writing would be my version of the rabbinate, a substitute for the Talmud I had studied so restively and the preaching to which I must have been inwardly inclined. Like the callow heroes of so many nineteenth-century novels, I could only find myself by making my way to the big city.

As an undergraduate at Columbia I discovered the West Side, and despite periods when I hated New York and wanted nothing more than to live elsewhere, the West Side has essentially been my home ever since. When my wife and I moved back to New York with a six-week-old child in 1966, there were still large rent-controlled apartments with high ceilings and spectacular views in once-elegant, well-constructed prewar buildings. Flats that sell today for half a million dollars could be had then for a few hundred a month, if you could find them—which often meant months of scanning the ads in the *Times*, pounding the pavements, and haggling with agents, supers, and departing tenants—then perhaps paying some money "under the table," a pittance by today's standards.

The West Side was then spiraling downward into a different kind of slum from where I had grown up. The Lower East Side had always been poor; its tiny apartments had airless rooms with windows looking out on narrow shafts; its population at the turn of the century had been more dense than Calcutta's. The

West Side had its low-rise tenements on Amsterdam and Columbus Avenues but also its grand residential buildings sliding inexorably into shabby gentility. The neighborhood was still dotted with Irish bars, remnants of the old blue-collar population that had given way in the 1950s to Puerto Ricans, for whom the neighborhood was a big step up from the grim poverty of the island.

The ethnic and generational mix was one of the strengths of the neighborhood, yet it was becoming more explosive every year. As the old German Jews in their ten-room apartments were dying off, the fear of crime was relentlessly driving the middle class to the Upper East Side, if they could afford it, or out of the city. Yet this gave the area a mild bohemian flavor, since it made room for students sharing the rent, for young couples living together, for junior academics from Columbia, for writers and musicians whose income was marginal or unpredictable. Despised by much of the middle class, neglected by landlords and city alike, this run-down neighborhood, once so correct and respectable, became a refuge for many who were in flight from the suburbs or from Flushing, from the Middle West or the South—a place where unpublished authors, undiscovered artists, and indigent young lovers could be poor and happy on nothing a year.

There was great housing, good shopping, and a zestful community spirit on the West Side in those years, but there was also a palpable tension on the street that could flare up at any moment into a menacing incident. I recall walking babysitters home at 2 A.M. with my fingers curled around my keys — to do maximum damage if I had to defend myself. I remember being relieved of the contents of my wallet by three young toughs in front of my building one June evening, and being dunned for a ten-dollar "loan" on Amsterdam Avenue by someone who offered me his gun, wrapped in a newspaper, as "collateral." Our parents were indignant that we were living in a combat zone. A friend had his car stolen off the street, stripped to a metal hulk, and dumped in what the police then called "Korea," a no-man's-land around Manhattan Avenue and 109th Street. I wasn't fazed by any of these incidents: they were the cost of doing business. If you stayed in the neighborhood, you had to do it ALL.

The other side was the pleasure of being close to the center of the city yet living in what often felt like a small village, a cultural mix that was also a ghetto full of people of one's own choosing. In those days every few blocks along Broadway became a world unto itself, with its own supermarkets, banks, dry cleaners, theaters, its own sandbox on Riverside Drive, where the child-people and the dog-people battled for turf.

Outsiders were incredulous when I said I lived in a small town, but there were times when I didn't venture south of Columbus Circle for six months at a time; whenever I did, the crowds made my head spin. Central Park and Riverside Park gave the neighborhood a pastoral quality that made it possible for us to raise children in the city, while the overflow from Columbia gave the area a cultural intensity that we rarely associate with trees, light, and air.

Many of these same qualities can still be found on the Upper West Side. But the cost of housing and the spiraling commercial rents have changed everything. The slowly graying population of an earlier era hangs in, but the yuppies are gradually making the neighborhood their own. As sushi bars and designer ice-cream spread, as boutiques sit astride bodegas and numbers joints compete for space with outdoor cafés, the contrasts from block to block become more striking than ever. But the neighborhood is becoming more distinctively middle class than it was even in its heyday. Many of the low-rise buildings once inhabited by the respectable poor have been

swept up in the co-op gold rush, as Columbus and now Amsterdam Avenues are being gentrified beyond recognition.

The mix of people on and off Broadway on a Saturday afternoon is still exhilarating—yuppies in jogging suits, fierce pensioners wheeling their carts like weapons at Fairway, students browsing along the shelves at Shakespeare and Company, Korean greengrocers, three or four to a block, displaying their wares in all seasons, winos roosting on benches in the middle of the traffic island, young couples with strollers braving the crowd in an ever-expanding Zabar's. There's probably no neighborhood in New York with a busier street life at virtually any hour.

Yet the changes accelerate from week to week. Much has been improved in this upward push, especially for those who can afford it. Rows of brownstones, built originally as town houses for Our Crowd, have been rescued from crime and decay and turned into our most beautiful urban blocks. One stretch of Broadway between 104th and 108th Street, long a dead space in which few businesses really thrived, has now become Restaurant Row, where spiffy East Side types, hard-bitten locals, and Columbia students mingle without visible ill will. On the same streets, a legion of homeless people panhandle for their next meal. Festering SROs and residence hotels are renovated into expensive condos yet little new housing is provided for those who are displaced. Meanwhile, the aspiring young who are transiently poor must move in with their parents, take on exorbitant sublets, or hunt up housing in distant parts of the city.

Those of us who were already there, who held on when the neighborhood—and the city—hit bottom, managed to survive in this game of musical chairs, while losing the mobility we once prized. The casualties of gentrification can be seen on every block, and it is easy to detest the kind of money that's moving in. Yet for me the neighborhood remains a re-creation of the kind of community I dimly experienced as a child. There the immigrant experience provided a set of common bonds: a shared culture, common religion, family ties, and similar hopes for a better future. Here too a common culture binds people together: cosmopolitanism, professionalism, political liberalism, some involvement with books and the arts, an unusual degree of civic-mindedness, a sense of having seceded from the cruder aspects of the American Dream. In short, the *Times*-reading, college-educated professional and academic class, the fruits of the immense expansion of higher education after World War Two. Once most of these people would have been bound for the suburbs; now, with wives working as well as husbands, the city attracts them in ever-greater numbers.

Having survived the depredations of crime and decay, the West Side must now endure the improvements wrought by wealth and greed. The special organic qualities of the three neighborhoods I have described were in part due to their stagnation, which I experienced as stability. Now all three are being buffeted to different degrees by the fabled "rebirth" of New York, as new investment, new construction, and shifts in population disrupt patterns that had persisted for decades. On the Lower East Side and Upper West Side, the pressure comes from soaring real estate values, reflecting larger changes in the city's economic life: the shift from an industrial base, with many blue-collar jobs, to a service economy employing more professionals, as well as the growth of foreign investment. In Flushing it comes from a large influx of intensely entrepreneurial Chinese and Koreans who are emulating the migratory patterns and social mobility of earlier immigrant groups.

The security and stability of a neighborhood can be a nurturing form of community; but at their worst they become exclusionary, almost xenophobic, incubating the kind of anger and hatred which recently surfaced in Howard Beach. The good citizens on Gladwin Avenue in Flushing no doubt felt threatened by the prospect of a welfare house for homeless babies on their well-kept block. No doubt the location was chosen with little sensitivity to the community's fears. Some neighbors merely protested; others allegedly burned the place out. Like some of our soldiers in Vietnam, they risked destroying the block in order to "save" it.

Only dying cities remain the same, preserving old neighborhoods under glass as museum pieces and tourist attractions while the real activity of the city, if there is any, takes place offstage. New York has always been a changing city, but for many years it was thought to be a city in decline, distrusted by many Americans as an offshore island closer to Europe than to our own heartland.

Foreigners have come to love New York because they find it dynamic, diverse, and immensely energizing. They have made the city a place to park their capital, and often themselves, contributing much to the partial, one-sided economic boom. Now that New York has become even more of a world capital, especially in the arts, in finance, and in everything related to communication and style, the city's preeminence has become a mixed blessing to those who live here. Money is a great solvent, and neighborhoods can be colonized as dramatically as underdeveloped countries. As some blocks are rescued from decay, others are destroyed by the forces of development, and the city becomes more of a playground for the well-to-do.

Once community groups fought the neglect of their neighborhoods; now they battle to ward off unwanted attention. The spirit of the 1960s has left behind a reservoir of local energy that provides some civic resistance to the greed of private capital and the development-mindedness of politicians who are either corrupt or simply willing to give the city away if only to assure a solid tax base.

The city has absorbed great changes in the past; it will no doubt assimilate these as well. Yet everywhere we turn, the fabric of community life seems threatened. Living in New York, like living in the twentieth century, has often been horrible but never dull. Even under siege the city remains a wondrous place to live—appreciated by newcomers more than by hardened New Yorkers. To Fritz Lang, arriving for the first time in New York Harbor, the skyline of the city was like the face of the future; it was the image that inspired his film *Metropolis*. Once a rarity on film, the city has now become a favorite haunt of filmmakers, though the images they convey can be spooky (*After Hours*), chicly superficial (*Desperately Seeking Susan*), or lovingly elegiac (*Hannah and Her Sisters*). They celebrate these mean streets as if they could disappear at any moment. At the present rate of change, such films could soon become as much a remembrance of things past as *The Naked City*. □

Robert Lekachman

THE WEST SIDE OF MY YOUTH

I was born in 1920 in the old Women's Hospital of St. Luke's at 110th Street and Amsterdam Avenue. Two-thirds of a wretched century later, I reside one block west and five blocks north on Broadway and 115th Street, overlooking the Columbia University campus and the two buildings that engaged my youthful energies as a member of the Columbia College class of 1942—Hamilton Hall, where most undergraduate humanities and social science classes met, and Butler Library, named inevitably after Nicholas Murray Butler, tyrant of all that he surveyed.

With two involuntary exceptions, mine has been a West Side life. From the time I was five until I was twenty-two, my parents for inscrutable reasons occupied a house in Sea Cliff, a disagreeably anti-Semitic north shore of Long Island bedroom village. At 18, I partially escaped by commuting daily on the Long Island railroad and the Seventh Avenue IRT to Columbia College. Problems of unemployment for me and my peers were solved by World War II. A group of my neighbors sent me the familiar greetings, which led to four safe but boring years as a regimental clerk, typing with mounting virtuosity payrolls, morning reports and, in Guam, the Philippines, and Okinawa, casualty reports and letters of condolence. As part of the early occupation forces in Japan, I developed a new specialty— composition of citations for Silver and Bronze Stars. Although the heroic deeds recited were often imaginary, the medals were each worth five points in the accounting that determined just when each of us would be shipped home to be discharged into the bosom of the fat civilian economy.

This is all by way of excusing my absences from "home." The word demands exegesis. As an unhappy child, I saw New York, an undifferentiated entity, as my goal. Occasional expeditions to the opera and the theater reinforced my perception that here were centered all the delights of civilization, none of them visible in Sea Cliff. What focused my aspirations was Columbia College. Living outside of the metropolitan area, I was ineligible for free tuition at City College. Harvard was beyond my dreams, but Columbia represented an attainable pinnacle of academic status. In 1938, when the economy was staggering out of a sharp recession superimposed upon continuing depression, most of my classmates (no women of course) were grateful commuters, particularly Jews, who treasured admission to WASP culture the more because Columbia had an all but officially announced Jewish quota.

Columbia College was small, some 1,500 students, and so was the graduate school. In the heyday of general education, the stars of the faculty did not disdain teaching humanities or contemporary civilization to freshmen and sophomores. The teachers I recall with gratitude include Mark Van Doren, Moses Hadas, the sociologist Robert Lynd of Middletown fame, and, Franco devotee though he was, the extraordinarily gifted lecturer Carlton Hayes. Lionel Trilling and Jacques Barzun taught a legendary colloquium section, limited to fifteen aspiring aesthetes. John Herman Randall and Irwin Edman attracted admirers to the philosophy department. Imagine. People talked seriously about Plato, Beethoven, Dutch naturalists, French Impressionists, John Dewey, and Karl Marx. In the fashion of the young, they vented opinions on books they hadn't read or, if read, absorbed, and on art and music, with which their familiarity was recent and superficial. Still, this was the company I aspired to keep forever and ever. I was sufficiently overawed by the cultural pretensions of some of my contemporaries to discard the notion of becoming an eminent literary critic or a trailblazing novelist. I took the way Richard Nixon was later to deny ever pursuing, the easy way. I became an economist on the excuse that after the revolution the new regime would certainly enlist planners and social scientists.

As luck would have it, I did become a writer in a much easier competition. Few social scientists, and even fewer economists, compose readable prose. As for the revolution, it appears to be on indefinite hold.

Columbia is embedded in Morningside Heights, separated from Harlem by the barrier of Morningside Park. To this day, mean-spirited souls call the area West Harlem. In 1938, scarcely a black face was to be seen. Still, the menace was there. At an orientation session we were warned not to venture into Morningside Park, lest Harlemites of unfriendly disposition do us violent damage. I remember a single black classmate, an amiable soul who went wrong, became a Republican, and worked in recent years for Virginia's impeccably reactionary Senator Paul Trible. Columbia was less political than City College. There were no alcoves in which our own Daniel Bells, Irving Kristols, and Irving Howes split Marxist hairs. There was a Young Socialist chapter. Stalinists had seized the high ground—the mimeograph machine, in the American Student Union. But it is even clearer now in the pages of a reunion brochure than at the time that most of the Columbia lads wanted to be doctors, lawyers, at a pinch dentists or accountants.

Half a century ago, the Columbia campus was uncrowded and architecturally decent, if less than distinguished. Low Library and Butler Library faced each other on the north-south axis, and Earl Hall and the Chapel were symmetrically anchored on the west and east. Dormitories, office, and classroom buildings, even the science labs, were in a consistent medium-rise, Italianate style. Space was sufficiently cheap and funds for construction sufficiently scarce so that tennis courts were strewn between 114th and 120th streets. Practically nobody had money. But food and beer, the strongest beverage drunk in my

circle, were cheap. One could eat large quantities of moderately digestible egg foo young, chow mein, and chop suey at the New Asia. The West End and the Gold Rail dispensed watery beer in premises uncleaned since their creation. In the nose of memory, I can still smell the Gold Rail's aroma of sour pickles, stale beer, unkempt waiters, dirty glasses, and unclean tables and chairs. So delightful to adjourn there with Moses Hadas after an instructive colloqium discussion of Boswell's Samuel Johnson or Jonathan Swift's utopias and dystopias. Alas, after a single beer—I didn't really want a second—I had to hurry lest I miss the last train to Sea Cliff.

My definition of the West Side stretched from 125th Street, where the best Chinese restaurant crouched, to Columbus Circle. In between were numerous cinemas, including the Loew's Beacon between 74th and 75th Streets on Broadway. Like other palaces—the Paradise on Bronx's Champs Elysees, the Grand Concourse, and the Valencia in Brooklyn—the Beacon was magnificently vulgar, a triumph of glitz surmounted by a genuinely fake starry ceiling. In those days beyond recall, one waited *inside* the theater and once seated bathed in the full measure on a Saturday afternoon of cartoon, serial episode, newsreel, trailer of coming attractions, and *two* feature films—on one memorable occasion Boris Karloff as Frankenstein's lovable monster and Bela Lugosi as Bram Stoker's addict of beef tea, Dracula.

Families lived inexpensively in decently maintained rental housing. The merchants who served them, including Columbus Circle entrepreneurs, were a relaxed collection of tavern keepers, cafeteria operators (Bickford was a name to conjure with), grocers, butchers, hardware purveyors, clothiers, dealers in toasters, radios, and vacuum cleaners, and produce vendors. Rents were low for both commercial and residential tenants because vacancy rates were high. Landlords humbly painted their premises annually and, in response to market exigencies, offered free rent to new tenants for one, two, sometimes three months. No need for rent control. A fair definition of tenant heaven is a vacancy rate higher than 10 percent. No co-ops, no condos confused traditional animosities between landlords and tenants.

I do not describe utopia. Most families struggled on the edge of indigence, beset by layoffs, temporarily rescued by WPA jobs, and inspirited less by practical benefits from federal and local government than by the sense that Franklin Roosevelt in the White House and Fiorello LaGuardia in

City Hall were on their side. It's rather harder for the casualties of the 1980s economy to enlist Ronald Reagan and Edward Koch as allies.

For Columbia's lumpen intellectuals, leisure for theoretical discussion simply continued a curriculum undistorted by vocational aspiration. Some of us, it is true, were the children of businessmen and potential heirs to moneymaking enterprises. My own father was the proprietor of a commercial printing plant, usually on the edge of bankruptcy. Scorning business, most of us had only the dimmest possible notion of what we were going to do in our lives after college.

The 1980s are something else. Structures of impeccably bad taste have replaced tennis courts and open space. Uris Hall, home to the School of Business and testimonial to one of the city's affluent developers; the Mudd engineering building; the Law School, a boxlike contemporary atrocity decorated by a wildly inappropriate sculpture; and Ferris Booth and Carman Hall, student center and dormitory respectively, celebrate the vulgarity of the university's trustees and administrators.

Columbia College, conceding that it could not attract students of adequate talent from only half the gene pool, now admits women in competition with still all-female Barnard. Its venerable humanities and contemporary civilization courses are taught mostly by preceptors, graduate students whose title trades dignity for adequate pay and status. Despite access to the entire gene pool, remedial education is necessary. A baby humanities course equips freshmen who read slowly and write badly to handle the real thing. Football players are frequent enrollees. Since the team has not won a game in several years and this fall threatens to break Northwestern's record losing streak, the admissions office seems to have admitted young men whose academic deficits are matched by slowness of foot, clumsiness of hand, and inadequate ferocity.

Nevertheless, there are continuities in the university neighborhood. Although, in its relentless search for student and faculty housing, Columbia has acquired and converted single-room-occupancy apartment buildings into dormitories—commuting is déclassé—the territory of university dominion, roughly between 110th and 125th Streets, is still a highly miscellaneous area, housing upper-middle-income professional types, senior citizens desperately clinging to rent-controlled or stabilized apartments, perpetual graduate students, local merchants, and an increasingly black, Hispanic, and Asian population.

Columbia's aspirations to gentrify the area thus far have been only moderately successful. Chock

Full O'Nuts continues mysteriously to occupy the southwest corner of Broadway and 116th Street, though its customers are few and its decor depressing. The West End survives as an expanded combination of bar-and-grill and nightly jazz club. The New Asia, now the Moon Palace, cooks on, offering of course Szechuan dishes as complements to Cantonese standbys. The Gold Rail perished, to be reincarnated as an immaculate Hunan Gardens. Where a Rexall drug emporium flourished on 110th Street and Broadway, another Chinese restaurant caters to the insatiable West Side appetite for takeout. Discount druggists have more than filled the Rexall gap. The Mill, a combined stationery, newspaper, and short-order establishment, recently was celebrated as a survivor by the "Living" section of the *New York Times*. There are yuppie touches: Steve's and Häagen-Dazs ice cream shops, David's cookies, Sir George shoes; but between the university and 96th Street, the area remains full of cleaners, shoe stores, pizza parlors, supermarkets, opticians, and similar establishments of traditional rather than yuppie aspect.

South of 96th Street, all is transformed. On Broadway old movie theaters and other low-rise structures have been demolished so that glitzy high-rise condos, each usually endowed with state-of-the-art security, health club facilities, and a concierge at the service of lucky inhabitants, can be marketed at vast prices to the huge yuppie community of buyers. Look-alike structures with names like Montana, Princeton, New West, Bromley, Savannah, and, less imaginatively, Broadway vie for patronage. Only yesterday the developers killed the Thalia theater, from time immemorial a legend among highbrow moviegoers. The restaurants of Hunan Gulch in the 90s are supplemented by popular Japanese newcomers.

Condos rise also on Amsterdam and Columbus Avenues. There the restaurant scene is wild. All is

concept—overpriced, overcrowded restaurants offer Mexican, Greek, Cuban, "continental," Chinese, Japanese, and unidentifiable culinary treats.

Long ago Robert Moses' Coliseum at Columbus Circle destroyed a lower-middle-class residential and commercial neighborhood; only fair that Morton Zuckerman, megadeveloper and magazine owner, will destroy it and erect two enormous towers guaranteed to cast perpetual shadow on the statue of Columbus and much of Central Park. Somewhat later Lincoln Center, the Rockefellers' tacky salute to the performing arts, displaced another group of average citizens. Where did they go? Who knew, who cared? Relentless gentrification has turned many older buildings, on West End Avenue in particular, into co-ops.

The West Side, which half a century ago harbored people engaged in useful occupations, now is filled with the beneficiaries of the age of information—lawyers, investment bankers, advertising and public relations wizards, computer adepts, interior decorators, political campaign consultants, and other manipulators of paper and symbols. For the most part, their activities subtract from the sum of human welfare and their incomes seem to rise in direct relation to the damage that they inflict and the waste of resources they bring about.

If Columbia University has its way, gentrification will move relentlessly north of 96th Street all the way to 125th Street. To many of its unhappy neighbors, the university seems to be a massive real estate conglomerate that happens incidentally to offer classes and degrees to students who will be customers for the upscale clothes, electronics, personal care, expensive leisure, workout facilities, and food that comprise the wave of the present—the world of the yuppie.

I cannot conclude this memoir without comment on the political scene, then and now. In the wake of Adlai Stevenson's honorable defeats by a national hero with whom the electorate enjoyed a political romance unmatched until the emergence of Ronald

Reagan, West Side politics were inspired by Stevenson to undertake an exciting wave of reform, led by a certain William Fitts Ryan. Ryan, in 1956 an assistant district attorney in Frank Hogan's much overrated Manhattan DA's office, was the scion of a highly political family with connections both in the south, the birthplace of Ryan's mother, and in the north, notably to Franklin and Eleanor Roosevelt. Ryan became district leader and then in 1960 congressman, a position he held until his death in 1972. Reform politics in the Ryan era were squeaky clean, highly contentious, and genuinely participatory. Meetings of the now defunct Riverside Democrats frequently ended at three in the morning.

Similar events occurred in reform clubs further south. Such bursts of energy are fated to burn out. Still, a pity. For the young on sexual hunts, reform clubs were a dignified alternative to singles bars, let alone the personals in the *Village Voice* and the *New York Review of Books*. In those days, district leaders worked at their jobs and harassed the sleepy city bureaucracy into reluctant action.

Reform politics flourished during the Lindsay era. Indeed, alumni of the West Side clubs like Mitchell Ginsburg, Human Resources Commissioner, and Jerry Kretchmer, Environmental Protection czar, occupied positions of great responsibility. Though no longer proud of his political origins, the egregious Ed Koch won publicity and public office by defeating Carmine De Sapio, the walking symbol of machine politics, by the cry of reform. Alas, as events in Queens and the Bronx glaringly reveal, the machines are back. Nowhere are reform clubs strong.

They left a heritage in the human form of superior politicians, alumni of the 1950s and 1960s, who vastly improve upon their predecessors. Ted Weiss, a courageous liberal, occupies more or less Bill Ryan's congressional district—its boundaries have been repeatedly altered. Franz Leichter, probably the legislature's

most valuable member, is a state senator. Ed Sullivan, a former teacher, sits in the Assembly as representative of a district, mostly black, that includes Morningside Heights. Ruth Messenger gives Ed Koch almost daily fits. It can be plausibly argued that the reform movement improved the quality of state and national government.

Unfortunately, it failed to transform municipal politics. On the current evidence, corruption, conniving, and favor-swapping are as prevalent as they were in the bad old days of Bill O'Dwyer. A pessimist may say that corruption is more expensive to the taxpayers now than it was in the pre-Lindsay days. One could pay off loyal campaign workers of sketchy education with low-paid jobs. Now such loyalists expect to head the Parking Violations Bureau, the Department of Transportation, and other agencies. The scale of corruption has predictably risen with the wild pace of Manhattan development. Variances, tax breaks, subsidies to the Donald Trumps: these are benefits paid for not usually by bribes, but by huge campaign contributions. Whether Ed Koch is personally honest or not is a trivial question. He is the developers' mayor. They financed him, elected him, reelected him, and reelected him yet again.

In sum, the West Side of Manhattan is far richer now than it was fifty or thirty years ago. It is also less humane, less concerned with the community, glitzier, and increasingly less interesting. For the deterioration, blame can be widely assigned. The Rockefellers demolished a neighborhood to construct Lincoln Center. Columbia University has done its considerable best to shrink the scale of low-income housing within its domain. Politicians have given developers practically a free ride. But worst of all, nowhere in sight are the heirs to the reform movement which for a few years generated a sense of community around which human atoms could rally.

Mind you, I am not moving. Where are things better? □

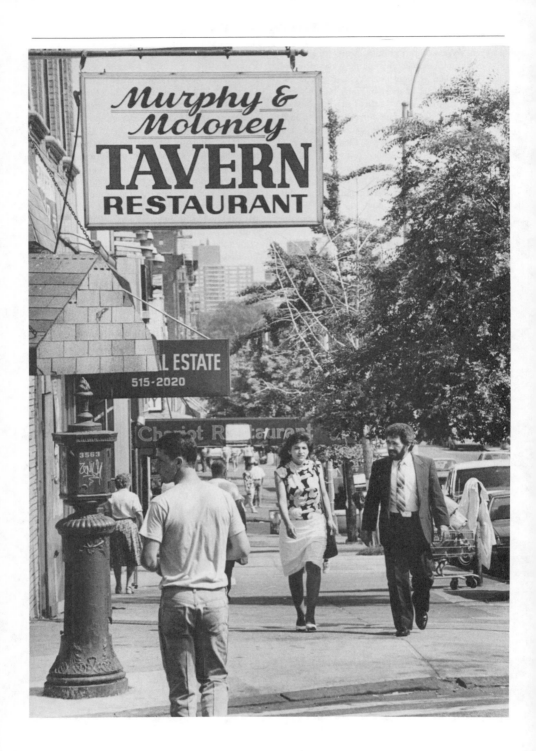

Leonard Kriegel

IN THE COUNTRY
OF THE OTHER

A Journey Back to the North Bronx

The legacy is invariable—a brief pang of guilt followed by overwhelming relief at my own escape from the northeast Bronx. I come off the Henry Hudson Parkway and where the traffic light flags me down, at the pocked and rutted joining of Gun Hill Road and Mosholu Parkway, I feel myself sucked back into old wars that seem so permanent a part of my memory. Only this is not my Bronx, I remind myself, as I stare at the massive battlements of Tracy Towers Houses, a state-subsidized medieval fortress built in the 1970s. My gaze shifts to the classical spire of De Witt Clinton High School, illuminated by the blue March sky and the unusually warm sun. Erase the concrete brutality of Tracy Towers and the landscape is fit for Constable. As the light changes, I gun the motor and my eye catches a cluster of students charging across the road. My mind

transforms faces and colors into those of my adolescence—from black to white, from Puerto Rican to Italian, from Jamaican to Jew. Only the inevitability of struggle has not changed. And that is what I always find myself seeking when I come back to the neighborhood.

I inventory the neighborhood, as I always do. A left at Van Cortlandt Park East takes me past the graffiti-dripping red brick of the P.S. 80 schoolyard. At the narrow avenue named by a city bureaucrat— his sense of history matched only by his sense of humor—after the Comte de Rochambeau, who led the French armies fighting alongside Americans struggling for independence, I make a sharp right. And it is after this turn that I once again think of myself as a spy in the country of the Other.

I write about The Bronx—probably more often

than I should. But I don't live there. Not anymore. And whenever I come back to the neighborhood, I secretly congratulate myself on having left it in 1957, when I was a twenty-four-year-old recently married graduate student who wanted to teach the glories of Whitman and write with the honesty of Orwell. Modest ambitions to have pulled from streets that served as a farm system for the moneyed technicolor fantasies of Hollywood producers and the equally moneyed, equally technicolor fantasies of Seventh-Avenue fashion designers. Melnick and Marshall, Klein and Lauren—they, too, had learned their lessons on Rochambeau Avenue. Stand with your own or stand alone.

And on 206th Street. And on Bainbridge Avenue. And on Hull Avenue. And on that smooth, grassy parkway named for yet another member of the French nobility, the Comte de Mosholu. And on Jerome Avenue. Movies and fashion enough there. The old saw still accurate—you can take the boy out of The Bronx, but you can't take The Bronx out of the boy. You might succeed in teaching him how to place these streets in a book. Ten years ago, I had done that in *Notes for the Two-Dollar Window*, a plea for the neighborhood's losers, the Jews and Italians and Irish who had been left behind. A bitter love letter to the neighborhood. But I was smart enough to make it a love letter from a distance. From Manhattan, where I still lived.

And the mayoral reign of Ed Koch had certainly given us an interesting variation on the old saw: Apparently, you *could* take New York out of The Bronx. In its way, fitting enough. Even when the neighborhood—what old guidebooks call the Norwood section of The Bronx—bubbled over with optimism and recited its litany of streets named after heroes and events of the War of Independence and the War of 1812—Steuben Avenue, Gun Hill Road, Gates Place, Knox Place, Perry Avenue, Decatur Avenue, Bainbridge Avenue—we were not altogether certain that those of us who lived there could claim New York. New York was "downtown"; New York was "sophisticated"; and New York belonged to "them." It still did. Only now people like me were part of "them."

Which accounted for why I thought of myself as a spy. Our Bronx had always been the borough of the Great Denial. It simply didn't count for much. And the people who lived there knew they didn't count for much as far as "real" New Yorkers were concerned. Staten Island and Queens had been pulled into New York's psyche kicking and screaming, the one content to remain a psychological vassal to New Jersey (the only borough in the city where jokes about New Jersey are not considered funny), the other swollen

with itself, a knuckle on that finger of land known as Long Island pointing back toward Europe. Brooklyn had never allowed itself to be defined by Manhattan. Even a casual visitor to Bay Ridge or Boro Park or the recently gentrified Park Slope envied the sense of neighborhood he discovered in Brooklyn. And the man or woman who lives in Manhattan is *the* New Yorker personified, one whose soul beds down in dreams with the souls of ancient Thebans and Cairenes, urban standard-bearers to the world. In Manhattan, one learns to mythicize not the landscape but the self, like joggers in Central Park who buttress each other's egos with references to "the wall."

But The Bronx shames even memory. It has been the city's basket case for so long now that it is allowed little in the way of individuation. Only in dying has The Bronx been collectivized into an American object lesson. Only when its ravaged streets are featured in a movie like *Fort Apache: The Bronx* or its burning tenements are used by Howard Cosell to illuminate a dull interlude in the World Series is The Bronx made part of this America. Even its name is clipped, a blubbery invitation to nose-thumbing: "The Bronx / No thonx," wrote Ogden Nash, and those few of us who had heard of the *New Yorker* winced with how little we mattered to our sophisticated cousins in Manhattan.

At best, The Bronx was a place to come from for writers of memoirs and novelists smart enough to understand that even as they wrote of their origins, life was richer for their having gotten out in time. After all, "creative people"—which is how they were known in the neighborhood—didn't move from Manhattan to The Bronx. That traffic had always been one way. The only upscale part of the borough, Riverdale, didn't even consider itself part of The Bronx at all. Residents of those shaded, tree-lined streets were ours only legally. Spiritually, they were as far removed from our plebeian streets as were people living in Bucks County, Pennsylvania. Riverdale, New York—that was the postal address they preferred. Diplomats lived in Riverdale; doctors and dentists and lawyers and stockbrokers and belt manufacturers who spoke proper English lived in Riverdale; Toscanini had lived in Riverdale. And Riverdale, these people reminded us, had little in common with The Bronx. New York geography had always been a question of psychology rather than place.

W hen we moved there in 1937, the neighborhood was a way station for first- and second- and third-generation Italian and Jewish and Irish immigrant families. In the 1930s and 1940s, they moved to these streets because the neighborhood was cleaner, its sense of deprivation virtually nonexistent, its graffiti localized to the tunnel of Williamsbridge Oval Park: "Mickey does it! Why don't you?"

What the neighborhood shared with other neighborhoods in The Bronx was its incorrigibly optimistic architecture, so much more playful in its aspirations than the heavy stones of Manhattan. The dullness of Park Avenue and the staid thickness of West End Avenue were not to be found in the Art Deco lobbies and mock-Tudor apartment buildings that sheltered cab drivers and plumbers, furriers and garment cutters, bus drivers and subway conductors.

The people who "worked for the city" were the ones we envied—if "envy" is the correct word for what we felt about our own—for they possessed what our fathers lacked: Security. And they also possessed the distinction of being employed by those who lived in Manhattan.

But if we were not altogether certain that we belonged to New York, we were still New Yorkers. We were the first or last subway stop on the IND's D Train. We were wooed by politicians and visiting dignitaries who knew enough about this city's priorities to make an obligatory run up the Grand Concourse. They sought out the borough's splendors, rather than self-righteously clucking over its burnt-out husks, as Carter and Reagan did, pledging to make those savage streets gentle again—and then forgetting their very existence. A darker-skinned borough now—and easy enough to ignore.

We were provincials. And we had no illusions about our provincialism. But we mattered. Or so we believed. We even had our moments in the sun, when The Bronx stood at the center of the nation. Some of the attention was embarrassing, such as that time in 1948 when two children claimed to have been visited by the Virgin in a yard near Bedford Park Boulevard. Even my Catholic friends were suspicious. "It's the goddamn Concourse," said Billy to me. "How could she choose the Concourse?" But if apparitions of the Virgin were questionable, the Yankees weren't. Some of us hated them. But they had the look and feel of winners to the rest of America. The Yankees mattered.

And our votes mattered. Politicians wooed The Bronx because the borough housed working people who were unionized and who believed that they had as much right as anyone else to share in the American pie. They voted. In 1948, the first hint I had that the cause of the workingman was not as hopeless as Gallup and his pollsters predicted came from my younger brother, who followed Truman's motorcade up the Grand Concourse and conducted his own poll of those lining the sidewalks. Truman was in, he assured me.

Despite such occasional victories, the neighborhood was no place for prophets or seers. It had an ingrained sense of boundaries, as did all city neighborhoods. The Bronx had parks and The Bronx had politics and the two were intricately related. Even today, when they are not being indicted, the borough's politicians still brag that 20 percent of The Bronx is green parkland. And the truth was I could go from the wilds of Bronx Park to the smooth lawns of Mosholu Parkway to the chestnut trees of Van Cortlandt Park without ever losing sight of green. Where but in The Bronx could one have found Communists erecting the doomed Allerton Avenue co-ops to rival the successful Socialist Amalgamated Housing Co-op that wedged its promise between Mosholu Parkway and Van Cortlandt Park? Politics, parks, trade unionism—plebeian and provincial, but it worked.

But on my way to Manhattan I had passed the parks as well as the provincialism by. My occasional sentimentality about the people who still lived here was no more than a writer's strategy. And I knew it. It might have been meaningful had I been able, as my journalist son had done a year ago, to follow two cops from roof to roof, hunting not for my past but for the future that had come to the neighborhood. It was my son, Mark, not I, who journeyed with Officers Zielinsky and Slattery of the 52nd Precinct on rooftop forays in which they tried to spot adolescent "steerers" directing traffic to the crack sellers on De Kalb Avenue or Knox Place. For they now "do drugs" in the neighborhood, our own mundane passions having given way to what my son terms "the Hula-Hoop of urban narcotics."

I find myself wondering whether he could see the windows of his grandmother's apartment as he followed Officers Zielinsky and Slattery. The reason I still travel to the neighborhood every three or four weeks is that my 87-year-old mother still lives there, sharing an apartment with my 80-year-old uncle, once a furrier, a radical, a passionate trade unionist. And now a legally blind emphysema-racked survivor out of habit. Together, they live in the same apartment to which we moved in 1937, when I was four. My mother returned there from our own small apartment on 206th Street after my father died in 1976. It is better for an old woman waiting to die to live with an old man waiting to die—although neither my mother nor my uncle can tell you why.

Despite the drug problem, these are not the mean streets. They never were. The neighborhood has escaped the fate of all other Bronx neighborhoods south of Fordham Road. I still see shoppers on Bainbridge Avenue, a great many of them. Old women mix with young mothers pushing strollers and baby carriages. Fitting ardor for the tasks of young motherhood. I have not seen so many young women pushing baby carriages since I left the neighborhood thirty years ago. Bouffant hair, blond and redhead, clearskinned and freckled, these are not the daughters of the women's movement. They have not yet learned that their bodies are their own—and no one has yet convinced them that biology is not destiny.

The daughters of Ireland, they have come to the neighborhood from both the southern counties and Ulster. And now, with the men they marry and the children they bear, they are staking their claim to a neighborhood most of my own Irish friends left when I did. They are new immigrants, fleeing the Beirutization of Belfast and Dublin's lack of economic opportunity. And now they are "rescuing" the neighborhood, the old-timers say. As I drive through these streets, I watch them walk through their new America, watch their unconcealed pleasure at the prospects before them, their acceptance of a promise that is still coming.

The presence of the new Irish immigrants is everywhere, in the voices still filled with the lilt of Ireland, in the surprising number of pubs that seem to breed through exilic mitosis on Bainbridge Avenue and Gun Hill Road and Webster Avenue. In the space of a single avenue block, I count four of them. Irish watering holes. Gold shamrocks and green awnings and the thrust of memory frozen into the very congeniality and peace that was lacking. When I enter a pub or luncheonette and engage them in conversation, I hear them fondling memories of life back there, the way my father would fondle celebrations of holidays on a farm in Galicia—for the moment ignoring the cossacks lurking in the wings. A subtle sense of betrayal. Maybe it could have been different for them, for my father, and for me. History, I have read, has many cunning corridors—and all of them seem to lead to fantasy.

Manhattan bars offer a currency of the contemporary. What's in, what's out. What appeals to the young. What has passed *us* by. In the neighborhood, the names of bars evoke instant nostalgia: Murphy & Maloney, The Green Derby Pub, Ireland 32. Another old saw: Jews own candy stores, Italians own barber shops, the Irish own bars. Ethnic identities—a minor tale of capital.

I pull into an empty space in front of a bar-and-restaurant whose name I instantly distrust— Greentree on the Oval. There used to be a bike store on this spot. For twenty-five cents a child could buy two hours of time to teach himself to ride a two-wheeler on the quarter-mile dirt track of the Oval, the WPA's great gift to the neighborhood. The new gold sign stands out from the red brick of the entrance to the bar.

Three men are working on setting a window in the store next door. They are each in their late twenties, each Irish. I get out of my car. Lunch is served at the Greentree from 12:00 on. It is now 11:40. A man around my age, dark red hair slicked back in the fashion of movie gangsters in the 1940s, an unlit cigarette dangling from his lips, joins the group. I drift over to them. The men installing the window are enjoying their work, enjoying the warm March morning, enjoying the sight of the young mothers marching past with baby carriages and infants in sling pouches.

"There used to be a poolroom here," I offer, slapping at my sweating brow with a handkerchief. Sam Pistone owned the poolroom. And when the Sunday *News* featured a full-page color photo of Pius XII in all his finery, some steady customer pasted it to the poolroom door, where it remained, colors shining through dirt and grime, until I left the neighborhood. Sam looked like the Pope's twin.

The three men smile. The man with the slicked-back hair frowns, then grudgingly says, "Gone twenty years. Junk now. Acres and acres of junk."

"Things change," one of the workingmen says, his brogue thickening my absurd pleasure in knowing that someone else remembers Sam's poolroom. "Things change," the others say in unison.

Only one neighborhood hand is in the bar when I enter it at 12:00. A man in his late sixties, he nods as if we knew each other. The bar is horseshoe-shaped, solidly unfashionable—a relief after the red brick entrance and gold sign. The bartender turns out to be the man who knew the fate of Sam's poolroom. He ties his apron on and takes his place behind the bar. The bar has a pleasant feel to it and that soft, beery smell I still associate with bars in The Bronx.

In the dining room, an attractive Irishwoman in her twenties wipes off the table at which I seat myself, hands me a menu, and, in a brogue even more delightful than that of the man outside, asks, "Do you know what it is you want, sir? Or shall I run through the specials?"

She is from a small town a few miles south of the Ulster border. But she has no politics. She has come to America to get away from such things, to enjoy herself.

The Jews and Italians used to be the new people in the neighborhood. The Irish and Germans were already there when we arrived. The Germans disappeared, except for scattered groups who kept the Lutheran church on 206th Street functioning. And now the Jews who remained were old, their children having followed the American dream elsewhere. The Italians seemed altogether invisible. Hispanic pockets flourished north of Gun Hill Road and dotted the streets below Gun Hill off Webster Avenue. But it was the Irish who dominated the neighborhood now, the newest as well as the oldest of the new people.

The neighborhood is still distinct and insular, I discover, as I drift through these streets in the days that follow. The people living here seem engaged in the same search we undertook. They are moving up, looking for the rewards of Americanization. The allure of crack should be sufficient testimony to that. They, too, are hungry for the nation's pleasures. They, too, watch the 6:00 P.M. news and wonder what it is they are missing out on.

Only their connection to this America is tenuous, ill-defined. I watch three teenagers practice shooting a hockey puck from one side of Perry Avenue to the other. They should be in school at this 11:00 A.M. hour on a late-March day. But they aren't. And I am pleased to see them drive the puck, slashing at it. Street hockey was always an Irish game—"seeded by the geometry of the city," I wrote in *Notes*. And frozen in time, I think now. The game remains. And these teenagers look like the older brothers of the boys who taught me street hockey when I moved to 206th Street at the age of eight. They eye me suspiciously as I drive slowly by. My eyes lock with those of the oldest boy, who tightens his grip on the hockey stick he holds away from his shoulder like a rifle at parade rest. He does not wear skates. None of the boys has skates.

I turn left at 205th Street and drive halfway down the block. I park directly in front of the flagstone entrance of the Public Library. Built in 1953, it was once the neighborhood's pride. Now its flagstone is graffiti-slashed. And its windows are thick sheets of plastic, a scratched and faded insurance policy designed to keep vandals and the world at bay. Like Tracy Towers, the library has about it the look of a besieged outpost.

In bold black lettering that reminds me of an eye doctor's chart, a sign in the window proclaims: "This is your Library. It's up to you to keep it clean!" The library is scheduled to open at 12:30. I watch an old woman with swollen ankles painfully mount the three steps, ignoring the pantomimed imprecations of the guard who suddenly appears behind the door to wave her away. Like the old

woman, the guard is white-haired. He waves at her as if he were shooing a dog. He points to the sign depicting the library's hours. The old woman stares at him silently. A thin black woman, neatly dressed and very proper-looking, mounts the stone steps, a paper bag from the McDonald's on Bainbridge Avenue in her hand. The guard opens the door to let her in. They smile at each other. The old woman with swollen ankles watches. Then she makes her painful way down the three steps.

I get out of my car. The small park behind the library is empty, despite the warmth of the morning. The orange-tinted brick of the building below the library shines in the springtime sun. It has recently been steam-cleaned. All over the neighborhood, buildings are being steam-cleaned. The bricks of the neighborhood are warm and colorful—a fitting architecture for working people filled with a sense of moving up, of making life better for their sons and daughters. An optimistic architecture. Apartment building entrances in which blue ceramic Greek vases embrace stone clusters of grapes. Concrete lions invite one into Tudor and medieval fantasies. Decoration to suggest possibility, that which had been approved by history beckoning us on in the guise of the new.

Only such fantasies are now challenged by graffiti. Initials and names spin like rogue comets out of control, pressing their claims against the impermanence of stone and brick. Overwhelming it—so that before one can become used to the steam-cleaned brick some local Kilroy has savaged his presence onto it, a "creative" burst of anger with no other achievement in sight. Kilroy was here, there, and everywhere. But our neighborhood Kilroys have been nowhere. It is these streets alone they claim.

Which is why, I try to tell myself, men have always stamped their signatures on the works of others. Signatures for which they are praised by those who insist on seeing them as signs of life, as demands to be heard, as a noble defiance of the aspirations society deems acceptable.

There is probably something to the argument. But I retreat back into my own provincial longings. I prefer the ceramic vases and the stone lions and the grapes and the green-and- orange Art Deco entrances—embellishments of an architecture that promised working people they might yet become what they could not altogether envision becoming. These mock-Tudor apartment buildings, these turrets leaning into the emptiness of sun and sky and now overwhelmed by forests of television antennas— emblems of aspirations that reflected our sense of moving up. Better that than initials fixed to such casual hatred.

"It's getting better," I hear from the old people. "The neighborhood's moving up again." And it is easy enough to feel the rising sense of optimism in these streets. The neighborhood has survived the ravages that afflicted most of the rest of The Bronx. As its residents tell me, things *are* getting better. Buildings are being steam-cleaned; new full-pane vinyl and aluminum windows are replacing the old-fashioned wooden windows that were so difficult to open—a boon for people like my mother, who can now more easily watch the life passing in the streets below. Elevators that have not worked for years are being repaired. There is scaffolding everywhere in the neighborhood—the visible symbol of improvement.

The northeast Bronx is to be condoized and co-oped. And yet, that does not seem to disturb the people in the neighborhood, anymore than the way the graffiti return as soon as the bricks have been cleaned. Somehow, it does not matter, just as it does not matter that everyone I speak to warns me to avoid the walks and public buildings of the Oval after dark. Nothing is more important than that the people in the neighborhood believe once again that their corner of The Bronx has a future.

Curiously enough, politics does not seem to enter into that future. No one I speak to is interested in the scandals of the Koch administration or the dethroning of Stanley Friedman and Stanley Simon. The neighborhood will absorb Koch and Friedman and Simon and whatever or whoever replaces Koch and Friedman and Simon as it absorbs the inevitable resurfacing of graffiti—with a shrug of the shoulders and a sense that what happens happens. And there does not seem to be very much in the, way of organized opposition to the "threat" of co-oping and condoizing. If anything, the people to whom I speak are eager to travel the way they are convinced the rest of New York has already traveled.

On a small patch of earth in front of a two-story house on Hull Avenue, a cherry tree blooms. Five years ago, I would have thought of how incongruous that tree was. Now it seems lovely and natural. Other than their graffiti, these houses are respectable, well cared for, like their owners.

A lean Hispanic boy of twelve or thirteen is dribbling a basketball in the small yard of P.S. 56. Aware that I am watching him from my car, he switches hands, slapping the ball behind his back, then spinning to the basket. I smile, he laughs. Behind him, neatly painted on a concrete wall intended for handball, a large American flag with thirteen stars for the original colonies. I like the way the boy's angular body spins out of it. And I laugh, thinking that I have found the perfect Hollywood fade-out for a neighborhood that never hungered for perfection. There are those problems that call to mind only plodding rewards. Waving to the boy, I drive away, no longer content to be a spy in the country of the Other.   □

Rosalyn Drexler

LIFE AND GAMES IN THE WEST BRONX

My aunt and her friends played Mah Jongg in Van Cortlandt Park. They'd bring their card tables, folding chairs, beach chairs (the striped-awning kind), food, and ice-water, then settle in for the day. They were Russian émigrés who had found their niche in the West Bronx. My mother had two sisters, both older than she. This was their crowd. My mother, a shy person, wasn't included. She'd sit to the side watching, with me beside her. We had an activity of our own: I'd tell her stories and she'd write them down. My handwriting was very poor and hers was beautiful. She was my first and only collaborator.

In the late 1930s it was like country up there; people grew tomatoes in empty lots, and I and my friends'd roast spuds in the hot ashes of open fires. The park didn't have a highway to divide it yet and a path led down to the Van Cortlandt Park Lake, with benches at each side all along the way. I remember hiding behind such a bench to watch two of my friends make love: in those days that meant hugging and kissing, period.

Wintertime we'd go ice-skating on the lake. The first time I tried to ice-skate was in a back-lot on our block in the East Bronx, not far from Claremont Park. The winter cold would freeze the rain over, creating a ready-made lake for us. My "skates" were two wooden cheese boxes that I had begged from a salesman at Daitch's (in those days, a neighborhood dairy) on Bathgate Avenue. Bathgate was the scene of the big outdoor market, where Mother bought me tiny doll clothes for my celluloid dolls, about a hand high with movable arms and legs and faces as cute as Betty Boop's. Afterwards we'd lunch at a nearby deli, and I'd order my favorite food: chopped herring salad with a big slice of challah, and a glass of sour milk.

Along the highways into Manhattan, boys would hawk song sheets with the latest hits. Everyone must have been hot to sing, there were no car radios: what were they supposed to do while waiting for traffic to unjam, or for a light to change? Imagine hundreds of drivers anxiously grasping their steering wheels, a song sheet propped in front of them, singing "Donkey Serenade," or "Indian Love Call."

My rich Uncle Moe bought me a song sheet; that, and my first bicycle, which my father bought at a discount from my grandfather's second-hand store, made me the envy of my friends. I gave them rides and let them borrow song sheets, but still they hated me for my comparative affluence, and for that added bit of mobility afforded by my crummy bike.

Rich Uncle Moe (he was in the wholesale coat-manufacturing business) would appear in his long gray car of foreign make to take our family for a ride through Crotona Park. He'd treat us to ice-cream cones, then we'd tootle through the park licking them, and enjoying the view. Sometimes we'd drive to a golf range where Uncle Moe would rent golf clubs and pails of golf balls and under his tutelage we'd hit the balls as far as we could.

Mother said that some day I'd be another Deanna Durbin. All I had to do was study the lyrics on the song sheets. Prepare for the big break. So I did:

"They say some day you'll find/all who love are blind. . . ./So I smile and say/When a lovely flame dies/Smokes get in your eyes." I didn't quite understand the words but became deadly afraid of falling in love and losing my sight.

Mother really believed I'd be a star some day, so when my cousin Chico (cousin through marriage) of the Marx Brothers came to town to stay at the Warwick Hotel not far from Central Park South, Mom dressed me up to impress him. I wore a plaid dress with a high bodice and flared skirt. My hair was long and pulled back, my eyes blue, and my face was dimpled. I believe I was almost thirteen, perhaps less. Mother asked me to sing for him. The selection was "A Heart That Is Free," made popular by Deanna Durbin . . . a song way up in the high register! What a strain. I got through it. Chico took me into another room supposedly to discuss my career, and felt me up. It embarrassed me. "I don't have too much up there," I said. Obviously it was enough for him. Well actually I was mortified. Mother had too much respect for the guy just because he was successful; she'd believed in his good intentions. One good thing though, I was always taken to see the Marx Brothers films; brought up on that kind of humor: the wordplay, the inspired non sequiturs, the irreverence. This influenced my work a great deal.

My best friend in The Bronx was Ray. She had a sister Shirley, a father who worked in chenille (he brought chenille bathrobes home with him); there was also a retarded brother whose main occupation was shredding paper and throwing it to the street from the fire escape. Their mother was away somewhere . . . they said that she was sick.

Our clotheslines were attached to the same pole, and we'd chat as we hung clothes out: I recall the creaky sound of the clothesline as it went around the pulley, and the smell of air and sun on the clothes. Ray and me, we'd giggle together and run up and down the street for the pure physicality of it. We had a crush on the same boy, Solly. Solly had two brothers. When we went to the city pool in Claremont Park, they'd push us screaming into the water, and then dive in and try to "duck" us. We'd play ring-a-levio too, where someone was "it," and the rest of us ran to hide. It was very exciting, this hiding, and waiting in the dark behind some large object, or jammed behind the stairwell of a dimly lit hallway till one of us was discovered and tapped three times, to be "it."

Shirley and Ray were the proud possessors of a

rare commodity, a hand-wound victrola. Sometimes they'd put a record on it, open the window and lean out calling for me to listen. We often communicated this way, shouting out the window. I especially enjoyed hearing the "Blue Danube Waltz," or Caruso singing an aria from "The Pearl Fishers." Once again my tastes were being formed, an education gained unawares. I loved Ray, and later named my first child after her. A number of years ago I met Shirley in the subway while waiting for a train. She told me that Ray was in a mental hospital. Sometimes I think about Ray, about meeting her and she's okay, and we're friends again.

It was the Depression. We ate cheap—matzo-brei three times a day: broken pieces of matzo added to beaten eggs and milk in a bowl, then fried in butter. Milk came in bottles (Grade A and Grade B . . . Grade A had more cream). An egg man came once a week to sell eggs fresh off the farm. A scissors man came 'round to sharpen old knives and scissors for the housewives. There was an old-clothes man who came around to buy used clothes cheap. And the iceman, with his calipers, holding a dripping piece of ice on his back (protected with an old piece of rug), would bring us the big twenty-five-cent block to put in the icebox. Beggars would come to the backyard singing for their supper, and we, the children, would be allowed to toss a few coins down to them. Mother said it was a mitzvah . . . blessed to give. Even when we had very little ourselves, she'd make sandwiches for the people who came to our door asking for food. That was her way.

I recently took a car trip through the East Bronx and the West Bronx. It looked like an entirely different culture, with the same poverty. I saw the same green parks as a refuge from the granite gray of the streets, but no sense of leisure, unless an addict nodding out in the street is leisure, unless the homeless sleeping in doorways is leisure. There was still dancing in the streets: the young continue to have spirit; but today it is only one step away from warfare in the streets, which has a drop-dead beat all its own. Nothing stays the same, but it doesn't necessarily get better. More often it gets worse. There are two to three million homeless in the United States: my mother and others like her, making sandwiches to share with the hungry who come to the door, would certainly die of exhaustion today.   □

Jerome Charyn

"THE ROUGH ADVENTURE OF THE STREET. . . ."

"Cities, like dreams," Calvino tells us, "are made of desires and fears, even if the thread of their discourse is secret, their rules are absurd, their perspective deceitful, and everything conceals something else" (*Invisible Cities*).

Calvino is right, of course. New York is the ultimate dream city: monstrous, rude, gentle, brilliant, and dumb. It has all the arrogance and snobbery of a small village, and the pure delight of an empire sitting by the sea. It can never be adequately defined or circumscribed, because it's a city that didn't grow out of an idea that made practical sense. The Dutch arrived like phantoms, thinking they were traders, and did not realize that they'd been seduced by a very strange island. They never conquered Manhattan. They built a tiny settlement at the edge of the island, called it New Amsterdam, and forgot they'd ever left home. It was a magic harbor. The British took it from them, renamed the island, but they couldn't really turn it into an English town. New York had its own peculiar babble, its own peculiar tongue.

It was a mythical landscape: Europe's dream and desire of a fabulous kingdom, a kingdom of unlimited wealth. But this *new world* of New Amsterdam and New York wasn't so readily decipherable. It had convicts, rabbis, merchants, witches, soldiers, slaves. It was a village that grew into a gigantic Monopoly board. Somehow it always stank of wealth.

And it didn't matter who were its kings. The English, the Dutch, or even the French, who could have crept down from Canada (New France) to steal the whole pie. The island always withstood authority and centers of power, even if it was King George's own capital of British America during the Revolutionary War. The Tories danced on this island throughout most of the revolution, while American soldiers died on prison ships in the harbor. Tory landlords discovered the miracle of real estate. They charged fortunes for tiny houses and tents. But there was an anarchy in King George's village that went much deeper than any idea of the Crown.

New York has always been a curious mixture of law *and* disorder. It's no accident that the worst gangs the world has ever seen came out of an old slophouse called the Brewery over a hundred and fifty years ago. It was a "housing project" in lower Manhattan for poor blacks, the immigrant Irish, dwarfs, beggars, the lame, and the blind. There were at least two murders a night inside the Brewery. There were mad, raving songs. There was highway robbery in the halls. There was child prostitution. There was arson. There was rape. And yet somehow the Brewery learned to police itself. Its tenants managed to survive . . . except for those two murders a night.

The Irish moved out of the Brewery, entered politics, and soon controlled the town. For a while it seemed as if the Irish had established their own state on the island of Manhattan. They managed politics, the police, and crime. Irish spinster ladies taught in the schools. Irish priests invented their own little Vatican. Irish gangs destroyed their Republican rivals and transformed the Democrats into a party of immigrants and thieves. The thieves were often compassionate. They would steal your money and give your daughter a jar of milk.

The Irish didn't have palaces on Fifth Avenue. They never entered Wall Street. They weren't land speculators or millionaires. But the Irish ran New York. They fashioned its day-to-day existence. They built its underground railroads and its bridges. They'd fled the Old World during potato famines, until there were more Irish in New York than in all of Dublin. And then . . . .

The Italians and the Russian Jews arrived. They lived in their own little Breweries. They scratched, they starved, they finagled, they married, they stole, they died, they danced with the Irish, and then pushed the Irish out of the way. And suddenly New York was a Jewish-Italian town. With Arnold Rothstein. Fannie Brice. Fiorello LaGuardia (who was Italian and Jewish). Lucky Luciano. Arthur Miller. Lauren Bacall. Danny Kaye. Diane Arbus. Norman Mailer. Martin Scorsese. Robert De Niro. Barbara Streisand. John Gotti. Ed Koch . . . .

But the honeymoon is over. At the very point of their "apotheosis," the Jews in New York have become a dying breed. And the Italians are sinking into the suburbs. Now we have the Chinese, the Koreans, Cambodians, West Indian blacks . . . and God knows what complexion New York will have in fifty years. But it doesn't matter.

A Chinese mayor in 2035 will have to live with the same anarchy that tugs at the city's heart. Because underlying the city's fabric is a kind of dream song that doesn't pay much attention to

spectacular rises and falls. It's a type of murderous energy that has little to do with race or religion, City Hall, or the New York Stock Exchange.

Now, in 1987, New York wears an odd metaphysical mask: blacks have grown invisible. Harlem is like a burnt-out Vietnamese village with bits of decoration at its borders. Black children ride on the trains, beating out songs on their seats, "rapping" about those moonscapes they live in. No one really listens. A few of the children become graffiti artists, breakdancers, or comedians, like Eddie Murphy, but the rest are stranded on their moonscapes: concrete bunkers we call housing developments.

Yet those are the lucky ones, in a way. At least they have an address. In New York, an "address" is harder and harder to find, particularly for Latinos and blacks. Who wants to build low-income housing when realtors can make fortunes building towers for the rich? It's part of the same metaphysics. As the poor multiply, so do the rich. The middle class have become their own small underprivileged country. Shoemakers disappear. Corner groceries are a relic of a different past. Every block in Manhattan needs an ice-cream parlor. The realtors and the young rich want to sculpt the city into a fairyland of fashion shops. And so we have a fake seaport, a convention center that looks like an isolated tomb of glass, a vertical shopping mall at Herald Square that has its own imbecilic theme song: whole floors dedicated to different city neighborhoods. It looks and feels like a home for androids. Who goes there?

A black man I discovered selling tiny bottles of perfume outside on the corner seemed to have much more expertise and enthusiasm than any of the human mannequins behind those glass walls.

And so, it would seem, this endless construction, the desire to build vertical and horizontal towers, and entomb ourselves in glass, has a chance of turning Manhattan into a moonscape for the rich.

But not even all that glass, that constant duplication of boxes shooting into the sky, can destroy the anarchy that exists inside Manhattan's grid.

Under the streets there's an entire system of abandoned subway stations, abandoned tunnels, abandoned tracks, a Plutonian world that mocks all the massive building above ground. Pluto prefers his own republic. A few yards from the Yale Club is a door that leads to an "outland" of tunnels under Grand Central Station. Various drifters have their own "streets" within these tunnels. There's even a Burma Road.

If you want to "discover" New York, go into the dunes: visit those caves in the South Bronx where breakdancing began as ritualized warfare between rival gangs. Or stroll down Ninth Avenue, which hasn't been gentrified, and one can still feel an electric charm, a *sense* of neighborhood with some of the anarchy a street ought to have. The old and the young mixing, mingling, with all kinds of quarrels and courtship rites.

Or go to Brighton Beach, where the Russian Jews have descended, drinking borscht and wearing 1950s' American clothes. Visit Mafia country in Bath Beach, where the young bloods stand in front of restaurants wearing their silkiest shirts. Travel to the Lower East Side, where the Chinese, the Latinos, and elderly Jews occupy the parks and the streets as if they'd all come out of a single crib.

Go up to the Grand Concourse and discover Art Deco buildings that some merchant prince built for his favorite daughter fifty years ago. THE CAROLINE or THE BEVERLY will be chiseled in stone above the front door . . . .

Museums and opera houses cannot get you into the blood of a town. They are splendid attempts at order in a disordered world. But we have to be Marco Polo in Manhattan, and risk that rough adventure of the street.   □

A DISSENT ROUND TABLE

ARE THERE SOLUTIONS?

In March of 1987 Dissent *organized, under the leadership of editor Fred Siegel, a round-table discussion on the problems of New York, with emphasis on the possibilities of solutions. We print below a transcript, sharply reduced for reasons of space. The round table was held at the Cooper Union and we wish to thank its vice president, Alan Green, for providing the meeting room. Participants were: Angelo Falcón, Institute for Puerto Rican Policy; Dan Feldman, State Assembly member from Brooklyn; Nathan* Glazer, *Professor of Education and Sociology, Harvard University; John Jeffries, assistant professor, Columbia University School of Architecture and Planning; Daniel McCarthy, Municipal Research Institute; Ruth Messinger, New York City Council member; Jan Rosenberg, Department of Sociology, Long Island University; Sol Stern, special assistant to the City Council President; David Tobis, Welfare Research Institute; and Don Wycliff,* New York Times *Editorial Board.*

Fred Siegel: The ice of the Reagan Age is cracking. It hasn't fully melted, but even before the Iragua affair there was a sense that the Republican agenda had run out of steam. Beset by an accumulation of social problems, the Reagan administration and conservatism generally have been floundering ever since their 1984 triumph.

The feeling many people have is that reform opportunities come in cycles, and that we now face a period of opportunity for liberals. The danger is that if liberals fail to deliver the goods or to take advantage of this opportunity, the cynicism that follows will be even deeper than the cynicism we've just been through.

After all the scandals, Mayor Koch is still running at a 55 percent approval rating. In the conservative eras of the 1920s and 1950s there were reform movements waiting to challenge the machines. What's striking in 1987 is that, despite the scandals and the very real failures of the Koch administration, there is no alternative yet on the horizon. New York had

two-party competition through the 1920s; this was followed by an era in which Republican fusion tickets—Republicans allied with labor or liberals, as with LaGuardia and Lindsay—supplied the opposition. Then, following Lindsay, you had Democrats fending off Democratic reformers. Many of those reformers achieved power; today, as the joke goes, the two-party system is Democrats versus prosecutors.

The Democrats today aren't really a coherent party. Formally New York resembles a one-party state. But in fact the party is little more than a collection of cliques, each with its own pipeline to the treasury; or it is an incumbent-protection society. Politics has largely been reduced to small groups able to organize for their own interest, so that politics becomes an extension of business.

Ruth Messinger: I think it's too facile to say the challengers aren't there. They are, but this is a very difficult city in which to organize; the structure of government, both formal and informal, has built up in ways that protect incumbency and frustrate insurgency. The formal structure is clear, and is now a matter at least under some debate. By informal I mean both the role that money plays in politics—which is almost unbelievable—and the impact of the waves of corruption and its exposure. These revelations create additional cynicism, which translates into frustration and apathy.

I don't think it's fair to say that the desire to challenge doesn't exist. In my judgment the questions are of critical mass: how do groups find out what they have in common, how do you build coalitions with sufficient numbers and sufficient conviction that can make a challenge?

Fred Siegel: What are the structures that frustrate coalitions?

Ruth Messinger: County leader politics; the degree to which the dominant majority black and Latin segments of this population have been disenfranchised. The person who is supposed to be closest to you is your City Council member. But we each represent 210,000 people!

In the City Council there are *very* few insurgents. It's kind of a chicken-and-egg problem, but this has fed the tendency of the City Council over the last fifteen years to acquiesce to a strong mayor. The council has more than enough power in the City Charter to be a strong legislature. It is frustrated to some extent by the diffusion of accountability created by the current structure and power of the Board of Estimate. But I think that it's frustrated as well by the size of those districts and the extraordinary difficulty of building serious challenges and moving ideas.

Sol Stern: But how would you explain the fact that, after the scandal in Queens, with the county leader and borough president known to be a crook, the machine these crooks represented had virtually no opposition at the next election? Whatever you might think of the new Queens Borough President Claire Schulman, she was literally picked by the same party leaders who had so loyally supported Manes. In the Bronx, only eight years ago you had a reform borough president—Bobby Abrams. Now virtually the entire Bronx organization is

in jail or about to go to jail and there is still little in the way of insurgency. It can't be simply because of the power of incumbency or money. Money was also important ten, fifteen years ago. It can't be simply because of television.

Ruth Messinger: Well maybe it can't be simply because of those things, but I think that those *are* things that have changed extraordinarily in the last two decades. I don't think that this city is lacking insurgent groups trying to build coalitions. Angelo Falcon represents one such effort. The various challenges from the Brooklyn blacks are another. They are frustrated by the perceived difficulty of different groups agreeing on a sufficiently common agenda to do something together.

But also I think you have to look seriously at money. There *was* a challenge to Claire Schulman. The question is not what people thought about Claire or her challenger; the question is where money moved very fast.

Nathan Glazer: The discussion is taking off on the problem of why there's no strong alternative where so many people are involved in corruption. But I think there is a previous, related question: What policy or what policies are out there for the insurgents to offer? One policy is to say: "We'll be more honest," or "We'll listen to people more"—a change in personnel. That's always available to reformers, and in New York, with its history of machine abuses, that's been an almost sufficient agenda. But it always requires something else, and it's the something else that seems to have disintegrated.

Martin Shefter's book on the fiscal crisis argues that there are waves of reform, bringing government which responds to new people coming to the city by providing social services. Then that frightens the business classes, or leads to near bankruptcy, and there is a period of "fiscal responsibility." We're coming toward the end of a period of fiscal responsibility. But in the present situation, with a 22-billion dollar budget and very large sums already devoted to welfare, education, and whatever, can you imagine anyone arguing that the time has come to start spending more? Doing more means spending more money. As

L. to r., Sol Stern, Nathan Glazer, Angelo Falcón

soon as anyone says that, I think he's almost out of the political game.

This is a city with the highest city and state income taxes in the country, with the most elaborate, costly social services. So one problem is defining an alternative to a period of fiscally responsible government that hasn't particularly reduced taxes, [but] has been friendly to business and development so that many companies are still willing to shoulder the enormous burdens of doing business in New York. It takes one third more to build anything, taxes are extravagant—it's really a credit to New York that anyone still wants to build or invest here.

In sum, what would the insurgents say, what would they do? What will be their policy aside from "Get the rascals out," a good slogan but not a policy?

Don Wycliff: It strikes me that to talk about conservatism and liberalism in New York City is almost meaningless because so many normally liberal elements are invested in the status quo. The housing situation, rent control, the way the school system operates—everybody has an investment in major governmental institutions remaining the way they are. Insurgents are disarmed at the beginning. If there's going to be ferment, I think it's going to come from outsiders, from new immigrants,

whether from other parts of this country or other parts of the world. These people are making things happen in some of the city's neighborhoods, maybe about the only interesting things happening.

John Jeffries: I just want to pick up on two things with respect to alternatives. Unfortunately in New York City that's a rather easy abstract question to deal with: for groups that don't benefit from existing circumstances, an alternative would be any situation that allows them to benefit more. That leaves aside the question of spending more money. But in the weaker case, an alternative policy would be one in which those people who bear the brunt of sacrifices, both cyclical and structural, bear them less frequently. That is, if we can find ways to have cyclical and structural change such that the burdens had a more random incidence, that would be an alternative situation.

Fred Siegel: I don't think John has answered Don Wycliff's point. If tomorrow the city was hit with a tidal wave or an earthquake that produced the level of homelessness and dislocation we now have, emergency powers would be invoked to override the ordinary clash of political interests and to ration essential supplies. Yet nowhere in the political culture of New York is there a willingness to override

L. to r., Dan Feldman, Dan McCarthy

ordinary interests no matter how severe the social emergency.

New York has not developed a housing policy that links development in Manhattan with the needs of the outer boroughs. I know linkage has belatedly begun here in New York. One way for liberals to indicate that linkage will not just be business as usual, would be to tie an excess-profits tax on Manhattan development to a reorganization of the rent control system. The city in particular, and reform more generally, doesn't have to be held up to ridicule because of a rent control system that provides subsidized rents for Faye Dunaway and Mia Farrow, good liberals though they may be.

Our policies lack equity. On the one hand, people say there is a homeless crisis. On the other hand, we continue to distribute housing as if there were no crisis. There is no demand to demonstrate need before someone can move into a subsidized Mitchell-Lama building, or a child inherit a rent-controlled apartment. In fact, with all the statistics it gathers, the city doesn't even know what the incomes are of its rent-controlled tenants. On the federal level, liberals looking to meet social needs have begun arguing for dedicated funding—for instance, taxing the Medicare benefits of well-to-do recipients in order to expand the benefits for those worst off. Couldn't something similar be done with subsidized housing,

so that the wealthy who enjoy those benefits are taxed to aid the victims of the housing crisis? That would indicate something more then business as usual.

Dan Feldman: Look, there are many other irrationalities. In 1985 I noticed that you can't use federal money except for *temporary* housing for the homeless. That was a problem nationwide. I went to the city's Human Resources Administration and said, "Go to New York City's congressional delegation and tell them to change that. Why spend $30,000 in rent for a welfare hotel, when you could use that money to build something? It's crazy." The response that I got was, "You're not familiar with what you're talking about, so shut up and go away."

There are so many irrational pieces in the system. Before you get to the level of my voting against rent control—I wouldn't just be defeated, I'd be hanged from the nearest lamp post—before you can get to that there are a million irrationalities blocking progress. So I don't know if you even need to ask enormous political courage of New York's representatives. There are so many plain old sane things to do before you get to that point. There are so many things that we won't challenge, and it's partly, as far as I'm concerned, partly attributable to the Rawlsian nonsense which has stifled

L. to r., Fred Siegel, John Jeffries, Dan Feldman

a lot of debate: You can only make changes that benefit the most disadvantaged. Let's say that you talk about decriminalizing all drugs, and you get the predictable opposition from the right. But you also get the opposition from the left, that more people will probably become addicts. And they won't accept the answer that "Yeah, but if we had prohibition we'd have fewer alcoholics, and you know what harm that does to society." Now we're in a situation where if you tell a kid to work in McDonald's for $5.00 an hour, he's going to say "Forget it, I'm going to sell drugs for $1,000 a week." The massive social harm that the criminality of drug abuse implies, you're not allowed to raise that, because you'd probably have more addicts if drugs were legal.

Ruth Messinger: I don't think it's true that in order to put through an innovative idea you have to agree to change some existing policy. I really go back to what John said, and a little bit of what Don said: the examples are out there. Very often when you talk about them people respond to you as if you were discussing something that couldn't exist within at least 5,000 miles of these shores, whereas they exist in other cities, where there are successful minority administrations, and administrations the same color and sex as ours, but where they're trying different things.

Fred Siegel: Ruth, some examples.

Ruth Messinger: Well, you mentioned linkage, and I think that's a good example because it is a policy that in New York City is now (a) more rhetoric than reality; and (b) based on a totally different set of notions of exchange— "We'll give you this if you do that"—than exists in other places. In San Francisco you don't put up commercial space downtown without paying for day care. But New York has day-care slots available for only 18 percent of the eligible children. So why wouldn't you want to do that tomorrow? And you don't need to undo rent control to adopt successful innovation from other cities.

Sol Stern: I agree with Ruth that there are a lot of very easy things to do that we are not doing. We don't have to debate whether we can do something like decriminalizing drugs, which is certainly utopian whether it's right or wrong, or even having a fair rent allocation system or taking back some of the money from the rent control subsidy. Let me give you an example. With all this reporting on the dropout rate,

L. to r., Angelo Falcón, Ruth Messinger, Jan Rosenberg, Don Wycliff

there was a piece in the *Times* about Thomas Jefferson High School. The school started out four years ago with nine hundred kids in the entering class, and there are now sixty in the senior class! A prima facie case that this is a school for failure. Whatever the reason, and you can argue about the reasons, one doesn't need a better case to say, "Shut it down." And you create something in its place that we have evidence has worked. There are thirteen alternative high schools in the city, serving only 2 percent of the city's high school students, and *they work*. I've been to some of them.

What's mind-boggling to me is, where are all the parents in that district? Where is the screaming and hollering from the minority community that's victimized by an institution like Thomas Jefferson, saying: "Anything is better than this." Break it up and create four or five alternative schools. Board of Education President Bobby Wagner has said alternative schools don't cost any more; space is not really a problem; and there is a track record. It is simply a question of inertia that we don't have more than thirteen alternative high schools in

this city. So there are many examples like that, before we even get to the issue of money.

But let's get back to the issue of money Nat Glazer has raised. He said we can't spend more. In a city in which the median income of renters is about $12,000 a year, you have no alternative but to spend more unless you want to see the housing crisis literally destroy the social fabric of the city. You have to figure out ways to spend more money on low-income housing or the welfare housing grant.

David Tobis: That was the point I wanted to make: *We have to spend more*, because if we don't we're only going to be dealing on the margins of the problems. You can take money that's currently allocated to subsidize the real estate interests and the banks and the stock markets in the city—Ruth Messinger has done a wonderful study documenting hundreds of millions of dollars that could be gotten from subsidies now provided for people that don't need the subsidies. You can't solve the problems of poverty in the city without spending more money. Forty percent of the children in the city are now living below the

L. to r., Dan McCarthy, David Tobis

poverty level. That's a tremendous constituency, their families and the schools they're in. Those people want more spent to meet their needs, and the issue is how to organize them and make them into a constituency that could support the expenditures.

Don Wycliff: I have to confess I get very worried immediately, not when somebody says spend more, but when somebody talks about how to organize the poor and make them into a constituency. Sol Stern's question is the key one: Why aren't those parents screaming like crazy? It just blows my mind to see how supine the black political constituency in this city is. I don't understand it, frankly. And the Hispanic political constituency as well. But as soon as somebody *else* starts trying to energize them, I get very worried and suspicious.

Fred Siegel: But Don, right now black levels of political participation in New York are *higher* than white levels of political participation. So it's not just the question of political participation.

Jan Rosenberg: Education is one of the issues that raise this question of critical mass in just the ways we've been talking about. It touches the lives of many segments of the population. And it puzzles me, too, that people

aren't more organized around what I see as some of the threats to education.

There are proposals circulating about ways to randomly redistribute children in high schools in the city. That seems to me to undermine some of the strong programs that have been created, rather than creating more of the magnet programs that have in fact drawn students from a variety of neighborhoods and from some variety of backgrounds—though they've left large segments of the poor and underclass untouched. These schools provide models of success that Ruth was talking about. We need to look hard at what's worked, and try to understand that there's been a lot of money spent and some things *have* worked. And I don't think that is widely enough known—I think, in terms of building enough political will to go forward, that's essential.

Fred Siegel: Is more money required? If so, where will it come from?

Sol Stern: Or what are the consequences of *not* spending the money? If we don't spend the money, what is the scenario? What are the consequences to the city of 40 percent of the children living in poverty, of a hundred thousand families doubled up in housing? Why is it inconceivable to build a constituency to spend more money on social issues if you put it in the right perspective? You have a president who built a constituency for spending a lot more money on an issue he was able to define as key to the national interest. In 1975 the city convinced people to make sacrifices so that the city could survive. Why is it inconceivable that you could build a constituency for spending more money, given the alternatives, continuing with 40 percent of the kids in poverty and an enormous homeless problem?

Dan Feldman: One answer is that the public cynicism about the efficacy of government is so great that if you tell them, "Give us more money and we'll be able to do this," they'll say, "Baloney, you won't. We don't trust you."

Don Wycliff: I agree, and I'm troubled because we've gotten to the point of "Can we do it without spending more money?" and I still haven't heard what we're going to do.

Sol Stern: Well, build low-income housing and raise the welfare grants for housing, that's two areas; bring the welfare grant somewhere a little closer to the level of poverty; get more people who are in fact entitled to a welfare grant, given their income status, and who are now excluded—get them into the welfare system. On the national scene, we're beginning to get a liberal/conservative consensus on welfare reform. Not that everyone is agreeing on this buzz-work about obligation, or that welfare mothers will either have to go to work, or report to work training, or go back to school; but there is a general consensus that this won't be cheap. We're going to have to spend a lot of money for day care and some social services. So there is a consensus there on more money and what to use it for.

Angelo Falcón: But isn't that welfare reform movement being sold, whatever the substance of it, as more of a punitive thing: "We're going to put these people in line."

I think that the level of tolerance for certain problems in this society has risen to a point where you'll see people dying on the streets and not make a connection between that and social policy. And that's been a long-term process over the 1970s, in terms of people redefining those issues away, and a tremendous assault on liberalism while, for example, the Reagan people and the right have been able to lower the levels of tolerance in terms of defense spending. They've been able to say, "Look, this is a matter of life and death, we've got to spend more money on arms because we have no choice."

I think liberalism has been transformed in another way. In New York, Puerto Ricans used to be able to rely on the fact that, look, we may have a chance to get in some more positions because every once in a while these white guys start fighting. Under Wagner some Puerto Ricans were brought in, then under Lindsay. Then all of a sudden that gets transformed with Koch in a way where the substance of reform isn't there but the form is there.

Koch still has a reform air—he's not perceived as a machine guy. If you're in government and you're battling with the guy you see the reality. But most people don't do that. On the surface he doesn't look like one of the machine, he doesn't look like a Meade Esposito. So I think that's clouded the issues.

Ruth Messinger: But Angelo, I think there are people at a lot of different income levels in different communities in the city who know that the services they're getting for their tax dollar have gone down. It's a question of changing the dominant message. I agree with what both Dan and Don said: you have to be clear about what you would do—and make it sound sufficiently compelling that people will pay for it, *and* you have to let people know that the burden of paying for it is not going to fall on exactly the same people who paid it before. But it's not that hard to do in this city.

First of all, there are a lot of innovative ideas. We have nine hundred schools open seven hours a day five days a week forty weeks a year. It took us forever to get some of them open from 3 to 6 P.M. School buildings ought to be community resources, to have a range of programs. You start moving senior citizens programs in there; you make what we mean by community schools. That's something for which people would want to see money allocated.

Now that doesn't mean that they want to shell it out of their pockets. So then I think you have a separate argument, which is, "Where is there money?" We've got in this city a set of protection societies for sources of income that we are choosing not to tap. We are paying money for every large development and to protect a hidden surplus of about a half a billion dollars a year.

Fred Siegel: Ruth, when you say there's a hidden surplus, does that come from the Financial Control Board?

Ruth Messinger: That comes originally from Dan McCarthy, and from virtually anybody that's ever looked at the budget. For several years we were under a tight monitoring system and things were touch-and-go. And then we started ending each year with a surplus.

The mayor advertises the surplus every year in July as if it were the greatest thing that had happened to the city. Running a surplus sounds like a good thing. But it's our tax money, and we're contributing it—under forced conditions—to pay for services, and they're building up a surplus. So for four years we ran a surplus of $400 or 500 million each year and rolled it over. And last year when some of us began to get wise we were given a set of projections that said things were different: impact of federal tax reform, the increase in the cost of living, lack of elasticity in some of our sources of income; next year—that's right now—will be *extremely* tight.

Well, it isn't extremely tight. They're still pretending that it's tighter than last year, but I think that's just to save face. I now believe the numbers will be exactly the same as before, and you have to believe that it's deliberate policy. There is this reservoir of funds we ought to have the right to touch, not overspend, not spend down to the last penny, but touch.

Nathan Glazer: What happens to this surplus? I've always believed that people in government are happy to spend money. So why don't they do it? I'm asking out of ignorance.

Ruth Messinger: We roll it over every year. The mayor says, "See, we haven't wasted it, we were just being cautious. We took in more than we thought, and we spent a little less than projected, but it's okay; it'll serve as a base for next year." Which would be reasonable if it happened once! I think you're asking a good

question, and I can't answer it: Why is there a commitment to an additional one-half billion dollars' worth of surplus when there are services that are desperately starving?

Dan McCarthy: The question of where the money is is a good one, but I have become increasingly skeptical as to whether dollars and budgets are the crucial issues in New York. I'm the author of the 10 percent Capital Gains Tax that will generate a half billion dollars for New York State this year. So I'm one of the last of the big spenders in New York City.

Nathan Glazer: The capital gains tax on real estate? That tax works?

Dan McCarthy: Yes, it works. I'm no longer as convinced, however, that dollars are the problem. I think that we have to address more clearly the failure of our existing institutions to make better use of the resources they now have. I've had the opportunity over the last few years to see the planning and leadership of some of the major institutions in the city. And whether that's churches or business interests or whatever, I think we have a failure of leadership, a great deal of complacency, and a real unwillingness to change.

The future of New York is black, Hispanic, and Asian. While that's often said, I don't believe it's completely understood. The real story of New York in the 1980s, I believe, is not the budget, it's not even corruption: it really is that this is the watershed period in the city's history when new people came to the fore and exercised their influence over the future direction of the city.

I've been reading two books recently; one is Carlyle's *French Revolution*, and the other is Sayre's *Governing New York City*. Institutions don't change unless there are major forces at work, and I think those forces are now coming to a head in New York and will shape the future, namely demographic forces. Rebuilding our existing institutions is crucial to the future.

One other point: I'm no longer as convinced as I once was that better political leadership will change this city. Change will come about through better civic leadership, media leadership, and journalism. The introduction of

Newsday in this city has done more to open up policy issues than any other single event.

David Tobis: Let's get back to the issue that Dan Feldman raised about the cynicism towards government—"Government can't do anything." The poverty rate for the elderly has been cut in half over the last twenty years because of government action: the establishment in the U.S. of Medicare and Social Security. When government chooses to act in a wise way, when there is an organized constituency, it makes a tremendous difference. There are things that the private sector does not do adequately, and then government takes the heat for it. One example is child welfare. Special Services for Children (SSC), the city agency that oversees the foster-care system run directly by private agencies, is repeatedly blamed, but is not provided with the resources to do its job, to monitor agencies adequately and to hold them accountable. When there aren't enough beds because agencies have not provided the beds for kids in foster care, the city gets the blame for that.

Don Wycliff: Wait a second, you have to explain that. Isn't the government legally responsible for those children?

David Tobis: Right, but the power does not rest with government. Government spends $350 million a year for foster-care services. But the control of what happens to those kids in foster care does not rest, and has never ultimately rested, with the city. Religious agencies run the majority of the system. The Wilder lawsuit has argued that the control of placement has rested with the agencies, and that they have discriminated on racial grounds; that the better agencies have not taken black and Hispanic kids. As a result, children received inadequate care. The city runs a very small piece of foster care—about 5 percent of the system—those beds were established in the late 1940s and mid-1960s, to take the kids that voluntary agencies refused to take. Over the 1930s, 1940s, and 1950s, the foster-care system moved from white to black. The voluntary agencies did not want to take the worst and most difficult cases. The city was forced to create its own system. The Wilder lawsuit will give the city greater control.

Ruth Messinger: Yes, but in defense of what Don is asking you, it *is* the city's responsibility. The city has chosen to discharge that responsibility through a contracting-out system that it defends by saying, "We are just not as good as the voluntary and religious agencies at being small, community-based, humane." That rhetoric, while it may have some basis in reality, also serves to diffuse accountability. The city can say: "Gosh, it's not our fault; we pay these people a lot of money and they're supposed to provide the service."

Dan Wycliff: But I don't elect the archbishop, I elect the mayor.

Angelo Falcón: I've seen many discussions like this, where you can make a very rational case why you need to spend more money. But when you get down to connecting with constituencies at the street level, it's a very different process. Every time there's talk about expanding a program, people in the Latino community say, "We're not going to get any of this stuff." So you're not going to get much of a response because the feeling is: "That money is going to be used by those other guys up there, like they've done in the past, and that's it. It's not going to filter down to us." So right there you're going to have trouble connecting on that issue with one large constituency in the city.

John Jeffries: At the very least, it should be more costly for people who benefit from the current context to operate the way they're operating. Underemployment, poverty, unemployment, etc., should be more evenly distributed across groups. And we have to talk more about the extent to which local governments, in the absence of state and federal aid, interest or intervention, can solve these problems.

The confusion of our alternative policy is very much a confusion about what a locality can do in the absence of federal policy and in the context of New York State policy. The economic policy for New York City is basically that the state gives the city money, and the city says, "Thank you very much, leave it by the door." We have to talk about whether or not there's a posture that produces better results.

Ruth Messinger: I think that what John is saying is critical. It is true that there are potholes to be filled, but we have an administration that finds it very comfortable to say, "The problem with providing services today is that there isn't any money." And when they're asked to amplify on that, they cite programs the federal government has cut. They don't argue with the state for alternative funding or cut some of our extraordinarily generous subsidies to real estate developers in order to use that money more equitably.

The best example is housing. It would be extraordinarily expensive for this city to undertake any expansion of the housing program. But we live in a city that has between sixty and one hundred thousand vacant city-owned apartments. In 1976 and 1977 the city said that a variety of strategies to fix up some of those apartments would never work. Then the city tried using federal money, announced that they were extraordinarily successful, that lo and behold low-income communities could manage their own housing, do some sweat equity, use government money, run their own buildings. And after we announced that that program was successful we then said we're not going to do any more, because the federal money has dried up.

Nathan Glazer: We have an interesting set of alternative explanations of what is going wrong here. I want to link two things said by Dan Feldman and Angelo Falcon: when you (Dan) said people don't trust government, I assume you meant middle-class people don't trust government; Angelo then said that low-income people don't trust government either. Well, that's a very hard thing to get around in building a coalition that argues that government should do more.

Now there's a second thing we've heard, going against simplistic views that we simply need more money: that there is some kind of incapacity in government, that even when it has it, it can't do it. Now why would city government be against fixing up city housing if there's federal money for it? Or if it won't cost that much, why wouldn't the city use money from other sources? Whenever I hear there's a failure of leadership I get a little worried because it's so indefinite. [What about] the Wollman Rink? Maybe it's the Wicks Law,

maybe its a failure of leadership, maybe there's a kind of culture of total incapacity where no one expects to be able to do anything and therefore they can't and have to be hit over the head by politicians. How did this culture develop and how does it get changed?

I understand the argument that you need more money. You put more people on, you fill more potholes, you place those foster kids more rapidly; whatever has to be done you do more of, faster. How do you do it *without* more money, and won't you have to do it that way, in view of the general suspicion of government?

While I have the floor I will say one more thing, because a few times people have raised the question of the ethnic and racial change that is occurring. Now this is going to link up directly with the question of what do people expect government to do, how do they trust government.

New immigrants are transforming the city, ninety thousand a year settling in New York. The Puerto Ricans, in 1980, according to the City Planning Commissioner, were 60 percent of all Hispanics; by now they are probably down to 50 percent of Hispanics. There is also the large black immigration from the Caribbean, the huge Asian immigration—let me tell you something interesting, they don't want government to do anything for them, they want government to stay out of their way. That's all they want. I recall a meeting with the mayor of Boston—I live in Cambridge—new immigrants coming in, Haitians, representatives of the community, and the mayor said, "What can we do for you?" And all they said was, "We can fix up the houses, we can handle it, don't do it! Get out of our way!"

On the one hand we say the city is changing, but it's not changing to constituencies that want more government.

Angelo Falcón: I think that's misleading. I will send you to the Upper West Side of Manhattan Dominican community and you'll get a very different reaction in terms of what government is about. You also have to be careful in terms of who are playing the broker roles, in terms of social classes, and how they're projecting a community that's very disorganized and newly settled. I think it's more complex.

Sol Stern: I'll make a couple of points. One on the culture of incompetence or incapacity. What institution has more notorious a culture of incapacity than the Defense Department? I mean, a sixty-four-dollar screw? This is an administration, or the last two administrations, that has never done anything right in the military field, until they took on Grenada. Yet they were able to swing a population around to the notion, "Let's flush more money down the drain." Why? Because they were able to convince people that it's a priority.

Now I don't think it's inconceivable in this city to get people convinced that it's a priority to spend more money on the underclass—when they decide that if we have a school system in which a third of the kids are on welfare, we can't use that school system, and therefore it's going to cost us seven or eight thousand dollars a year to send our kids to private schools. Eventually, how many kids can go to Stuyvesant High School? I'm talking about the white middle class, or the ethnic middle class.

Obviously you want at the same time to make sure government will function better, and I believe, by the way, that it will if it becomes a priority. □